AN INTRODUCTION
TO
ANALYSIS

Daniel Saltz

Associate Professor of Mathematics
San Diego State College

Prentice-Hall, Inc.

Englewood Cliffs, N.J.

PRENTICE-HALL INTERNATIONAL, INC., *London*
PRENTICE-HALL OF AUSTRALIA, PTY., LTD., *Sydney*
PRENTICE-HALL OF CANADA, LTD., *Toronto*
PRENTICE-HALL OF INDIA (PRIVATE) LTD., *New Delhi*
PRENTICE-HALL OF JAPAN, INC., *Tokyo*

Current printing (last digit):
11 10 9 8 7 6 5 4 3

Library of Congress Catalog No. 65-14936
Printed in the United States of America
C47784

To Joanne

PREFACE

This book is meant to introduce some of the important concepts and methods found in the calculus of one real variable, and to apply these concepts and methods to the construction of models found in such areas as business, the life sciences, and psychology. To keep on the main stream of the general ideas of calculus, the reader's attention is restricted to exponential and logarithmic functions, and to those functions which are obtained by taking powers and roots of ratios of polynomials. It is the author's belief that once these basic concepts are understood, it would require a minimum of labor to enrich the class of functions to the trigonometric, hyperbolic, their inverses, etc.—topics covered in most standard calculus books. It is assumed that the reader can handle elementary algebra.

The principal audience addressed is the nonmathematician, nonphysical scientist (with the possible exception of some areas of chemistry). The philosophy guiding the book is that to appreciate fully and to understand any model based on calculus—be it the demand equations in economics or probabilistic learning models—it is necessary first to have an appreciation of the underlying mathematical concepts. Hence, every effort has been made to avoid the "cookbook" approach, i.e., a listing of theorems with little interest in the their structure or proof. To be sure, not every interesting theorem can be proved at the level of this book, but those that cannot will be carefully stated, nevertheless, and references will be given so that the interested reader can ultimately investigate the proofs himself. Those theorems that can be proved will be proved, and whenever possible, theorems will be compared and related, especially where one theorem contributes to the proof of another. The book has examples to illustrate both the obvious and the subtle significances of theorems.

Chapter 1 is concerned with the underlying concept of the calculus: the concept of limit. It is intended to give the reader the correct sense of the meaning of limit and some techniques for evaluating limits. Some preliminary algebraic ideas that directly relate to the presentation of calculus are introduced (e.g., inequalities and the binomial theorem). A formal definition of limit appears in §1.6, but can be omitted on a first reading. Continuous functions are introduced, and the chapter ends with the derivative and its immediate applications to tangent line (geometrical) and rate of change concepts. Shorter examples appear from such disciplines as economics and psychology.

Chapter 2 applies the derivative to an investigation of monotone functions and the problem of finding the absolute extrema of a function of one variable. The ideas in turn are related to problems from business. Some theorems which appear in the theory of demand are presented, interpreted from the points of view of both the economist and the mathematician. These theorems are proved. The chapter concludes with a brief discussion of Walras's law and the problem of the existence of a solution to the equation of general equilibrium is discussed with the pertinent mathematical tools, especially fixed point theorems.

Chapter 3 is essentially a discussion of the definite integral, its implications to the area problem, and some techniques for evaluating the integral. The integral is defined as the appropriate limit of a sum, and uses a regular partition. A more general definition is mentioned briefly in §3.5. The exponential and logarithimic functions are introduced in §3.8 and §3.9.

Chapter 4 applies the concept of integral. The differential equation $y' = Ay$, where A is constant, is introduced and solved, and the used in numerous applications. The improper integral is introduced and used in a discussion of continuous probability. The end of Chapter 4 is an introduction to probability; such concepts as sample space, event space, random variable, probability function, distribution and density functions, and the normal distribution are discussed. The book concludes with an application of probability theory to a learning-theory model, an optimal inventory problem in business, and a problem in discrete and continuous time series.

The appendix contains proofs of some theorems stated, but not proved, in the body of the book, as well as some additional exercises in applying the mean-value theorem.

Set theory as a discipline in its own right does not appear; however, set theory is introduced as an integral part of the discussion of sample and event spaces in probability theory. Such ideas as union, intersection, complement, null event (rather than null set), etc., will be found in this section as well as some standard elementary theorems from set theory, often phrased in terms of event spaces.

Finally, the author wishes to express his thanks to Dr. Herbert Gindler for his constructive reading of parts of the manuscript and to Dr. Steve Hoffman for his patient search for errors.

DANIEL SALTZ

CONTENTS

Chapter *1*

INTRODUCTION

TO

DIFFERENTIAL CALCULUS

1.1. Functions and their graphs. Some important miscellany.

We shall concern ourselves with a particular type of relationship between numbers which we shall call a functional relationship. To explain the concept of function, suppose we have two boxes of objects, one box labeled "A" and the second box labeled "B". What we want to do is to pair off some of the objects in A with some of the objects in B; i.e., to each of certain objects in box A we shall associate some specific object in box B, but with one restriction: that, at most, one object in box B will be associated with a given object of box A. Such an identification is called a *function* from A to B. Observe that there is nothing in our construction of functions that would not allow us to identify a single object of box B with more than one object of box A.

Example 1.1.1. Let the objects in box A be $\{a, b, c\}$; let the objects in box B be the numbers $\{1, 2, 3\}$; and let us use the notation $f(a) = 1$ to indicate that object 1 in box B is associated with object a in box A by the *function f*. Then a typical function is f given by the correspondence $f(a) = 1$, $f(b) = 2$, $f(c) = 3$. Another distinct function g is given by $g(a) = 2$, $g(b) = 3$, $g(c) = 1$. Observe that the correspondence h, that associates 1 with a, 1 with b, and 1 with c is a function, and so we write $h(a) = h(b) = h(c) = 1$. The correspondence which associates 1 with a, 2 with a, and 3 with a is *not* a functional relationship from box A to box B, since we have violated the condition that, at most, one object in B will be associated with any given object in A.

We said above that it was only necessary that some of the objects of A be paired off with objects of B, so the correspondence K which associates 1 with a, and 3 with b, but makes nothing correspond with c is also a function.

We write $K(a) = 1$, $K(b) = 3$. We call the set of objects in A that the function associates with objects in B the *domain* of the function. In Ex. 1.1.1, the domain of f, g, and h is $\{a, b, c\}$; the domain of K is $\{a, b\}$. The set of objects in B that is associated with elements of A is called the *range* of the function. In our examples, the range of f and g is $\{1, 2, 3\}$; the range of h is $\{1\}$; and the range of K is $\{1, 3\}$. A function associates *every* element in its domain with the appropriate element in its range. We say that $f(x)$ *is undefined at* $x = a$, or, $f(a)$ *is undefined*, if a is not in the domain of f. We shall soon examine more examples illustrating these concepts.

The specific "boxes" with which we shall be interested are collections of "real" numbers. We shall outline this system briefly. The **natural numbers** are the numbers 1, 2, 3, ... (the three dots, "...", shall mean "and so on"). The **integers** adjoin to the natural numbers to give the system ..., -4, -3, -2, -1, 0, 1, 2, 3, 4, ... The **rational numbers** are defined to be the numbers of the form p/q, where p and q are integers, and $q > 0$. For example, 1/2, 3/8, $-7/15$, 3/47 are all rational numbers. In fact, since every integer p can be written as $p/1$, we see that every integer is also a rational number. The **irrational numbers** are numbers which are real but not rational. Numbers like π, $\sqrt{2}$, $\sqrt{7}$ are irrational. [We shall not prove this.] The **real numbers** are those numbers that can be written as decimals of the form $\pm n \, . \, abcd \ldots$ where n is a non-negative integer, and a, b, c, d, etc. are any of the digits from 0 to 9, and the dots "..." signify that the expansion may continue indefinitely or stop. The rationals and the irrationals together form the reals.

We next construct a geometrical analog to the real numbers which we shall call the **real line**. Draw a horizontal straight line (obviously, all that we can actually draw on paper is a segment of that line). Pick a point on this line, and label it 0. Pick a point distinct from 0 and to its right, and label it 1. Then the length of the interval between 0 and 1 will be a unit of length. Reproduce this length indefinitely to either side of zero and label the points 2, 3, 4, ... to the right of 1, and -1, -2, -3, ... to the left of 0 (see Fig. 1.1.1). Observe that the dis-

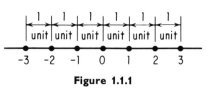

Figure 1.1.1

tinction here between 1 and -1 is the direction from 0 from which they are measured. The fundamental principle is that to each real number there corresponds a unique point on the line, and that to each point on the real

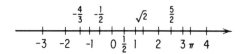

Figure 1.1.2

line there corresponds a unique real number. The line may be pictured as in Fig. 1.1.2. The arrow points in the direction of increasing numbers.

Next, construct a vertical line perpendicular to the given line, intersecting it at 0, and label it the same way as the horizontal line is labeled, using the same unit interval, with increasing values pointing up. Call the horizontal line the x-axis and the vertical line the y-axis. We are now in a position to label points in the plane. From the point P, draw a perpendicular to the x-axis, and suppose this perpendicular intersects the x-axis at $x = a$. Construct a perpendicular from P to the y-axis, and suppose the point at which it intersects this axis is $y = b$ (see Fig. 1.1.3). We call the value "a" the x-coordinate of P, the value "b" the y-coordinate of P. We label P with the pair of real numbers (a, b) in that order; i.e., x-coordinate first, y-coordinate second. Observe that for each point P there are unique real numbers $x = a$, $y = b$ such that P can be labeled (a, b), and for each pair of real numbers (a, b), there is a unique point in the plane with coordinates (a, b). In this way, we have identified all points in the plane with pairs of real numbers. This scheme will be necessary when we wish to graph functions. Example 1.1.2 illustrates some points in the plane.

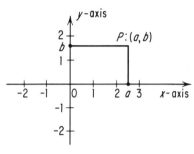

Figure 1.1.3

Example 1.1.2.

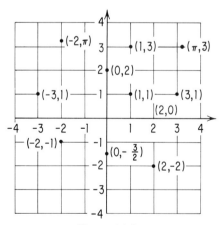

Figure 1.1.4

In the following examples we shall give some numerical functions; i.e., functions whose range and domain will be real numbers.

Example 1.1.3. $f(x) = x$. In the notation of Ex. 1.1.1, this is the function which makes each x correspond to the same number x. Similarly, $f(0) = 0$, $f(-1) = -1$, $f(7) = 7$, $f(125) = 125$, etc. It is legitimate to call this relation a function, since to every real number x we associate exactly one real number, namely the number x itself. The domain of the function is the entire x-axis, and the range is the entire y-axis.

Example 1.1.4. $g(x) = x^2 + 1$. Some typical values are

$$g(-1) = (-1)^2 + 1 = 2, \quad g(0) = 1, \quad g(1) = 2, \quad g(\sqrt{2}) = 3, \quad \text{etc.}$$

Observe that this is a functional relation, since to each x there corresponds exactly one value, x^2, and hence exactly one value $x^2 + 1$. The domain is the entire x-axis. Observe, however, that $f(x) = -2$ has no real solution, since $x^2 + 1 = -2$ implies that $x^2 = -3$, and there is no real number x whose square is -3. To find the range we must ask for what y the equation $y = x^2 + 1$ has a solution x, where x is in the domain of g; the totality of such y is the range of $g(x)$. Clearly, $y = -2$ is not in the range. The equation $y = x^2 + 1$ when solved for x is $x = \pm\sqrt{y - 1}$ which is meaningful if and only if the radicand $y - 1$ is non-negative; i.e., $y - 1 \geq 0$. So the range is the set of all y such that $y \geq 1$. We shall exhibit the graph of this function later. Observe that $g(1) = g(-1) = 2$, but this does not violate the definition of function.

Example 1.1.5. $f(x) = \sqrt{x}$. This function is not defined at $x = -1$, since there is no real number whose square is -1. In fact, since the domain is the set of all x such that $\sqrt{x}$ is defined, the domain of f is the set of all x such that $x \geq 0$. For each such x there corresponds exactly one number $\sqrt{x}$.

Example 1.1.6. $f(x) = 2$. This says that to each x we associate the same number 2. So, $f(-1) = 2$, $f(0) = 2$, $f(1{,}000{,}000) = 2$. The domain is the set of all real x, the range is the set containing the single number $y = 2$.

Example 1.1.7. We next define a special function called the **absolute value** of x, written $f(x) = |x|$. It is defined by cases according to the sign of x as follows:

$$|x| = \begin{cases} x, & \text{if the number } x \text{ is zero or positive (i.e., if } x \geq 0) \\ -x, & \text{if the number } x \text{ is negative (i.e., if } x < 0) \end{cases}$$

For example, since $-2 < 0$, then $|-2| = -(-2)$. Since $-5 < 0$, we have $|-5| = -(-5) = 5$. The reader should observe that $|7| = |-7| = 7$, $|-2| = |2| = 2$, and in general, $|a| = |-a| \geq 0$ for *any* a. Thus, we see that $\sqrt{x^2} = |x|$.

Example 1.1.8.

$$f(x) = \frac{x^2 - 1}{x - 1}$$

We know that

$$\frac{x^2 - 1}{x - 1} = \frac{(x + 1)(x - 1)}{x - 1}$$

If $x - 1 \neq 0$, that is, if $x \neq 1$, then

$$\frac{(x + 1)(x - 1)}{x - 1} = x + 1$$

(division by 0 is *not* permitted). But

$$f(1) = \frac{0}{0}$$

which is meaningless; i.e., $f(1)$ is undefined (recall this means that 1 is *not* in the domain of f). For $x \neq 1$, $f(x) = x + 1$ which is everywhere defined. Hence, the domain of f is all x except $x = 1$.

The concept of function is really a very natural one for many areas of application. For instance, when the physicist says that the position of a particle can be given as a function of time, he is asserting that there is some relation connecting time with the position of the particle, and that at a given time, the particle is to be found in no more than one position. When the economist says that demand is a function of price, he means that price and demand are related in such a way that to each price (in some domain of prices), there corresponds no more than one demand. Observe however that the same demand might result from different prices (the analogy here is that there corresponds, at most, one y to each x, but different x's might correspond to the same y).

Example 1.1.9. In the early learning-theory-model proposed by L. L. Thurston (The Learning Curve Equation, *Psychological Bulletin*, 1917 (14)), the quantity x, the number of times one must practice an act (in order to be able to complete that act successfully) was related to y, the number of successful acts, by the equation

$$y = \frac{a(x + b)}{x + c}$$

where a, b, and c are certain empirical constants. Thus, the number of successful acts is functionally related to the number of practice acts; i.e.,

$$G(x) = \frac{a(x + b)}{x + c}$$

Example 1.1.10. A question of considerable interest to the psychologist is the reliability of a test; i.e., whether a test measures what it is intended to measure. A test is said to be *lengthened by a factor of n* if $(n - 1)$ new tests, each one somehow equivalent to the original test, have been added to the original test, and the entire aggregate is given as a single new test. Hence, a test is lengthened by a factor of n if it is replaced by a new but equivalent test n times as long as the original test. Let r be the measure of the reliability of the original test; the Spearman-Brown formula asserts that reliability of the test after it has been lengthened by a factor of n is given by a function $f_n(r)$, and that under suitable conditions,

$$f_n(r) = \frac{nr}{1 + (n - 1)r}, \qquad 0 \le r \le 1$$

All functions we shall henceforth consider in this book are numerical functions. The expression "*y* is a function of *x*" shall mean that there is a function, say *f*, which makes correspond values *y* to certain values *x*, and we write this expression as $y = f(x)$. There is nothing special about the symbol *f*, so $y = g(x)$ or $y = \theta(x)$ would also designate "*y* is a function of *x*".

Notation like "$y = y(x)$" is often used in mathematical literature. Though logically faulty, the notation is highly suggestive. The logical difficulty is that the *y* on the right of the equality, representing the *function*, is conceptually different from the *y* on the left side of the equality, representing the *real number* on the *y*-axis obtained by applying the function to *x*. The notation is suggestive, because it implies that the result of applying the function to *x* (i.e., *y*(*x*)) is exactly *y*. With this word of caution, the symbol $y = y(x)$ will appear occasionally where circumstances make it useful.

To each *x* we associate the value $y = f(x)$ and plot the point $P: (x, f(x))$. The set of all points $(x, f(x))$ traced out in the plane as *x* varies over the domain of *f* is called the **graph** of *f*.

Example 1.1.11. We graph in Fig. 1.1.5 the functions of Exs. 1.1.3–1.1.8. Observe the domain and range of the respective function in each graph.

The first class of functions that we shall consider in the calculus will be the polynomial functions (in one variable). Let $a_0, \ldots, a_n$ be $n + 1$ real numbers, which we shall think of as fixed. Suppose further that $a_0 \ne 0$. The expression

(1.1.1) $$P(x) = a_0 x^n + a_1 x^{n-1} + \cdots + a_{n-1} x + a_n$$

is called a **polynomial in x of degree n.** It is a function of *x*. (Why?)

Example 1.1.12.
(i) $P(x) = x^2 - 2x + 1$ is a polynomial of degree 2;
(ii) $P(x) = x^{15} - 3x^6 + x$ is a polynomial of degree 15;
(iii) $P(x) = 2$ is a polynomial of degree 0.

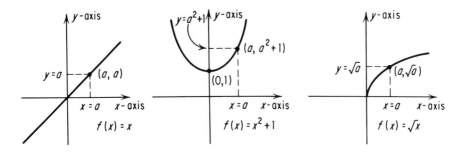

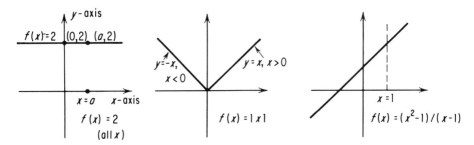

Figure 1.1.5

In (ii), the reader should observe that

$$P(a + b) = (a + b)^{15} - 3(a + b)^6 + (a + b)$$

and

$$P(1 + h) = (1 + h)^{15} - 3(1 + h)^6 + (1 + h)$$

Let $P: (a, b)$ and $Q:(c, d)$ be two arbitrary points in the plane. We wish to find the distance D between P and Q. As in Fig. 1.1.6, construct the right triangle PQR with hypotenuse the segment between P and Q. In the diagram, R is the point (c, b). The theorem of Pythagoras tells us that

$$PQ^2 = PR^2 + RQ^2$$

where PQ is the length of the segment from P to Q, with PR and RQ defined similarly. In Fig. 1.1.6 $c > a$, $d > b$, $PR = c - a$, and $RQ = d - b$. More precisely, since in general we would not know whether $c > a$ or $c < a$, we would set $PR = |c - a|$ to guarantee that $PR > 0$. Similarly we would set $RQ = |d - b|$. Hence,

Figure 1.1.6

$D^2 = |c - a|^2 + |d - b|^2.$ But $|c - a|^2 = (c - a)^2,$ $|d - b|^2 = (d - b)^2.$
(Why?) Hence,

(1.1.2) $$D = \sqrt{(c - a)^2 + (d - b)^2}$$

is the *distance between the points* (a, b) *and* (c, d), and hence also the distance between (c, d) and (a, b).

Formula (1.1.2) is also valid, though more simple, if the line segment is parallel to an axis. In fact, if the line through P and Q is parallel to the y-axis, then $a = c$, and we can see immediately that the distance between P and Q is $|d - b|$, which is exactly what we obtain if we set $a = c$ in (1.1.2).

Example 1.1.13. Find the distance between $(-1, 2)$ and $(3, 5)$. The required distance is

$$D = \sqrt{(-1 - 3)^2 + (2 - 5)^2} = \sqrt{16 + 9} = 5$$

Example 1.1.14. A circle can be defined as the locus of all points in a plane at a fixed distance, say r, from a fixed point, say (h, k) (see Fig. 1.1.7). We use (1.1.2) to find the algebraic equation of the circle. Let (x, y) be any point on the circle; then the distance from (x, y) to (h, k) is given by $D = \sqrt{(x - h)^2 + (y - k)^2}$, and this quantity has the constant value of r, so that

$$r = \sqrt{(x - h)^2 + (y - k)^2}$$

or

(1.1.3) $$r^2 = (x - h)^2 + (y - k)^2$$

Hence (1.1.3) is the equation of the circle of radius r and center (h, k). If the center of the circle is $(0, 0)$, the circle has the special form $r^2 = x^2 + y^2$.

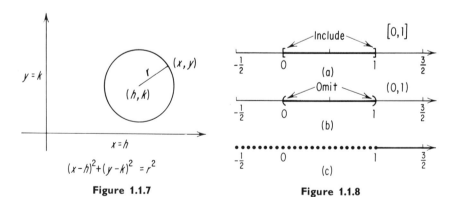

Figure 1.1.7   Figure 1.1.8

We conclude §1.1 with some miscellany. First, we give some very important definitions that will appear repeatedly throughout this book.

We say that the set of all x such that $a \leq x \leq b$ (where a and b are fixed numbers, with $a < b$) is the **closed interval from a to b**, and we designate this interval by the symbol $[a, b]$. The set of all x such that $a < x < b$ is called the **open interval from a to b**, and is designated by (a, b). These differ in that a closed interval includes both endpoints, whereas an open interval excludes both endpoints. Figure 1.1.8(a) shows the closed interval from 0 to 1; Fig. 1.1.8(b) shows the open interval from 0 to 1. We will call the set of all x such that $x \geq a$ (or $x \leq b$) a closed half-line, and the set of all x such that $x > a$ (or $x < b$) an *open half-line*. In Fig. 1.1.8(c), the bold line beginning at and including 1 is the closed half-line $x \geq 1$, whereas the dotted line beginning at but excluding 1 is the open half-line $x < 1$.

We say that I *is a closed interval* if there are distinct numbers a and b such that I is the set of all x for which $a \leq x \leq b$. In a completely analogous way we define I as an open interval, or an open or closed half-line.

Finally, we indicate a procedure for solving algebraic inequalities. This will be important, for example, when we investigate the domain of certain functions (see Prob. 1.1.16). We illustrate the procedure by Ex. 1.1.17.

We first remind the reader of the following facts from algebra, which we shall state as an axiom.

Axiom 1.1.1. Let a, b, c, u, and w be (real) numbers.
(i) If $a < b$, then $a + c < b + c$, and $a - c < b - c$.
(ii) Suppose $u > 0$. If $a < b$, then $au < bu$.
(iii) Suppose $w < 0$. If $a < b$, then $aw > bw$.

Example 1.1.15.
(a) Since $10 > 2$, it follows that $10 + 37 > 2 + 37$, and $10 - 18 > 2 - 18$;
(b) $2 < 10$, and hence $2 + 37 < 10 + 37$, and $2 - 18 < 10 - 18$;
(c) $-1 < 2$, and hence $-1 + 5 < 2 + 5$;
(d) $-2 < 4$, and hence $-2 - 1 < 4 - 1$;
(e) $6 > 2$, and hence $6 \cdot 3 > 2 \cdot 3$;
(f) $6 > -4$, and hence $6 \cdot 5 > -4 \cdot 5$;
(g) $6 > 2$, and $-3 < 0$, from which it follows that $6 \cdot (-3) < 2 \cdot (-3)$;
(h) Since $-1 > -3$ and $-4 < 0$, it follows that $-1 \cdot -4 < -3 \cdot -4$.

Example 1.1.16. If $3 - 2x < -5$, then $(3 - 2x) - 3 < -5 - 3$, $-2x < -8$, and (multiplying by $-\frac{1}{2}$) $x > 4$.

The inequality $a < x < b$ means $a < x$ *and* $x < b$ simultaneously, and in particular requires $a < b$. Also, $a \leq b$ means $a < b$ *or* $a = b$ (clearly, not both). Axiom 1.1.1 remains valid if " $<$ " is replaced by " $\leq$ ".

If $a \geq 0$, then $|a| = a > -a = -|a|$. But if $|a| = a$, then $|a| \geq a$, and if $a > -|a|$, then $a \geq -|a|$. Consequently if $a \geq 0$, then $|a| \geq a \geq -|a|$. Next, if $a < 0$, then $|a| = -a > a = -|a|$. Again, $|a| > a$ implies $|a| \geq a$ and

$a = -|a|$ implies $a \geq -|a|$, so that if $a < 0$, then $|a| \geq a \geq -|a|$. Hence we see that for all (real) a, $|a| \geq a \geq -|a|$.

From this we see also that for any (real) numbers a and b, $|a| \geq a \geq -|a|$ and $|b| \geq b \geq -|b|$. By Axiom 1.1.1(i), it follows that

$$|a| + |b| \geq a + b \geq -(|a| + |b|)$$

We have proved that if a and b are any real numbers,

(1.1.4) $|a + b| \leq |a| + |b|$ (triangle inequality)

Example 1.1.17. We solve the inequality $f(x) = x^2 - 2x - 3 > 0$. Observe that $x^2 - 2x - 3 = (x - 3)(x + 1)$. We shall reduce the problem to that of investigating the factors of $f(x)$, namely $u(x) = x - 3$ and $w(x) = x + 1$. We see that $f(x) > 0$ when $u(x)$ and $w(x)$ have the same sign, so we must investigate the sign of $u(x)$ and $w(x)$. We have that $u(x) > 0$ when $x - 3 > 0$, or, $x > 3$; also, $u(x) < 0$ when $x - 3 < 0$, or, $x < 3$. And $u(x) = 0$, when $x = 3$. In Fig. 1.1.9, we write beside $u(x)$ the sign of $u(x)$ corresponding to the appropriate x.

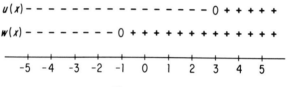

Figure 1.1.9

Next, $w(x) > 0$ when $x > -1$; $w(x) < 0$ when $x < -1$; $w(x) = 0$ when $x = -1$. In Fig. 1.1.9 we write beside $w(x)$ the sign of $w(x)$ corresponding to the appropriate x.

By inspecting Fig. 1.1.9, we see that $u(x)$ and $w(x)$ have the same sign when $x < -1$ or when $x > 3$. Hence, $f(x) > 0$ when $x > 3$ or $x < -1$; i.e., $f(x) > 0$ on the open half-lines $x > 3$ and $x < -1$.

Though the problem does not ask for the solution to $f(x) < 0$, we have all the necessary information to solve this inequality. Observe that $f(x) < 0$ when $u(x)$ and $w(x)$ are of opposite sign. From Fig. 1.1.9, we see this happens in the open interval $-1 < x < 3$. Hence, $f(x) < 0$ when x is in the open interval $-1 < x < 3$.

PROBLEMS

1.1.1. Let $f(x) = x^3 - x^2 + x + 1$. Find $f(0), f(1), f(-1), f(2), f(-2)$.

1.1.2. Let

$$f(x) = \frac{1}{x-1}, \quad g(x) = \frac{1}{\sqrt{x-1}}, \quad h(x) = \sqrt{x-1}$$

Evaluate $f(0)$, $f(-1)$, $g(10)$, $h(10)$. What can be said about the values $f(1)$, $g(-1)$, $g(-2)$, $h(-1)$, $h(-2)$? Give the domains of the functions f, g, and h and sketch their graphs. If the domains are half lines or intervals, state whether they are open or closed or neither.

1.1.3. Consider the relationship $x^2 + y^2 = 1$. Can y be expressed as a function of x? (i.e., is there a function f such that $y = f(x)$?) (*Hint:* solve for y.)

1.1.4. Draw the graph of

$$y = \frac{x^2 - 9}{x - 3}$$

1.1.5. Plot the points $(1, 0)$, $(0, 1)$, $(5, -3)$, $(-3, 5)$. Observe that in general the point (a, b) is distinct from the point (b, a).

1.1.6. Any three points in a plane which do not lie on a common line can be thought of as the vertices of a triangle. Show that each of the following sets form right triangles with vertices A, B, and C.

(a) $A:(1, 0)$, $B:(5, 3)$, $C(4 - 4)$
(b) $A:(0, 1)$, $B:(2, 3)$, $C(0, 5)$

1.1.7. Consider the relation $y = (x/|x|)$. Explain why y is a function of x for $x \neq 0$. What is wrong at $x = 0$? Call this function F; i.e., $F(x) = (x/|x|)$, $x \neq 0$. Find $F(-2)$, $F(-1)$, $F(1)$, and $F(2)$. Sketch the graph. State the domain and range of F.

1.1.8. Let

$$f(x) = \sqrt{x}, \quad g(x) = \frac{1}{x}$$

Let c and h be real numbers, $h \neq 0$. Evaluate

$$\frac{f(c + h) - f(c)}{h}, \quad \frac{g(c + h) - g(c)}{h}$$

1.1.9. Let $f(x) = |x|$, and let h be a real number, $h \neq 0$. Evaluate

$$\frac{f(h) - f(0)}{h}$$

1.1.10. Consider the sets of Ex. 1.1.1; box A contains $\{a, b, c\}$, and box B contains $\{1, 2, 3\}$. How many functions are there with domain A and range B, if we require that distinct values of B are associated with distinct values of A?

1.1.11. Find the center and radius of the circle $x^2 + y^2 - 2x - 4y = 1$. (*Hint:* complete the square in x and y.)

1.1.12. Show that if point $P : (x, y)$ is equidistant from the point $(0, 4)$ and the x-axis, then $x^2 - 8y + 16 = 0$. Is the converse true?

1.1.13. (a) When does $|5 - 2x|$ equal $5 - 2x$?
        (b) When does $|5 - 2x|$ equal $2x - 5$?

1.1.14. Draw the graph of the function $f(x) = n$ if $n \le x < n + 1$, and n is an integer.

1.1.15. Solve each of the following inequalities. Indicate whether your solutions are open or closed intervals or half-lines

(a) $x^2 - x \ge 0$ (b) $x^2 - 2x + 1 \ge 0$

(c) $x^2 - 4 \le 0$ (d) $x^3 + 2x > 0$

(e) $(x - 1)(x - 2)(x - 3) < 0$ (f) $\dfrac{(x + 5)(x - 1)}{x^2 - 4} \ge 0$

1.1.16. Find the domain of each of the following:

(a) $f(x) = \sqrt{x^2 - x - 2}$ (b) $g(x) = \dfrac{1}{\sqrt{x^3 - 2x^2 - 15x}}$

(c) $y(x) = \sqrt{-x^2 - x + 2}$ (d) $W(x) = \sqrt{x^4 + x^2}$

Problems 1.1.17–1.1.19 relate to the reliability function of Ex. 1.1.10.

1.1.17. Show that the range of $f_n(r)$ is the closed interval $[0, 1]$; i.e., $0 \le f_n(r) \le 1$, for all r in $0 \le r \le 1$.

1.1.18. Let $R = f_n(r)$. Show that $f_{1/n}(R) = r$.

1.1.19. Define

$$F_n(r) = n\left[\frac{1}{f_n(r)} - 1\right]$$

Show that $F_n(r) = F_m(r)$, for all m and n. Why is $F_n(r)$ a useful function for the psychologist?

1.1.20. Verify that (1.1.2) remains valid if the line segment is parallel to the x-axis and determine the form (1.1.2) takes for such segments.

1.1.21. If a and b are any real numbers, prove $||a| - |b|| \le |a - b|$. (*Hint:* Observe $a = b + (a - b)$, and $b = a + (b - a)$, and use (1.1.4).)

1.2. The slope of a tangent line. Derivatives.

Consider the following geometrical problem. Given a function $y = f(x)$, we wish to define a line *tangent* to the graph of the function at the point $(a, f(a))$. We know from plane geometry that a line is determined by one point on the line and some measure of the direction of the line. Hence, we will know the tangent line if we can determine the angle θ the line makes with the x-axis (see Fig. 1.2.1), since we already know a point on the line is $(a, f(a))$.

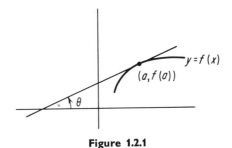

Figure 1.2.1

Of course the tangent line and the graph of the function $y = f(x)$ must share the given point. However, the angle θ is not a desirable measure of angle, so we introduce the following equivalent measure.

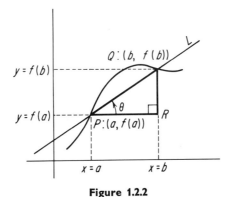

Figure 1.2.2

Given a (necessarily non-vertical) straight line L through the points $P:(a, f(a))$ and $Q:(b, f(b))$, construct the right triangle PQR of Fig. 1.2.2. We define the slope $m(L)$, or simply m if no confusion can arise, of the line L as:

(1.2.1)
$$m(L) = \frac{f(b) - f(a)}{b - a}$$

Those of you who know trigonometry will recognize $m(L) = \tan\theta$, where θ is the angle between the line L and the x-axis measured counterclockwise from the x-axis (see Fig. 1.2.2). By using arguments from plane geometry which involve similar triangles, one can show that for a given line L, the value of $m(L)$ is unique; i.e., it is independent of the particular points on the line chosen to evaluate $m(L)$ (see Fig. 1.2.3). For every non-vertical line L we get a unique value for $m(L)$. Restricting our attention to θ ($0° \le \theta < 180°$), one can show that $0° \le \theta < 90°$ if and only if $m(L) \ge 0$, and $90° < \theta < 180°$ if and only if $m(L) < 0$, and that $m(L) = 0$ if and only if $\theta = 0°$, or what amounts to the same thing, if L is parallel to the x-axis (see Prob. 1.2.2). Observe that parallel lines have the same slope (see Prob. 1.2.1). Observe, also, that

$$\frac{f(b) - f(a)}{b - a} = \frac{-[f(a) - f(b)]}{-(a - b)} = \frac{f(a) - f(b)}{a - b}$$

so that the roles of $(a, f(a))$ and $(b, f(b))$ in (1.2.1) may be interchanged.

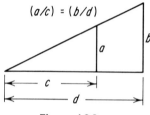

Figure 1.2.3

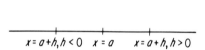

Figure 1.2.4

We now return to the problem of defining the tangent line T to the graph of $y = f(x)$ at $x = a$ (i.e., at the point on the graph, $(a, f(a))$, corresponding to $x = a$). What we must find to know the line T is $m(T)$. We shall investigate the specific equation of T in a subsequent section.

Let h be an arbitrary (positive or negative *but non-zero*) number. Then $b = a + h$ is a point to the right of a if $h > 0$, and $b = a + h$ is a number to the left of a if $h < 0$ (see Fig. 1.2.4).

Let us first assume $h > 0$, so that $b = a + h$ is to the right of a. The point on the graph corresponding to $b = a + h$ is then $Q:(a + h, f(a + h))$. Draw the line L through P and Q, and observe that

$$m(L) = \frac{f(a + h) - f(a)}{h}$$

We are assuming that $f(x)$ is defined in an open interval containing $x = a$. If the point Q is taken closer to P, e.g., Q^1 in Fig. 1.2.5, the line through the new point Q^1 and P is a better approximation to the line T. We are led to define the *slope of the line T tangent to the graph of $f(x)$ at the point $(a, f(a))$*, or simply at $x = a$, as

(1.2.2) $$m(T) = \lim_{Q \to P} m(L) = \lim_{h \to 0} \frac{f(a + h) - f(a)}{h}$$

where $\lim\limits_{h \to 0}$ is read "the limit as h tends to 0" or "the limit as h approaches 0", and is meant to include both the case $h \to 0$ with $h > 0$ *and* $h \to 0$ with $h < 0$.

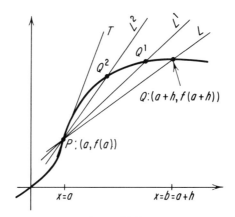

Figure 1.2.5

Also, in the notation $h \to 0$, we **do not set h = 0.** By "the limit" we mean that

$$\frac{f(a + h) - f(a)}{h}$$

takes on values all arbitrarily close to the number $m(T)$ if h is chosen sufficiently close to 0, though not equal to 0, with both $h > 0$ and $h < 0$ considered.

If (1.2.2) exists, we define the *line T as the line tangent to the graph of $f(x)$* at $(a, f(a))$ if the line T passes through $(a, f(a))$ and has the slope given by (1.2.2). [The reader should observe that we are disregarding vertical tangent lines, for which (1.2.2) does *not* exist (see Prob. 1.2.2). In Prob. 1.2.10 the reader will be asked to construct a suitable definition for "vertical tangent".]

Example 1.2.1. Find $m(T)$ for the line tangent to the graph of $f(x)$ x^2 at x 1. We must evaluate, with h 0, h 0,   0,

$$m(T) = \lim_{h \to 0} \frac{f(1 + h) - f(1)}{h} = \lim_{h \to 0} \frac{(1 + h)^2 - 1^2}{h}$$

$$= \lim_{h \to 0} \frac{2h + h^2}{h} = \lim_{h \to 0} \frac{h}{h}(2 + h)$$

Since we have required $h \neq 0$, we see that $h/h = 1$, and so the limit becomes

$$m(T) = \lim_{h \to 0} (2 + h) = 2$$

since $2 + h$ can be made to stay arbitrarily close to 2 by taking positive or
negative values of h sufficiently close
to 0 (see Fig. 1.2.6).

Example 1.2.2. Find the slope of
the line tangent to the graph of $f(x) =$
x^2 at $x = 0$; i.e., find $m(T)$ for $x = 0$.
For $h > 0$ or $h < 0$ but $h \neq 0$, we
must evaluate

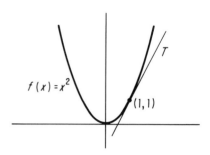

Figure 1.2.6

$$m(T) = \lim_{h \to 0} \frac{f(0 + h) - f(0)}{h} = \lim_{h \to 0} \frac{h^2}{h}$$

Since $h \neq 0$,

$$\frac{h^2}{h} = h; \quad \text{hence} \quad m(T) = \lim_{h \to 0} h = 0$$

that is, h can be made to stay arbitrarily close to 0 by taking h sufficiently
close to 0 through both positive and negative values of h, $h \neq 0$. Hence $m(T)$,
the slope of the line tangent to $f(x) = x^2$, at $x = 0$, is equal to 0.

Example 1.2.3. Find $m(T)$ for $f(x) = ax + b$ at any value $x = c$. Here a
and b are to be thought of as fixed numbers, i.e., a and b are constants.

$$m(T) = \lim_{h \to 0} \frac{f(c + h) - f(c)}{h} = \lim_{h \to 0} \frac{[a(c + h) + b] - [ac + b]}{h}$$

$$= \lim_{h \to 0} a \frac{h}{h} = \lim_{h \to 0} a = a$$

Hence, $m(T) = a$. Again we used the fact that $h \neq 0$ to write $a(h/h) = a$. So
$m(T) = \lim_{h \to 0} a = a$ means that $m(T) = a$ can be made to stay arbitrarily close
to a by taking h sufficiently close to 0; but since $a = a$, this is certainly true,
and for this particular situation has nothing to do with h at all.

Example 1.2.4. Let $f(x) = 3x - 7$. Find $m(T)$ at any point $x = a$.

$$m(T) = \lim_{h \to 0} \frac{[3(a + h) - 7] - [3a - 7]}{h} = \lim_{h \to 0} 3 \frac{h}{h} = 3$$

Again, $h \neq 0$ implies $h/h = 1$. The function $f(x) = 3x - 7$ corresponds to the
function $f(x) = ax + b$ of Ex. 1.2.3 with $a = 3$, $b = 7$. We should observe
from Ex. 1.2.3 that with $a = 3$, $m(T) = 3$, which is exactly our conclusion in
this example.

Example 1.2.5. Find $m(T)$ for $f(x) = \sqrt{|x|}$ at $x = 0$. Here, $m(T)$ is given by

$$\lim_{h \to 0} \frac{f(0 + h) - f(0)}{h} = \lim_{h \to 0} \frac{\sqrt{|h|}}{h} = \lim_{h \to 0} \frac{|h|^{1/2}}{h}$$

But, for $h > 0$,

$$\frac{|h|^{1/2}}{h} = h^{(1/2)-1} = h^{-1/2} = (1/\sqrt{h})$$

Hence

$$m(T) = \lim_{h \to 0} \frac{1}{\sqrt{h}}$$

if this expression has meaning. We see that for $h > 0$, as h becomes small, $1/\sqrt{h}$ becomes very large, and hence approaches no number $m(T)$; i.e., the limit *does not exist.*

The expression

$$\lim_{h \to 0} \frac{f(a + h) - f(a)}{h}$$

plays an important role in mathematics and gets a special name: *the **derivative** of $f(x)$ at $x = a$,* and is written $f'(a)$; i.e.,

(1.2.3)
$$f'(a) = \lim_{h \to 0} \frac{f(a + h) - f(a)}{h}$$

Owing to historical accident, there are many notations for the derivative. Some of the more commonly used are:

$$f'(a) = Df(a) = D_x f(a) = Df(x)|_{x=a} = \frac{d}{dx} f(x)|_{x=a} = \frac{df(x)}{dx}\bigg|_{x=a} = \frac{d}{dx} f(a)$$

In terms of this new notation, observe that in Ex. 1.2.1, we computed $f'(1)$, where $f(x) = x^2$ (or, in terms of other notation, we computed

$$Dx^2|_{x=1} \quad \text{or} \quad \frac{dx^2}{dx}\bigg|_{x=1}$$

to be 2. In Ex. 1.2.2, we found that $f'(0) = 0$ where $f(x) = x^2$, or, $Dx^2|_{x=0} = 0$. Example 1.2.3 shows that if $f(x) = ax + b$, than $f'(c) = a$ for any real number c. In Ex. 1.2.5, we found that if $f(x) = \sqrt{|x|}$, then $f'(0)$ is undefined [i.e., 0 is not in the domain of $f'(x)$].

If we compare (1.2.2) and (1.2.3), we can summarize as follows: *the geometrical interpretation of $f'(a)$ is that it represents the slope of the (non-vertical) line tangent to $y = f(x)$ at the point $(a, f(a))$* (see Fig. 1.2.7).

If in the expression for $f'(a)$ the quantity a is variable, then f' is a function of a. Replacing a by x, we get $f'(x)$, a new function of x derived from $f(x)$ by taking the limit in (1.2.3). This limit can be written

(1.2.4)
$$f'(x) = \lim_{h \to 0} \frac{f(x + h) - f(x)}{h}$$

Example 1.2.6. If $f(x) = x^2$, find $f'(x)$. We have:

$$f'(x) = \lim_{h \to 0} \frac{(x + h)^2 - x^2}{h}$$

$$= \lim_{h \to 0} \frac{2xh + h^2}{h}$$

$$= \lim_{h \to 0} (2x + h) = 2x$$

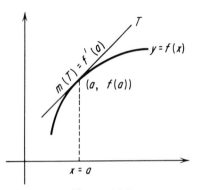

Figure 1.2.7

We have used the fact that $h \neq 0$ to write $h/h = 1$, and we still consider $h \to 0$ for $h > 0$, and $h < 0$.

If $f'(a)$ exists, we say that $f(x)$ is *differentiable at* $x = a$. If $f'(x)$ does not exist for some $x = a$ (i.e., if a is not in the domain of $f'(x)$), we say $f(x)$ is *not differentiable at* $x = a$. From Ex. 1.2.5, we see that $\sqrt{|x|}$ is not differentiable at $x = 0$.

PROBLEMS

1.2.1. Let L and J be two parallel lines. Show that $m(L) = m(J)$.

1.2.2. Let the line L intersect the x-axis at an angle θ. Show that if $\theta = 0$, then $m(L) = 0$; if $0° < \theta < 90°$, then $m(L) > 0$, if $90° < \theta < 180°$, then $m(L) < 0$ and if $\theta = 90°$, then $m(L)$ is undefined.

1.2.3. Let $f(x) = |x|$. Show that $f(x)$ is not differentiable at $x = 0$, but $f'(x) = 1$ if $x > 0$ and $f'(x) = -1$ if $x < 0$.

1.2.4. Find $f'(x)$ for each of the following functions:

(a) $f(x) = x^2 + 1$ (b) $f(x) = \sqrt{x}$

(c) $f(x) = \dfrac{1}{x}$ (d) $f(x) = \dfrac{1}{\sqrt{x}}$

(e) $f(x) = \dfrac{1}{x-1}$ (f) $f(x) = ax^2 + bx + c$ a, b, c constant.

1.2.5. Use the result of Prob. 1.2.4(c) to find the slopes of the lines tangent to $f(x) = 1/x$ at $x = -1$, $x = 2$, and $x = -2$. Sketch the graph of $f(x) = 1/x$. What can be said about the construction of a tangent line at $x = 0$?

1.2.6. Use the result of Prob. 1.2.4(b) to find the slope of the tangent line to $f(x) = \sqrt{x}$ at $x = 1$, $x = 4$, and $x = 9$. Sketch the graph of $f(x) = \sqrt{x}$ (see Ex. 1.1.5). In terms of Prob. 1.2.4(b), what can be said about $f'(0)$? Compare this with Ex. 1.2.5. In terms of your sketch of $\sqrt{x}$, what can be said about the construction of a tangent line at $x = 0$?

1.2.7. Consider the function $f(x) = x^2 + 1$. Use (1.2.3) to evaluate $f'(0)$ and $f'(1)$. Compare this with what you get by setting $x = 0$ and $x = 1$ in the result of Prob. 1.2.4(a).

1.2.8. Suppose we are given a function $y = f(x)$ with the known properties that $f(0) = 1$ and $f'(0) = 3$. Evaluate

$$\lim_{h \to 0} \frac{f(h) - 1}{h}$$

1.2.9. Define

$$f(x) = \begin{cases} 0, & x \neq 1 \\ 1, & x = 1 \end{cases}$$

Observe that this is a function. Draw the graph of $f(x)$. Using (1.2.4), investigate $f'(1)$.

1.2.10. The line T is a *vertical tangent* line to the graph of $f(x)$ at $(a, f(a))$ if

$$\lim_{h \to 0} \frac{h}{f(a+h) - f(a)} = 0$$

and T then has equation $x = a$. Show that $f(x) = x^{2/3}$ has a vertical tangent at $x = 0$.

1.3. Velocity, acceleration. Rate of change.

To the non-mathematician the major interest in calculus is in its varied powerful applications. We shall save most of these applications until we have more information about the derivative. However, we shall introduce briefly what was historically one of the earliest uses of the derivative.

If an object is in motion, we assert that the distance s traveled by the object after t units of time have elapsed will be a function of the time t (i.e., to each time t, we associate at most one value of the distance traveled s), and so we may represent distance by $s(t)$.

Suppose a particle moves in a straight line according to a known law of motion $s(t)$. The classical definition of average velocity, which we shall denote by $\bar{v}$ (read "v-bar") is:

$$\bar{v} = \frac{\text{change in distance corresponding to a change in time}}{\text{change in time}}$$

Suppose in particular we wish to evaluate $\bar{v}$ as time varies from $t = a$ to $t = b$. The corresponding distances are $s(a)$ and $s(b)$, so

$$(1.3.1) \qquad \bar{v} = \frac{s(b) - s(a)}{b - a}$$

Example 1.3.1. A particle falls so that the distance it has fallen, s feet, at time t seconds, is given by $s(t) = 32t^2$. What is the average velocity of the particle from time $t = 1$ to time $t = 2$? We see that

$$\bar{v} = \frac{s(2) - s(1)}{2 - 1} = 32 \cdot 4 - 32 \cdot 1$$

$$= 32(4 - 1) = 32 \cdot 3 = 96 \text{ ft/sec}$$

Given $s(t)$ we wish to define the instantaneous velocity v of a particle at the instant the time is $t = c$. If we look at a time near $t = c$, say $t = c + h$, then the average velocity $\bar{v}$ of the particle from time $t = c$ to time $t = c + h$ is:

$$\bar{v} = \frac{s(c + h) - s(c)}{h}$$

where $h = $ (final time) $-$ (initial time) $= (c + h) - c = h$ is the change in time. It seems reasonable that as the change in time becomes smaller and smaller, the corresponding average velocities are better and better approximations to the *instantaneous velocity* at $t = c$. We are led to define the instantaneous velocity v at time $t = c$ as the limit of the average velocities from $t = c$ to $t = c + h$, as h tends to 0:

$$v = \lim_{h \to 0} \frac{s(c + h) - s(c)}{h}$$

If we indicate the time at which we wish to evaluate v simply as t, the instantaneous velocity at time t is:

$$(1.3.2) \qquad v(t) = \lim_{h \to 0} \frac{s(t + h) - s(t)}{h}$$

By comparing (1.3.2) with (1.2.3), we see that $v(t) = s'(t)$. Average acceleration, $\bar{a}$, and instantaneous acceleration at time t, $a(t)$, can be defined in a completely analogous manner, simply by substituting v for s and a for v in our previous arguments. This is because acceleration is nothing but the rate of change of velocity. Hence, (1.3.1) and (1.3.2) become:

(1.3.3)
$$\bar{a} = \frac{v(b) - v(c)}{b - c}$$

where $\bar{a}$ is the *average acceleration* over the time interval from $t = c$ to $t = b$, and

(1.3.4)
$$a(t) = \lim_{h \to 0} \frac{v(t + h) - v(t)}{h}$$

where $a(t)$ is the *instantaneous acceleration* at time t.

Comparing (1.3.4) and (1.2.3) we see that $a(t) = v'(t) = s''(t)$, where $s''(t)$ indicates two successive differentiations of $s(t)$; the first time getting $v(t)$ and the second time $v'(t) = a(t)$. s'' is called the second derivative of s; more will be said of this later. Summarizing, we see that:

(1.3.5)
$$\begin{cases} v(t) = s'(t); \text{ i.e., velocity is the derivative of distance} \\ a(t) = v'(t); \text{ i.e., acceleration is the derivative of velocity} \end{cases}$$

Example 1.3.2. Suppose distance is given by $s(t) = t^2$. Find $\bar{v}$ and $\bar{a}$ from $t = 1$ to $t = 2$; find $v(t)$ and $a(t)$; and find $v(0)$, $v(1)$, $a(0)$, $a(1)$.

Solution: First, we see that $\bar{v}$ is given by (1.3.1) as

$$\bar{v} = \frac{s(2) - s(1)}{2 - 1} = 4 - 1 = 3$$

If we look at (1.3.3), we see that before we can find $\bar{a}$ we must know v. From (1.3.5), $v(t) = s'(t) = (d/dt)t^2$. Recall that in Ex. 1.2.6, we found that if $f(x) = x^2$, then $f'(x) = 2x$. Hence, if $s(t) = t^2$, then $s'(t) = 2t$. Hence, $v(t) = 2t$. By (1.3.3)

$$\bar{a} = \frac{v(2) - v(1)}{2 - 1} = 2 \cdot 2 - 2 \cdot 1 = 2$$

From (1.3.4),

$$a(t) = \lim_{h \to 0} \frac{v(t + h) - v(t)}{h} = \lim_{h \to 0} \frac{2(t + h) - 2t}{h} = \lim_{h \to 0} \frac{2h}{h} = 2$$

and so acceleration is constant. Summarizing, $\bar{v} = 3$, $\bar{a} = 2$, $v(t) = 2t$, and $a(t) = 2$. Hence, $v(0) = 2 \cdot 0 = 0$, $v(1) = 2 \cdot 1 = 2$, $a(0) = 2$, and $a(1) = 2$.

The linear velocity of a particle is the rate of change of the distance of the particle with respect to time; i.e., the symbol ds/dt may be thought of as rate of change of s with respect to t. This gives us still another interpretation of the derivative, which we generalize as follows: suppose a quantity w is known to vary with another quantity u, and suppose this is given by $w = G(u)$. Then we define $G'(u) = dG(u)/du$ as the *rate of change of w with respect to u*.

Example 1.3.3. The total cost of producing and marketing x units of a commodity is assumed to be a function of x alone, that is, independent of time and other commodities. Designate this function by $s(x)$. It is natural to assume that if no commodities are produced, there is no cost; i.e., $s(0) = 0$. The *average cost* to produce x units, $\bar{s}(x)$, is given by

$$\frac{s(x) - s(0)}{x - 0} = \frac{s(x)}{x}$$

The rate of change of total cost with respect to the number of units produced is called *marginal cost*, and can be expressed as $s'(x)$, the derivative of $s(x)$ with respect to x.

PROBLEMS

1.3.1. Suppose the distance a particle has traveled in t seconds is given by $s(t) = \sqrt{t}$. Find the velocity of the particle (see Prob. 1.2.4) and the acceleration of the particle at an arbitrary time t. Find $\bar{v}$ and $\bar{a}$ as the particle goes from time $t = 9$ to time $t = 16$.

1.3.2. A ball is thrown straight up in the air so that its distance s above the ground at time t is given by $s(t) = 128t - 16t^2$.

(a) Find $\bar{v}$ over the time interval $t = 0$ to $t = 1$.
(b) Find $\bar{v}$ over the time interval $t = a$ to $t = a + h$.
(c) Find $v(a)$, the instantaneous velocity at time a.
(d) Find the maximum height that the ball goes.

1.3.3. Let A be the area of a square of side x. Find the rate of change of A with respect to x when $x = 10$.

1.3.4. Let A be the area of a circle of radius r. Show that the rate of change of area with respect to the radius is given by the circumference of the circle.

1.3.5. A spherical balloon has air pumped into it so that at time t, the radius r is given by $r(t) = \frac{1}{2}t$. How fast is the balloon expanding; i.e., how fast is the volume increasing? (*Recall:* the volume v of a sphere with radius r is $v = \frac{4}{3}\pi r^3$.)

1.3.6. Water is being pumped from a tank so that the volume of water V in gallons t minutes after the pumping has begun is given by

$$V(t) = 100(10 - t)^2$$

Find the average rate at which the water is drained for the first 5 minutes, then for the first 10 minutes. Find the rate at which the water is being drained at $t = 5$, and then at $t = 10$.

1.3.7. A particle moves so that its distance s at time t is $s(t) = at^2 + bt + c$ (a, b, c constant). Find the velocity (see Prob. 1.2.4(f)) and the acceleration of the particle.

1.3.8. Suppose the total cost of producing x units of a commodity (see Ex. 1.3.3) is given by $s(x) = 2x^3$. Find the average and marginal costs of producing 100 units of the commodity.

1.4. The equation of a straight line. Tangent lines.

In §1.2 we considered non-vertical straight lines which passed through two points on the graph of some given function $y = f(x)$, and straight lines that were tangent to the graphs of given functions at specified points. We found that we could determine the line if we knew a point on the line and its slope. The problem in §1.2 was to find the proper slope. We shall now investigate the general problem of determining the equations of lines.

Suppose we are given a point (a, b) and a number m; we want the line through (a, b) with slope equal to the given value m. Call the line so determined L. The question is: Given an arbitrary x, what is the corresponding value of y such that (x, y) is on L?

Since m is assumed to exist, L is not a vertical line (see Prob. 1.2.2). We will approach the problem by putting the point (x, y), distinct from (a, b), on the line and then investigating the properties it must possess to be on the line. Since m is independent of the choice of points on L from which it is evaluated, we shall use the known point (a, b) and the unknown point (x, y) to evaluate the known value m. We have $m = (y - b)/(x - a)$, or

$$(1.4.1) \qquad\qquad y - b = m(x - a)$$

It is important to realize that in (1.4.1), a, b, and m are known, and x and y are the coordinates of an *arbitrary* point on the line L (see Fig. 1.4.1).

If we know two distinct points, (a, b) and (c, d), then $m = (d - b)/(c - a)$, provided $c \neq a$, and the equation becomes

$$(1.4.2) \qquad\qquad y - b = \frac{d - b}{c - a}(x - a)$$

Hence, as we could have predicted from plane geometry, two points also give the equation of a unique line.

If we are given a specific point $(0, b)$ (i.e., a point whose first coordinate is 0), then we see that it is the point at which the line crosses the y-axis. If this line has slope m, then from (1.4.1) we see $y - b = m(x - 0)$, and so

(1.4.3) $y = mx + b$

Compare this with Ex. 1.2.3; b is called the y-intercept, and the form (1.4.3) is called the y-intercept equation for the line (see Fig. 1.4.2). Observe also

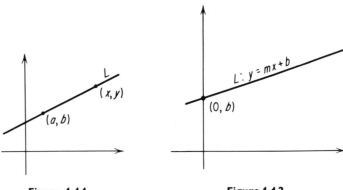

Figure 1.4.1   Figure 1.4.2

that from (1.4.3) we see immediately that for all non-vertical lines, y is expressible as a function of x.

Example 1.4.1. Find the y-intercept form of the line through $(2, 1)$ and $(-1, 4)$. Clearly $m = [1 - 4]/[2 - (-1)] = -1$, so by (1.4.1), the line has the equation $y - 1 = -1(x - 2)$, or, $y - 1 = -x + 2$, or, finally, in the form of (1.4.3), $y = -x + 3$. The reader should verify that the point $(-1, 4)$ could have been used instead of $(2, 1)$ in (1.4.1).

Example 1.4.2. Is the point $(4, 2)$ on the line of Ex. 1.4.1? If so, it must satisfy $y = -x + 3$; i.e., it must be that $2 = -4 + 3$. Since $2 \neq -1$, the point $(4, 2)$ is not on the line.

Example 1.4.3. Find the equation of the line through $(5, 1)$ and $(7, 1)$. Here, $m = 0$, so, by (1.4.1), $y - 1 = 0(x - 5) = 0$. Hence the line has equation $y = 1$.

Example 1.4.4. Identify the graph of the relation $3x + 2y = 1$. Here, $2y = 1 - 3x$, or, $y = -\frac{3}{2}x + \frac{1}{2}$. From (1.4.3), we see that this is a line with slope $-\frac{3}{2}$ and y-intercept $\frac{1}{2}$ (see Fig. 1.4.3).

We will now consider the vertical line (i.e., the line parallel to the y-axis) passing through the point $(3, 0)$. Observe that the y coordinate of the line is arbitrary, and that every point of this line has first coordinate 3. The equation of the line is simply $x = 3$ (see Fig. 1.4.4). In general, then, the vertical line passing through $(a, 0)$ has equation $x = a$. We should observe that the vertical line has *no slope*, and is a flagrant violator of the conditions necessary for a relation to be functional. For the line $x = 3$, a vast number of y values correspond to the single value $x = 3$. The reader should also observe that *all lines which have functional representations are lines with slope, and can all be put in the form $y = mx + b$.*

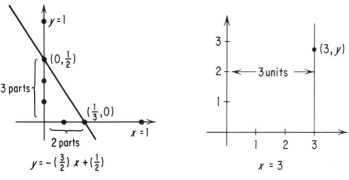

Figure 1.4.3   Figure 1.4.4

What is the equation of the line tangent to the graph of $f(x)$ at $(a, f(a))$? From (1.4.1), we see the equation is:

(1.4.4) $$y - f(a) = f'(a)(x - a)$$

Example 1.4.5. Find the equation of the line tangent to the graph of $f(x) = x^2$ at $x = 5$. From Ex. 1.2.6, $f'(x) = 2x$, and hence $f'(5) = 10$. Clearly $f(5) = 25$. From (1.4.4), the line has equation $y - f(5) = f'(5)(x - 5)$, so, $y - 25 = 10(x - 5)$, or, $y = 10x - 25$ is the required line.

PROBLEMS

1.4.1. Find the equation of the lines through the specified points:

    (a) $(1, 4)$ and $(3, -2)$
    (b) $(2, -4)$ and $(-6, -4)$
    (c) $(-\frac{1}{2}, 1)$ and $(1, 2)$
    (d) $(1, 1)$ and $(1, 6)$
    (e) (a, b) and $(0, d)$, $a \neq 0$, $b \neq 0$, $d \neq 0$.

1.4.2. Find the equation of the line through $(2, -1)$ and parallel to the line $y = -2x + 1$.

1.4.3. Find the tangent line to the graph of each of the following functions at the indicated points (see Prob. 1.2.4):

(a) $f(x) = x^2 + 1$ at $x = 2$
(b) $f(x) = \sqrt{x}$ at $x = 4$
(c) $f(x) = 1/x$ at $x = 1$
(d) $f(x) = \sqrt{|x|}$ at $x = 0$
(e) $f(x) = ax^2 + bx + C$ at $x = 1$

1.4.4. In each of the following, determine whether or not the three given points all lie on the same line.

(a) $P(1, 0)$, $Q(0, 1)$, and $R(2, -1)$
(b) $P(-2, 1)$, $Q(0, 5)$, and $R(-1, 2)$
(c) $P(0, -1)$, $Q(-1, -3)$, and $R(1, 1)$

1.5. Limits

The derivative defined in §1.2 is a special case of limit. A more general problem is to investigate the symbol $\lim\limits_{x \to c} f(x)$ and the numbers $f(x)$ as x takes values near c, or, as "x tends to c". Again, "x tending to c" is meant to signify that x takes values near c with $x < c$ and with $x > c$, but $x \neq c$. Here we assume that $f(x)$ is defined in an open interval containing c, except possibly at $x = c$.

For instance, let $f(x) = 2x + 5$, and consider $\lim\limits_{x \to 1} f(x)$. Observe that $f(2) = 9$, $f(3/2) = 8$, $f(5/4) = 7 + \frac{1}{2}$, $f(9/8) = 7 + \frac{1}{4}$, $f(17/16) = 7 + \frac{1}{8}$, $f(33/32) = 7 + \frac{1}{16}$. We see that as x tends to 1 (written "$x \to 1$") from values greater than 1, $f(x)$ tends to 7 (written "$f(x) \to 7$"). Also, $f(0) = 5, f(1/2) = 6$, $f(3/4) = 6 + \frac{1}{2}, f(7/8) = 6 + \frac{3}{4}, f(15/16) = 6 + \frac{7}{8}$. We see here that $f(x) \to 7$ as $x \to 1$ for values of x less than 1. Hence, we write $\lim\limits_{x \to 1} (2x + 5) = 7$. In general, we define:

Definition 1.5.1. Let $f(x)$ be defined in some open interval containing $x = c$, though not necessarily at $x = c$. The symbol $\lim\limits_{x \to c} f(x) = L$ means that the numbers $f(x)$ can be made to stay arbitrarily close to L if only we take x sufficiently close to c, for values of x both greater than and less than c, but $x \neq c$.

This will serve as a working definition of limit. A more formal definition will appear in §1.6.

The reader may have observed that in the example above, the limit 7 is exactly what we would have obtained by evaluating $f(x) = 2x + 5$ at $x = 1$ i.e., $\lim\limits_{x \to 1} f(x) = f(1)$. A reasonable question to ask is if this is always the case. The answer is an emphatic no, as some of the next examples will show. In fact, functions with the property $\lim_{x \to c} f(x) = f(c)$ are called *continuous*, and will be discussed in §1.7.

Example 1.5.1. $\lim_{x \to 2} x^2 = 4$, since x^2 can be made to stay arbitrarily close to 4 by taking x sufficiently close to 2, if $x \neq 2$.

Example 1.5.2. Let

$$f(x) = \frac{x^2 - 1}{x - 1}$$

Observe that $f(1)$ does not exist since division by 0 is not permitted. Consequently, if $\lim_{x \to 1} f(x)$ exists, it cannot be $f(1)$. Observe that

$$\lim_{x \to 1} \frac{x^2 - 1}{x - 1} = \lim_{x \to 1} \frac{(x + 1)(x - 1)}{x - 1}$$

and since $x \neq 1$, we have that $[(x - 1)/(x - 1)] = 1$,

$$\lim_{x \to 1} \frac{x^2 - 1}{x - 1} = \lim_{x \to 1} (x + 1) = 2$$

The reader should convince himself that $\lim_{x \to 1} (x + 1) = 2$ whether $x \to 1$ for values $x > 1$ or $x < 1$; again, this limit 2 does not equal the undefined $f(1)$.

Example 1.5.3. Let

$$g(x) = \begin{cases} \dfrac{x^2 - 1}{x - 1}, & x \neq 1 \\ 3, & x = 1 \quad \text{(i.e., } g(1) = 3\text{)} \end{cases}$$

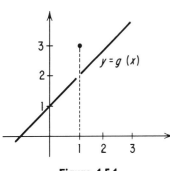

Figure 1.5.1

Observe that $g(x)$ is not the same function as $f(x)$ of Ex. 1.5.2, since $g(1) = 3$ but $f(1)$ is undefined. Let us evaluate $\lim_{x \to 1} g(x)$. In this evaluation we can always assume $x \neq 1$, and hence all the calculations to evaluate the limit are identical to the calculations of Ex. 1.5.2. But since $g(1) = 3$ by definition of $g(x)$, we see that $\lim_{x \to 1} g(x) = 2 \neq 3 = g(1)$. So, the limit *does* exist, the value $g(1)$ is meaningful, but the limit is not equal to $g(1)$. The graph of $g(x)$ is drawn in Fig. 1.5.1.

Example 1.5.4. Let $H(x) = 1/x$. What is $\lim_{x \to 0} H(x)$? Observe that $H(1/2) = 2$, $H(1/4) = 4$, $H(1/1000) = 1000$, $H(10^{-20}) = 10^{20}$. In fact, as

$x \to 0$, $x > 0$, $H(x)$ becomes arbitrarily large, and as $x \to 0$, $x < 0$, $|H(x)|$ takes on arbitrarily large values. Hence, $\lim_{x \to 0} H(x)$ *does not exist.*

In our discussion of limit up to this point, we have assumed that $f(x)$ is meaningful for values $x < a$ and $x > a$. Since we are interested in $\lim_{x \to a}$, it is actually enough that $f(x)$ be meaningful for values $x < a$ and $x > a$ with x near a in some sense. We have, in fact, assumed that the domain of $f(x)$ includes some open interval containing a, except possibly a itself. This is certainly going to be the case if the domain of $f(x)$ is the entire x-axis, with the possible exception of $x = a$, and this is the case for many of the functions with which we deal.

There are functions whose domain is *not* the entire x-axis; e.g., $g(x) = \sqrt{x}$ (why?). Suppose we have a function f with domain an interval I or a half-infinite line J. The question is this: If the domain of $f(x)$ is the interval I of all numbers x from $x = a$ to $x = b$ with $a < b$ (with no commitments as to whether I is open or closed, if, indeed it is either) how shall we consider $\lim_{x \to a}$ since $f(x)$ is not even meaningful for $x < a$, and how shall we consider $\lim_{x \to b}$ if $f(x)$ is not meaningful for $x > b$? In the event that this occurs (i.e., in the event that $f(x)$ is not defined in an open interval containing the value of x at which we wish to evaluate the limit) we make the following definition.

Definition 1.5.2. Let the domain of $f(x)$ be an interval (perhaps open, perhaps closed, perhaps neither) with endpoints a and b, $a < b$. Then at the endpoints a and b, we say that $\lim_{x \to a} f(x) = L$ if the values of $f(x)$ can be made to stay arbitrarily close to L by taking x sufficiently close to a, for $x > a$ and $x \ne a$ [i.e., $x \ne a$ and x in the domain of $f(x)$], and we say that $\lim_{x \to b} f(x) = K$ if the values of $f(x)$ can be made to stay arbitrarily close to K by taking x sufficiently close to b, for $x < b$ and $x \ne b$ [i.e., $x \ne b$ and x in the domain of $f(x)$].

Example 1.5.5. Let $f(x) = 1$ for $0 \le x \le 1$ (notice that $f(x)$ is defined only on the closed interval $0 \le x \le 1$). We wish to investigate $\lim_{x \to 1} f(x)$. Since $x = 1$ is an endpoint of the interval on which $f(x)$ is defined, we must use Def. 1.5.2, *not* Def. 1.5.1. We see that $\lim_{x \to 1} f(x)$ means to take the limit as $x \to 1$ with $x < 1$, $x \ne 1$. Hence, the limit *exists* and equals 1. If we wish to evaluate $\lim_{x \to \frac{1}{2}} f(x)$, we use Def. 1.5.1, since $f(x)$ *is* defined in an open interval containing $x = \frac{1}{2}$ (e.g., $x = \frac{1}{2}$ is in the open interval $I: \frac{1}{4} < x < \frac{3}{4}$, and I is contained in the domain of f, $0 \le x \le 1$). Of course, $\lim_{x \to \frac{1}{2}} f(x) = 1$.

Example 1.5.6. Set $f(x) = 1/x$, $0 < x \leq 1$. Here the domain is the interval $0 < x \leq 1$. To investigate $\lim_{x \to 0} f(x)$, we use Def. 1.5.2 and investigate $\lim_{x \to 0} (1/x)$ with $x > 0$. But as $x \to 0$, $x > 0$, we see that $1/x$ becomes large, so no limit exists. This is *not* the function $H(x)$ of Ex. 1.5.4, since the domain of $H(x)$ is *all* x except $x = 0$. To investigate $\lim_{x \to 0} H(x)$, we used Def. 1.5.1.

Definition 1.5.3. If the domain of $f(x)$ is a half line of the form $J: x \geq A$ (or $x > A$), we say that $\lim_{x \to A} f(x) = M$ if the values of $f(x)$ can be made to stay arbitrarily close to M by taking x sufficiently close to A, with $x > A$ and $x \neq A$ [i.e., $x \neq A$ and x in the domain of $f(x)$]. If the domain of $f(x)$ is a half line of the form $I: x \leq B$ (or $x < B$), we say $\lim_{x \to B} f(x) = N$ if the values of $f(x)$ can be made to stay arbitrarily close to N by taking x sufficiently close to B with $x < B$ and $x \neq B$ [i.e., $x \neq B$ and x in the domain of $f(x)$].

Example 1.5.7. Let $f(x) = \sqrt{x}$. The domain of $f(x)$ is $J: x \geq 0$. So by Def. 1.5.3, for $x \neq 0$ in the domain of f (i.e., for $x > 0$), as $x \to 0$, we see that $\sqrt{x} \to 0$, so $\lim_{x \to 0} \sqrt{x} = 0$.

Example 1.5.8. Let $g(x)$ be defined as follows:

$$g(x) = \begin{cases} \sqrt{x}, & x \geq 0 \\ -1, & x < 0 \end{cases}$$

This function is not the same as $f(x)$ in Ex. 1.5.7, since $f(x)$ is *not* defined for $x < 0$, but $g(x)$ is. The domain of $g(x)$ is the entire x-axis, and so $\lim_{x \to 0} g(x)$ means that we must consider $x > 0$, and $x < 0$, but $x \neq 0$ (see Fig. 1.5.2). For $x > 0$, $g(x) \to 0$ as $x \to 0$, but for $x < 0$, $g(x) \to -1$ as $x \to 0$. Hence, $g(x)$ does *not* have a limit as $x \to 0$, since $\lim_{x \to 0} g(x)$ must be a single unique number found by taking $x \to 0$ for *both* $x < 0$ and $x > 0$, $x \neq 0$.

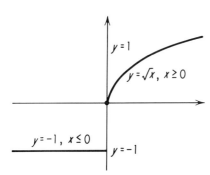

Figure 1.5.2

We shall also consider the following limit process: What value, if any, does $f(x)$ approach as x becomes large? Consider $H(x) = 1/x$. Here $H(10) = 1/10$, $H(100) = 1/100$, $H(10^{10}) = 1/10^{10}$. In fact, as x becomes very large, $1/x$ tends to 0. We write

$$\lim_{x \to \infty} \frac{1}{x} = 0$$

to signify this. In general, we define:

Definition 1.5.4. We write $\lim\limits_{x \to \infty} f(x) = L$ to mean that the values of $f(x)$ can be made to stay arbitrarily close to L by taking x sufficiently large.

Of course the symbol $f(\infty)$ is meaningless since ∞ is not a real number. In a completely analogous way we can define $\lim\limits_{x \to -\infty} f(x) = L$.

Example 1.5.9. Let A be any real number. Then,

$$\lim_{x \to \infty} \frac{1}{x + A} = 0$$

In fact,

$$\lim_{x \to \infty} \frac{1}{x^c + A} = 0$$

for any real $c > 0$.

The following theorem on limits is of great importance. Unfortunately we do not have the machinery to prove the theorem, but it should be completely understood.

Theorem 1.5.1. Suppose $\lim\limits_{x \to c} f(x)$ and $\lim\limits_{x \to c} g(x)$ exist. Let A be any real number. Then the following are true:

(i) $$\lim_{x \to c} A = A$$

i.e., the limit of a constant function is just that constant function.

(ii) $$\lim_{x \to c} \{f(x) \pm g(x)\} = \left\{\lim_{x \to c} f(x)\right\} \pm \left\{\lim_{x \to c} g(x)\right\}$$

i.e., the limit of a sum (or difference) of functions is the sum (or difference) of the limits.

(iii) $$\lim_{x \to c} \{f(x) \cdot g(x)\} = \left\{\lim_{x \to c} f(x)\right\} \cdot \left\{\lim_{x \to c} g(x)\right\}$$

i.e., the limit of a product is the product of limits.

(iv) $$\lim_{x \to c} \frac{f(x)}{g(x)} = \frac{\lim\limits_{x \to c} f(x)}{\lim\limits_{x \to c} g(x)} \quad \text{provided} \quad \lim_{x \to c} g(x) \neq 0$$

i.e., the limit of a quotient is the quotient of the limits, provided the limit in the denominator is not zero.

Observe that Thm. 1.5.1 gives no information if one or both of the limits fail to exist.

Example 1.5.10. Let $f(x) = x$, $g(x) = 1/x$. What is $\lim_{x \to 0} f(x)g(x)$? We see that $\lim_{x \to 0} g(x)$ does not exist (see Ex. 1.5.4). Hence, Thm. 1.5.1, (iii), *does not apply.* But $\lim_{x \to 0} f(x)g(x) = \lim_{x \to 0} x \cdot (1/x)$, and since the symbol $x \to 0$ automatically insures $x \neq 0$, we have $x \cdot (1/x) = 1$, so $\lim_{x \to 0} f(x)g(x) = 1$. Consequently, though one function in a product may fail to have a limit, the product *may* have a limit, but Thm. 1.5.1 cannot be used to find that limit.

Example 1.5.11. Let $f(x) = 1$, and $g(x) = 1/x$. What is $\lim_{x \to 0} f(x)g(x)$? Here, $\lim_{x \to 0} f(x)$ exists and is equal to 1, but $\lim_{x \to 0} g(x)$ does not exist. Thus, Thm. 1.5.1 does *not* apply. But here we see that $\lim_{x \to 0} f(x)g(x) = \lim_{x \to 0} 1/x$ does *not* exist (see Ex. 1.5.4).

Example 1.5.12. Let $f(x) = 1/x$, $g(x) = -1/x$. Clearly neither $\lim_{x \to 0} f(x)$ nor $\lim_{x \to 0} g(x)$ exist. Again Thm. 1.5.1 does not apply. But

$$\lim_{x \to 0} \{f(x) + g(x)\} = \lim_{x \to 0} \{1/x - 1/x\}$$

and since $x \to 0$ implies $x \neq 0$, $1/x - 1/x = 0$, so $\lim_{x \to 0} \{f(x) + g(x)\} = \lim_{x \to 0} 0 = 0$. Hence, though each of two functions may fail to have a limit, their sum may have a limit. Again, Thm. 1.5.1 cannot be used to find that limit.

Example 1.5.13. Evaluate $\lim_{x \to 2} [x^2(x + 3) + (1/x)]$. We can write

$$\lim_{x \to 2} [x^2(x + 3) + (1/x)] = \lim_{x \to 2} [x^2(x + 3)] + \lim_{x \to 2} (1/x)$$

$$= \left[\lim_{x \to 2} x^2 \right]\left[\lim_{x \to 2} (x + 3) \right] + \left[\lim_{x \to 2} (1/x) \right]$$

by using Thm. 1.5.1, *provided* that each limit in the decomposition exists and that the limit that appears in any denominator is not zero. This is certainly the case here, and hence $\lim_{x \to 2} [x^2(x + 3) + (1/x)] = (4 \cdot 5) + \frac{1}{2} = \frac{41}{2}$.

Example 1.5.10 can be slightly rephrased to exhibit what is called a *proof by contradiction.* We are given a certain collection of hypotheses (i.e., assumptions) from which we wish to deduce some proposition. We assume the proposition to be false and attempt to deduce from this that one of our hypotheses is contradicted, or that a theorem we know to be true turns out to be false; i.e., we try to show that assuming our proposition to be false leads to an impossible situation. We illustrate this in the next example.

Example 1.5.14. For our hypotheses, we accept that $\lim_{x \to 0} x = 0$ and $\lim_{x \to 0} (x/x) = 1$ (i.e., we assume these limit statements to be known, or previously proved). We can use the same argument as in Ex. 1.5.10 to show that $\lim_{x \to 0} (x/x) = 1$. We wish to prove the proposition: $\lim_{x \to 0} 1/x$ does not exist (i.e., we show in a different way what we have already observed in Ex. 1.5.4). Suppose the statement "$\lim_{x \to 0} (1/x)$ does not exist" is false. Then it must be that $\lim_{x \to 0} (1/x)$ *does* exist; call this limit A. We hope that the assertion $\lim_{x \to 0} (1/x) = A$ will lead to a contradiction of something we know or assume to be true.

Since $\lim_{x \to 0} (1/x) = A$ and $\lim_{x \to 0} x = 0$, we can use Thm. 1.5.1 (iii) to conclude that

$$\lim_{x \to 0} (x/x) = \lim_{x \to 0} x \cdot \lim_{x \to 0} (1/x) = 0 \cdot A = 0$$

But we have assumed that $\lim_{x \to 0} (x/x) = 1$ and since $1 \neq 0$, we have reached a contradiction. Hence the statement $\lim_{x \to 0} (1/x) = A$ is untenable, and consequently $\lim_{x \to 0} (1/x)$ does not exist.

Finally, suppose that the domain of $f(x)$ is the closed interval $a \leq x \leq b$. What meaning can we give $f'(a)$? By Def. 1.5.2, the quantity $\lim_{h \to 0} f(a + h)$ must be evaluated for $h > 0$. Hence, to be consistent with Def. 1.5.2, we shall say

Definition 1.5.5. If the domain of $f(x)$ is the closed interval $[a, b]$, then

$$f'(a) = \lim_{h \to 0} \frac{f(a + h) - f(a)}{h} \qquad \text{evaluated only for } h > 0$$

$$f'(b) = \lim_{h \to 0} \frac{f(b + h) - f(b)}{h} \qquad \text{evaluated only for } h < 0$$

PROBLEMS

1.5.1. Evaluate $\lim_{x \to 1} (x^5 - 2x^4 + 3x^3 - x^2 + 2x + 1)$.

1.5.2. Evaluate "$\lim_{x \to 1}$" for each of the following:

$$\text{(a)} \quad f(x) = \frac{x - 1}{x + 1}$$

(b) $g(x) = \dfrac{x^3 - x}{x - 1}$

(c) $h(x) = \dfrac{1}{x} - \dfrac{1}{x - 1}$

1.5.3. Evaluate

$$\lim_{x \to \infty} \frac{x^2 - 2x + 1}{2x^2 + x - 1}$$

(*Hint:* First multiply numerator and denominator by $1/x^2$.)

1.5.4. Evaluate

$$\lim_{x \to 2} \frac{x^2 + x - 6}{x - 2}$$

1.5.5. Evaluate

$$\lim_{x \to 2} \frac{x^2 + x - 6}{x + 2}$$

1.5.6. Evaluate

$$\lim_{x \to c} \frac{(1/x^2) - (1/c^2)}{x - c}$$

1.5.7. Evaluate

$$\lim_{h \to 0} \frac{(5 + h)^2 - 25}{h}$$

1.5.8. Evaluate

$$\lim_{x \to \infty} \frac{6x^5 + x^3 - 5}{5x^5 - 2x^2 + x - 10}$$

(*Hint:* Multiply the numerator and denominator by the appropriate value.)

1.5.9. Evaluate

$$\lim_{n \to \infty} 2^{-n}, \quad \lim_{n \to \infty} 2^{-1/n}, \quad \lim_{n \to \infty} 2^{(n+1)/n}$$

where n is an integer.

1.5.10. Suppose that we are given a function $g(x)$ with the property that

$$\lim_{x \to 0} g(x) = 5$$

Define

$$f(x) = \begin{cases} xg(x), & x \neq 0 \\ 0, & x = 0 \end{cases}$$

Find $f'(0)$.

1.5.11. Let $f(x) = n$ if $n \le x < n + 1$, n an integer. Evaluate

$$\lim_{x \to \frac{1}{2}} f(x), \quad \lim_{x \to \frac{3}{4}} f(x), \quad \lim_{x \to m} f(x)$$

where m is an integer.

1.5.12. Let $f(x)$ be as in Prob. 1.5.11, but now defined only for $1 \le x \le 2$ (i.e., we are restricting the domain to be *only* those x on the interval $1 \le x \le 2$). Evaluate, if they exist, $\lim_{x \to 1} f(x)$ and $\lim_{x \to 2} f(x)$. Compare this to Prob. 1.5.11, in which the domain of the function is the entire x-axis.

1.5.13. Find

$$\lim_{x \to \infty} (\sqrt{x^2 + 1} - x)$$

1.5.14. Let

$$F(x) = \begin{cases} 1, & 0 \le x \le 1 \\ 2, & 1 < x \le 2 \end{cases}$$

Does $F(x)$ have a limit at $x = 0$, at $x = 2$, at $x = 1$? Compare your result at $x = 1$ with Ex. 1.5.5.

1.5.15. Show that

$$\lim_{x \to \infty} [\sqrt{x(x + b)} - x] = b/2$$

1.5.16. If the domain of $f(x)$ is the half line $x \ge a$, construct a suitable working definition for $f'(a)$ taking into account the endpoint problem. Use this to investigate $f'(0)$ if $f(x) = \sqrt{x}$, $x \ge 0$.

1.5.17. Let $f(x) = x^2 + 1$, $0 \le x \le 1$. Use Def. 1.5.5 to find $f'(0)$ and $f'(1)$.

1.6. The definition of limit.†

Heuristically, $\lim_{x \to c} f(x) = L$ says that $f(x)$ can be made to stay arbitrarily close to L if x is sufficiently close to c, but $x \ne c$. We shall suppose for simplicity that $f(x)$ is defined throughout some interval containing c, but not necessarily at $x = c$. We can rephrase our heuristic definition to read: The distance between the numbers $f(x)$ and L can be made to stay arbitrarily small if the distance between x and c is sufficiently small but positive.

Let us investigate the notion of "distance." The distance between the numbers 8 and 2 is simply the length of the interval (hence it is positive) between $x = 8$ and $x = 2$, which is $8 - 2 = 6$ (see Fig. 1.6.1). Clearly, this should be the distance between 2 and 8, but $2 - 8 = -6$.

---

† This section may be omitted without loss of continuity.

We can avoid the problem by saying that the distance between 2 and 8 is $|8 - 2| = |2 - 8| = 6$ (see Ex. 1.1.7 for the definition of $|x|$). In general, the distance between numbers a and b is $|b - a| = |a - b|$.

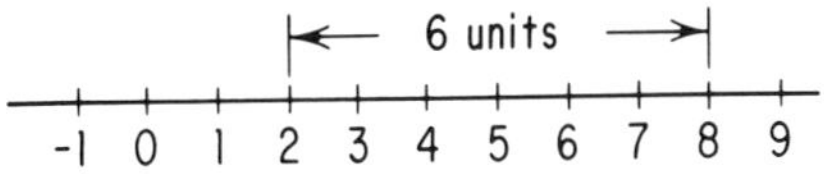

Figure 1.6.1

Assume that $f(x)$ is defined in some open interval containing $x = c$, but not necessarily at $x = c$. Hence, $f(x)$ is defined for values $x > c$ and $x < c$ if x is sufficiently close to c. $\lim_{x \to c} f(x) = L$ now reads: $|f(x) - L|$ can be made to stay arbitrarily small if $|x - c|$ is sufficiently small but positive. For instance, if the limit is L we require that there must be a number A such that $|f(x) - L| < 1$ if $0 < |x - c| < A$, and a number B such that $|f(x) - L| < 1/10$ if $0 < |x - c| < B$, and a number C such that $|f(x) - L| < 10^{-10}$ if $0 < |x - c| < C$, and in general, that for every $\varepsilon > 0$ there must correspond a $\delta > 0$ such that $|f(x) - L| < \varepsilon$ if $0 < |x - c| < \delta$. We formalize this by defining:

Definition 1.6.1. Let $f(x)$ be defined in some open interval containing $x = c$, but not necessarily at c. $\lim_{x \to c} f(x) = L$ means that to each arbitrary number $\varepsilon > 0$ there corresponds a $\delta > 0$ (which usually depends on ε) such that $|f(x) - L| < \varepsilon$ if $0 < |x - c| < \delta$.

This definition gives us no method for calculating the limit; it simply lists requirements that any conjectured limit must satisfy.

Example 1.6.1. Verify that $\lim_{x \to 1} (2x + 5) = 7$. Here, $f(x) = 2x + 5$, the conjectured limit L is 7, and $c = 1$. By Def. 1.6.1, we see that for each arbitrary $\varepsilon > 0$ we must find a $\delta > 0$ such that if $0 < |x - 1| < \delta$ then

$$|f(x) - L| = |(2x + 5) - 7| = |2x - 2| < \varepsilon$$

Observe that $|2x - 2| = 2|x - 1|$ and that $2|x - 1| < \varepsilon$ is equivalent to $|2x - 2| = 2|x - 1| < \varepsilon$. But $2|x - 1| < \varepsilon$ is satisfied if $0 < |x - 1| < \varepsilon/2$. Hence, if $0 < |x - 1| < \varepsilon/2$, then $|2x - 2| < \varepsilon$. We choose $\delta = \varepsilon/2$ in order to meet the requirement of Def. 1.6.1.

Because in problems dealing with limits it is often necessary to evaluate inequalities involving absolute values, we shall illustrate briefly the technique for solving such inequalities.

Example 1.6.2. Find the values x for which $|2x - 1| < 3$. There are two possibilities. If $2x - 1 \geq 0$, then $|2x - 1| = 2x - 1$, and so $|2x - 1| < 3$ is equivalent to $2x - 1 < 3$. If, on the other hand, $2x - 1 < 0$, then

$$|2x - 1| = -(2x - 1)$$

and so $|2x - 1| < 3$ becomes $-(2x - 1) < 3$, or $2x - 1 > -3$. Both cases can be summarized by saying that $|2x - 1| < 3$ is equivalent to

$$-3 < 2x - 1 < 3$$

Adding 1 across the inequality we obtain $-2 < 2x < 4$, and dividing by 2 finally yields $-1 < x < 2$. So the inequality $-1 < x < 2$, is equivalent to the inequality $|2x - 1| < 3$.

Example 1.6.3. Show that $\lim_{x \to 2} x^2 = 4$ where $f(x) = x^2$, $L = 4$, and $c = 2$.

We must show that for arbitrary $\varepsilon > 0$, there exists a corresponding δ such that $0 < |x - 2| < \delta$ implies $|x^2 - 4| < \varepsilon$. We see that

$$|x^2 - 4| = |(x + 2)(x - 2)| = |x + 2| \cdot |x - 2|$$

Hence, $|x^2 - 4| < \varepsilon$ is equivalent to $|x + 2| \cdot |x - 2| < \varepsilon$. We are free to choose $|x - 2|$ as small as we please and so choose $|x - 2| \leq 1$. This says *the δ we ultimately pick must be ≤ 1.* Now $|x - 2| \leq 1$ implies by calculations similar to those in Ex. 1.6.2 that $-1 \leq x - 2 \leq 1$, so $1 \leq x \leq 3$, and finally $3 \leq x + 2 \leq 5$. Clearly $-5 < 3$, so we have that $|x - 2| \leq 1$ implies $-5 \leq x + 2 \leq 5$, or, $|x + 2| \leq 5$. Hence,

$$|x^2 - 4| = |x + 2| \cdot |x - 2| \leq 5|x - 2|$$

so if $5|x - 2| < \varepsilon$, then we are assured that $|x^2 - 4| < \varepsilon$. But $5|x - 2| < \varepsilon$ is satisfied if $|x - 2| < \varepsilon/5$. If $\varepsilon/5 \leq 1$, we can choose $\delta = \varepsilon/5$. In all cases, we can pick δ the smaller of the numbers 1 and $\varepsilon/5$.

Finally, it is possible to consider functions whose domain is an interval I (open or closed), and to construct an appropriate $\varepsilon - \delta$ definition of limit at $x = a$ and at $x = b$. The heuristics have already been discussed in §1.5; we shall give no formal definition for this case. The reader should realize that such a definition is necessary, since in the formal $\varepsilon - \delta$ definition of limit given above, we have assumed $f(x)$ to be defined in an open interval containing c (here, we speak of "$\lim_{x \to c}$") but with c *not* an endpoint, whereas in the case just described, a and b *are* endpoints.

PROBLEMS

1.6.1. Show that $\lim_{x \to 3} (x + 6) = 9$.

1.6.2. Show that $\lim_{x \to 2} (5x - 4) = 6$.

1.6.3. Show that $\lim_{x \to 3} x^2 = 9$.

1.6.4. Show that $\lim_{x \to c} x^2 = c^2$ for any c.

1.6.5. Show that $\lim_{x \to 2} x^3 = 8$.

1.6.6. Prove Thm. 1.5.1 (i).

1.6.7. Prove Thm. 1.5.1 (ii). [*Hint:* Call $\lim_{x \to c} f(x) = A$, $\lim_{x \to c} g(x) = B$, and prove $\lim_{x \to c} f(x) \pm g(x) = A \pm B$. Use (1.1.4).]

1.6.8. Show that for any real $a \neq 0$, $\lim_{x \to a} \dfrac{1}{x} = \dfrac{1}{a}$.

1.7. Continuity

Definition 1.7.1. Let $f(x)$ be a function defined on an open interval containing $x = c$; then $f(x)$ is said to be **continuous** at $x = c$ if it satisfies *each* of the following properties:

      (a) $f(c)$ is defined [i.e., c is in the domain of $f(x)$]
      (b) $\lim_{x \to c} f(x)$ exists, and is equal to L
      (c) $L = f(c)$

Intuitively, "a function is continuous at $x = c$" means that, if x varies slightly from c, then $f(x)$ varies slightly from $f(c)$.

Suppose that the domain of $f(x)$ is an interval $I: a \leq x \leq b$ or a half-line of the form $J: x \geq A$ or, perhaps, $K: x \leq B$. Then we see that $f(x)$ is *not* defined in an open interval containing a or b or A or B, so Def. 1.7.1 cannot be applied in these cases. Recall that in Defs. 1.5.2 and 1.5.3 we have already discussed the meaning of limit on domains like I, J, and K. To be consistent, we say,

Definition 1.7.2.
(i) Let the domain of $f(x)$ be $a \leq x \leq b$. Then $f(x)$ is **continuous** at $x = a$ if $\lim_{x \to a} f(x)$ exists (as in Def. 1.5.2), and has the value $f(a)$. Also, $f(x)$ is *continuous at $x = b$* if $\lim_{x \to b} f(x)$ exists (as in Def. 1.5.2), and has the value $f(b)$.
(ii) Let the domain of $f(x)$ be the half line $x \geq A$. Then we say $f(x)$ *is continuous at A* if $\lim_{x \to A} f(x)$ exists (as in Def. 1.5.3), and has the value $f(A)$.
(iii) Let the domain of $f(x)$ be the half-line $x \leq B$. Then we say $f(x)$ *is continuous at B* if $\lim_{x \to B} f(x)$ exists (as in Def. 1.5.3), and has the value $f(B)$.

At all other points in the domain of $f(x)$, Def. 1.7.1 is applicable.

In Ex. 1.5.1, we saw that for $f(x) = x^2$, $\lim\limits_{x \to 2} f(x) = 4 = f(2)$. Hence $f(x) = x^2$ is continuous at $x = 2$. In fact, we see that for any c,

$$\lim_{x \to c} f(x) = \lim_{x \to c} x^2 = c^2 = f(c)$$

so $f(x) = x^2$ is continuous everywhere (i.e., it is continuous for all c). If $g(x) = 2x + 1$, we see that $\lim\limits_{x \to 1} g(x) = 3 = g(1)$, $\lim\limits_{x \to 3} g(x) = 7 = g(3)$, $\lim\limits_{x \to -1} g(x) = -1 = g(-1)$, and, in fact, $\lim\limits_{x \to c} g(x) = 2c + 1 = g(c)$, so $g(x) = 2x + 1$ is also continuous everywhere. Similarly, for a non-negative integer n and any constant A, the function $p(x) = Ax^n$ is continuous everywhere.

By specializing Thm. 1.5.1, we get:

Theorem 1.7.1. If $f(x)$ and $g(x)$ are each continuous at $x = c$, then:

(a) $f(x) \pm g(x)$ is continuous at $x = c$
(b) $f(x)g(x)$ is continuous at $x = c$
(c) $f(x)/g(x)$ is continuous at $x = c$, provided $g(c) \neq 0$

Furthermore, if for some constant k, $f(x) = k$, then $f(x)$ is continuous everywhere. A function that is constant is continuous for all x.

Example 1.7.1. Set $f(x) = x^2$ and $g(x) = 3x + 1$. Then, $\lim\limits_{x \to 2} x^2 = 4 = f(2)$, and $\lim\limits_{x \to 2} (3x + 1) = 7 = g(2)$. Hence, $f(x)$ and $g(x)$ are each continuous at $x = 2$. Theorem 1.7.1(b) assures us that $f(x) + g(x)$ is continuous at $x = 2$; i.e., $\lim\limits_{x \to 2} [f(x) + g(x)] = f(2) + g(2) = 11$. But this is clear, since

$$f(x) + g(x) = x^2 + 3x + 1 \quad \text{and} \quad \lim_{x \to 2} (x^2 + 3x + 1) = 11$$

as the theorem predicted.

Example 1.7.2. Consider the polynomal

$$P(x) = a_0 x^n + a_1 x^{n-1} + \cdots + a_{n-1} x + a_n, \qquad a_0 \neq 0$$

We see that it is continuous everywhere, since $a_0 x^n$, $a_1 x^{n-1}$, $\ldots$, $a_{n-1} x$ and a_n are each continuous everywhere, and $P(x)$ is the sum of such functions.

Definition 1.7.3. A function is *discontinuous* at $x = c$ if it is not continuous at $x = c$.

The following examples are functions which have some discontinuities.

Example 1.7.3. Let

$$f(x) = \frac{x^2 - 1}{x - 1}$$

From Ex. 1.5.2 we recall that $f(1)$ is undefined, so even though $\lim_{x \to 1} f(x)$ exists, we see that condition (a) of Def. 1.7.1 is violated, and the function is discontinuous at $x = 1$. The reader should convince himself that $f(x)$ is continuous everywhere except at $x = 1$.

Example 1.7.4. We investigate continuity at $x = 1$ of the function $g(x)$ of Ex. 1.5.3. Here we see that condition (a) of Def. 1.7.1 is satisfied with $g(1) = 3$; condition (b) is satisfied with $\lim_{x \to 1} g(x) = 2$. But condition (c) is violated, so this function is discontinuous at $x = 1$. It is continuous everywhere else, however.

Example 1.7.5. We want to determine whether the function $H(x) = 1/x$ of Ex. 1.5.4 is continuous at $x = 0$. Both conditions (a) and (b) of Def. 1.7.1 are violated, so $H(x)$ is discontinuous at $x = 0$. H is continuous everywhere else. The reader should observe that the function $f(x)$ in Ex. 1.5.6 is also discontinuous at $x = 0$.

Example 1.7.6. We want to determine whether the function $f(x) = \sqrt{x}$ with domain the half-line $x \geq 0$ is continuous at $x = 0$. Here we must use Def. 1.7.2. By the result of Ex. 1.5.7, $\lim_{x \to 0} \sqrt{x} = 0$, and since $\sqrt{0} = 0$, we have $\lim_{x \to 0} \sqrt{x} = \sqrt{0}$. Thus, this function is continuous at $x = 0$.

Theorem 1.7.2. The following equations are equivalent to Def. 1.7.1, and each asserts that $f(x)$ is continuous at $x = c$:

(a) $\lim_{h \to 0} f(c + h) = f(c)$

(b) $\lim_{x \to c} [f(x) - f(c)] = 0$

(c) $\lim_{h \to 0} [f(c + h) - f(c)] = 0$

The following theorem relates derivatives to continuity.

Theorem 1.7.3. If $f(x)$ has a derivative at $x = c$, then it is necessarily continuous at $x = c$.

Proof.

$$f'(c) = \lim_{h \to 0} \frac{f(c + h) - f(c)}{h}$$

exists by assumption. We observe that

$$\lim_{h \to 0} [f(c + h) - f(c)] = \lim_{h \to 0} \frac{f(c + h) - f(c)}{h} \cdot h$$

$$= \lim_{h \to 0} \frac{f(c + h) - f(c)}{h} \cdot \lim_{h \to 0} h$$

$$= f'(c) \cdot 0 = 0$$

We have used Thm. 1.5.1 (iii). Hence, we conclude that

$$\lim_{h \to 0} [f(c + h) - f(c)] = 0$$

so by Thm. 1.7.2(c), $f(x)$ is continuous at $x = c$.

The converse of Thm. 1.7.3 is *not* true. For example, $f(x) = |x|$ is continuous everywhere, but $f'(0)$ is undefined (see Prob. 1.2.3).

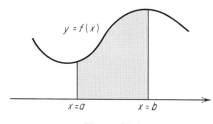

$y = f(x)$

$x = a$ $x = b$

Figure 1.7.1

We study continuous functions because they have extremely important properties. For instance, if we consider the region bounded by the graph of a function $f(x)$, the x-axis and the vertical lines $x = a$ and $x = b$ (see Fig. 1.7.1), we shall see in a later section that this region always has an area if $f(x)$ is continuous. We shall state another important property of continuous functions.

Definition 1.7.4. A function is said to be continuous on an interval $I: a \le x \le b$ if it is continuous at each point in I, with continuity at endpoints defined as in Def. 1.7.2.

Theorem 1.7.4. Let $f(x)$ be continuous on a closed interval $I: a \le x \le b$. Then there exist numbers (not necessarily unique) c and d, where $a \le c \le b$ and $a \le d \le b$, such that $f(c)$ is the minimum value of $f(x)$ for all x in I, and $f(d)$ is the maximum value of $f(x)$ for all x in I. Hence, $f(c) \le f(x) \le f(d)$ for all x in I.

We do not have the necessary tools to prove this theorem. The reader will find a proof in the appendix to Chapter 1, *Differential and Integral Calculus*, vol. 1, by Richard Courant (see the bibliography). We shall need this theorem later.

Example 1.7.7. Define

$$f(x) = \begin{cases} 1/x, & 0 < x \le 1 \\ 0, & x = 0 \end{cases}$$

This function is defined on the entire interval $I: 0 \le x \le 1$, but it is *not* continuous at $x = 0$ (see Ex. 1.7.5 and Ex. 1.5.14). As x takes on values closer to 0, $f(x)$ takes on larger values. Hence, there is *no* number d such that $f(d)$ is the maximum value of $f(x)$ for all x in the interval $0 \le x \le 1$. However, $f(0) = 0$ is the minimum value of the function on $0 \le x \le 1$, since for $0 < x < 1$, $(1/x) > 1$.

Example 1.7.8. In Ex. 1.3.3, we defined total cost, $S(x)$. It is reasonable to assume that $S(x)$ is continuous everywhere in its domain; i.e., as $x \to a$, $S(x) \to S(a)$. Heuristically, this means that a small change in the number of units produced is accompanied by a small change in cost. Again referring to Ex. 1.3.3, it is interesting to observe that Thm. 1.7.3 assures us that if the marginal cost is simply meaningful for some value $x = a$ of units produced (i.e., if $S'(a)$ exists), then the function representing total cost, $S(x)$ is continuous at $x = a$.

PROBLEMS

1.7.1. Determine whether the function

$$f(x) = \begin{cases} \dfrac{x^2 + 2x - 3}{x + 3}, & x \ne -3 \\ -4, & x = -3 \end{cases}$$

is continuous at $x = -3$.

1.7.2. Consider the function $f(x) = n$ if $n \le x < n + 1$, with n an integer. Is $f(x)$ continuous at $x = 1$? If not, what conditions of Def. 1.7.1 are violated.

1.7.3. Determine whether each of the following functions is continuous at the value or values indicated.

(a) $f(x) = \dfrac{x - 1}{x}$ at $x = -1$, $x = 1$, $x = 0$;

(b) $g(x) = x^2 + 2$ at $x = -1$, $x = 1$, $x = 0$;

(c) $F(x) = \begin{cases} \sqrt{x}, & \text{if } x \ge 0 \\ 0, & \text{if } -1 \le x < 0 \end{cases}$ at $x = -1$, $x = 1$, $x = 0$;

(d) $G(x) = \begin{cases} 1 & \text{if } x \ge 1/10 \\ -1 & \text{if } 0 < x < 1/10 \end{cases}$ at $x = 0$, $x = 1$, $x = 1/10$

(e) $W(x) = \dfrac{3x - 2}{x - 4}$ at $x = -3$

1.7.4. Explain why Thm. 1.7.2 is valid.

1.7.5. The function $f(x) = x$ is continuous on $I: 0 \le x \le 1$. Hence, by Thm. 1.7.4, there are numbers c and d such that $f(c)$ is the minimum value of $f(x)$ on I and $f(d)$ is the minimum value of $f(x)$ on I. Determine c and d. Are there also values c and d with the properties described above for $f(x)$ if x is in the interval $0 < x < 1$?

1.7.6. Let

$$G(x) = \frac{x^2 - 9}{x - 3}   \text{ for } x \ne 3$$

Define $G(x)$ at $x = 3$ so that it will be continuous at $x = 3$.

1.7.7. Determine whether the function in Ex. 1.5.6 is continuous at $x = 0$.

1.7.8. Let $f(x) = x^{14} - 3x^{12} + 10x^2 + 2, 0 \le x \le 1$. Show that $|f(x)| < 16$ for all x in $[0, 1]$. [*Hint:* Use (1.1.4).]

1.7.9. Suppose that we know that the functions $f(x)$ and $g(x)$ have the same domain and that $f(x) > g(x)$ for all x in this common domain. Suppose also that both functions are continuous at the point $x = c$. Show that

$$W(x) = \frac{1}{f(x) - g(x)}$$

is continuous at $x = c$.

1.8. The binomial theorem.

It is relatively simple to carry out the details to show that

$$(x + y)^2 = x^2 + 2xy + y^2$$

a little more complicated to show that $(x + y)^3 = x^3 + 3x^2y + 3xy^2 + y^3$, and unpleasant to expand $(x + y)^{21}$ by repeated multiplication. The binomial theorem gives a single expression for $(x + y)^n$ where n is any positive integer. The proof of this theorem is algebraic, and can be found in any standard college algebra text.

We shall need the following definitions.

Definition 1.8.1.

(i) $n! = 1 \cdot 2 \cdot 3 \cdot \,\cdots\, \cdot (n - 1) \cdot n$

and is called *n-factorial*;

(ii) $0! = 1$ (remember this is a definition);

(iii) $\binom{n}{k} = \dfrac{n!}{k!(n-k)!}$

and is called a **binomial coefficient**;

(iv) $x^0 = 1$ for any real number $x \neq 0$.

Example 1.8.1.

$$\frac{n!}{1!(n-1)!} = \frac{1 \cdot 2 \cdot 3 \cdot \ \cdots \ \cdot (n-1) \cdot n}{1 \cdot 2 \cdot 3 \cdot \ \cdots \ \cdot (n-1)} = n$$

Theorem 1.8.1. (The binomial theorem). Let n be any positive integer and let x and y be any two non-zero real numbers. Then

$$(1.8.1) \quad (x+y)^n = x^n + \binom{n}{1}x^{n-1}y + \binom{n}{2}x^{n-2}y^2 + \cdots + \binom{n}{n-1}xy^{n-1} + y^n$$

To emphasize the symmetry of the equation, we could write (1.8.1) in the equivalent form

$$(1.8.2) \quad (x+y)^n = \binom{n}{0}x^n y^0 + \binom{n}{1}x^{n-1}y^1 + \binom{n}{2}x^{n-2}y^2 + \cdots$$

$$+ \binom{n}{n-1}x^1 y^{n-1} + \binom{n}{n}x^0 y^n$$

The reader should verify that (1.8.1) and (1.8.2) are identical. From (1.8.2) we observe the following characteristics of the equation: The powers of x begin at n and descend to 0, the powers of y begin at 0 and ascend to n, the sum of the exponents appearing in any summand is n, the lower entry in each binomial coefficient corresponds to the exponent of y in that summand, the top entry of each binomial coefficient minus the lower entry in the same coefficient is the exponent of x in that summand, and the lower entries in the binomial coefficients go from 0 to n as we go from one summand to the next.

Example 1.8.2. Use (1.8.1) to expand $(x+y)^2$. Here $n = 2$.

$$(x+y)^2 = x^2 + \binom{2}{1} xy + y^2 = x^2 + 2xy + y^2$$

since

$$\binom{2}{1} = \frac{2!}{1!(2-1)!} = 2$$

Example 1.8.3. Use (1.8.1) to expand $(x + y)^3$. Here $n = 3$.

$$(x + y)^3 = x^3 + \binom{3}{1}x^2y + \binom{3}{2}xy^2 + y^3$$

$$= x^3 + \frac{3!}{1!2!}x^2y + \frac{3!}{2!1!}xy^2 + y^3$$

$$= x^2 + 3x^2y + 3xy^2 + y^3$$

PROBLEMS

1.8.1. Find $(a + b)^4$, $(a - b)^4$, $(a^2 + 2b)^3$.

1.8.2. Write an expression for $(x + h)^n - x^n$ where n is any positive integer.

1.8.3. Find $(2a - 3b)^5$, $\left[\frac{2}{3}a^2 - \sqrt{b}\right]^3$, $\left(\frac{2}{a} + \frac{1}{b}\right)^4$

1.9. Techniques for differentiation. Higher order derivatives.

If one had to differentiate the function given by $\sqrt[5]{x^{15} + 3\sqrt{x}}$, the expression for the derivative would look like:

$$\lim_{h \to 0} \frac{\sqrt[5]{(x + h)^{15} + 3\sqrt{x + h}} - \sqrt[5]{x^{15} + 3\sqrt{x}}}{h}$$

The calculations are clearly unpleasant. What we seek are ways to differentiate such functions which do not involve explicitly using the definition of a derivative. Given differentiable functions $f(x)$ and $g(x)$, we seek expressions for the derivative of their sum, difference, product, quotient, and powers.

Important: *In all the subsequent theorems in §1.9, §1.10, and §1.11, we shall once and for all assume that the functions we are dealing with have derivatives at common points, and the theorems are valid at such points*; i.e., if $f'(c)$ is defined but $g'(c)$ is not, the theorem is *not* necessarily true at $x = c$.

Theorem 1.9.1. The function $f(x) = x^n$, when n is a fixed positive integer, has a derivative at every x given by

(1.9.1) $$Dx^n = nx^{n-1}$$

Proof. By (1.2.4),

$$Dx^n = \lim_{h \to 0} \frac{(x + h)^n - x^n}{h}$$

Using (1.8.1), we see that

$$(x + h)^n - x^n = -x^n + (x + h)^n$$

$$= -x^n + x^n + nx^{n-1}h + h^2 \left[\binom{n}{2} x^{n-2} + \binom{n}{3} x^{n-3} h + \cdots + h^{n-2} \right]$$

$$= nx^{n-1}h + h^2 \cdot \begin{bmatrix} \text{an expression involving binomial co-} \\ \text{efficients, powers of } x \text{ and powers of } h \end{bmatrix}$$

Hence,

$$\lim_{h \to 0} \frac{(x + h)^n - x^n}{h} = \lim_{h \to 0} \frac{nx^{n-1}h + h^2 \cdot \begin{bmatrix} \text{expression involving binomial coeffi-} \\ \text{cients, powers of } x, \text{ and powers of } h \end{bmatrix}}{h}$$

$$= \lim_{h \to 0} \left\{ nx^{n-1} + h \cdot \begin{bmatrix} \text{expression involving binomial coeffi-} \\ \text{cients, powers of } x, \text{ and powers of } h. \end{bmatrix} \right\}$$

$$= nx^{n-1} + 0 = nx^{n-1}$$

Example 1.9.1.

(i) $$Dx^2 = 2x^{2-1} = 2x$$

(ii) $$Dx^5 = 5x^{5-1} = 5x^4$$

(iii) $$\frac{dx^{10}}{dx} = 10x^9$$

(iv) $$\frac{dx}{dx} = Dx^1 = 1 \cdot x^{1-1} = x^0 = 1$$

We remark that (1.9.1) can also be written

$$\frac{dx^n}{dx} = nx^{n-1} \quad \text{or} \quad \frac{d}{dx} x^n = nx^{n-1}$$

Theorem 1.9.2. If A is any constant, then

(1.9.2) $$D[A \cdot f(x)] = A \cdot Df(x)$$

or

$$\frac{d}{dx} Af(x) = A \frac{d}{dx} f(x)$$

Proof. Call $G(x) = A \cdot f(x)$. We want $DG(x)$. By definition,

$$DG(x) = \lim_{h \to 0} \frac{G(x + h) - G(x)}{h} = \lim_{h \to 0} \frac{A \cdot f(x + h) - Af(x)}{h}$$

$$= \lim_{h \to 0} A \frac{f(x + h) - f(x)}{h}$$

$$= \lim_{h \to 0} A \cdot \lim_{h \to 0} \frac{f(x + h) - f(x)}{h} \qquad \text{by Thm. 1.5.1 (iii)}$$

$$= A \cdot Df(x) \qquad \text{by Thm. 1.5.1 (i) and (1.2.3)}$$

Example 1.9.2.

(i) $D5x^7 = 5Dx^7 = 5 \cdot 7x^6 = 35x^6$

(ii) $D\pi x^5 = \pi Dx^5 = 5\pi x^4$

Theorem 1.9.3. The derivative of a sum is the sum of the derivatives; i.e.,

(1.9.3) $D\{f(x) + g(x)\} = \{Df(x)\} + \{Dg(x)\}$

Proof. Call $F(x) = f(x) + g(x)$. We then want to find $DF(x)$. Observe that $F(x + h) - F(x) = \{f(x + h) + g(x + h)\} - \{f(x) + g(x)\}$. Then,

$$DF(x) = \lim_{h \to 0} \frac{F(x + h) - F(x)}{h}$$

$$= \lim_{h \to 0} \frac{\{f(x + h) + g(x + h)\} - \{f(x) + g(x)\}}{h}$$

$$= \lim_{h \to 0} \frac{\{f(x + h) - f(x)\} + \{g(x + h) - g(x)\}}{h}$$

$$= \lim_{h \to 0} \left\{ \frac{f(x + h) - f(x)}{h} + \frac{g(x + h) - g(x)}{h} \right\}$$

$$= \lim_{h \to 0} \frac{f(x + h) - f(x)}{h} + \lim_{h \to 0} \frac{g(x + h) - g(x)}{h}$$

$$\text{[by Thm. 1.5.1 (ii)]}$$

$$= \{Df(x)\} + \{Dg(x)\} \qquad \text{[by (1.2.3)]}$$

Theorem 1.9.4. The derivative of a difference is the difference of the derivatives; i.e.,

(1.9.4) $D[f(x) - g(x)] = [Df(x)] - [Dg(x)]$

Proof.

$$D[f(x) - g(x)] = D\{f(x) + [-g(x)]\}$$
$$= Df(x) + D[(-1)g(x)] \qquad [\text{(by (1.9.3)}]$$
$$= Df(x) - Dg(x) \qquad [\text{(by (1.9.2)}]$$

For the sake of completeness, we prove:

Theorem 1.9.5. Let c be an arbitrary but fixed real number, and let $f(x) = c$ for all x. Then $Df(x) = 0$ for all x.

Proof. Set $f(x) = c$. Then, $f(x + h) = c$, so

$$Dc = \lim_{h \to 0} \frac{c - c}{h} = \lim_{h \to 0} 0 = 0$$

It is possible to sharpen Thm. 1.9.5 to read, "If $f(x) = c$ for all x in some open interval I contained in the domain of $f(x)$, then $f'(x) = 0$ on I". To prove this, use the proof of Thm. 1.9.5, but choose h so small that $x + h$ is in I for x in I.

Example 1.9.3. Combining the results of Thms. 1.9.1 through 1.9.5, we have

(i)
$$D(x^3 - 2x^2 + 4x + 1) = Dx^3 - D2x^2 + D4x + D1$$
$$= Dx^3 - 2Dx^2 + 4Dx + D1$$
$$= 3x^2 - 4x + 4$$

(ii) $$D(ax^2 + bx + c) = 2ax + b \qquad (a, b, c \text{ constants})$$

(iii) $$D(a_0x^n + a_1x^{n-1} + \cdots + a_{n-1}x + a_n) = na_0x^{n-1}$$
$$+ (n - 1)a_1x^{n-2} + \cdots + a_{n-1}$$

From Ex. 1.9.3 (iii) we see that a polynomial of degree n has a derivative everywhere, and the derivative is a polynomial of degree $n - 1$. Theorem 1.7.3 gives us another proof that a polynomial is continuous everywhere.

If we are given $y = f(x)$, we see that $f'(x)$ is just a new function of x; in fact, a function derived from $f(x)$. We can write $g(x) = f'(x)$. Clearly, $g(x)$ might also have a derivative, $g'(x)$. If so we call it the *second* derivative of $f(x)$, written $f''(x)$. The second derivative is then the derivative of the first derivative, $(d/dx)[(d/dx)f(x)]$, or, $D[Df(x)]$, and is written $d^2f(x)/dx^2$ or $D^2f(x)$.

Example 1.9.4. If $f(x) = x^3 - 2x^2 + 4x + 1$, we have that

$$df(x)/dx = f'(x) = 3x^2 - 4x + 4$$

and

$$d^2f(x)/dx^2 = f''(x) = D(3x^2 - 4x + 4) = 6x - 4$$

Example 1.9.5. Let
$$f(x) = x^3, \text{ then}$$
$$f'(x) = 3x^2, \text{ and}$$
$$f''(x) = 6x$$

Again, it is possible that the function $f''(x)$ has a derivative; if so we call it the *third* derivative of $f(x)$, written $f'''(x)$. So,
$$f'''(x) = (d/dx)(d^2 f(x)/dx^2) = D[D^2 f(x)]$$
and is written
$$f'''(x) = d^3 f(x)/dx^3 = D^3 f(x)$$

In general, we denote the *nth derivative of $f(x)$ by*
$$f^{(n)}(x) \quad \text{or} \quad d^n f(x)/dx^n \quad \text{or} \quad D^n f(x) \quad \text{or} \quad (d^n/dx^n)f(x)$$

and define the symbol to be the derivative of the $(n-1)$st derivative; i.e.,

(1.9.5) $$D^n f(x) = D[D^{n-1} f(x)]$$

whenever it exists.

Example 1.9.6. Let $f(x) = x^5 - 3x^2$. Then

$$f'(x) = 5x^4 - 6x$$
$$d^2 f/dx^2 = D^2 f = f''(x) = 20x^3 - 6$$
$$d^3 f/dx^3 = D^3 f = f'''(x) = 60x^2$$
$$d^4 f \, dx^4 = D^4 f = f^{(4)}(x) = 120x$$
$$d^5 f/dx^5 = D^5 f = f^{(5)}(x) = 120$$
$$d^6 f/dx^6 = D^6 f = f^{(6)}(x) = 0$$
$$d^n f/dx^n = D^n f = f^{(n)}(x) = 0 \qquad n \geq 6$$

Example 1.9.7. Let the position of a particle at time t be given by $s(t)$. Then its velocity is given by $s'(t)$ and its acceleration by $s''(t)$, the second derivative of $s(t)$. [See §1.3, especially (1.3.5)].

PROBLEMS

1.9.1. Find the slope of the line tangent to the graph of
$$f(x) = x^5 - 2x^4 + 3x^2 + x - 5 \qquad \text{at } x = 1$$

1.9.2. A particle moves so that its distance at time t is given by $s(t) = 128t - 16t^2$. Find the velocity and acceleration of the particle at an arbitrary time t.

1.9.3. If the total cost of producing x units of a commodity is given by $S(x) = x^3 - \frac{1}{2}x^2 + 7x$, find the marginal cost when 10 units have been produced (see Ex. 1.3.3).

1.9.4. Let $f(x) = x^6 + 3x^4 - 2x + 1$. Find $f'(x)$, $f''(x)$, $f'''(x)$, $f^{(4)}(x)$, and $f^{(5)}(x)$.

1.9.5. Find the points on the graph of $y = 2x^3 - 3x^2 - 12x + 20$ where the tangent line is parallel to the x-axis.

1.9.6. Find $(d/dx)(x + 1)^4$ by using (1.8.1). Then find $(d^2/dx^2)(x + 1)^4$. (*Hint:* Write $(x + h + 1)^4$ as $([x + 1] + h)^4$.)

1.9.7. Find $(d/dx)(x^2 - 1)^4$ by using (1.8.1). Then find $(d^2/dx^2)(x^2 - 1)^4$.

1.9.8. Find $D[(x + 3)(x - 1)]$.

1.9.9. Find all points on the graph of $f(x) = (\frac{1}{3})x^3 + (\frac{1}{2})x^2 - 3x + 1$ where the tangent line is parallel to the line $y = -x$.

1.9.10. Let $f(x) = x^4 + x^2 - 1$. Find the slope of the line tangent to the graph of $f'(x)$ at $x = 1$.

1.9.11. Find $D\{x^5(x^2 - 3x + 1) + x^2\}$.

1.9.12. (a) Find
$$\lim_{h \to 0} \frac{[2 + h]^5 - 32}{h}$$
(b) Find
$$\lim_{h \to 0} \frac{[1 + h]^{10} - 1}{h}$$

1.9.13. Suppose $f'(x)$ exists, and $f(x) \neq 0$. Show that
$$D\frac{1}{f(x)} = -\frac{Df(x)}{[f(x)]^2}$$

1.9.14. Suppose $f'(x)$ exists, and k is a constant, $k \neq 0$. Show that
$$D\frac{f(x)}{k} = \frac{Df(x)}{k}$$

1.9.15. Let the domain of $f(x)$ be the closed interval $a \leq x \leq b$, and suppose $f(x)$ is constant on its domain. Use Def. (1.5.5) to prove $f'(a) = f'(b) = 0$.

1.10. Composition of functions. The chain rule.

The easiest way to explain the composition of functions is by illustration.

Example 1.10.1. Set $f(u) = u^2 + 1$. We now consider the case that u is also a function. Set $u = g(x) = \frac{1}{2}(x - 1)$. Then by direct substitution, $f(u) = f[g(x)]$; i.e., we evaluate $f(u)$ at $u = g(x)$. This means that every instance of u is to be replaced by $g(x)$, so, since $f(u) = u^2 + 1$, we have that

$$f[g(x)] = [g(x)]^2 + 1 = \left[\frac{(x-1)}{2}\right]^2 + 1 = \tfrac{1}{4}(x^2 - 2x + 5)$$

Observe that our final expression for $f[g(x)]$ involves only x. In fact, if we write $w(x) = \tfrac{1}{4}(x^2 - 2x + 5)$, we see that $f[g(x)] = w(x)$. We call $w(x)$ the composition of $f(u)$ and $g(x)$. In particular,

$$\begin{aligned}
f[g(0)] &= w(0) = \tfrac{5}{4} \\
f[g(1)] &= w(1) = \tfrac{1}{4}(1^2 - 2\cdot 1 + 5) = 1 \\
f[g(-1)] &= w(-1) = 2
\end{aligned}$$

and so on.

Let us evaluate $f[g(0)]$ in a different but equivalent way. Since $g(x) = \tfrac{1}{2}(x - 1)$, then $g(0) = -\tfrac{1}{2}$. Thus $f[g(0)]$ is the same as $f(u)$ evaluated at $u = g(0) = -\tfrac{1}{2}$. This gives $f[g(0)] = f(-\tfrac{1}{2}) = (-\tfrac{1}{2})^2 + 1 = \tfrac{5}{4}$. Observe that $dw(x)/dx = \tfrac{1}{2}(x - 1)$.

Example 1.10.2. Set $F(u) = 2u(u - 1)$, and let $u = G(x) = 6x + 1$. Then $F[G(x)]$ is the value of $F(u)$ evaluated at $u = G(x)$. So,

$$\begin{aligned}
F[G(x)] &= 2 \cdot G(x) \cdot [G(x) - 1] \\
&= 2(6x + 1)[(6x + 1) - 1] \\
&= 12x(6x + 1) \\
&= 72x^2 + 12x
\end{aligned}$$

If we write $W(x) = 72x^2 + 12x$, then $F[G(x)] = W(x)$. We see that W is the composition of F and G. Observe that:

$$W'(x) = \frac{d}{dx}\, W(x) = \frac{d}{dx}\,(72x^2 + 12x) = 144x + 12$$

In Ex. 1.10.1, we had that

$$\begin{aligned}
f(u) &= u^2 + 1, \quad u = g(x) = \tfrac{1}{2}(x - 1) \\
f[g(x)] &= w(x) = \tfrac{1}{4}(x^2 - 2x + 5)
\end{aligned}$$

and

$$\left(\frac{d}{dx}\right) f[g(x)] = \frac{d}{dx}\, w(x) = \frac{x-1}{2}$$

Knowing only that $f(u) = u^2 + 1$ and $u = g(x) = \tfrac{1}{2}(x - 1)$, we can directly evaluate $w'(x)$ *without ever explicitly knowing* $w(x)$ and avoid all the algebra and substitutions necessary to evaluate $w(x)$ by using the following theorem, the chain rule.

Theorem 1.10.1   (The Chain Rule).   Let $u = g(x)$ have a derivative $g'(x) = dg(x)/dx$ defined on the interval $a \le x \le b$ [i.e., the interval $a \le x \le b$ is in the domain of $g'(x)$], and let the range of $g(x)$ be the interval $A \le u \le B$.

Let the function $y = f(u)$ have a derivative $f'(u) = df(u)/du$ defined on the interval $A \le u \le B$. Let $W(x) = f[g(x)]$. Then

$$(1.10.1) \qquad W'(x) = \frac{df[g(x)]}{dx} = \frac{df(u)}{du} \cdot \frac{dg(x)}{dx}$$

where it is understood that $u = g(x)$; and $W'(x)$ is defined on the interval $a \le x \le b$.

Remarks. In Thm. 1.10.1, our concern with the domains and ranges of the derivatives is to guarantee that it is meaningful to talk about the composition function $W(x)$ and its derivative $W'(x)$. If the domain of $f(x)$ and the range of $g(x)$ did not properly match, we might fall on some value of $g(x)$, say $g(c) = s$, such that s would not be in the domain of $f(u)$; i.e., $f[g(c)] = f(s)$ might be meaningless, and hence $f'[g(x)]$ would be meaningless at $x = c$.

If we have a function F, let us introduce the notation $D_z F$ to mean the derivative of F with respect to z; e.g., if we have a composition function $f[g(x)]$, $D_x f[g(x)]$ means the derivative of that function with respect to x. With this notation we can write (1.10.1) as $D_x f[g(x)] = D_u f(u) \cdot D_x g(x)$ with $u = g(x)$; i.e., the derivative of the composition function is simply the product of its constituent parts.

The theorem is proved in Appendix A.

Example 1.10.3. As in Ex. 1.10.1,

$$f(u) = u^2 + 1 \quad \text{and} \quad u = g(x) = \frac{x-1}{2}$$

So

$$D_u f(u) = \frac{d}{du}(u^2 + 1) = 2u$$

and

$$D_x g(x) = \frac{d}{dx}\frac{x-1}{2} = \frac{1}{2}$$

From Ex. 1.10.1, we know that $f[g(x)]$ is a function only of x, which we called $w(x)$. By (1.10.1), $w'(x) = (d/dx)f[g(x)] = 2u \cdot \frac{1}{2} = u$. But $u = \frac{1}{2}(x-1)$ so $w'(x) = \frac{1}{2}(x-1)$. This is the same result we obtained in Ex. 1.10.1 by explicitly evaluating $w(x)$ and then taking its derivative.

Example 1.10.4. As in Ex. 1.10.2, $F(u) = 2u(u-1) = 2u^2 - 2u$, and $u = G(x) = 6x + 1$. By the chain rule,

$$W'(x) = \frac{d}{dx} F[G(x)] = \frac{d}{du} F(u) \cdot \frac{d}{dx} G(x)$$

$$= (4u - 2) \cdot 6 = 24u - 12$$

Since $u = g(x) = 6x + 1$,

$$W'(x) = 24(6x + 1) - 12 = 144x + 12$$

which is the same result we obtained in Ex. 1.10.2 by explicitly differentiating $F[g(x)]$.

Example 1.10.5. Let $f(u) = u^3 - 3u^2 + 2u + 1$, and $u = g(x) = x^2 + x - 1$. Then, if we form $f[g(x)]$, we have from (1.10.1)

$$\frac{d}{dx} f[g(x)] = \frac{df(u)}{du} \cdot \frac{dg(x)}{dx}$$

$$= (3u^2 - 6u + 2)(2x + 1)$$

$$= [3(x^2 + x - 1)^2 - 6(x^2 + x - 1) + 2][2x + 1]$$

The last expression could be simplified, of course.

Example 1.10.6. Evaluate $(d/dx)(x^3 + 5)^{17}$. Here we set $f(u) = u^{17}$ and $u = g(x) = x^3 + 5$. From (1.10.1),

$$\frac{d}{dx}(x^3 + 5)^{17} = \frac{d}{dx} f[g(x)] = \frac{df(u)}{du} \cdot \frac{dg(x)}{dx}$$

$$= (17u^{16})(3x^2)$$

$$= 51x^2(x^3 + 5)^{16}$$

For completeness we state the following theorem without proof. (The proof is given in Appendix A.)

Theorem 1.10.2. Let $f(u)$ and $g(x)$ be functions of u and x, respectively, and let the range of $g(x)$ be in the domain of $f(u)$; hence $f[g(x)]$ is defined for all x in the domain of $g(x)$. Suppose A is a number such that $f(u)$ is continuous at $u = A$, and suppose $A = g(B)$ for some $x = B$. Further suppose that $g(x)$ is continuous at $x = B$. Then, the composite function $f[g(x)]$ is continuous at $x = B$.

Roughly, we are asserting that if each of two functions is continuous, then so is their composition. An interesting consequence of this is:

Theorem 1.10.3. If $g(x)$ is continuous at $x = a$, then $|g(x)|$ is also continuous at $x = a$.

Proof. Let $f(u) = |u|$; then $f(u)$ is continuous for all u. Let $u = g(x)$ be continuous at $x = a$. Then by Thm. 1.10.2, $f[g(x)] = |g(x)|$ is continuous at $x = a$.

PROBLEMS

1.10.1. For each of the following, find $f[g(x)]$ explicitly, and then compute $(d/dx)f[g(x)]$ from your value for $f[g(x)]$. Then use (1.10.1) to evaluate $(d/dx)f[g(x)]$.

(a) $f(u) = u^2 + 3u - 1$　and　$u = g(x) = 2x + 1$
(b) $f(u) = u^2$　and　$u = g(x) = x^2 + 2x + 3$
(c) $f(u) = u + 1$　and　$u = g(x) = x^3 + 3x^2 + x - 5$

1.10.2. Use (1.10.1) to evaluate $(d/dx)(x^2 + 1)^{30}$ and $(d/dx)(x^8 - 3)^{27}$.

1.10.3. Let $f(x) = 3x - 7$. Find $g(x)$ such that $f[g(x)] = x$. Verify that $g[f(x)] = x$. Such a g is called the *inverse* of f.

1.10.4. Set $f(x) = x^2 - 1$. Solve the equation $f[f(x)] = -1$.

1.10.5. (a) Suppose $f(u)$ and $u = g(x)$ satisfy the equation $f[g(x)] = x$, and that both $f(x)$ and $g(x)$ have derivatives everywhere. Show that

$$\frac{dg(x)}{dx} = \frac{1}{df(u)/du}$$

evaluated at $u = g(x)$.
(b) Let $f(u) = u^2 + 2u + 2$, $u \geq -1$. Suppose further that $u = g(x)$ satisfies the equation $f[g(x)] = x$. Use (a) to find $g'(x)$.

1.10.6. Let $f(x)$ be a function such that $f'(x) = x^5$. Find $(d/dx)f(x^2)$. (*Hint:* Set $g(x) = x^2$.)

1.10.7. Set $F(x)$ be such that $F'(x) = x^2 + 1$. Find

$$\frac{d}{dx} F\left(\frac{x+1}{x-1}\right)$$

1.10.8. For the reliability function of Ex. 1.1.10,

$$f_n(r) = \frac{nr}{1 + (n-1)r}$$

show that $f_n[f_n(r)] = f_{n^2}(r)$. What does this say about reliability?

1.11. More techniques for differentiation.

In §1.9, we found formulas for derivatives of sums, differences, and constant multiples of functions. We next look at products. Remember that all the theorems are valid at all points at which $f'(x)$ and $g'(x)$ exist (see the remarks in §1.9).

Theorem 1.11.1 (Product rule). The derivative of a product is given by

(1.11.1) $$D[f(x)g(x)] = f(x)Dg(x) + [Df(x)]g(x)$$

or $(fg)' = fg' + f'g$.

Proof. Since we are assuming that both f' and g' exist (recall our omnipresent hypothesis of §1.9), we know that $(f + g)'$ exists and that

$$(f + g)' = f' + g'$$

Hence, by the chain rule, $D(f + g)^2$ exists and

$$D(f + g)^2 = 2(f + g)(f + g)' = 2(f + g)(f' + g')$$

An analogous statement holds for $D(f - g)^2$. Since we have the identity†

$$f \cdot g = \tfrac{1}{4}(f + g)^2 - \tfrac{1}{4}(f - g)^2$$

we have by our previous remarks

$$
\begin{aligned}
(f \cdot g)' &= \tfrac{1}{4}D(f + g)^2 - \tfrac{1}{4}D(f - g)^2 \\
&= \tfrac{1}{4} \cdot 2(f + g)(f' + g') - \tfrac{1}{4} \cdot 2(f - g)(f' - g') \\
&= \tfrac{1}{2}(ff' + gf' + g'f + gg') - \tfrac{1}{2}(ff' - gf' - g'f + gg') \\
&= gf' + g'f = fg' + f'g
\end{aligned}
$$

as desired.

Example 1.11.1.
$$
\begin{aligned}
Dx^2(x^2 - x + 1) &= x^2 D(x^2 - x + 1) + (Dx^2)(x^2 - x + 1) \\
&= x^2(2x - 1) + (2x)(x^2 - x + 1) \\
&= 4x^3 - 3x^2 + 2x
\end{aligned}
$$

Clearly,

$$x^2(x^2 - x + 1) = x^4 - x^3 + x^2$$

and

$$D(x^4 - x^3 + x^2) = 4x^3 - 3x^2 + 2x$$

In this example, it is probably better not to use the product rule. This will not always be the case.

Example 1.11.2. Let x represent the quantity of some commodity demanded by the market and $p(x)$ the price per unit of that quantity. (The reader should convince himself that functional notation is justified.) The classical definitions from economics are that *total revenue $R(x)$* is equal to $x \cdot p(x)$, and that *marginal revenue with respect to demand* is the rate of change of the total revenue with respect to demand. Hence, marginal revenue is simply $R'(x)$.

---

† The reader can expand the right side to convince himself of this identity.

By the product rule, we see that marginal revenue is given by

$$R'(x) = xp'(x) + p(x)$$

Under some conditions it is better to think of demand x as a function of price p; we will write this as $x(p)$. We can interpret the function $x(p)$ as the number of people that will buy the commodity if it were offered at price p. For instance, if 100 people will buy the commodity priced at \$2, we write $x(2) = 100$ (people); if 76 people will buy the commodity priced at \$ $(\frac{3}{2})$ = \$1.50, we write $x(\frac{3}{2}) = 76$ (people), and so on. *Total revenue* $S(p)$ now expressed *as a function of* p is given by $S(p) = p \cdot x(p)$, and *marginal revenue with respect to price* is the rate of change of total revenue with respect to price, $S'(p) = dS/dp$. Again by the product rule,

$$S'(p) = p(dx/dp) + x(p)$$

Theorem 1.11.2. The quotient rule. If $g(x) \neq 0$, the derivative of a quotient of functions is given by

$$(1.11.2) \qquad D\left[\frac{f(x)}{g(x)}\right] = \frac{g(x)Df(x) - [Dg(x)]f(x)}{[g(x)]^2}$$

The proof will appear as an exercise.

Example 1.11.3.

$$D\frac{1}{x} = \frac{xD1 - (Dx) \cdot 1}{x^2} = -\frac{1}{x^2}$$

Example 1.11.4.

$$D\frac{1}{x^2} = \frac{x^2 \cdot D1 - (Dx^2) \cdot 1}{x^4} = \frac{-2x}{x^4} = -\frac{2}{x^3}$$

Example 1.11.5. For any positive integer n, we see that

$$D\left[\frac{1}{x^n}\right] = \frac{x^n \cdot D1 - (Dx^n) \cdot 1}{(x^n)^2} = \frac{-nx^{n-1}}{x^{2n}} = nx^{n-1-2n} = -nx^{-n-1}$$

We used (1.9.1) in these calculations. Since $(1/x^n) = x^{-n}$, where $-n$ is negative (n was assumed positive), this example shows that for any positive integer n, $Dx^{-n} = -nx^{-n-1}$. Hence, *Thm. 1.9.1 is still valid if n is negative.*

Example 1.11.6. We use Ex. 1.11.5 to find $D(1/x)$. We write

$$D(1/x) = Dx^{-1} = -1x^{-2} = -(1/x^2)$$

which is the same result as in Ex. 1.11.3.

Example 1.11.7.

$$D\frac{x^2 + 2x + 3}{x + 1} = \frac{(x + 1)D(x^2 + 2x + 3) - [D(x + 1)][x^2 + 2x + 3]}{(x + 1)^2}$$

$$= \frac{(x + 1)(2x + 2) - (x^2 + 2x + 3)}{(x + 1)^2}$$

$$= \frac{x^2 + 2x - 1}{(x + 1)^2}$$

Theorem 1.11.3. Let n be any integer, then the derivative of the nth power of $f(x)$ is given by

(1.11.3) $$D[f(x)]^n = n[f(x)]^{n-1}Df(x)$$

Proof. We use the chain rule. Set $G(u) = u^n$ and let $u = f(x)$. Then $G(u) = G[f(x)] = [f(x)]^n$, and so $D[f(x)]^n = dG[f(x)]/dx$. By (1.10.1),

$$\frac{d}{dx} G[f(x)] = \frac{d}{du} G(u) \cdot \frac{d}{dx} f(x)$$

$$= nu^{n-1} \frac{d}{dx} f(x)$$

$$= n[f(x)]^{n-1} \frac{d}{dx} f(x)$$

By (1.9.1) and Ex. 1.11.5, we see that $(d/du)G(u) = nu^{n-1}$ is valid for any integer.

We have so far observed that $Dx^n = nx^{n-1}$ is valid for any integer. We shall later see that Thm. 1.11.3 is still valid if n is a rational number; i.e., $n = p/q$ where p and q are integers and $q > 0$. In this form, the derivative reads $Dx^{p/q} = (p/q)x^{(p/q)-1}$. In fact, $Dx^n = nx^{n-1}$ if n is *any fixed* real number! We shall state this as a theorem (it will be proved in §3.9).

Theorem 1.11.4. For any fixed real number r and differentiable function $f(x)$,

(1.11.4) $$Dx^r = rx^{r-1}$$

(1.11.5) $$D[f(x)]^r = r[f(x)]^{r-1}Df(x)$$

Example 1.11.8. $Dx^\pi = \pi x^{\pi-1}$.

Example 1.11.9. We find $D(x^2 + 2x + 3)^{\sqrt{2}}$. In (1.11.5), set

$$f(x) = x^2 + 2x + 3 \quad \text{and} \quad r = \sqrt{2}$$

Hence,

$$D(x^2 + 2x + 3)^{\sqrt{2}} = \sqrt{2}(x^2 + 2x + 3)^{\sqrt{2}-1}(2x + 2)$$

Example 1.11.10. $D\sqrt{x} = Dx^{1/2} = (\frac{1}{2})x^{-1/2} = 1/2\sqrt{x}$. [Compare this with Prob. 1.2.4(b).]

Example 1.11.11. Find $D\{(x^2 + 1)^5(2x - 7)^{10}\}$. We use the product rule (1.11.1):

$$\begin{aligned}
D\{(x^2 + 1)^5(2x - 7)^{10}\} &= (x^2 + 1)^5 \cdot D(2x - 7)^{10} + [D(x^2 + 1)^5](2x - 7)^{10} \\
&= [(x^2 + 1)^5 \cdot 10(2x - 7)^9 \cdot 2] \\
&\quad + [5(x^2 + 1)^4 \cdot 2x(2x - 7)^{10}] \\
&= 10(x^2 + 1)^4(2x - 7)^9[2(x^2 + 1) + x(2x - 7)] \\
&= 10(x^2 + 1)^4(2x - 7)^9(4x^2 - 7x + 2)
\end{aligned}$$

PROBLEMS

1.11.1. Use methods of this section to do Prob. 1.2.4 (b) through (e).

1.11.2. Find the derivative of each of the following:

(a) $f(x) = x/(x - 1)$ (b) $f(x) = x/\sqrt{x - 1}$

(c) $f(x) = [(x + 3)/(x + 2)]^2$ (d) $f(x) = (x + 1)\sqrt{x}$

(e) $f(x) = (x^5 - x^4 + 1)^{10}$ (f) $f(x) = (x - 1)^3/(x + 1)^4$

(g) $f(x) = x^2(x + 1)^{-1}$ (h) $f(x) = (x^3 - 1)^5 \cdot \sqrt[3]{x^2 + 2}$

(i) $f(x) = \sqrt{x^2 + 2} + [1/\sqrt{x - 2}]$ (j) $f(x) = \sqrt{x + \sqrt{x}}$

1.11.3. Find the slope of the line tangent to the graph of $f(x) = x/(x^2 + 1)$ at $x = 0$; at $x = 1$. Write the equations of the tangent lines to the corresponding points on the graph.

1.11.4. The distance a particle moves at time t is given by $s(t) = \sqrt{2t^2 + 1}$. Find the velocity and acceleration of the particle.

1.11.5. Find $D\{\sqrt[3]{x}\}$ and $D\{\sqrt[3]{x - 5}\}$. Discuss the tangent lines to the graphs of $\sqrt[3]{x}$ and $\sqrt[3]{x - 5}$ at $x = 0$ and $x = 5$, respectively.

1.11.6. Use (1.11.5) to find $D[(x + 2)/(x - 2)]^{\pi}$.

1.11.7. Set $f(x) = (1 + x)/(1 - x)$, find $f'(x)$, $f''(x)$, and $f'''(x)$.

1.11.8. Find $f'(x)$ if:

(a) $f(x) = x^3(1 - x^3)^3$
(b) $f(x) = (x + 2)(x - 5)^{-8}$
(c) $f(x) = (x^4 - 12x^2)/(x^2 - 4)^2$
(d) $f(x) = \sqrt{x}\,(x + 1)^{n+1}$
(e) $f(x) = (x^2 + 5x - 7)/(x^2 + 1)^2$
(f) $f(x) = [(x^5 + 1)/x] + \sqrt{(x + 3)/x}$

1.11.9. Find

$$\lim_{h \to 0} \frac{[1 + 2(x + h)]^{10} - [1 + 2x]^{10}}{h}$$

1.11.10. Prove Thm. 1.11.2. (*Hint:* First write

$$D\left[\frac{f(x)}{g(x)}\right] = \lim_{h \to 0} \left\{ \frac{1}{h}\left[\frac{f(x + h)}{g(x + h)} - \frac{f(x)}{g(x)}\right]\right\} = \lim_{h \to 0} \frac{f(x + h)g(x) - f(x)g(x + h)}{h \cdot g(x + h)g(x)}$$

Add $-g(x)f(x) + g(x)f(x)$ to the numerator; do some factoring; and take the limit.)

1.11.11. Consider the function $f(x) = x^x$ where $x > 0$. It might be conjectured that $Df(x) = x \cdot x^{x-1}$. Explain why Thm. 1.11.4 does *not* imply this result.

1.11.12. (This problem is based on Ex. 1.11.2.) Suppose the price of a commodity with demand x is $p(x) = 8/(2 + x)$. Find the total and marginal revenues.

1.11.13. The demand for a commodity as a function of price is given by $x(p) = (8 - 2p)/p$. Find the total and marginal revenues (see Ex. 1.11.2). Compare your result with the result of Prob. 1.11.12.

1.12. Implicit functions. Implicit differentiation.

Up to now we have considered exclusively functions of x given *explicitly* in terms of x. For instance, in the expression $y = x + 1$, y is clearly a function of x, and we would ordinarily write $y = G(x) = x + 1$. Suppose the same relation had been written $y - x - 1 = 0$. This y is the same as the one in $y = G(x) = x + 1$, so we see that the relation $y - x - 1 = 0$ *implicitly* gives y as a function of x. By direct substitution, we write the relation as

$$G(x) - x - 1 = 0.$$

Example 1.12.1. Consider $xy - x = 1$. If we solve explicitly for y, we obtain $x(y - 1) = 1$, $y = 1 + 1/x$. Hence, $y = F(x) = 1 + 1/x$. With this

$F(x)$, we can write $xy - x = 1$ as $xF(x) - x = 1$. Since $F(x) = 1 + 1/x$, we have $F'(x) = (-1/x^2)$.

In the equation $x^5y^2 - \sqrt{xy - y} + (x/y)^{10} + 172 = 0$, it would be impossible to solve explicitly for $y = f(x)$. However, the method of implicit differentiation gives us a technique for finding $f'(x)$ *without ever explicitly finding $f(x)$*. We appeal to the following: if $P(x) = Q(x)$ and $P(x)$ has a derivative, then $Q(x)$ has a derivative, and $P'(x) = Q'(x)$. (Why?)

Let us return to Ex. 1.12.1. Here $xy - x = 1$. Let us assume that $y = F(x)$. Then by substitution, $xF(x) - x = 1$. Hence,

$$D\{xF(x) - x\} = D1$$

We evaluate:

$$
\begin{aligned}
D\{xF(x) - x\} &= D\{xF(x)\} - Dx \\
&= xDF(x) + \{Dx\}F(x) - Dx \qquad \text{[using (1.11.1)]} \\
&= xF'(x) + F(x) - 1
\end{aligned}
$$

Since $D1 = 0$, we obtain

$$xF'(x) + F(x) - 1 = 0$$

or

$$F'(x) = \frac{1 - F(x)}{x}$$

Hence, we found $F'(x)$ without explicitly knowing $F(x)$, though our answer involves $F(x)$. This is not necessarily undesirable.

Example 1.12.2. Consider the graph of the relation $xy - x = 1$. Find the slope of the tangent line to the graph at $x = 1$. Here, $1 \cdot F(1) - 1 = 1$, so $F(1) = 2$. We have already observed that $F'(x) = [1 - F(x)]/x$. Hence, $F'(1) = 1 - F(1) = 1 - 2 = -1$, which is the desired slope.

Finally, we saw in Ex. 1.12.1 that $F(x) = 1 + 1/x$, so that

$$F'(x) = [1 - F(x)]/x$$

becomes

$$F'(x) = \frac{1 - (1 + 1/x)}{x} = -\frac{1}{x^2}$$

which is the same result as in Ex. 1.12.1.

Example 1.12.3. A typical problem appearing in calculus texts is: "If $x^2 + y^2 = 1$, find dy/dx", which means: "Suppose $y = G(x)$ in the equation $x^2 + y^2 = 1$; write $x^2 + [G(x)]^2 = 1$ and find $G'(x)$". If we carry out the formal calculations required, we get: $D\{x^2 + [G(x)]^2\} = D1$. We simplify: $D\{x^2 + [G(x)]^2\} = Dx^2 + D[G(x)]^2 = 2x + 2G(x)G'(x)$. Here we used (1.9.3) and (1.11.5). Hence, we finally obtain

$$x + G(x)G'(x) = 0$$

or

(A) $$G'(x) = -x/G(x)$$

Suppose we next solve $x^2 + y^2 = 1$ explicitly for y. We obtain $y^2 = 1 - x^2$,
so $y = \pm\sqrt{1 - x^2}$. But here y is *not* a
function of x, since for, say $x = 0$, we
get $y = 1$ or $y = -1$; i.e., for this x
we get *two* values y. It would seem
that, since y is not a function of x,
setting $y = G(x)$ is *not* proper, and
equation (A) above fails. As we
shall now see this is not the case,
and equation (A) *is valid* if it is properly interpreted.

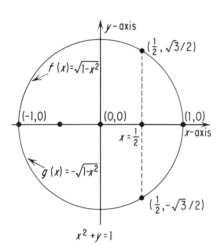

Figure 1.12.1

The expression $y = \pm\sqrt{1 - x^2}$
gives rise to two distinct functions, $f(x) = \sqrt{1 - x^2}$ and $g(x) =
-\sqrt{1 - x^2}$. The graph of $f(x)$ is
the top semi-circle of the circle $x^2
+ y^2 = 1$ and $g(x) = -\sqrt{1 - x^2}$ is
the bottom semi-circle (see Fig.
1.12.1).

Using (1.11.5), we see that $f'(x) = -x/\sqrt{1 - x^2}$ and $g'(x) = x/\sqrt{1 - x^2}$.
Hence $f'(1/2) = -1/\sqrt{3}$ and $g'(1/2) = 1/\sqrt{3}$. Suppose next we look at
$x^2 + y^2 = 1$ and set $x = 1/2$. We would then find that $y = \sqrt{3}/2$ or
$y = -\sqrt{3}/2$; observe that $f(1/2) = -\sqrt{3}/2$ and $g(1/2) = -\sqrt{3}/2$. Again, look
at equation (A); if we set $y = G(x)$ to obtain

(B) $$G'(x) = -x/y$$

and take $y = f(1/2) = \sqrt{3}/2$, equation (B) becomes

$$G'(1/2) = -\frac{1/2}{\sqrt{3}/2} = -\frac{1}{\sqrt{3}}$$

which is *exactly* $f'(1/2)$. If in (A) we set $y = G(x)$ to obtain (B), and take
$y = g(1/2) = -\sqrt{3}/2$, then equation (B) becomes

$$G'(1/2) = -\frac{-1/2}{\sqrt{3}/2} = \frac{1}{\sqrt{3}}$$

which is *exactly* $g'(1/2)$.

Hence, equation (A) is correct again if properly interpreted. Given $x = 1/2$, we get two values for $G'(x)$, one corresponding to the top semi-circle, $y = f(x)$, and the other corresponding to the bottom semi-circle, $y = g(x)$. The specific value of $G(x)$ you use depends on whether you are interested in the top or bottom semi-circle. In fact, if we write

$$G'(x) = -x/y$$

where y is the value corresponding to x in $x^2 + y^2 = 1$, we see that

$$y = \pm\sqrt{1 - x^2}$$

so

$$G'(x) = -\frac{x}{\pm\sqrt{1 - x^2}} = \mp\frac{x}{\sqrt{1 - x^2}}$$

If we choose the negative value above, we see that $G'(x) = f'(x)$, whereas if we choose the positive value, we see that $G'(x) = g'(x)$.

Example 1.12.4. Let $f(x) = x^{2/3}$. Find $f'(x)$ without using (1.11.5). Since $f(x) = x^{2/3}$, we see that by cubing each side, $[f(x)]^3 = x^2$. Hence,

$$D[f(x)]^3 = Dx^2$$

This becomes $3[f(x)]^2 Df(x) = 2x$, so,

$$Df(x) = \frac{\frac{2}{3}x}{[f(x)]^2} = \frac{\frac{2}{3}x}{x^{4/3}} = \frac{\frac{2}{3}}{x^{1/3}} = \frac{2}{3}x^{-1/3}$$

Example 1.12.5. Let p and q be integers, with $q > 0$. Set $f(x) = x^{p/q}$. We can duplicate the details of Ex. 1.12.4 to show that $f'(x) = (p/q)x^{(p/q)-1}$. We leave the details as a problem.

Example 1.12.6. A pebble is dropped into a pond causing a circular ripple. A measuring device indicates that at the time the radius is 5 inches, the radius is changing at the rate of 2 in./sec. How fast is the area changing at this instant of time? Clearly, both the area and the radius are changing with time, and hence both depend on time. So we shall write the area as $A(t)$ with the usual meaning that area A is a function of time t. Similarly we shall write $R(t)$ for the radius. It is well known that $A = \pi R^2$; substituting the functions, this becomes $A(t) = \pi[R(t)]^2$. The problem tells us that at the time that $R = 5$, the radius is changing at the rate of 2 in./sec; i.e.,

$$\frac{dR(t)}{dt}\bigg]_{R=5} = 2 \text{ in./sec}$$

We are asked to find $dA(t)/dt$ when $R = 5$. (See §1.3.) Observe that:

$$A(t) = \pi[R(t)]^2$$

implies

$$\frac{dA(t)}{dt} = \frac{d}{dt}\pi[R(t)]^2 = \pi\frac{d[R(t)]^2}{dt}$$

By (1.11.5),

$$\frac{d[R(t)]^2}{dt} = 2R(t)\frac{dR(t)}{dt}$$

Hence,

$$\frac{dA(t)}{dt} = 2\pi R(t)\frac{dR(t)}{dt}$$

is the general relationship between

$$\frac{dA(t)}{dt} \quad \text{and} \quad \frac{dR(t)}{dt}$$

To solve our particular problem, we see that

$$\frac{d}{dt}A(t)\bigg]_{R=5} = 2\pi\cdot5\cdot2 = 20\pi \text{ in./sec}$$

Once we know $A(t) = \pi[R(t)]^2$, the relationship between dA/dt and dR/dt follows and is completely determined.

Example 1.12.7. We have a tank whose shape is a right circular cone of height 10 ft and whose base has a radius of 2 ft. Water is poured into the tank in such a way that the volume of water is increasing at the rate of 3 cu ft/min at the instant that the water level is 8 ft. How *fast* is water level rising at this instant? The cone is pictured in Fig. 1.12.2, in which h is the height of water at an arbitrary time, and r is the corresponding radius of the top of the water. The volume of water V in the tank is the difference in the volumes of the cone of radius 2 and height 10 and the cone of the radius r and height $10 - h$, hence, from the formula for the volume of a right circular cone, $\frac{\pi}{3}$ (radius)$^2 \cdot$ height, the volume of water in the tank is

$$3V = \pi\cdot2^2\cdot10 - \pi r^2(10 - h)$$
$$= 40\pi - \pi r^2(10 - h)$$

Next we see that h and r are not independent; in fact, by similar triangles,

$$\frac{10}{2} = \frac{10 - h}{r}$$

or

$$r = \tfrac{1}{5}(10 - h)$$

(see Fig. 1.12.3).

Hence,

$$3V = 40\pi - \frac{\pi(10 - h)^2}{25}(10 - h)$$

or

$$3V = 40\pi - (\pi/25)(10 - h)^3$$

Since volume and height are changing with time, we write $V(t)$ and $h(t)$, and consequently

(A) $3V(t) = 40\pi - (\pi/25)[10 - h(t)]^3$

By (1.11.5), it follows that

(B) $3\dfrac{dV(t)}{dt} = \dfrac{3\pi}{25}[10 - h(t)]^2 \cdot \dfrac{dh(t)}{dt}$

at *any* instant of time.

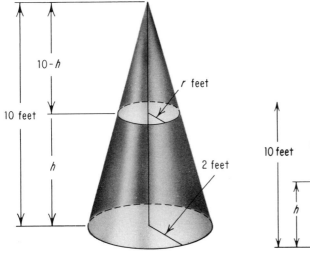
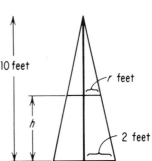

Figure 1.12.2   **Figure 1.12.3**

Re-reading the problem, we see that we are given $dV(t)/dt = 3$ gal/min when $h = 8$, and we wish to find $dh(t)/dt$. In the computations above, *we first found a relation between $V(t)$ and $h(t)$ from which we deduced a relationship between dV/dt and dh/dt.* Specifically, equation (A) is a relationship between V and h, from which we *deduced* (B), the relationship between dV/dt and dh/dt. Thus, from equation (B), we see that at the instant that $h = 8$,

$$9 = \frac{3\pi}{25}[10 - 8]^2 \cdot \frac{dh}{dt}$$

so, finally,

$$\frac{dh(t)}{dt} = \frac{75}{4\pi} \frac{ft}{min}$$

PROBLEMS

1.12.1. Consider the equation $(1 + x)y^2 - x = 0$.

(a) Solve this *explicitly* for y. Observe that you obtain two functions. Write them both explicitly and graph them. Find the derivative of each function.

(b) Use implicit differentiation to find $F'(x)$, assuming that y can be written as $F(x)$. Find $F'(1)$. Explain your answer in terms of (a).

1.12.2. Let $f(x) = x^{p/q}$, where p and q are integers, with $q > 0$. Prove that $f'(x) = (p/q)x^{(p/q)-1}$. (*Hint:* See Ex. 1.12.4 and Ex. 1.12.5.)

1.12.3. In each of the following use implicit differentiation to find dy/dx, and leave your answer in terms of x and y:

(a) $y^4 + x^2 y^2 = 10$ (b) $\sqrt{x} + \sqrt{y} = \sqrt{a}$
(c) $y^2 = (x + 1)/(x - 1)$ (d) $x^3 + y^2 = 1$
(e) $x^2 y + xy^2 = 6$ (f) $x^2 + y^2 = xy$

1.12.4. Find the slope of the tangent line to each of the following curves at the point or points indicated:

(a) $x^2 - 2xy + y^2 + 2x + y - 6 = 0$ at $(2, 2)$
(b) $x^2 y^2 - y - 2 = 0$ at $(1, -1)$ and $(1, -2)$
(c) $x^3 + y^3 = 18xy$ at $(8, 4)$
(d) $xy^{1/2} - yx^{1/2} = 0$ at $(1, 1)$
(e) $\dfrac{x - y}{x - 2y} = 2$ at $(3, 1)$

1.12.5. A ladder 5 ft long rests against a vertical wall. Assume the ground is horizontal. The ladder slides down the wall in such a way that at the instant the foot of the ladder is 4 ft from the wall, the foot of the ladder is moving 2 ft/sec. How fast is the top of the ladder descending the wall at this instant?

1.12.6. A particle moves in the circular path $x^2 + y^2 = 25$ in such a way that when the particle is at the point $(3, 4)$, the component of the velocity in the direction of the x-axis is -10 ft/sec. Find the component of the velocity in the direction of the y-axis at this point.

1.12.7. A man 6 ft tall walks at the rate of 4 ft/sec toward a streetlight that is 24 ft tall. How fast is the length of his shadow changing?

1.12.8. Water is withdrawn from a conical reservoir 6 ft in diameter and 8 ft deep at the constant rate of 3 cu ft/min. The vertex of the cone faces down. How fast is the water level falling at the instant the level is 4 ft deep?

1.12.9. Two trucks have a common starting point, but one moves southward at 30 mph and the other westward at 40 mph. At end of one hour, how fast are the trucks moving away from each other?

1.12.10. A piece of ice is in the shape of a sphere. If the ice melts at the rate of 5 cu in./min, how fast is the radius changing at the instant that the radius is 4 in.? If the surface area is decreasing by 2 sq in./min, how fast is the radius changing (again assuming the ice melts at the rate of 5 cu in./min)?

1.12.11. A light source hangs from the parabola $y^2 = x$ in such a way that it always casts a thin beam of light perpendicular to the x-axis, striking the x-axis at a point P (see Fig. 1.12.4). The light source slides down the parabola so that the velocity of the light source in the y-direction is -10 ft/sec. Find the velocity of the point of light on the x-axis (i.e., the velocity of the point P) at the instant $x = 4$.

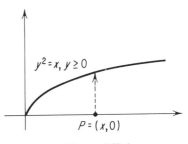

Figure 1.12.4

1.12.12. A point moves along the curve $y^2 = x^3$ in such a way that its distance from the origin increases at the constant rate of 2 units per second. Find dx/dt at $(2, 2\sqrt{2})$.

1.12.13. A particle is projected horizontally from a platform 2 ft above the ground. Directly above the platform and 6 ft from the ground is a light-source. Assuming the velocity of the particle at time $t = 1$ is 2 ft/sec, find the velocity of the shadow of the particle at time $t = 1$. Assume that the particle moves *only* horizontally.

1.12.14. The marginal revenue corresponding to a demand of $x = 2$ is known to be 10. If the price corresponding to demand $x = 2$ is $8, what is the rate of change of price (with respect to demand) corresponding to demand $x = 2$? (See Ex. 1.11.2.)

Chapter 2

APPLICATIONS

OF THE

DERIVATIVE

In §1.3, we saw the derivative used to define instantaneous velocity and instantaneous acceleration. We also saw dy/dx interpreted as the rate of change of y with respect to x. In this chapter we pursue more uses of the derivative.

2.1. Preliminary remarks on evaluating functions.

In the succeeding sections we shall often be required to evaluate polynomials at various specific values of x. To aid in this computation, we shall present an algebraic technique sometimes called *synthetic substitution*.

Example 2.1.1. We will illustrate the technique by considering

$$f(x) = -x^5 - 2x^4 + x^2 - 3$$

and evaluating $f(5)$.

Step 1. Write the coefficients of $f(x)$ next to each other on a line in the order of *descending* powers of x, placing a 0 wherever a power of x is missing. This line of numbers will be referred to as line 1.

For our particular example, this becomes:

(line 1) -1 -2 0 1 0 -3

Step 2. Copy the first term appearing in line 1 onto line 3.

Step 3. To evaluate $f(5)$, multiply the first term appearing in line 3 (in our example, -1) by the value at which we wish to evaluate the function, 5, and put this result ($-1 \cdot 5 = -5$) in the second line below the second term in line one, and add, giving -7. Then multiply the result of this addition, (-7), by the value at which we wish to evaluate the function, 5, and place the result (-35) on line 2 below the third number on line 1 and again add. Continue this process. The number under the last entry is the value of the function. Hence, $f(5) = -4353$ (see Fig. 2.1.1).

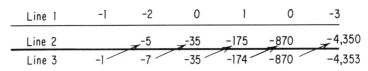

Line 1	-1	-2	0	1	0	-3
Line 2		-5	-35	-175	-870	-4,350
Line 3	-1	-7	-35	-174	-870	-4,353

Figure 2.1.1

Example 2.1.2. We evaluate $g(2)$ if $g(x) = 2x^8 - x^6 - 29x^4 + 14x$. The result (shown in Fig. 2.1.2) is $g(2) = 12$. In practice we omit the arrows between lines 3 and 2.

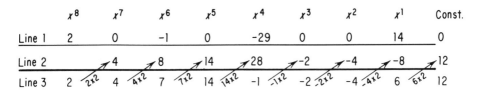

	x^8	x^7	x^6	x^5	x^4	x^3	x^2	x^1	Const.
Line 1	2	0	-1	0	-29	0	0	14	0
Line 2		4	8	14	28	-2	-4	-8	12
Line 3	2	4	7	14	-1	-2	-4	6	12

Figure 2.1.2

Let us see why this technique works. Let the polynomial you wish to evaluate be $P(x) = a_0x^n + a_1x^{n-1} + a_2x^{n-2} + \cdots + a_n$. Line 1 is then: $a_0\, a_1\, a_2 \ldots a_n$. Suppose we wish to evaluate $P(x)$ at $x = B$; i.e., $P(B)$. We first multiply $a_0 \cdot B$ and then add the product to the second element on line 1, a_1 to get $a_0B + a_1$. This sum is now multiplied by B to get

$$(a_0B + a_1)B = a_0B^2 + a_1B$$

which is added to the third element of line 1, a_2, to get: $a_0B^2 + a_1B + a_2$. Next, we again multiply by B to get

$$(a_0B^2 + a_1B + a_2)B = a_0B^3 + a_1B^2 + a_2B$$

which we add to the fourth element of line 1, a_3, to get

$$a_0B^3 + a_1B^2 + a_2B + a_3$$

Continuing, we finally get:

$$a_0B^n + a_1B^{n-1} + a_2B^{n-2} + \cdots + a_n$$

which is precisely $P(B)$, the value we wish to compute.

PROBLEMS

2.1.1. Given $f(x) = x^7 - 2x^6 + 4x^5 - 6x^4 + 10x^2 - 8$, find $f(1)$ and $f(2)$.

2.1.2. Given $f(x) = x^5 - x^4 + 3x^3 - 8x^2$, find $f(2)$ and $f'(2)$.

2.1.3. For the function given in Prob. 2.1.2, find $g''(2)$ and $g'''(2)$.

2.1.4. Let $g(x) = -40 + x^6$; find $g(-2)$.

2.1.5. Evaluate the polynomial $P(x) = x^4 - 44x^2 + 300$ at $x = 6$.

2.1.6. Let $F(x) = 6x^4 + x^3 + 4x^2 + x - 2$, find $F(-1)$, $F(0)$, and $F(-2/3)$.

2.2. Strictly increasing and strictly decreasing functions.

A function $y = f(x)$ is said to be **strictly increasing**, which we shall abbre-

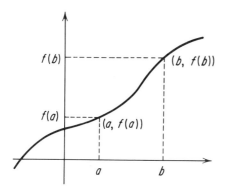

Figure 2.2.1

viate by **S.I.**, if as x increases, $f(x)$ increases as well. We see that geometrically, $f(x)$ is **S.I.** if the graph of $f(x)$ "rises" as it "moves" from left to right. Analytically we *define* $f(x)$ *to be* **S.I.** if whenever $b > a$, we have $f(b) > f(a)$ (see Fig. 2.2.1). Similarly, $f(x)$ is said to be **S.I.** on an (open or closed) interval I or half-line J if whenever $b > a$ for a and b points on I (or J, respectively), we have $f(b) > f(a)$ (see Fig. 2.2.2). Clearly, a function which is **S.I.** on I (or J) need not have this property elsewhere.

Example 2.2.1. The function $f(x) = 3x - 1$ is **S.I.** To see this, pick a and b any two numbers with $a < b$. Since $3 > 0$, we have that $3a < 3b$, and finally $3a - 1 < 3b - 1$. Since $f(a) = 3a - 1$ and $f(b) = 3b - 1$, we have $f(a) < f(b)$.

Example 2.2.2. The function $g(x) = x^2$ is **S.I.** provided $x > 0$. To see this, pick a and b any two

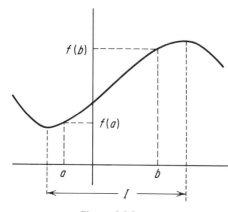

Figure 2.2.2

numbers on the half-line $x > 0$, with $a < b$; i.e., a and b satisfy $0 < a < b$. By Axiom 1.1.1, if we multiply by $a > 0$ we obtain $0 < a^2 < ab$. If we next multiply by $b > 0$, we obtain from $0 < a < b$ the inequality $0 < ab < b^2$. Putting these inequalities together, we have $0 < a^2 < ab < b^2$; i.e., if $0 < a < b$, then $a^2 < b^2$. But $g(a) = a^2$ and $g(b) = b^2$, so we have shown that if $0 < a < b$, then $g(a) < g(b)$; i.e., $g(x)$ is **S.I.** if $x > 0$.

A function $y = f(x)$ is said to be *strictly decreasing*, abbreviated **S.D.**, if as x increases, $f(x)$ *decreases*; i.e., geometrically, the graph of $f(x)$ "drops" as it "moves" from left to right. Analytically, we say that $f(x)$ is **S.D.** if whenever $b > a$ we have $f(b) < f(a)$ (see Fig. 2.2.3). We can define **S.D.** for intervals and half-lines as we did for **S.I.** functions; i.e., by requiring the definition hold for all $b > a$ on the interval or half-line (see Fig. 2.2.4).

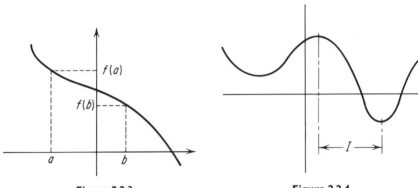

Figure 2.2.3   **Figure 2.2.4**

Example 2.2.3. Let $F(x) = 1 - 2x$. Then $F(x)$ is **S.D.** To see this, suppose that $a < b$. We must show $F(a) > F(b)$. Now $a < b$ implies that $-2a > -2b$, since $-2 < 0$; hence, $1 - 2a > 1 - 2b$. But $F(a) = 1 - 2a$ and $F(b) = 1 - 2b$, so we have $F(a) > F(b)$.

Example 2.2.4. The function $G(x) = x^2$ is **S.D.** provided $x < 0$. To see this, pick any a, b with $a < b$ and a, b in the region $x < 0$; i.e., $a < b < 0$. Since $b < 0$, we have that $ab > b^2$. Also, since $a < 0$, we have $a^2 > ab$. Hence, for $a < b < 0$, we have $a^2 > ab > b^2$; i.e., $G(a) = a^2 > b^2 = G(b)$.

If we inspect the graph of a strictly increasing function (see Fig. 2.2.5), we see that all tangent lines to the graph have non-negative slope, whereas if we inspect the graph of a strictly decreasing function (see Fig. 2.2.6), we see that all tangent lines to the graph have non-positive slope. Of course we are assuming that these functions are differentiable. In fact, we see geometrically that if $f'(x)$ is defined at a point, say $x = c$, at which the function changes from increasing to decreasing (or from decreasing to increasing), then

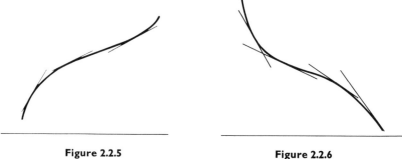

Figure 2.2.5   **Figure 2.2.6**

$f'(c) = 0$ (see Fig. 2.2.7). But the cautious reader should not read too much
into this observation. It is possible that $f'(c) = 0$ but that $f(x)$ *does not change*
from increasing to decreasing (or decreasing to increasing) at $x = c$. Specifically, $F(x) = x^3$ has the property that $F'(0) = 0$, but $F(x) = x^3$ is **S.I.** for
all x (see Ex. 2.2.9 and Fig. 2.2.8).

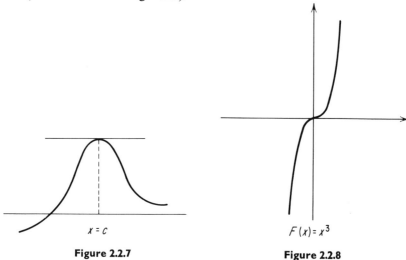

Figure 2.2.7   **Figure 2.2.8**

Unfortunately we do not have all the tools necessary to give a complete
analytic proof of what we have observed geometrically, though we can give a
partial proof. The complete proof follows from what is called the *mean
value theorem* which appears in the appendix.† We shall state the theorem in
Prob. 2.2.4 and let the reader apply it to complete the proof of the next theorem.

Theorem 2.2.1. (i) Let $f(x)$ be continuous on the closed interval $a \le x \le b$
and differentiable on the open interval $a < x < b$. Suppose further that

_____

† The reader is cautioned that to understand the proof in the appendix Thm. 2.4.2 is needed.

$f'(x) > 0$ for all x in the open interval $a < x < b$. Then for all x in the *closed* interval $a \leq x \leq b$, $f(x)$ is **S.I.**

(ii) Let $f(x)$ be **S.I.** on an interval I and suppose $f(x)$ is differentiable on this interval. Then $f'(x) \geq 0$ on the interval I. (i) and (ii) remain true if I is replaced by a half-line, or the entire x-axis.

Proof. Part (i) follows from the mean value theorem; we omit this part of the proof. To prove (ii), recall that $f(x)$ **S.I.** on I means that whenever a and b are points in I with $a < b$, we have $f(a) < f(b)$. Let $h = b - a > 0$; i.e., $b = a + h$. Then $a < b$ becomes $a < a + h$, or simply $h > 0$. Hence, $[f(a + h) - f(a)]/h$ is positive. But it is known in general (a proof is outlined in Prob. 2.2.8) that if a function $G(x)$ has the property that $G(x) > 0$ for all x in an open interval containing $x = c$, except possibly at $x = c$, and if $\lim\limits_{x \to c} G(x)$ exists and equals L, then $L \geq 0$. With x replaced by h, c replaced by 0, and $G(h) = [f(a + h) - f(a)]/h$ where a is considered fixed, we see that for $h > 0$,

$$\lim_{\substack{h \to 0 \\ h > 0}} \frac{f(a + h) - f(a)}{h} \geq 0$$

But since $f(x)$ is assumed to be differentiable on I, and a is a point in I, $f'(a)$ exists, and must equal

$$\lim_{\substack{h \to 0 \\ (h > 0)}} \frac{f(a + h) - f(a)}{h}$$

from which it follows that $f'(a) \geq 0$.

The reader should convince himself that the interval I can be replaced by a half-line or the entire x-axis.

Theorem 2.2.2. Theorem 2.2.1 still holds if the symbols "$f'(x) > 0$" "$f'(x) \geq 0$", and "**S.I.**" are systematically replaced by "$f'(x) < 0$", "$f'(x) \leq 0$", and "**S.D.**", respectively.

An open question is whether $f'(x)$ can occasionally be zero with $f(x)$ still known to be **S.I.** or **S.D.** The following corollary provides at least a partial answer.

Corollary 1. Let $f(x)$ be continuous on the closed interval $a \leq x \leq b$ and differentiable on the open interval $a < x < b$, and suppose c is in the open interval $a < x < b$ (i.e., $a < c < b$).

(i) If $f'(x) > 0$ for all $x \neq c$ on $a < x < b$, and if $f'(c) = 0$, then $f(x)$ is **S.I.** on the closed interval $a \leq x \leq b$.

(ii) If $f'(x) < 0$ for all $x \neq c$ on $a < x < b$, and $f'(c) = 0$, then $f(x)$ is **S.D.** on the closed interval $a \leq x \leq b$.

Proof. We shall prove only (i). Theorem 2.2.1(i) already insures us that for $\delta > 0$, $f(x)$ is **S.I.** in every interval of the form $a \le x \le c - \delta$ and $c + \delta \le x \le b$. If we can show that whenever $u < c$, we have $f(u) < f(c)$, and whenever $w > c$ we have $f(w) > f(c)$, we will also have that $a \le u < c < w \le b$ implies $f(u) < f(c) < f(w)$; i.e., $f(x)$ is **S.I.** on $a \le x \le b$. But $f(x)$ is continuous on $a \le x \le c$ and differentiable on $a < x \le c$, and hence differentiable on $a < x < c$. So, by Thm. 2.2.1(i), $f(x)$ is **S.I.** on the *entire closed interval* $a \le x \le c$; i.e., if $u < c$, then $f(u) < f(c)$. A similar argument holds for $c \le x \le b$.

Corollary 2. If $f(x)$ is continuous on the closed interval $a \le x \le b$ and differentiable on the open interval $a < x < b$ and $f'(x) > 0$ (or $f'(x) < 0$, respectively) on $a < x < b$, *except that* $f'(x) = 0$ *at a finite number of points in* $a < x < b$, $f(x)$ is still **S.I.** (or **S.D.**, respectively) on $a \le x \le b$.

Proof. This is essentially Cor. 1 applied a finite number of times.

Example 2.2.5. Consider the function $f(x) = 3x - 1$. Since $f'(x) = 3 > 0$, we see that $f(x)$ is **S.I.** everywhere. Compare this with Ex. 2.2.1.

Example 2.2.6. Consider $u(x) = x^2$. Since $u'(x) = 2x$ then $u(x)$ is **S.I.** when $u'(x) > 0$; i.e., when $x > 0$, and $u(x)$ is **S.D.** when $x < 0$. Compare this with Ex. 2.2.2 and Ex. 2.2.4.

Example 2.2.7. Consider $F(x) = 1 - 2x$. Here $F'(x) = -2$ and hence $F(x)$ is **S.D.**

To investigate increasing and decreasing functions, we remind the student that a method of solving algebraic inequalities was exhibited in §1.1.

Example 2.2.8. Determine where the function $f(x) = 2x^3 + 9x^2 + 12x + 6$ is **S.I.** and where it is **S.D.** We see that

$$f'(x) = 6x^2 + 18x + 12 = 6(x^2 + 3x + 2) = 6(x + 2)(x + 1)$$

Now $x + 2 > 0$ when $x > -2$ and $x + 2 < 0$ when $x < -2$; $x + 1 > 0$ when $x > -1$ and $x + 1 < 0$ when $x < -1$.

We see from Fig. 2.2.9 that $f'(x) > 0$ when $x > -1$ and $x < -2$, and $f'(x) < 0$ when $-2 < x < 1$. Hence, $f(x)$ is **S.I.** when $x > -1$ and $x < -2$, whereas $f(x)$ is **S.D.** when $-2 < x < -1$. Figure 2.2.10 is a sketch of the graph of $f(x)$. Observe that there are horizontal tangents to the graph at $x = -2$ and $x = -1$.

Example 2.2.9. Determine where $f(x) = x^3$ is **S.I.** and where it is **S.D.** Here, $f'(x) = 3x^2 > 0$ for all $x \ne 0$, and $f'(x) = 0$ at $x = 0$. Hence $f(x)$ is **S.I.** everywhere, but there is a horizontal tangent to the graph at $x = 0$. We have used Cor. 1 to Thm. 2.2.1. The graph of the function is sketched in Fig. 2.2.8.

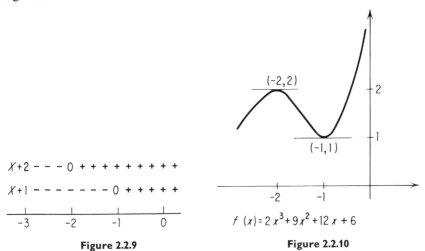

Figure 2.2.9   **Figure 2.2.10**

$f(x) = 2x^3 + 9x^2 + 12x + 6$

PROBLEMS

2.2.1. Find where each of the following functions is **S.I.** and where each ir **S.D.** Find all horizontal tangents.

(a) $f(x) = x^2 - 1$ (b) $f(x) = 1/x$
(c) $f(x) = x^2 - 4x + 3$ (d) $f(x) = x + (2/x)$
(e) $f(x) = x^5 + x^3$ (f) $f(x) = 3x^5 - 5x^3$
(g) $f(x) = 2x^3 + 2x^2 - 2x + 1$ (h) $f(x) = (x^3 - 3x^2 + 3x)^3$
(i) $f(x) = x^3 - 3x + 4$ (j) $f(x) = 3x^4 + 4x^3 - 36x^2$
(k) $f(x) = 3x^4 + 4x^3$ (l) $f(x) = 2x^3 + 3x^2 + 6x + 1$
(m) $f(x) = (6x^5 - 15x^4 + 10x^3)^3$ (n) $f(x) = 1 + 1/x + 1/x^2$

2.2.2. Consider the function $f(x) = 1/x$, where $-1 \le x \le 1$ and $x \ne 0$. Sketch the graph. Observe that $f'(x) = -1/x^2 < 0$ for all x in $-1 \le x \le 1$, if $x \ne 0$. Is $f(x)$ **S.D.**? How does it fit into Thm. 2.2.2(ii)?

2.2.3. Consider the function $g(x) = \sqrt[3]{x}$. Show that $g'(0)$ does not exist. Nevertheless, show that $g(x)$ is **S.I.** on the interval $-1 \le x \le 1$. Does this contradict Thm. 2.2.1(i)?

2.2.4. The **mean value theorem** states the following: Let $f(x)$ be continuous on the closed interval $a \le x \le b$ and differentiable on the open interval $a < x < b$. Draw the straight line L through $(a, f(a))$ and $(b, f(b))$. Then there is at least one point $x = c$, with $a < c < b$, such that the line tangent to the graph of $f(x)$ at the point $(c, f(c))$ is parallel to L (see Fig. 2.2.11).

Recall that two lines (not parallel to y-axis) are parallel if and only if they have the same slope. The slope of the non-vertical line L is given by

$$\frac{f(b) - f(a)}{b - a}$$

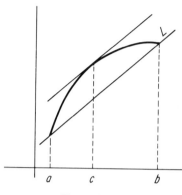

and the slope of the line tangent to the graph of $f(x)$ at $x = c$ is $f'(c)$. Hence, the analytic form of the theorem is as follows:

Theorem (Mean Value Theorem). Let $f(x)$ be continuous on $a \leq x \leq b$ and differentiable on $a < x < b$. Then there is at least one point $x = c$, with $a < c < b$, such that

Figure 2.2.11

$$\frac{f(b) - f(a)}{b - a} = f'(c)$$

A complete discussion and proof appear in the appendix. Use the mean value theorem to prove Thm. 2.2.1(i) and Thm. 2.2.2(i).

2.2.5. Let $f(x)$ be continuous on $a \leq x \leq b$, and suppose that $f'(x) = 0$ for every x in $a < x < b$. Use the mean value theorem (see Prob. 2.2.4) to show that $f(x)$ is identically a constant for all x in $a \leq x \leq b$.

2.2.6. Prove Cor. 1(ii).

2.2.7. Prove Cor. 2 in the special case that $f'(x) > 0$ on $a \leq x \leq b$ except at two points $x = r$ and $x = s$, and that $f'(r) = f'(s) = 0$.

2.2.8. Suppose that $\lim_{x \to c} G(x) = L$ and, for all x in some open interval I containing c, $G(x) > A$ for some constant A. Prove that $L \geq A$. [*Hint:* From Def. 1.6.1, we know that $\lim_{x \to c} G(x) = L$ means that for every $\varepsilon > 0$, there is a δ such that $|L - G(x)| < \varepsilon$ if $0 < |x - c| < \delta$. Pick δ so small that the x's satisfying $0 < |x - c| < \delta$ are in the given open interval I. The inequality $|L - G(x)| < \varepsilon$ can be expanded to read $-\varepsilon < L - G(x) < \varepsilon$, or, $G(x) - \varepsilon < L < G(x) + \varepsilon$. Since $G(x) < A$ for x in I, we have

$$L < G(x) + \varepsilon < A + \varepsilon$$

for every $\varepsilon > 0$; i.e., $L < A + \varepsilon$ for every $\varepsilon > 0$. This implies $L \leq A$ (since if $L > A$, then $L - A$ is positive, say $L - A = \alpha > 0$, and then $L = A + \alpha$, for $\alpha > 0$; but $L < A + \varepsilon$, for *all* $\varepsilon > 0$, thus making the assertion $L > A$ untenable)].

2.2.9. Let $f(x)$ be a function with the property that $f'(x)$ exists and $f'(x) > f(x)/x$, for all $x > 0$. Define $g(x) = f(x)/x$. Show that $g(x)$ is **S.I.** for all $x > 0$.

2.3. Some aspects of the theory of demand: an application to economics.†

We again use the notation of Ex. 1.11.2; p will denote the price of a commodity and $x(p)$ the corresponding demand function.

What is desired is a measure of the responsiveness of the consumer to price changes. Since there is no uniform set of units used in business (land is measured in acres, milk in quarts or gallons, steel by the ton), such a measure should be independent of particular units if it is to be applicable to all business areas. Next, percentage changes might be preferred to absolute changes. To illustrate, if the price of penny bubble gum drops one penny, the demand for the gum by bubble gum devotees would no doubt swell to great proportions, whereas a one penny drop in the retail price of a Rolls-Royce would probably draw only smiles. However, it is more reasonable to suppose that bubble gum devotees and Rolls-Royce fans would be stirred more equally if the price of each product would be reduced by 50 per cent.

We are led to use as our measure of responsiveness what we shall call *average (price) elasticity of demand for an item* w, call it Q, defined by

$$(2.3.1) \qquad Q = - \frac{\text{percentage change in the demand for } w}{\text{percentage change in the price of } w}$$

Remark: Since a rise in price is accompanied by a drop in demand for demand functions $x(p)$ that are **S.D.**, the numerator and denominator (2.3.1) are of opposite sign, so that $Q \geq 0$.

Example 2.3.1. Suppose that a demand function is given,

$$x(p) = 10 - p^2,$$

with the price $p = 2$; hence, demand is $x(2) = 6$. Suppose that the price is decreased by 5 per cent. We wish to find the average percentage change in demand relative to the percentage change in price as the price is decreased; i.e., we wish to find Q.

The new price is $2 - (5\%) \cdot 2 = 2 - 0.1 = 1.9$, and the new demand is $x(1.9) = 6.39$. Hence, the change in demand is

$$x(1.9) - x(2) = 6.39 - 6 = 0.39$$

and the percentage increase in demand is

$$\frac{x(1.9) - x(2)}{x(2)} = \frac{0.39}{6} = 6.5\%$$

---

† For a more complete discussion, see W. J. Baumol, *Economic Theory and Economics.* (Englewood Cliffs, N.J.: Prentice-Hall, Inc., 1961), especially Chapter 8.

The change in price is $1.9 - 2 = -0.1$, so the average change in price is $(-0.1)/2 = -5\%$. Hence, $Q = -(6.5\%)/-5\% = 1.3$. Observe that Q has no unit; i.e., it is a pure number.

We seek next a general formula for Q as price changes from $p = a$ to $p = b$. This results in a change of price equal to $b - a$, with a corresponding change of demand $x(b) - x(a)$. With this in mind, we can rewrite (2.3.1) analytically by imitating in spirit the details of Ex. 2.3.1 to obtain

$$(2.3.2) \qquad Q = -\frac{x(b) - x(a)}{x(a)} \bigg/ \frac{b - a}{a} = -\frac{a}{x(a)} \frac{x(b) - x(a)}{b - a}$$

Suppose next the initial price a changes to the new price $a + h$. Then (2.3.2) becomes

$$(2.3.3) \qquad Q = -\frac{a}{x(a)} \frac{x(a + h) - x(a)}{h}$$

We define **elasticity of demand with respect to price** when the price is a and the corresponding demand is $x(a)$, as the limit of Q as $h \to 0$ in (2.3.3). If we designate the elasticity of demand by the Greek letter η, we have at any arbitrary price p (assuming $x(p)$ differentiable),

$$(2.3.4) \qquad \eta = -\lim_{h \to 0} \frac{p}{x(p)} \frac{x(p + h) - x(p)}{h} = -\frac{p}{x(p)} \frac{dx(p)}{dp}$$

Price is often expressed as a function of demand, and is then written $p(x)$. Our object is to reformulate (2.3.3) in terms of the function $p(x)$. As demand changes from $x = \delta$ to $x = \beta$, the corresponding prices change from $p(\delta)$ to $p(\beta)$. Hence (2.3.2) becomes

$$Q = -\left(\frac{\beta - \delta}{\delta}\right) \bigg/ \left(\frac{p(\beta) - p(\delta)}{p(\delta)}\right)$$

$$(2.3.5) \qquad = -\frac{p(\delta)}{\delta} \frac{\beta - \delta}{p(\beta) - p(\delta)}$$

At an arbitrary demand δ, setting $\beta = \delta + h = x + h$, (2.3.5) becomes

$$(2.3.6) \qquad Q = -\frac{p(\delta)}{\delta} \frac{h}{p(\delta + h) - p(\delta)}$$

and so in the limit we get the **elasticity of demand corresponding to demand** $x = \delta$, η, is

$$\eta = -\lim_{h \to 0} \frac{p(\delta)}{\delta} \left[1 \bigg/ \left(\frac{p(\delta + h) - p(\delta)}{h}\right) \right]$$

i.e.,

(2.3.7)
$$\eta = -\frac{p(\delta)}{\delta}\frac{1}{p'(\delta)}$$

where $'$ represents differentiation with respect to x.

Example 2.3.2. Let a demand curve be given by $p = [8/(2 + x)]$, $0 \le x \le 6$. Find the elasticity of demand with respect to demand η at the endpoints of the given interval. Here,

$$\frac{dp}{dx} = \frac{-8}{(2 + x)^2}$$

and hence, by (2.3.7),

$$\eta = \frac{-8}{x(2 + x)}\frac{(2 + x)^2}{-8} = \frac{2 + x}{x}$$

We see that $\eta = \frac{4}{3}$ at $x = 6$. η is undefined at $x = 0$, and $\eta \to +\infty$ as $x \to 0$ (in such a problem, we use limit in the sense of Def. 1.5.2). Next, we compute η, using (2.3.4). First, solving the expression $p = 8/(2 + x)$ for x, we obtain $2p + xp = 8$, and so $x(p) = (8 - 2p)/p$, and $x'(p) = -8/p^2$. Hence by (2.3.4),

$$\eta = -\frac{p}{(8 - 2p)/p}\cdot-\frac{8}{p^2} = \frac{4}{(4 - p)}$$

Observe that $0 \le x \le 6$ implies $2 \le 2 + x \le 8$, which implies

$$\frac{1}{2} \ge \frac{1}{(2 + x)} \ge \frac{1}{8}$$

which, in turn, implies $4 \ge 8/(2 + x) \ge 1$; i.e., the domain of $x(p)$ is $4 \ge p \ge 1$. At $p = 1$, $\eta = 4/3$ (and $x = 6$), and as $p \to 4$, $\eta \to \infty$ (and $x \to 0$). We have measured the *same* responsiveness in terms of different variables. In fact, setting $p = 8/(2 + x)$ in the expression for η yields

$$\eta = \frac{4}{4 - p} = \frac{4}{4 - (8/[2 + x])} = \frac{4}{(8 + 4x - 8)/(2 + x)} = \frac{2 + x}{x}$$

which was our initial value for η.

Suppose the demand function $x(p)$ has as its graph a straight line parallel to the price axis, [see Fig. 2.3.1(a)], with equation $x(p) = a$, $0 \le p \le b$. For this demand function, $dx/dp = 0$, and hence $\eta = 0$ for all p in $[0,b]$. No matter what the price may be in this situation the demand does not change, so the public is completely unresponsive to price changes; i.e., elasticity of demand is 0.

In Fig. 2.3.1(b), we see that the price is not responsive to demand; i.e., demand changes, but price does not, and from (2.3.7), with $p(x) = b$, we see

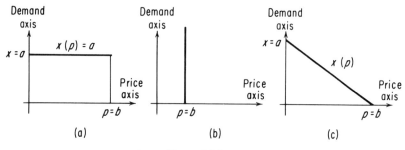

Figure 2.3.1

that since $p'(x) = 0$, elasticity of demand is undefined (some economists call this "infinite elasticity").

It is interesting to observe that for the general non-horizontal, non-vertical straight line demand curve, given by the function $x(p) = -(a/b)p + a$, $0 \leq p \leq b$, [see Fig. 2.3.1(c)], η is *not* constant. In fact, since $x'(p) = -a/b$, we may simplify (2.3.4) to $\eta = p/(b - p)$. At the left endpoint of the domain of $x(p)$, $p = 0$, we see that $\eta = 0$, and as $p \to b$, the right endpoint of the domain of $x(p)$, we see that $\eta \to \infty$ (observe that though $p = b$ is in the domain of $x(p)$, it is *not* in the domain of η).

What must be the structure of the demand function if the corresponding elasticity of demand is constant? We prove

Theorem 2.3.1. Let $x(p)$ be the demand function for some commodity, with domain $a \leq p \leq b$. We conclude that the product $p \cdot x(p)$ is constant throughout the interval $a \leq p \leq b$ if and only if $\eta = 1$ throughout the interval $a \leq p \leq b$.

Before proving this theorem, let us investigate its implications. The product $p \cdot x(p)$ represents the price of a commodity times its demand at that price; i.e., it represents the total amount the consumers would spend and therefore the producer will receive if the commodity is offered at price p. The quantity $a \cdot p(a)$ (i.e., the value of $p \cdot x(p)$ when $p = a$, the left endpoint of the domain of $x(p)$, i.e., the *lowest price* at which the commodity might be offered) is the consumers' initial outlay for the commodity. The theorem now asserts that if $\eta = 1$ for all p in $a \leq p \leq b$, then $p \cdot x(p)$ is constant, and hence equal to $a \cdot p(a)$; i.e., a fall in prices must result in an increase in purchase by exactly that amount needed to keep the consumers' total outlay the same as their initial outlay.

Proof of the theorem. We are not yet in a position to prove the entire theorem. We prove here that if $p \cdot x(p)$ is a constant c, then $\eta = 1$ for all p in $a \leq p \leq b$. We will prove the converse in Ex. 4.5.4. Suppose now that

$p \cdot x(p) = c$; then $x(p) = c/p$, and hence $x'(p) = -c/p^2$. By (2.3.4)

$$\eta = -\frac{p}{x(p)} x'(p) = \frac{c}{p \cdot x(p)} = \frac{c}{c} = 1$$

Theorem 2.3.2. Let $x(p)$ be a demand curve with domain $a \leq p \leq b$, and let $\eta(p)$ be the corresponding elasticity of demand at price p. Then: (a) $\eta < 1$ on $a \leq p \leq b$ (in which case $x(p)$ is called *inelastic*) implies that a rise in prices will *increase* consumer expenditure $p \cdot x(p)$; and, if a rise in prices will increase consumer expenditure, then $\eta \leq 1$, but, in view of Thm. 2.3.1, η cannot be identically one for all p on $a \leq p \leq b$. (b) $\eta > 1$ on $a \leq p \leq b$ (in which case $x(p)$ is called *elastic*) implies that a rise in prices will *decrease* consumer expenditure; and, if a rise in prices decreases consumer expenditure, then $\eta \geq 1$, but, in view of Thm. 2.3.1, η cannot be identically one for all p on $a \leq p \leq b$.

Remark: Observe that in terms of §2.2, Thm. 2.3.2 reads: on the interval $[a, b]$, (a) if $\eta < 1$, then $p \cdot x(p)$ is a **S.I.** function of p; and, if $p \cdot x(p)$ is a **S.I.** function of p, then $\eta \leq 1$, but not identically one; (b) if $\eta > 1$, then $p \cdot x(p)$ is a **S.D.** function of p; and, if $p \cdot x(p)$ is a **S.D.** function of p, then $\eta \geq 1$, but not identically one.

Proof of the theorem. In the spirit of the remark, we prove in (b) that $p \cdot x(p)$ is a **S.D.** function of p implies $\eta \geq 1$; the converse appears in Ex. 4.5.5. We shall leave (a) as an exercise. Since $p \cdot x(p)$ is **S.D.**, it follows from Thm. 2.2.2 that $D[p \cdot x(p)] \leq 0$, and hence, by the product rule,

$$p \cdot x'(p) + x(p) \leq 0$$

or, equivalently, $p \cdot x'(p) \leq -x(p)$. Dividing by $-x(p)$ yields

$$-[p/x(p)]x'(p) \geq 1$$

i.e., $\eta \geq 1$. (Recall that multiplying an inequality by a negative number changes the sense of the inequality.)

The elasticity Thm. 2.3.2 has an interesting application for a country X suffering from a "dollar shortage". The prime minister of country X might suggest as a solution that his nation's currency be devalued, thus making products cheaper to the American consumer, to create an increased flow of dollars to country X. An astute economist in country X might caution his prime minister that, among other problems, if the elasticity of demand for country X's exports is smaller than one, a decrease in prices will decrease consumer expenditure, and country X may end up obtaining fewer dollars than before.

PROBLEMS

2.3.1. Suppose the demand law is given by $x(p) = 3/p^4$. Show that $\eta = 4$. In general, if the demand law is given by $x(p) = ap^{-m}$, $m > 0$, show that $\eta = m$.

2.3.2. In Ex. 2.3.1, the demand curve is given by $x(p) = 10 - p^2$. Find η at $p = 2$.

2.3.3. Find the elasticity of demand in terms of x if the demand law is given by $p = 1/(1 + x^2)$.

2.3.4. Suppose that price and demand are connected by the relation $p^3 + x^3 = 9$. Find η when $p = 2$.

2.3.5. Suppose the demand law is given by $x = 100(30 - 2p)^3$. Find the average percentage change in demand relative to the percentage change in price as price changes from 1 to $\frac{3}{2}$. Find η at $p = 1$.

2.3.6. In an agricultural industry such as the citrus industry, a frost can do great harm to the citrus crop, affect the size of the crop, and so affect the selling price. If $x(p)$ denotes the demand as a function of price, and $p = f(s)$ indicates that price as a function of the crop size s express the elasticity of demand η in terms of s. Explain why you would expect $f(s)$ to be **S.D.**

2.3.7. Prove part (i) of Thm. 2.3.2.

2.3.8. A manufacturer finds that the demand law for his product is given by $x(p) = 100/p^7$. What should he do to the price of his product if he wishes to increase consumer expenditure? Repeat the problem for $x(p) = 73/\sqrt{p}$. In general, if $x(p) = ap^{-m}$, $m > 0$, for what m should he increase prices and for what m should he decrease prices to increase consumer expenditure?

2.3.9. Suppose we know that the supply of a quantity is functionally related to the interest rate i by the function $S(i)$. Define average interest elasticity of supply, and interest elasticity of supply in terms of i and $S(i)$. Assume that interest changes from $i = A$ to $i = B = A + h$.

2.4. The absolute and local extrema of a function.

Let us consider a function $f(x)$ with domain S, where S is perhaps an open or closed interval, perhaps a half-line, or perhaps the entire x-axis. We wish to determine the largest and smallest values attained by $f(x)$ on S if such values exist. To this end we define

Definition 2.4.1. Suppose we are given a function $f(x)$ with domain S. Then $f(x)$ has an **absolute maximum** $f(d)$ *on* S at $x = d$ if $f(d) \geq f(x)$ for every x in S. Similarly, $f(x)$ has an **absolute minimum** $f(c)$ *at* $x = c$ if $f(c) \le f(x)$ for every x in S. The word "absolute" will be omitted if there is no ambiguity.

We shall illustrate geometrically by examining the function $f(x)$ whose graph is illustrated in Fig. 2.4.1, with domain the interval from $x = a$ to $x = b$. As the diagram indicates, $f(d) = r$ and $f(c) = s$. Since $f(d) \ge f(x)$ for all x in the given interval, $f(d) = r$ is the maximum value of the function on its domain, the interval from a to b. In the terminology of §1.1 this is equivalent to saying that r is the largest number in the range of f. We say that $f(x)$ *has an absolute*

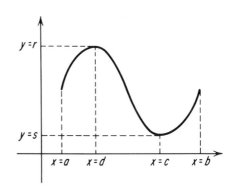

Figure 2.4.1

maximum at $x = d$ to indicate the x-coordinate at which $f(x)$ is largest. From Fig. 2.4.1, the reader should be able to derive the following information about the minimum:

(1) $f(c) = s$ is the absolute minimum of $f(x)$ on its interval domain; i.e., $f(c) \le f(x)$ for all x on the given interval.

(2) In view of (1), we can assert that $f(x)$ has an absolute minimum at $x = c$. The *value* of that minimum is given by (1).

(3) s is the smallest number in the range of f; this is equivalent to (1).

Definition 2.4.2. $f(x)$ is said to have an **absolute extremum** *at* $x = w$ if $f(x)$ has either an absolute maximum or an absolute minimum at $x = w$; i.e., if $f(w)$ is either the maximum or minimum of $f(x)$.

Of course, there is no guarantee that an arbitrary function $f(x)$ will have either an absolute maximum or an absolute minimum. We will illustrate functions which fail to possess absolute extrema in subsequent examples. But if our function is *continuous* and its domain is a *closed interval*, say $a \le x \le b$, then we are assured by Thm. 1.7.4 that there are numbers $x = c$ and $x = d$, $a \le c \le b$ and $a \le d \le b$, at which $f(x)$ takes on its minimum and maximum values, respectively. If $f(x)$ is not continuous or its domain is not a closed interval, anything can happen as far as absolute extrema are concerned. The next few examples will illustrate.

Example 2.4.1. Define

$$f(x) = \begin{cases} 1/x & \text{if } 0 < x \le 1 \\ 0 & \text{if } x = 0 \end{cases}$$

The domain of $f(x)$ is then the closed interval $0 \leq x \leq 1$ (see Fig. 2.4.2). This is exactly the function investigated in Ex. 1.7.7, and it is *discontinuous* at $x = 0$. Hence, Thm. 1.7.4 does not apply. We see directly that $f(x)$ has no maximum (the closer x is to 0, $x > 0$, the larger is the value of $f(x) = 1/x$, and there is *no* largest value). However, the function has an absolute minimum at $x = 0$, and $f(0) = 0$ is the minimum of $f(x)$ on $0 \leq x \leq 1$.

Example 2.4.2. Define

$$g(x) = \begin{cases} x & \text{if } 0 \leq x \leq 1, \text{ but } x \neq \tfrac{1}{2} \\ 1 & \text{if } x = \tfrac{1}{2} \end{cases}$$

The graph of the function is illustrated in Fig. 2.4.3. The function has as its domain the closed interval $0 \leq x \leq 1$, and is discontinuous at $x = \tfrac{1}{2}$.

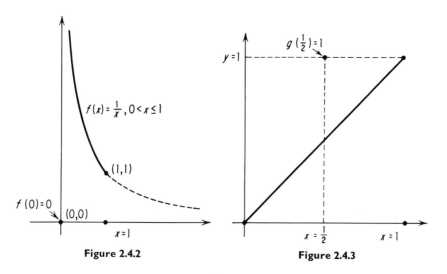

Figure 2.4.2   Figure 2.4.3

(Why?) Observe that $g(\tfrac{1}{2}) = g(1) = 1$ is the maximum value of $g(x)$ and $g(0) = 0$ is the minimum value of $g(x)$. Though Thm. 1.7.4 does not apply, a direct investigation has shown that *both* a maximum and minimum for $g(x)$ can be found. Observe that $g(x)$ has a maximum at $x = \tfrac{1}{2}$ and $x = 1$, but there is only one maximum value for $g(x)$, namely $g(\tfrac{1}{2}) = g(1) = 1$.

Example 2.4.3. Let $F(x) = |x|$. The domain of this function is the entire x-axis; again Thm. 1.7.4 does not apply, this time because its domain is not a closed interval. Observe that $F(x)$ is continuous for all x, with a minimum at $x = 0$, and $F(0) = 0$ is the minimum value of $F(x)$. It has no maximum (see the graph of F in Fig. 2.4.4.).

Example 2.4.4. Consider $G(x) = x$. The domain of $G(x)$ is the entire x-axis. It is of course continuous everywhere. It has no absolute extrema.

Example 2.4.5. Consider $u(x) = x$, where $0 < x < 1$. This function of course is not the function $G(x)$ of Ex. 2.4.4, since, for example, $G(10) = 10$, but $x = 10$ is not in the domain of $u(x)$; i.e., $u(10)$ is not defined. The graph of $u(x)$ is pictured in Fig. 2.4.5. The function $u(x)$ is continuous everywhere in its domain, the open interval $0 < x < 1$. Observe that the range of the function is the open interval $0 < y < 1$. The closer x is taken to 1, the greater is the value of $u(x)$, but there is *no* largest value of $u(x)$ ($u(1)$ is *not* defined).

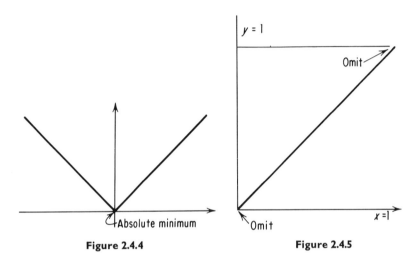

Figure 2.4.4   **Figure 2.4.5**

Hence, there is no absolute maximum value for $u(x)$. Similarly, the closer x is to 0, the smaller is the value of $u(x)$, but there is no smallest value, and hence $u(x)$ has no absolute minimum. (The observant reader should realize that the statement "$u(x)$ has no absolute extrema" is equivalent to "the range of $u(x)$, the open interval $0 < y < 1$, has no largest or smallest number".)

Example 2.4.6. Let $w(x) = 4x^3 - 3x^2$, $-\frac{1}{4} < x < \frac{3}{4}$. This function is continuous on the open interval $-\frac{1}{4} < x < \frac{3}{4}$. Again Thm. 1.7.4 does not apply. Nevertheless, it can be shown that there is an absolute maximum at $x = 0$, and $w(0) = 0$ is the absolute maximum of $w(x)$; and $w(x)$ has an absolute minimum at $x = \frac{1}{2}$, and $w(\frac{1}{2}) = -\frac{1}{4}$ is the absolute minimum of $w(x)$ (see the graph of $w(x)$ in Fig. 2.4.6). We shall return to this example later.

We next turn our attention to functions whose domains are closed intervals, that are continuous on their domains, and such that the function has a derivative everywhere on this domain except possibly at a finite number of points. Such functions necessarily have both an absolute maximum and an absolute minimum. (Why?) Various possibilities are illustrated in Fig. 2.4.7.

In Fig. 2.4.7, we graph six functions. From Fig. 2.4.7(a), we see that $f(x)$ has an absolute maximum at the left endpoint of its domain, $x = a$, and an absolute minimum at the right endpoint of its domain, $x = b$. From the pictured graph, $f(a) = v$ is the maximum value of $f(x)$ and $f(b) = u$ is the minimum value of $f(x)$.

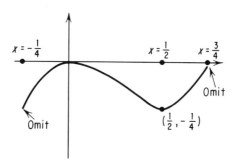

Figure 2.4.6

From Fig. 2.4.7(b), $g(a) = v$ is the maximum value of $g(x)$ and $g(b) = u$ is the minimum value of $g(x)$. Observe that $g(s)$ is smaller than all values $g(x)$ *provided x is taken "near"* s. Similarly, $g(t)$ is larger than all values $g(x)$ *provided x is taken "near"* t. The values $g(s)$ and $g(t)$ are certainly not absolute extrema, but they can be considered extrema relative to functional values nearby. We are led to define:

Definition 2.4.3. The function $f(x)$ is said to have a *local maximum at* $x = p$ if there exists an open interval I containing p such that $f(p) > f(x)$ for all x in I with $x \neq p$. Similarly, $f(x)$ has a *local minimum at* $x = q$ if there exists an open interval J containing q such that $f(q) < f(x)$ for all x in J with $x \neq q$. $f(x)$ has a *local extremum* at $x = r$ if $f(x)$ has either a local maximum or local minimum at $x = r$. We shall further require that if the domain of $f(x)$ is the interval from $x = a$ to $x = b$, then: if $f(x)$ has a *local* extremum at $x = r$, then $a < r < b$; i.e., a function cannot have a local extremum at an endpoint of its domain.

Returning to Fig. 2.4.7, we see that $h(x)$ has both a local and an absolute minimum at $x = c$, and $h(c)$ is the absolute minimum of $h(x)$, but $h(x)$ has only an absolute maximum at $x = b$, and $h(b)$ is the absolute maximum of $h(x)$. However, $F(x)$ has both a local and an absolute maximum at $x = d$, and both a local and an absolute minimum at $x = c$.

$G(x)$ has an absolute and local maximum at $x = d$, and an absolute maximum at $x = a$. Observe though that $G(a) = G(d) = v$ is the single number that is the absolute maximum of $G(x)$. Even though the absolute maximum of $G(x)$ may occur at different x, the absolute maximum of $G(x)$ is one number, the common value of G when evaluated at the points $x = d$ and $x = a$.

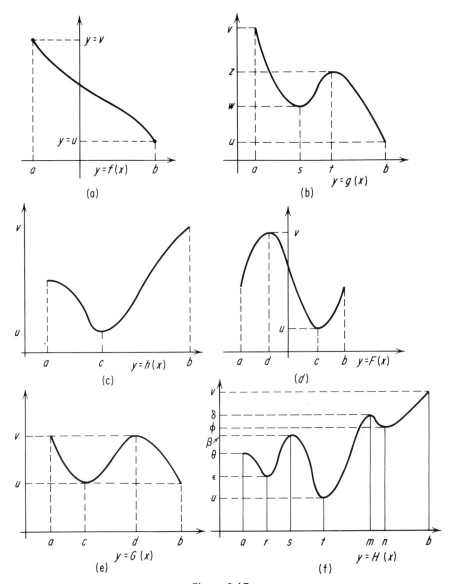

Figure 2.4.7

Observe that $H(x)$ has local maxima at $x = s$ and $x = m$, local minima at $x = r$, $x = t$, and $x = n$. The absolute maximum occurs at an endpoint $x = b$, and $H(b) = v$ is the absolute maximum of H. The absolute minimum is found at the same point as one of the local minima, $x = t$, and $H(t) = u$ is the absolute minimum of $H(x)$.

Remark. In Def. 2.4.3, many authors replace the word "local" by the word "relative".

The next theorem (which we shall not prove) gives us a rule for finding the absolute extrema for a continuous function whose domain is a closed interval, $a \leq x \leq b$.

Theorem 2.4.1. To find the absolute extrema of a continuous function $f(x)$ whose domain is closed interval $a \leq x \leq b$,

(1) find the location of all local extrema in $a < x < b$; suppose these local extrema are found at $x = r$, $x = s$, $x = t$, ...
(2) evaluate $f(r), f(s), f(t)$, ...
(3) evaluate $f(a)$ and $f(b)$

Then, the largest of the numbers computed in (2) and (3) is the absolute maximum of $f(x)$ and the smallest is the absolute minimum of $f(x)$.

Example 2.4.7. We apply Thm. 2.4.1 to find the absolute extrema of $g(x)$, whose graph is given in Fig. 2.4.7(b). From the graph,

(1) the local extrema occur at $x = s$ and $x = t$
(2) $g(s) = w$ and $g(t) = z$
(3) $g(a) = v$ and $g(b) = u$

It is clear from the graph that $u < w < z < v$. Hence, v is the absolute maximum of $g(x)$ and u is the absolute minimum of $g(x)$. This is the same result we obtained previously for $g(x)$.

Example 2.4.8. We apply Thm. 2.4.1 to find the absolute extrema of $H(x)$ whose graph is given in Fig. 2.4.7(f). From the graph,

(1) local extrema occur at r, s, t, m, and n
(2) $H(r) = \varepsilon$, $H(s) = \beta$, $H(t) = u$, $H(m) = \delta$, and $H(n) = \varphi$
(3) $H(a) = \theta$ and $H(b) = v$

By examining the y-axis in Fig. 2.4.7(f), we see that

$$u < \varepsilon < \theta < \beta < \varphi < \delta < v$$

Hence $H(t) = u$ and $H(b) = v$ are the absolute minimum and absolute maximum of $H(x)$, respectively.

Theorem 2.4.1 gives a complete procedure for finding absolute extrema; instruction (1) of the theorem is to "find the location of all local extrema". The question is: How do you find the x-values at which a given function has a local extremum? The clue is in the next theorem.

Theorem 2.4.2.† Suppose $f(x)$ has a local extremum at $x = c$, and suppose further that $f'(c)$ exists. Then, $f'(c) = 0$.

Before proving the theorem, we remark that its geometrical content is that if $f(x)$ has a local extremum at $x = c$, and if a tangent line can be drawn to the graph of $f(x)$ at $(c, f(c))$, then this tangent line is parallel to the x-axis.

Proof of the theorem. We prove the theorem for the case that the local extremum is a local maximum; a completely analogous argument holds for a local minimum. If $f(x)$ has a local maximum at $x = c$, then $f(c) > f(x)$ for all x near c. If we consider arbitrary $h > 0$ and $h < 0$, with h near 0, then $c + h$ is a number near c, so $f(c) > f(c + h)$, and hence $f(c + h) - f(c) < 0$. Let $R(h) = [f(c + h) - f(c)]/h$. By what we have already said, the numerator of R will be negative for $h > 0$ and for $h < 0$, provided h is near 0.

If $h > 0$, then $R < 0$. Since $f'(c)$ exists, $f'(c) = \lim_{h \to 0} R$ with $h > 0$. By the result of Prob. 2.2.8, $f'(c) \leq 0$.

If $h < 0$, then $R > 0$. Since $f'(c)$ exists, $f'(c) = \lim_{h \to 0} R$ with $h < 0$. Again using Prob. 2.2.8, $f'(c) \geq 0$.

The only way we can have both $f'(c) \leq 0$ *and* $f'(c) \geq 0$ is if $f'(c) = 0$. This proves the theorem.

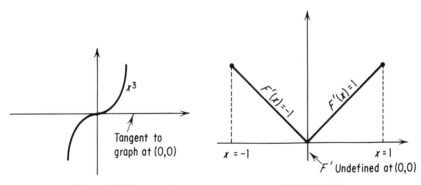

Figure 2.4.8   Figure 2.4.9

Unfortunately Thm. 2.4.2 does *not* assert that if $f'(d) = 0$, then a relative extremum will be found at $x = d$. In fact, the function $f(x) = x^3$ has as its derivative $f'(x) = 3x^2$. Consequently, $f'(0) = 0$, but since $f(x)$ is **S.I.**, it cannot have any local extrema (see Fig. 2.4.8). Nor does Thm. 2.4.2 tell us if it is possible for $f(x)$ to have a local extremum at a point at which f' does not

---

† With this theorem, the reader can now read the proof of the mean value theorem in the Appendix.

exist. A simple illustration, the function $F(x) = |x|$ with domain $-1 \leq x \leq 1$, shows that it is possible, since $F(x)$ has a local minimum at $x = 0$, though $F'(0)$ does not exist (see Fig. 2.4.9). What we can conclude is that *the values of x at which $f'(x) = 0$ or $f'(x)$ is undefined include all possible local extrema.*

The solutions to $f'(x) = 0$ and the x's at which $f'(x)$ is undefined may give extraneous values (i.e., values of x at which a local extremum is not found) as in $f(x) = x^3$ at $x = 0$, but including them in instruction (1) of Thm. 2.4.1 will cause no harm, since the functional values obtained by evaluating the function at these points will be discarded when in the last instruction of the theorem we keep only the largest and smallest values obtained in (2) and (3).

We modify Thm. 2.4.1 to read:

Procedure for finding the absolute extrema of a continuous function $f(x)$ that is differentiable at all but perhaps a finite number of points on its domain, the closed interval $a \leq x \leq b$:

(1) Find all x in $a < x < b$ that satisfy the equation $f'(x) = 0$ or at which $f'(x)$ is undefined; let $x = r$, $x = s$, $x = t$, ... be such x.
(2) Evaluate $f(r), f(s), f(t), \ldots$
(3) Evaluate $f(a)$ and $f(b)$
(4) The largest number of the numbers computed in (2) and (3) is the absolute maximum of $f(x)$ in $[a, b]$ and the smallest number is the absolute minimum.

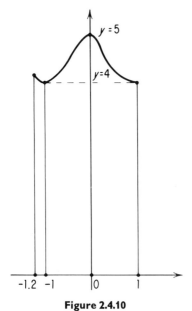

Example 2.4.9. Find the absolute extrema of the function

$$f(x) = x^4 - 2x^2 + 5, \qquad -1.2 \leq x \leq 1$$

Observe that $f'(x) = 4x^3 - 4x = 4(x^3 - x) = 4x(x + 1)(x - 1)$. Following (1) of the procedure, we see that $f'(x) = 0$ at $x = 0$, $x = +1$ and $x = -1$; $f'(x)$ is defined for all x in $-1.2 \leq x \leq 1$. Following (2), we find that $f(0) = 5$, $f(1) = 4$, and $f(-1) = 4$ (since $x = 1$ is the endpoint of the domain, we must compute $f(1)$ either in this step or in step (3) of the procedure). Following (3), $f(-1.2) = 4.1976$ and $f(1) = 4$. Clearly, $4 < 4.1976 < 5$. Thus, by (4), $f(-1) = f(1) = 4$ is the absolute minimum of $f(x)$, and $f(0) = 5$ is the absolute maximum of $f(x)$ (see the graph of the functions in Fig. 2.4.10).

Figure 2.4.10

Example 2.4.10. Let $v(x) = 4x^3 - 3x^2$, $-\frac{1}{4} \le x \le \frac{3}{4}$. To find the absolute extrema, we follow Procedure above.

(1) $v'(x) = 12x^2 - 6x = 6x(2x - 1)$; hence $v'(x) = 0$ when $x = 0$ or $x = \frac{1}{2}$.
(2) $v(0) = 0$, $v(\frac{1}{2}) = -\frac{1}{4}$.
(3) $v(-\frac{1}{4}) = -\frac{1}{4}$, $v(\frac{3}{4}) = 0$.
(4) $-\frac{1}{4} < 0$, so $v(\frac{1}{2}) = v(-\frac{1}{4}) = -\frac{1}{4}$ is the absolute minimum of $v(x)$ and $v(0) = v(\frac{3}{4}) = 0$ is the absolute maximum of $v(x)$.

Compare these results with $w(x)$ of Ex. 2.4.6. For $w(x)$, the domain is the open interval $-\frac{1}{4} < x < \frac{3}{4}$, which contains fewer points than the domain of $v(x)$, which is $-\frac{1}{4} \le x \le \frac{3}{4}$. Hence, $w(x)$ cannot have any absolute extrema that $v(x)$ does not have. Consequently, $w(0) = 0$ is the absolute maximum of $w(x)$ and $w(\frac{1}{2}) = -\frac{1}{4}$ is the absolute minimum of $w(x)$; since $-\frac{1}{4}$ and $\frac{3}{4}$ are *not* in the domain of $w(x)$, we do not evaluate $w(x)$ at these points (see Fig. 2.4.6).

Example 2.4.11. Find the absolute extrema of the function

$$g(x) = x^4 - 8x^2 + 12, \qquad -1 \le x \le 2$$

We follow the Procedure.

(1) $g'(x) = 4x(x + 2)(x - 2)$; hence $g'(x) = 0$ when $x = 0$, $x = +2$, or $x = -2$. However, -2 is not in the domain of $g(x)$, and so is discarded.
(2) $g(0) = 12$, $g(2) = -4$.
(3) $g(-1) = 5$ and $g(2) = -4$.
(4) $-4 < 5 < 12$.

Hence $g(2) = -4$ is the absolute minimum of $g(x)$ and $g(0) = 12$ is the absolute maximum of $g(x)$.

Example 2.4.12. Let $f(x) = 6x^{2/3}$, $-\frac{1}{2} \le x \le 1$. Find the local extrema.

(1) $f'(x) = 4x^{-1/3}$. There are no solutions to $f'(x) = 0$, but $f'(x)$ is undefined if $x = 0$.

(2) $f(0) = 0$.
(3) $f(-\frac{1}{2}) = (6/\sqrt[3]{4}) < 6$, $f(1) = 6$.
(4) $0 < (6/\sqrt[3]{4}) < 6$.

Hence, $f(0) = 0$ is the absolute minimum of $f(x)$, and $f(1) = 6$ is the absolute maximum of $f(x)$ (see Fig. 2.4.11).

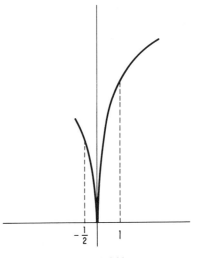

Figure 2.4.11

PROBLEMS

For each of the following functions, find the absolute maximum and absolute minimum in the specified domains.

2.4.1. $f(x) = x^3 - 3x^2$, $-1 \le x \le 3$

2.4.2. $f(x) = x^4 - 8x^2$, $-3 \le x \le 3$

2.4.3. $f(x) = 2x^3 - 7x^2 - 6x + 2$, $0 \le x \le 3$

2.4.4. $f(x) = \frac{1}{6}(x^3 - 6x^2 + 9x + 1)$, $0 \le x \le 2$

2.4.5. $f(x) = |x^{1/3}|$, $-1 \le x \le 2$

2.4.6. $f(x) = 1 - x^{2/3}$, $-1 \le x \le 1$

2.4.7. $f(x) = x^3$, $\frac{1}{2} \le x \le 1$

2.4.8. $f(x) = x^4 - 8x^2$, $-3 < x < 3$ (see Prob. 2.4.2)

2.4.9. $f(x) = x^3 - 3x^2$, $-1 < x < 3$ (see Prob. 2.4.1)

2.4.10. $f(x) = 8x^3 - 4x^2 + 72x$, $0 \le x \le 4$

2.4.11. $f(x) = x^3 + 3x + 7$, $0 \le x \le 1$

2.4.12. $f(x) = x^4 - 4x^2 - 4x$, $-1 \le x \le 2$
       [*Hint:* $(x + 1)$ is a factor of $f'(x)$.]

2.4.13. $f(x) = x^5 - 5x + 1$, $-2 \le x \le 2$

2.4.14. $f(x) = \sqrt{x}\,(x - 5)^{1/3}$, $0 \le x \le 6$

2.4.15. $f(x) = \sqrt[3]{x}\,\sqrt[3]{(x - 3)^2}$, $-1 \le x \le 4$

2.4.16. $f(x) = x^4 - 8x^3 + 22x^2 - 24x + 100$, $0 \le x \le 5$
       [*Hint:* $(x - 1)$ is a factor of $f'(x)$; use synthetic substitutions]

2.4.17. $f(x) = 6x^5 - 15x^4 - 10x^3 + 30x^2 + 100$, $-2 \le x \le 2$
       [*Hint:* $(x - 2)$ is a factor of $f'(x)$; use synthetic substitutions.]

2.4.18. $f(x) = 3x^4 - 18x^2 - 24x + 160$, $-3 \le x \le 3$
       [*Hint:* $(x + 1)$ is a factor of $f'(x)$; use synthetic substitutions.]

2.4.19. $f(x) = 3x^5 - 25x^3 + 60x + 10$, $-2 \le x \le 2$

2.4.20. $f(x) = 3x^5 - 25x^3 + 60 + 10$, $-3 < x \le 2$

2.5. More problems in absolute extrema.

Problems involving absolute extrema often arise in applications. If an object is in motion, the physicist often asks for the maximum velocity of the object or the maximum distance traveled by an object. In terms of §2.3 we might inquire about minimum average cost or maximum revenue. We shall illustrate with some examples. It will sometimes be necessary to investigate functions whose domain is a half-line. Strictly speaking, Thm. 2.4.1 does not apply, but for the particular functions we investigate we shall see that an absolute minimum or maximum will usually exist.

Example 2.5.1. Suppose $p(x)$, the price for the quantity x as a function of x is given by $p(x) = 6 - x^2$. Find the maximum total revenue if demand x varies so that $0 \le x \le \frac{5}{2}$. From Ex. 1.11.2, the total revenue $R(x)$ is given by: $R(x) = xp(x) = 6x - x^3$.

We see that $R'(x) = 6 - 3x^2 = 3(2 - x^2)$, so $R'(x) = 0$ when $x = \pm\sqrt{2}$. Again, $x = -\sqrt{2}$ can be ignored since it is not in the domain of $R(x)$. We evaluate $R(0) = 0$, $R(\sqrt{2}) = 4\sqrt{2}$, and $R(\frac{5}{2}) = -\frac{5}{8}$. The maximum total revenue then occurs when demand is $\sqrt{2}$, and the maximum total revenue is $4\sqrt{2}$.

Example 2.5.2. A photographer has a thin piece of wood 16 in. long. How should he cut the wood to make a rectangular picture frame that encloses the maximum area? Call the length of the required frame x and the width y. We wish to maximize xy, the area enclosed. The area becomes progressively larger as x and y are made larger of course, but we are restricted here by the total of 16 inches of wood to make up all the sides. The 16 inches then become the perimeter of the frame, and hence $2x + 2y = 16$, or, $x + y = 8$. The equation $x + y = 8$ is therefore a constraint on the possible dimensions of the rectangular frame.

The original problem can be rephrased to read: Maximize the product xy subject to the constraint $x + y = 8$. Next we see that our procedures are for maximizing functions of one variable, whereas xy depends on both x and y. We must either eliminate the x or y. Since $x + y = 8$, we have that $y = 8 - x$, and hence xy becomes $x(8 - x)$. The area subject to the given constraint is

$$A(x) = x(8 - x) = 8x - x^2$$

Since there are two sides of length x, we see that $0 \le 2x \le 16$, or, $0 \le x \le 8$. If $x = 0$ we have 0 area (if the rectangle has 0 length, it has 0 area), and if $x = 8$ we have 0 area (i.e., if $x = 8$, then $2x = 16$, so $y = 0$, and hence the rectangle has 0 width, and consequently 0 area). We also observe this analytically by seeing that $A(0) = A(8) = 0$. Hence $0 \le x \le 8$ is the domain of $A(x)$.

Finally, our problem is to find the absolute maximum of the function $A(x) = 8x - x^2$ in the closed interval $0 \le x \le 8$. Clearly, $A'(x) = 8 - 2x$, so $A'(x) = 0$ when $8 - 2x = 0$, $2x = 8$, or $x = 4$. $A'(x)$ is always defined. By the procedure of §2.4, we evaluate $A(0) = 0$, $A(8) = 0$, and $A(4) = 16$. Hence the maximum area is 16, and it occurs when $x = 4$. Since $x + y = 8$, then $y = 4$. Hence the rectangle with maximum area subject to the fixed perimeter is a square.

Example 2.5.3. Find the two non-negative numbers whose sum is 18 if the product of one by twice the square of the other is to be maximum. Call one number y, the other x. Then we wish to maximize $y \cdot 2x^2 = 2yx^2$ subject to the constraint $x + y = 18$. Since $y = 18 - x$, the problem is to maximize

$$f(x) = 2(18 - x)x^2 = 36x^2 - 2x^3$$

We next seek the domain of $f(x)$. Since x is assumed non-negative we have $x \ge 0$. Since $y \ge 0$ by assumption, we see from $x + y = 18$ that the largest value that x can have is 18. Hence, $0 \le x \le 18$.

We must maximize f in the closed interval $0 \le x \le 18$. Clearly,

$$f'(x) = 72x - 6x^2 = 6x(12 - x)$$

and so $f'(x) = 0$ has solutions $x = 0$ and $x = 12$. We compute $f(0) = 0$, $f(12) = 1728$ and $f(18) = 0$. Consequently, $f(x)$ has the absolute maximum value of 1728 attained when $x = 12$, and hence, since $x + y = 18$, when $y = 6$.

Example 2.5.4. Find the two *positive* numbers whose sum is 18 if the product of one by twice the square of the other is to be maximum. The only difference between this example and Ex. 2.5 3 is that the word "non-negative" in Ex. 2.5.3 has been replaced by the word "positive" in this example. The functions involved are very similar except that now the domain is the *open* interval $0 < x < 18$, since x positive does not permit $x = 0$, and if $x = 18$, then $y = 0$, which is not permitted. When we considered the closed interval in Ex. 2.5.3, we found the absolute maximum occurs at $x = 12$, and the absolute minimum occurs at $x = 0$ and $x = 18$, with $f(0) = 0 = f(18)$ and $f(12) = 1728$ the values of the extrema. From Fig. 2.5.1 (completely out of scale!), we

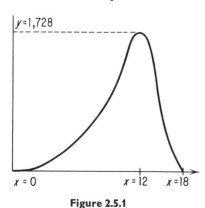

Figure 2.5.1

see that deleting the points $x = 0$ and $x = 18$ in no way alters the absolute maximum value of $f(x)$, and hence the function given by $36x^2 - 2x^3$,

$0 < x < 18$, assumes its absolute maximum at the same place as $36x^2 - 2x^3$, $0 \le x \le 18$. Thus, the answer to Ex. 2.5.4 is the same as the answer to Ex. 2.5.3.

Example 2.5.5. A manufacturer plans to construct a cylindrical can to hold 1 cubic foot of liquid. If the cost of constructing the top and bottom of the can is twice the cost of constructing the side, what are the dimensions of the most economical can?

Call c the cost of construction of a square foot of the side of the can. Then $2c$ is the cost of construction of a square foot of the top or bottom of the can. Let R be the radius of the can and H the height of the can, measured in feet. Then the volume of the can, a right circular cylinder, since the volume is known to be fixed at 1 cu ft, is given by $\pi R^2 H = 1$. The combined area of the base and top of the can is $2\pi R^2$, and hence the total cost of constructing the top and bottom of the can is $4c\pi R^2$; the total surface area of the cylinder is $2\pi RH$, and hence the cost of constructing this surface area is $2\pi cRH$. The total cost then is $4c\pi R^2 + 2\pi cRH$. The problem is to minimize $4c\pi R^2 + 2\pi cRH$, subject to the constraint $\pi R^2 H = 1$. Solving the constraint equation for H yields

(2.5.1) $$H = \frac{1}{\pi R^2}$$

so the quantity we wish to minimize, the total cost, becomes

$$G(R) = 4c\pi R^2 + \frac{2c}{R}$$

$$= 2c\left(2\pi R^2 + \frac{1}{R}\right)$$

where c is the *constant* cost of construction. If we analyze (2.5.1), it should be clear that the values of R can be chosen near 0 by taking H large, though $R \ne 0$, and that the values of R can become quite large by taking H sufficiently small. Hence the domain of $G(R)$ is $J : R > 0$, an open half-line. The results of §2.4 do not directly apply, but a direct analysis of $G(R)$ on its domain J will guarantee the existence of the desired absolute minimum. First, as $R \to 0$, $G(R)$ becomes arbitrarily large because of the $1/R$ term appearing. Hence, there is no minimum to $G(R)$ at $R = 0$. Next, as $R \to \infty$, $G(R)$ becomes arbitrarily large because of the R^2 term appearing. It is reasonable, therefore, to

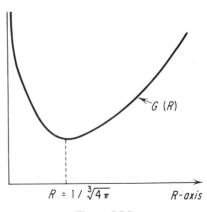

Figure 2.5.2

expect an absolute minimum which is also a local minimum. We shall next analyze $G'(R)$. We see that

$$G'(R) = 2c\left(4\pi R - \frac{1}{R^2}\right)$$

$G'(R)$ is undefined at $R = 0$, but by what we have said this value certainly will not contribute a minimum to $G(R)$, nor is it even in the domain of $G(R)$. We set $G'(R) = 0$. Finding a common denominator, and dividing by $2c$, this becomes,

$$\frac{4\pi R^3 - 1}{R^2} = 0$$

or

$$4\pi R^3 - 1 = 0$$

Thus,

$$R = \frac{1}{\sqrt[3]{4\pi}}$$

Observe that $G'(R) < 0$ when

$$2c\,\frac{4\pi R^3 - 1}{R^2} < 0$$

Since R^2 and c are positive, we divide by $2c$ and multiply by R^2 to obtain $G'(R) < 0$ when $4\pi R^3 - 1 < 0$, or, $R < (1/\sqrt[3]{4\pi})$. Hence $G(R)$ is **S.D.** for $R < (1/\sqrt[3]{4\pi})$. Similarly, the reader should convince himself that $G'(R) > 0$ when $R > (1/\sqrt[3]{4\pi})$, so $G(R)$ is **S.I.** for $R > (1/\sqrt[3]{4\pi})$. Hence, $R = (1/\sqrt[3]{4\pi})$ is the position of the local and absolute minimum of $G(R)$, and

$$G(1/\sqrt[3]{4\pi}) = 3c\,\sqrt[3]{4\pi}$$

is the minimum total cost (see Fig. 2.5.2). Finally, from (2.5.1), $H = (1/\pi R^2)$ and so, dividing by R,

$$\frac{H}{R} = \frac{1}{\pi R^3}$$

Since $R = (1/\sqrt[3]{4\pi})$, we have $R^3 = 1/4\pi$, so substituting, $H/R = 4$; i.e., the most economical can has a height H four times its radius R.

In many applications we deal with functions whose domain and/or range is some set of integers. For example, the cost of manufacturing n articles is a function of the integer n. Sometimes the methods outlined in §2.4 can be applied to such functions to locate extrema. Call the function whose extrema we seek $F(n)$, where n is a positive integer, $k \le n \le m$ (i.e., the domain of F is the set of positive integers n which lie between the fixed positive integers

k and m, so the domain of F is the set of integers $k, k + 1, k + 2, ..., m$). What we hope to do is to find a continuous function $G(x)$ where x is real and in $[k, m]$, and such that $G(n) = F(n)$ for all integer values n in $[k, m]$; i.e., we hope to find a continuous function G which agrees with F at all integer values in the domain of F. If such a G exists, we find its absolute extrema, and observe that the values $F(n)$ which are nearest the values of the absolute extrema of

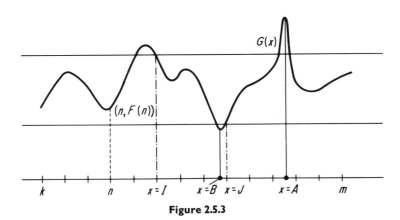

Figure 2.5.3

$G(x)$ must be the absolute extrema for $F(n)$. In Fig. 2.5.3, $G(A)$ is the absolute maximum of $G(x)$, and $F(I)$ is the value of $F(n)$ nearest $G(A)$, so $F(I)$ is the absolute maximum of $F(n)$. Similarly, $G(B)$ is the absolute minimum of $G(x)$, and therefore $F(J)$ is the absolute minimum of $F(n)$.

Example 2.5.6. A manufacturer determines that the demand for n lamps if each is priced at $\$p$ is given by the function $n = f(p) = 60 - \frac{1}{2}p$, where p is an even integer in the interval $[0, 120]$. Hence, the range of $f(p)$ is a set of integers, and if $n = f(p)$ for p an even integer in $[0, 120]$, we see that n is an integer in $[0, 60]$. We suppose next that our lamp manufacturer has determined the cost of producing n lamps to be $\$(140 + 25n)$. How many lamps should he manufacture to maximize his profit?

The total profit $F(n)$ obtained by producing n lamps at $\$p$ is

$$F(n) = np - (140 + 25n)$$
$$= n(120 - 2n) - (140 + 25n)$$
$$= -2n^2 + 95n - 140$$

We consider the function $G(x) = -2x^2 + 95x - 140, 0 \le x \le 60$, and observe that whenever $x = n$ is an integer, $G(n) = F(n)$, and that all points $(n, F(n))$ are on the graph of $G(x)$. Observe also that $G(\frac{1}{2}) = -43$, but $F(\frac{1}{2})$ is undefined. Since $G'(x) = -4x + 95 > 0$ if $x < 95/4$, and $G'(x) < 0$ if $x > 95/4$, we see by §2.2 that $G(x)$ is **S.I.** in $0 \le x \le 95/4$ and decreasing in $95/4 < x \le 60$.

Hence $G(x)$ has its absolute maximum at $x = 109/4$. A graph of $G(x)$ appears in Fig. 2.5.4. The dots on the graph indicate the points on the graph of $G(x)$ corresponding to integer values of x; i.e., for integers n, they are the points $(n, \; G(n)) = (n, \; F(n))$. We calculate to find $G(27) = F(27) = 1507$ and $F(28) = G(28) = 1453$. Since $G(27)$ is larger, a maximum profit of $1507 results from the production of 27 sets. It is only necessary to consider $F(27)$ and $F(28)$, since the function $G(x)$ and hence the function $F(n)$ is increasing for $x = n < 27$, so no value of $n < 27$ can possibly exceed $F(27)$; a similar remark holds for $n > 28$. Finally, since $n = 60 - \frac{1}{2}p$, we see that for $n = 27$ the price that must be charged to yield a maximum profit is $p = \$66$.

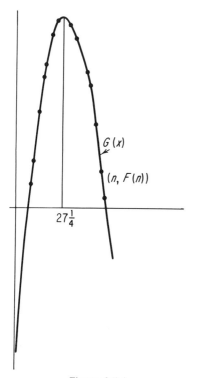

$G(x)$

$(n, F(n))$

$27\frac{1}{4}$

Figure 2.5.4

PROBLEMS

Problems 2.5.1–2.5.7 will deal with problems from §2.2 and from Ex. 1.3.3 and Ex. 1.11.2. For these problems, x will denote demand and p will denote price.

2.5.1. The demand law x in terms of price p is given by $x(p) = 5/p^6$. Determine when the elasticity of demand is greatest and when it is least on $p \geq 1$.

2.5.2. Suppose elasticity of demand η and price p are related by the equation $\eta^2 + p^2 - 2p = 3$. Determine when the elasticity of demand is greatest and when it is least on $0 \leq p \leq 3$ (keep in mind that $\eta \geq 0$).

2.5.3. Suppose the demand law is given by $p = (5 - x)^3$. Determine when the total revenue and marginal revenue are maximum and minimum in $0 \leq x \leq 5$.

2.5.4. Suppose the total cost of producing x units of a commodity is given by $S(x) = 2x^3 - 9x^2 + 12x$. Determine where the total cost and marginal cost are least and greatest on $0 \leq x \leq 3$.

2.5.5. Suppose the total cost $S(x)$ of producing x units is given by $S(x) = x^3 - 5x^2 + 6x$. Determine the minimum average cost for $1 \leq x \leq 4$.

2.5.6. Suppose that the total cost $S(x)$ of producing x units is given by $S(x) = 2x^4 - 6x^3 + 12x^2 - 2x + 1$. Determine the minimum and maximum marginal cost if $0 \leq x \leq 3$.

2.5.7. Determine the maximum total revenue if the demand law is given by $p(x) = 8/(4+x^2)$, $x \geq 0$. Sketch the graph of $p(x)$. Justify your answer.

2.5.8. Show that the rectangle with fixed perimeter which encloses the most area is a square.

2.5.9. Given $f(x) = 4x^5 + 5x^4 - 20x^3 + 40x^2 + 100x - 72$, find the maximum rate of change with respect to x of the slope of the tangent line to the graph of $f(x)$ on the interval $-2 \leq x \leq 1$.

2.5.10. The sum of one number, x, and three times a second number, y, is 80. Find the numbers if the product of x by the cube of y is maximum.

2.5.11. A triangular area is enclosed on two sides by a fence and on the third side by the straight edge of a river. The two sides of fence have equal length. Find the maximum area enclosed.

2.5.12. An open rectangular box is to be made from a sheet of tin 10 in. by 12 in. by cutting out a square from each corner and bending up the sides. Find how large a square should be cut from each corner if the volume of the box is to a maximum.

2.5.13. Find the dimensions of the right circular cylinder of largest volume that can be inscribed in a sphere of radius R.

2.5.14. A photographer finds that with a given mixture of chemicals he can expect a profit of 12¢ per photograph developed provided he develops no more than 1000 photographs. He finds that the profit decreases 0.01¢ for each photograph in excess of 1000, computed on the *total number* of photographs developed. How many photographs should he develop so as to have a maximum profit?

2.5.15. Find the area of the rectangle of maximum area that can be inscribed in the semi-circle given by $f(x) = \sqrt{R^2 - x^2}$ for fixed $R > 0$.

2.5.16. A post 6 ft high stands 4 ft from a wall. We want to place a ladder against the wall and have the ladder rest on the post. What is the shortest ladder that can be used?

2.5.17. A north-south street and an east-west street meet at a point P.

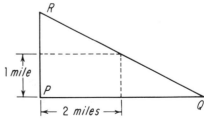

Figure 2.5.5

We wish to construct a diagonal road from a point R north of P to a point Q east of P but with the restriction that this road must pass through a point 2 miles east of P and 1 mile north of P. Where should R and Q be located so that the area of RPQ is a minimum (see Fig. 2.5.5)?

2.5.18. A thin piece of tin 100 sq in. in size is to be cut so as to construct an open box with a square base and sides perpendicular to the base. What should be the dimensions of the box if the box is to enclose the largest volume (ignore the waste in cutting)?

2.5.19. Bush and Mosteller proposed a learning model based on probability theory (see *A Stochastic Model with Applications to Learning*, Annals of Math. Stat., 1953, **24**, 559–685). Roughly, the probability of a particular event occurring when all events are equally likely is the frequency of that event relative to all possible outcomes; e.g., the "probability that a six appears on the roll of a die is 1/6" means that we expect the six to appear about one-sixth of the time relative to all possible outcomes of the roll of an "honest" die (more will be said of this in Chapter 4). For the learning model, we wish to estimate the probability p that a subject will make a certain response A. We suppose we have M observations, and of these the response A occurred n times (and hence failed to occur $M - n$ times). Then, if p denotes the probability of A (we wish to estimate somehow what this p should be), the *likelihood* that the response A occurs n times, $F(p)$, is given by $F(p) = p^n(1 - p)^{M-n}$, $0 \leq p \leq 1$. The *maximum likelihood estimate* of p is the value of p at which $F(p)$ assumes its absolute maximum on its domain, $0 \leq p \leq 1$. Show that the maximum likelihood estimate of p is $p = (n/M)$. Interpret this result.

2.5.20. A manufacturer finds that his costs to produce x articles a day, $0 \leq x \leq 100,000$, break down into (1) a fixed cost to employees of \$1200/day, (2) a fixed unit production cost of \$1.20/day per article, and (3) a maintenance cost of \$$x^2$/day. Hence, the total cost $F(x)$ (in dollars) per article produced, x, is

$$F(x) = \frac{1200}{x} + 1.2 + \frac{x^2}{100,000}$$

(Why?) How many articles should be produced each day to minimize cost?

2.5.21. In an experiment conducted by Neifeld and Poffenberger (A Math Analysis of Work Curves, *Journal of Psych.*, 1928, **1**, 448–456), it was found that the number of units of work per second y performed in n seconds by a subject making a series of arm contractions is given by the equation

$$y = an^3 + bn^2 + cn + d, \qquad n \geq 0$$

where a, b, c, and d are empirical constants that vary with the subject. We suppose for this problem that for a particular subject, $a = 4, b = -30, c = 27,$ and $d = 130$ (the reader can decide at the conclusion of the problem whether these are realistic constants). Find the maximum work per second done in the first 5 seconds.

2.6. An inventory problem.

We will next use the methods of §2.4 to investigate the following inventory problem. A retailer is faced with the problem of deciding how much inventory he should stock. If he carries a small inventory, he saves money on so-called *carrying costs*, such as storage costs, maintenance costs, and, if his goods are perishable, the cost of ruined articles, etc. If his inventory is too small, he will have to reorder frequently, and pay a penalty for many small orders; such *reorder costs* can become prohibitive if our retailer consistently understocks. Our retailer's problem is: What is the optimal inventory?

We shall use the following notation:

$x =$ the number of units of the commodity delivered per shipment
$u =$ the total carrying cost (in say dollars) spent in holding one unit of the commodity one year
$s =$ number of units the retailer plans to sell over the entire year.

To use methods of calculus, we assume x is defined in an interval or half-line, so that our units for x must be say pounds, or fluid ounces, or the like. We first analyze the carrying costs of the inventory. Suppose that our retailer expects to sell 10,000 units annually and accepts one initial shipment of 10,000 units. Assuming a uniform demand, his inventory should drop to 0 by the year's end (this, of course, is a convenient fiction, since no businessman would allow all his stock to be sold before reordering), and so his average inventory stock is $(10,000 + 0)/2 = 5000$ units. If he accepts two shipments of 5000 units, one shipment per six month period, then his inventory would drop uniformly from 5000 to 0 in 6 months (over each 6 month period), so his average inventory is $(5000 + 0)/2 = 2500$ units. In general then, if our retailer orders x units per shipment, his average inventory level will be $(x + 0)/2 = x/2$ units. Since it costs u dollars to hold each unit, his total *carrying cost* will be $xu/2$ dollars for the year.

Next, if the retailer expects to sell s units, and receives x units per shipment, he will require s/x shipments. For example, if 10,000 units are to be sold annually, and each shipment involves 1000 units, then $10,000/1000 = 10$ shipments will be required.

Let a represent all fixed shipping costs (i.e., those costs that are independent of x); and let b be the cost of shipment per unit, so that the cost of shipping x units is bx. Therefore, the cost of delivering x units is $a + bx$ dollars. The total annual reordering cost will equal the number of shipments, s/x, multiplied by the total cost per shipment, $a + bx$, and hence equals

$$\frac{s(a + bx)}{x} = \left[\frac{sa}{x}\right] + sb$$

The total cost to the retailer, $G(x)$, is the sum of the total carrying cost and reordering cost, and hence, for $x > 0$,

$$G(x) = \tfrac{1}{2}xu + \frac{sa}{x} + sb$$

To minimize the total cost $G(x)$; i.e., to find the number of units per shipment to order which will minimize total cost, we solve $G'(x) = \tfrac{1}{2}u - (sa)/x^2 = 0$ to obtain $x = \sqrt{2sa/u}$. Since $G'(x) < 0$ for $0 \le x < \sqrt{2sa/u}$ (why is this so?) we see that $G(x)$ is **S.D.** for $0 \le x < \sqrt{2sa/u}$; and since $G(x) > 0$ for $x > \sqrt{2sa/u}$, we see that $G(x)$ is **S.I.** for $x > \sqrt{2sa/u}$, so that $G(\sqrt{2sa/u})$ is the absolute minimum of $G(x)$. Observe that this says that inventory should increase in proportion to the *square root* of projected total sales.

PROBLEM

2.6.1. Verify that $G'(x) < 0$ for $0 \le x < \sqrt{2sa/u}$, and that $G'(x) > 0$ for $x > \sqrt{2sa/u}$, and that $G'(x) = 0$ for $x = \sqrt{2sa/u}$.

2.7. Intermediate value theorem, a fixed point theorem; an application to general equilibrium in economics.

We first pursue a further investigation into the nature of continuous functions. The theorem which we shall exhibit without proof is the so-called *intermediate value theorem* which asserts

Theorem 2.7.1. Let $f(x)$ be a function continuous on a closed interval $a \le x \le b$. Let w be any number between the numbers $f(a)$ and $f(b)$. Then there is a number u on the interval $a < x < b$ such that $f(u) = w$.

Let us pursue the meaning of this theorem by restating it in other ways. Loosely speaking, the theorem asserts that a function that is continuous on an interval $a \le x \le b$ assumes every value between $f(a)$ and $f(b)$. The following are equivalent restatements (all assume $f(x)$ is continuous on $a \le x \le b$):

(1) Every number between $f(a)$ and $f(b)$ is in the range of $f(x)$.

(2) If $f(a) < f(b)$ and w is any number such that $f(a) < w < f(b)$, then there exists a number u in $a < x < b$ such that $f(u) = w$.

(3) If $f(a) < f(b)$ and w is any number such that $f(a) < w < f(b)$, then the line $y = w$ intersects the graph of $f(x)$ (see Fig. 2.7.1). Clearly, similar statements hold if $f(a) > f(b)$.

A proof of Thm. 2.7.1 can be found, for instance, in *Advanced Calculus* by A. E. Taylor (Ginn and Company, 1955) in Chapter 3.

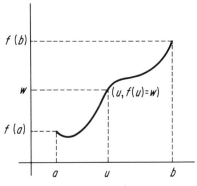

Figure 2.7.1

Example 2.7.1. The equation $2x^7 + x - 1 = 0$ has a solution in the interval $0 < x < 1$. To see this, set $f(x) = 2x^7 + x - 1$, and observe that this polynomial is continuous everywhere, so in particular on the interval $0 \le x \le 1$. Next, observe that $f(0) = -1$ and $f(1) = 2$. Since 0 is between $f(0) = -1$ and $f(1) = 2$ (i.e., $-1 < 0 < 2$), Thm. 2.7.1 asserts that there exists a number u in $0 < x < 1$ such that $f(u) = 0$; i.e., such that $2u^7 + u - 1 = 0$. Thus, $x = u$ is the desired solution.

We can use the intermediate value theorem to prove a so-called **fixed point theorem.** Geometrically, the fixed point theorem we shall prove asserts that if $f(x)$ is continuous with domain the interval $0 \le x \le 1$ and with range a subinterval of the interval $0 \le y \le 1$, then the graph of $f(x)$ must touch the line $y = x$ (see Fig. 2.7.2). Notice the graph of $f(x)$ must intersect the line $y = x$ at some point of the form (u, u), and at $x = u$, we have $f(u) = u$. The point $x = u$ is called a **fixed point of the function.** Analytically, we shall prove

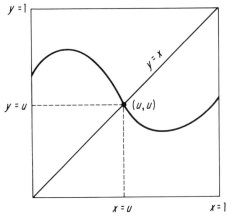

Figure 2.7.2

Theorem 2.7.2. Let $f(x)$ be defined and continuous on the interval $0 \le x \le 1$, and let the range of $f(x)$ be some subinterval of the interval $0 \le y \le 1$ (hence, $0 \le f(x) \le 1$ for all x in $[0, 1]$). Then there is at least one point u in the interval $[0, 1]$ at which $f(u) = u$.

Proof. Define the new function $G(x) = f(x) - x$. Since $G(x)$ is the difference of continuous functions, it is continuous.

First we investigate the behavior of $f(x)$ at $x = 0$. Observe that either $f(0) = 0$ or else $f(0) > 0$, since $f(x) \ge 0$ for all x in $[0, 1]$. If $f(0) = 0$, we are done; simply set $u = 0$. The troublesome possibility then is that $f(0) > 0$; we shall return to this possibility in a moment.

At $x = 1$, we see that either $f(1) = 1$ or $f(1) < 1$, since $f(x) \le 1$ for all x in $[0, 1]$. If $f(1) = 1$, we are done; simply set $u = 1$.

Let us examine the two troublesome cases: $f(0) > 0$ and $f(1) < 1$. If $f(0) > 0$, then $G(0) = f(0) - 0 = f(0) > 0$. If $f(1) < 1$, then $G(1) = f(1) - 1 < 0$. Hence, 0 must be between $G(0)$ and $G(1)$; i.e., $G(1) < 0 < G(0)$. But $G(x)$ is continuous, so by Thm. 2.7.1, there is a number u in $[0, 1]$ at which $G(u) = 0$. Since $G(u) = f(u) - u$ and $G(u) = 0$, it follows that $f(u) = u$, which proves the theorem.

A perhaps unexpected application of a fixed point theorem is to be found in economics, though the particular fixed point theorem used is a streamlined version of Thm. 2.7.2. The ideas involved can nevertheless be outlined.

Suppose we have an economy with 5276 commodities; our list of commodities would include money, of course, as well as stocks and bonds, houses, consumer goods, etc. A typical commodity on this list, say houses, might be item 35. We will assume (that is to say, the mathematical model we are creating to describe the economy has built into it the assumption) that the *demand* for houses depends on the prices of *each of the* 5276 items on the market, as well as a few non-commodity type influences such as the stock of cash in existence (which might be listed as item 5277 to keep our records straight). Call $D(35)$ the demand for commodity 35; i.e., $D(35)$ is the demand for houses. We are asserting that $D(35)$ depends on $P(1)$, the price of commodity 1, $P(2)$, the price of commodity 2, ..., to $P(5276)$, the price of commodity 5276, $P(5277)$, the price of the stock of cash in existence, and perhaps a few more. Hence, $D(35)$ depends on at least 5276 variables! Similar statements apply to $D(1)$, the demand for commodity 1, $D(2)$, the demand for commodity 2, ..., to $D(5276)$, the demand for commodity 5276.

Next we have a similar set of *supply* equations. If $S(35)$ denotes the supply of houses, we shall assume $S(35)$ depends on $P(1)$, $P(2)$, $P(3)$, ..., $P(5277)$, where the P's have the same meaning as above. This gives us a list of supply equations in which each of $S(1)$, $S(2)$, ..., $S(5276)$ depends on $P(1)$, $P(2)$, ..., $P(5277)$, and perhaps a few more.

The economy is said to be in *general equilibrium* if the supply for each item and its demand are equal; i.e., if we look at each commodity k, we have general equilibrium if $D(k) = S(k)$.

If we look at the set of equations $D(k) = S(k)$, and observe that each of the values $D(k)$ and $S(k)$ depend on $P(1)$, $P(2)$, ..., $P(5277)$, ..., we are facing a massive collection of 5276 equations in at least 5277 unknowns.

Using some assumptions from economics, one of them being Walras' law (see Section 3 of Chapter 12 in *Economic Theory and Operation Analysis* by W. J. Baumol,† for a more complete discussion of Walras' law), we can reduce the system to as many unknowns as equations; in our particular example, we would have 5276 equations in 5276 unknowns. General equilibrium will be realized if there are numbers $P(1)$, $P(2)$, ..., $P(5276)$ which will satisfy every one of the equations $D(1) = S(1)$, $D(2) = S(2)$, ..., $D(5276) = S(5276)$ *simultaneously!*

The question of whether such numbers $P(1)$, $P(2)$, ..., $P(5276)$ exist which *simultaneously* satisfy the 5276 equations $D(k) = S(k)$ is far from trivial.

Consider a simple one-commodity situation, and label this commodity 1; Suppose at price $P(1) = p$ the demand $D(1)$ is given by $D(1) = 900 - p$ and the supply $S(1)$ is given by $S(1) = 1000 - p$. Our equilibrium equation is simply $D(1) = S(1)$, and hence equilibrium occurs if $900 - p = 1000 - p$. But this equation says $100 = 0$, which is absurd and so the assumption that we can have equilibrium is untenable.

We shall next consider equations under which general equilibrium is realized. We shall suppose in our purely fictional model that we have a two commodity economy, with $P(1) = p$ and $P(2) = q$, the prices of commodities 1 and 2, respectively. We suppose that our supply functions $S(1)$ and $S(2)$ each depend on the prices p and q according to the equations

$$S(1) = 12 - 5p + q \quad \text{and} \quad S(2) = 5 + 2p + q$$

Similarly our demand functions $D(1)$ and $D(2)$ each depend on the same prices p and q according to the equations

$$D(1) = 2 - 3p + 5q \quad \text{and} \quad D(2) = 2 + p + 3q$$

Equilibrium is realized if there exist prices p and q such that $S(1) = D(1)$ and $S(2) = D(2)$ simultaneously. This leads to the equations

$$12 - 5p + q = 2 - 3p + 5q$$
$$5 + 2p + q = 2 + p + 3q$$

or

$$p + 2q = 5$$
$$-p + 2q = 3$$

---

† See the bibliography.

If we add these equations we obtain $4q = 8$ or $q = 2$; substituting into either equation gives $p = 1$. Hence, at prices $p = 1$ and $q = 2$, general equilibrium is realized.

In general then, we expect that more assumptions will be necessary to insure a set $P(1), ..., P(5276)$ which solves the equilibrium equations. We shall outline a recent proof of the *existence* of a solution to the equilibrium equations based on a modification of a model displayed by Lionel McKenzie (see "On the Existence of a General Equilibrium for a Competitive Market," *Econometrica*, **27**, 54–71, January, 1959). To simplify the model, we shall restrict our attention to the one variable case, though the McKenzie model assumes a system of demand equations in many variables. Let

P_d = the demand price,
P_s = the supply price (i.e., the price at which the seller is willing to supply),
Y_d = the demand quantity,
Y_s = the supply quantity.

The economic assumptions are sets of inequalities which assert (1) that production is proportional to demand, using no more than available resources, and (2) we are assuming a "perfect competition" economy, so profits are zero. Essentially, we assume that the demand quantity is a continuous function of the demand price, and write $Y_d = D(P_d)$ and we assume that the supply quantity is a continuous function of the supply price, and we write $Y_s = S(P_s)$. Our object is to show that the economy is in general equilibrium; i.e., there is a value $P = P_s = P_d$ such that $S(P) = D(P)$. We assume it is possible to solve $Y_s = S(P_s)$ for P_s to obtain the continuous function $P_s = G(Y_s)$ [specifically, we assume a continuous inverse function exists; see (3.9.1)]. This leads us to the equations

$$Y_d = D(P_d) \qquad P_s = G(Y_s)$$

Our model guarantees that there are values of Y_d and Y_s that coincide. Then

$$G[D(P_d)] = P_s$$

Since $G[D(P_d)]$ is continuous (recall Thm. 1.10.2), an appeal to the appropriate fixed point theorem guarantees a value P such that $G[D(P)] = P$. At this price, the demand conditions, the production conditions, and the no-profit conditions are satisfied.

PROBLEMS

2.7.1. Let $f(x)$ be defined and continuous for all x, and let a be a fixed positive constant. Suppose further that $f(-1) = 2a$, $f(0) = 0$, $f(1) = 4a$. Define $g(x) = f(x) - a$. Show that $g(x) = 0$ has at least two solutions.

2.7.2. Let $f(x)$ be defined and have a continuous derivative on $a \leq x \leq b$. Suppose that $f(a) = 0 = f(b)$, and that $f(x)$ changes sign on $a \leq x \leq b$. Define $g(x) = f'(x) + 2f(x)$. Show that $g(x) = 0$ has at least one solution on $a \leq x \leq b$. (*Hint:* Apply Thm. 1.7.4 and Thm. 2.4.2 to f, and then Thm. 2.7.1 to g.)

2.7.3. Let $f(x)$ have the property that $f(x)$ is continuous and $f(x) < 0$ for $0 < x \leq 1$, and $f(0) = 1$. Use Thm. 2.7.1 to show that $f(x)$ cannot be continuous at $x = 0$.

Chapter 3

INTEGRATION

3.1. Summations.

Suppose we have 35 numbers that we wish to add. We might call the first number a, the second number b, the third c, and so on. Unfortunately, there are not enough letters in the alphabet to represent all 35 numbers, so we will adopt the following more versatile notation: We call the first number a_1, the second a_2, the third a_3, ..., the 17th number a_{17}, ..., the 35th number a_{35}. With this notation, a_n is the nth number in the set we are adding; in other words, the nth summand is a_n.

The desired sum is then $a_1 + a_2 + a_3 + \cdots + a_{34} + a_{35}$. This notation is abbreviated once more by using the following notation:

$$\sum_{k=1}^{35} a_k = a_1 + a_2 + a_5 + \cdots + a_{34} + a_{35}$$

and

$$\sum_{k=1}^{35} a_k$$

is read: The sum of all numbers a_k, starting at the position designated by the value of k appearing at the bottom of the $\sum$, namely $k = 1$, and ending at the value appearing at the top of the $\sum$ notation, namely, 35; i.e., the sum of a_k from $k = 1$ to $k = 35$. Then

$$\sum_{k=15}^{23} a_k$$

is the sum of all numbers a_k starting with $k = 15$ and ending with $k = 23$, and hence

$$\sum_{k=15}^{23} a_k = a_{15} + a_{16} + \cdots + a_{22} + a_{23}$$

Example 3.1.1.

$$\sum_{k=1}^{6} k^2 = 1^2 + 2^2 + 3^2 + 4^2 + 5^2 + 6^2$$

Here, $a_k = k^2$. In particular, $a_1 = 1$, $a_2 = 2^2$, $a_3 = 3^2$, $a_4 = 4^2$, ... Next,

$$\sum_{k=1}^{100} 1/2^k = 1/2 + 1/2^2 + 1/2^3 + \cdots + 1/2^{99} + 1/2^{100}$$

where, $a_1 = 1/2$, $a_2 = 1/2^2 = 1/4$, $a_3 = 1/2^3 = 1/8$, and in general, $a_k = 2^{-k}$.

We generalize this as follows: Suppose we are given a set of N numbers, $A_1, A_2, A_3, ..., A_{N-1}, A_N$. We define:

(3.1.1) $$\sum_{k=1}^{N} A_k = A_1 + A_2 + \cdots + A_{N-1} + A_N$$

We now prove some useful theorems.

Theorem 3.1.1. Let $A_1, A_2, ..., A_N$ and $B_1, B_2, ..., B_N$ be two sets of N numbers. Then

(3.1.2) $$\sum_{k=1}^{N} (A_k + B_k) = \sum_{k=1}^{N} A_k + \sum_{k=1}^{N} B_k$$

Proof. By (3.1.1),

$$\sum_{k=1}^{N} (A_k + B_k) = (A_1 + B_1) + (A_2 + B_2) + (A_3 + B_3) + \cdots + (A_N + B_N)$$

$$= (A_1 + A_2 + A_3 + \cdots + A_N) + (B_1 + B_2 + B_3 + \cdots + B_N)$$

$$= \sum_{k=1}^{N} A_k + \sum_{k=1}^{N} B_k$$

Theorem 3.1.2. Let c be any fixed constant, and $A_1, A_2, ..., A_N$ be a set of numbers. Then

(3.1.3) $$\sum_{k=1}^{N} (cA_k) = c \sum_{k=1}^{N} A_k$$

Proof.

$$\sum_{k=1}^{N} (cA_k) = (cA_1) + (cA_2) + (cA_3) + \cdots + (cA_N)$$

$$= c(A_1 + A_2 + A_3 + \cdots + A_N) = c \sum_{k=1}^{N} A_k$$

Theorem 3.1.3. Let $A_1, A_2, ..., A_N, A_{N+1}$ be a set of $N + 1$ numbers. Then

(3.1.4) $$\sum_{k=1}^{N} (A_{k+1} - A_k) = A_{N+1} - A_1$$

i.e., the sum of the first N consecutive differences is just the $(N + 1)$st term of the set minus the first term.

Proof.

$$\sum_{k=1}^{N} (A_{k+1} - A_k) = (A_2 - A_1) + (A_3 - A_2) + (A_4 - A_3) + \cdots$$
$$+ (A_N - A_{N-1}) + (A_{N+1} - A_N)$$
$$= -A_1 + (A_2 - A_2) + (A_3 - A_3) + \cdots$$
$$+ (A_N - A_N) + A_{N+1}$$
$$= A_{N+1} - A_1$$

Example 3.1.2. We wish to find an expression involving N which gives the value of the sum of the first N positive integers. In symbols, we wish to evaluate

(a)
$$\sum_{k=1}^{N} k = 1 + 2 + 3 + \cdots + (N - 1) + N$$

Clearly, this sum is not affected if we write it in the reverse order,

(b)
$$\sum_{k=1}^{N} k = N + (N - 1) + (N - 2) + \cdots + 3 + 2 + 1$$

If we add line (a) to line (b) we get:

$$2 \sum_{k=1}^{N} k = \underbrace{(N + 1) + (N + 1) + \cdots + (N + 1)}_{N \text{ times}} = N(N + 1)$$

and hence

(3.1.5)
$$\sum_{k=1}^{N} k = \tfrac{1}{2} N(N + 1)$$

In particular,

$$\sum_{k=1}^{37} k = 1 + 2 + 3 + \cdots + 36 + 37 = \tfrac{1}{2} \cdot 37 \cdot 38 = 703$$

Example 3.1.3. We next wish to evaluate

$$\sum_{k=1}^{N} k^2 = 1^2 + 2^2 + \cdots + N^2$$

i.e., the sum of the squares of the first N integers. The approach will be to evaluate

$$\sum_{k=1}^{N} \{(k + 1)^3 - k^3\}$$

two ways, one by expanding $(k + 1)^3$ explicitly, subtracting k^3 and summing; the other by using (3.1.4). A comparison of these results will yield

$$\sum_{k=1}^{N} k^2$$

First we shall make the following convention: we shall use $\sum$ systematically to replace

$$\sum_{k=1}^{N}$$

From the binomial theorem (see Thm. 1.8.1), we expand to get

$$(k+1)^3 - k^3 = k^3 + 3k^2 + 3k + 1 - k^3 = 3k^2 + 3k + 1$$

Hence

$$\sum \{(k+1)^3 - k^3\} = \sum \{3k^2 + 3k + 1\}$$

$$= \sum 3k^2 + \sum 3k + \sum 1 \qquad \text{from (3.1.2)}$$

$$= 3 \sum k^2 + 3 \sum k + \sum 1 \qquad \text{from (3.1.3)}$$

From (3.1.5.),

$$\sum k = \tfrac{1}{2}N(N+1)$$

also

$$\sum 1 = \underbrace{1 + 1 + \cdots + 1}_{N \text{ times}} = N$$

and hence

(a) $$\sum \{(k+1)^3 - k^3\} = 3 \sum k^2 + \tfrac{3}{2}N(N+1) + N$$

Next we evaluate $\sum \{(k+1)^3 - k^3\}$ by using (3.1.4). Let $A_k = k^3$ in (3.1.4):

(b) $$\sum \{(k+1)^3 - k^3\} = (N+1)^3 - 1^3 = N^3 + 3N^2 + 3N + 1 - 1$$

$$= N^3 + 3N^2 + 3N$$

Observe that the left sides of (a) and (b) are identical, so the right sides of these equations must be equal also. Hence,

$$3 \sum k^2 + \tfrac{3}{2}N(N+1) + N = N^3 + 3N^2 + 3N$$

If we multiply the last expression by 2, expand $3N(N+1)$, and transpose we get

$$6 \sum k^2 = 2N^3 + 3N^2 + N = N(N+1)(2N+1)$$

or finally

(3.1.6) $$\sum_{k=1}^{N} k^2 = \tfrac{1}{6}N(N+1)(2N+1)$$

Example 3.1.4.

$$\sum_{k=1}^{N} k^3 = \left[\frac{N(N+1)}{2} \right]^2$$

The verification is left as an exercise in the problem set.

Example 3.1.5. For fixed numbers $a \neq 0$ and $r \neq 0$, consider the series $a + ar + ar^2 + ar^3 + \cdots + ar^N$. Observe that if we multiply any term by r, we get the next term of the series. Such a series is called a *geometric series*, and it can be written as

$$\sum_{k=1}^{N+1} ar^{k-1}$$

To find the sum in closed form, write $S_N = a + ar + ar^2 + \cdots + ar^N$, multiply S_N by r to obtain $rS_N = ar + ar^2 + ar^3 + \cdots + ar^{N+1}$, and observe that

$$S_N - rS_N = a - ar^{N+1}$$

Hence, $S_N(1 - r) = a(1 - r^{N+1})$ or finally

(3.1.7)
$$\sum_{k=1}^{N+1} ar^{k-1} = S_N = \frac{a(1 - r^{N+1})}{1 - r}$$

PROBLEMS

3.1.1. Evaluate each of the following sums:

(a) $S_N = 1 + 2 + 3 + \cdots + 152 + 153$
(b) $S_N = 1^2 + 2^2 + 3^2 + \cdots + (152)^2 + (153)^2$
(c) $S_N = \frac{1}{2} + \frac{1}{4} + \frac{1}{8} + \cdots + 1/2^N$
(d) $S_N = 2 + 6 + 18 + 54 + \cdots + 2\{3^{25}\}$

3.1.2. Derive the result of Ex. 3.1.4; i.e., that

$$\sum_{k=1}^{N} k^3 = \left[\frac{N(N+1)}{2}\right]^2$$

Hint: Consider

$$\sum_{k=1}^{N} \{(k+1)^4 - k^4\}$$

3.1.3. Evaluate the sum $1 \cdot 2 + 2 \cdot 3 + \cdots + n(n+1)$.

3.1.4. A sequence $a_1, a_2, \ldots, a_{k-1}, a_k, \ldots$ in which each successive term is obtained by *adding* a fixed number to the previous term (i.e., $a_k = a_{k-1} + d$ for a fixed d, where $k = 1, 2, 3, \ldots$) is called an **arithmetic progression.** It could be written as

$$a_1, \quad a_2 = a_1 + d, \quad a_3 = a_2 + d = a_1 + 2d$$

and in general,

$$a_k = a_1 + (k-1)d$$

Evaluate

$$\sum_{k=1}^{N} (a_1 + (k-1)d)$$

3.1.5. Evaluate the sum $3 \cdot 1 + 4 \cdot 2 + 5 \cdot 3 + 6 \cdot 4 + \cdots + 35 \cdot 33$.

3.1.6. Write the following series explicitly for $n = 5$ and $n = 7$:

$$\sum_{k=1}^{n} \frac{1}{n} f\left(6 + \frac{k}{n}\right)$$

where f is a function of x.

3.1.7. Repeat Prob. 3.1.6 for (a) $f(x) = 3x + 2$, and (b) $f(x) = x^2$. In each case, derive a sum that depends only on n.

3.1.8. Let A_1, A_2, ..., A_n be a set of n real numbers. Show that

$$\left| \sum_{i=1}^{n} A_i \right| \leq \sum_{i=1}^{n} |A_i|$$

When does equality hold? [*Hint:* Consider (1.1.4).]

3.2. Some brief remarks on sequences and their limits. The geometric series.

In §3.1 we used the symbol A_k to represent the kth number in a set of numbers. In fact, to each number k we associated some real number A_k. Hence, in terms of §1.1 we have constructed a *function* which we could write as $A(k)$, whose domain is some set of positive integers and whose range is some set of real numbers. If the domain of $A(k)$ is all positive integers, then the sequence of numbers (writing as before $A(k) = A_k$)

$$A_1, A_2, A_3, A_4 \ldots, A_{n-1}, A_n, A_{n+1}, \ldots$$

is called an **infinite sequence**, or briefly, a **sequence**. The sequence

$$A_1, A_2, A_3, \ldots, A_{n-1}, A_n, \ldots$$

is abbreviated by the symbol $\{A_n\}$, where A_n is the nth term of the sequence.

Example 3.2.1. The numbers $1, 1/2, 1/3, \ldots, 1/n, \ldots$ form an infinite sequence $\{1/n\}$, with $A(n) = A_n = 1/n$. Notice all the values of A_n are distinct.

Example 3.2.2. The numbers, $1, 1, 1, 1, 1, 1, \ldots 1, \ldots$, form an infinite sequence, $\{B_n\}$, $B_n = 1$ for all n (it is the analogue of the constant function $f(x) = 1$). It is an infinite sequence all of whose terms are identical.

Example 3.2.3. The numbers $2, 0, 2, 0, \ldots$ form an infinite sequence $\{D_n\}$ with $D_n = 1 + (-1)^{n+1}$.

Example 3.2.4. The sequence

$$\left\{\frac{n^2 - 1}{n^2 + 2}\right\}$$

is the sequence 0, 1/2, 8/11, 5/6, ...

The analogue of (1.5.1) for sequences is:

Definition 3.2.1. Let $\{A_n\}$ be an infinite sequence. We define

$$\lim_{n \to \infty} A_n = L$$

to mean that the numbers A_n can be made to stay arbitrarily close to L by taking n sufficiently large.

We remark that Thm. 1.5.1 remains valid with $\lim_{x \to c}$ *replaced by* $\lim_{n \to \infty}$ *and with* $f(x)$ *and* $g(x)$ *replaced by two infinite sequences* $A(n)$ *and* $B(n)$, *respectively.* In particular,

Theorem 3.2.1. Let $\{A_n\}$ and $\{B_n\}$ be sequences such that $\lim_{n \to \infty} A_n$ and $\lim_{n \to \infty} B_n$ exist, and let c be any constant. Then

(1) $\lim_{n \to \infty} cA_n = c \lim_{n \to \infty} A_n$

(2) $\lim_{n \to \infty} (A_n \pm B_n) = \lim_{n \to \infty} A_n \pm \lim_{n \to \infty} B_n$

(The limit of a sum (or difference) is the sum (or difference) of the individual limits.)

(3) $\lim_{n \to \infty} A_n B_n = \lim_{n \to \infty} A_n \cdot \lim_{n \to \infty} B_n$

(The limit of a product is the product of the limits.)

(4) $\lim_{n \to \infty} A_n/B_n = \lim_{n \to \infty} A_n / \lim_{n \to \infty} B_n$ if $\lim_{n \to \infty} B_n \neq 0$.

(The limit of a quotient is the quotient of the limits, provided the limit in the denominator is not zero.)

Example 3.2.5. With $A_n = 1/n$ as in Ex. 3.2.1, we see that

$$\lim_{n \to \infty} A_n = \lim_{n \to \infty} 1/n = 0$$

since $1/n$ can be made arbitrarily close to 0 by taking n sufficiently large. Hence, $\lim_{n \to \infty} 1/n^2 = \lim_{n \to \infty} 1/n \cdot 1/n = \lim_{n \to \infty} 1/n \cdot \lim_{n \to \infty} 1/n = 0 \cdot 0 = 0$. Similarly, $\lim_{n \to \infty} c/n = 0$ where c is any constant [by Thm. 3.2.1, (1)].

Example 3.2.6. With $B_n = 1$ for all n, as in Ex. 3.2.2, we see that $\lim_{n \to \infty} B_n = 1$, since B_n can be made to stay arbitrarily close to 1 by taking n sufficiently large; in fact, $B_n = 1$ for *every* n.

Example 3.2.7. With D_n defined as in Ex. 3.2.3, we assert $\lim\limits_{n\to\infty} D_n$ does *not* exist. Suppose we try 2 as the limit. No matter how large an n we choose, there will be values (in fact, an infinite number of values) $k > n$ for which $D_k = 0$, and for these values D_k does *not* stay arbitrarily close to 2, since $D_k = 0$ is always 2 units from the proposed limit 2. No matter what number we try as the proposed limit, a similar difficulty will arise.

The following two examples will illustrate a general procedure for finding limits of ratios of polynomials in the integer variable n. We write $A_n \to L$ as $n \to \infty$ to mean $\lim\limits_{n\to\infty} A_n = L$.

Example 3.2.8. We investigate $\lim\limits_{n\to\infty} (n^2 - 1)/(n^2 + 2)$. The largest exponent appearing in either the numerator or denominator is 2 (it happens to appear in both the numerator and denominator). We divide the numerator and denominator by n raised to the largest exponent determined, 2, obtaining

$$\frac{(n^2 - 1)\cdot 1/n^2}{(n^2 + 2)\cdot 1/n^2} = \frac{1 - (1/n^2)}{1 + (2/n^2)} \to 1 \qquad \text{as } n \to \infty$$

so

$$\lim_{n\to\infty} \frac{n^2 - 1}{n^2 + 2} = 1$$

Example 2.3.9. Find

$$\lim_{n\to\infty} \frac{n^3 + n - 1}{n^4 + 2n + 1}$$

This time the largest exponent is 4; we divide numerator and denominator by n^4 to obtain

$$\frac{(n^3 + n - 1)\cdot 1/n^4}{(n^4 + 2n + 1)\cdot 1/n^4} = \frac{(1/n) + (1/n^3) - (1/n^4)}{1 + (2/n^3) + (1/n^4)} \to \frac{0}{1} = 0 \qquad \text{as } n \to \infty$$

so

$$\lim_{n\to\infty} \frac{n^3 + n - 1}{n^4 + 2n + 1} = 0$$

Theorem 3.2.2. If r is any number such that $|r| < 1$, then $\lim\limits_{n\to\infty} r^n = 0$.

Proof. Since $|r| < 1$, it follows that $1/|r| > 1$. Hence, we can write

$$1/|r| = 1 + h$$

for the appropriate positive number h. Hence, with (1.8.1),

$$\left(\frac{1}{|r|}\right)^n = \frac{1}{|r|^n} = (1 + h)^n = 1 + nh + \binom{n}{2}h^2 + \binom{n}{3}h^3 + \cdots + h^n$$

so

$$\frac{1}{|r|^n} = 1 + nh + \text{(terms involving positive multiples of powers of the positive number } h\text{)}$$

$$> 1 + nh$$

Hence,

$$0 < |r|^n < \frac{1}{1 + nh}$$

But

$$\lim_{n \to \infty} \frac{1}{1 + nh} = 0$$

and so $0 \le \lim_{n \to \infty} |r|^n \le 0$ which implies that $\lim_{n \to \infty} |r|^n = 0$, which in turn implies $\lim_{n \to \infty} r^n = 0$.

We turn next to a special sequence of special interest. We define:

$$S_1 = a$$

$$S_2 = a + ar$$

$$S_3 = a + ar + ar^2 = \sum_{k=1}^{3} ar^{k-1}$$

$$S_4 = a + ar + ar^2 + ar^3 = \sum_{k=1}^{4} ar^{k-1}$$

$$\vdots$$

$$S_n = a + ar + ar^2 + \cdots + ar^{n-1} = \sum_{k=1}^{n} ar^{k-1}$$

We have thus constructed a sequence $\{S_n\}$, whose nth term is a geometric series. The sequence $\{S_n\}$ is called an **infinite geometric series**.

Theorem 3.2.3. Let $|r| < 1$. Then, with $\{S_n\}$ defined as above,

(3.2.1) $$\lim_{n \to \infty} S_n = \lim_{n \to \infty} \sum_{k=1}^{n} ar^{k-1} = \frac{a}{1 - r}$$

Proof. From (3.1.7), setting $n = N + 1$, we see that

$$S_n = \frac{a(1 - r^n)}{1 - r} = \frac{a}{1 - r} - \frac{a}{1 - r}r^n$$

Hence,

$$\lim_{n \to \infty} S_n = \lim_{n \to \infty} \frac{a}{1-r} - \lim_{n \to \infty} \frac{a}{1-r} \cdot r^n$$

$$= \frac{a}{1-r} - \frac{a}{1-r} \lim_{n \to \infty} r^n$$

But since $|r| < 1$, $\lim\limits_{n \to \infty} r^n = 0$. (See Thm. 3.2.2.) This yields the desired result.

Example 3.2.10. We investigate the repeating decimal 0.33333 .... Write:

$$a_1 = 0.3 = \tfrac{3}{10}$$
$$a_2 = 0.03 = \tfrac{3}{10} \cdot (1/10)$$
$$a_3 = 0.003 = \tfrac{3}{10} \cdot (1/10^2)$$
$$\vdots$$
$$a_n = 0.\underbrace{00 \cdots 0}_{n-1 \text{ zeros}}3 = \tfrac{3}{10} \cdot (1/10^{n-1})$$

Then $a_1 + a_2 + \cdots + a_n = \tfrac{3}{10} + \tfrac{3}{10} \cdot 1/10 + \tfrac{3}{10} \cdot (1/10^2) + \cdots + \tfrac{3}{10} \cdot (1/10^{n-1})$. This is a geometric series (see Ex. 3.1.5) with $a = \tfrac{3}{10}$ and $r = \tfrac{1}{10}$ and $N = n - 1$. Hence

$$\underbrace{0.333 \cdots 3}_{n \text{ terms}} = a_1 + \cdots + a_n = \sum_{k=1}^{n} \frac{3}{10} \frac{1}{10^{k-1}}$$

So, using (3.2.1) above,

$$0.3333 \cdots = \lim_{n \to \infty} \sum_{k=1}^{n} a_k = \lim_{n \to \infty} \sum_{k=1}^{n} \frac{3}{10} \cdot \frac{1}{10^{k-1}} = \frac{\tfrac{3}{10}}{1 - \tfrac{1}{10}} = \frac{1}{3}$$

PROBLEMS

3.2.1. Evaluate each of the following limits when they exist:

(a) $\lim\limits_{n \to \infty} \dfrac{n^5 - 4n^6 + 5n^7}{n^7}$

(b) $\lim\limits_{n \to \infty} \dfrac{-3n^4 + n^2 - 100{,}000}{-6n^4 - n^2 + 10{,}000}$

(c) $\lim\limits_{n \to \infty} \dfrac{n^{16} - 1}{1 - n^{16}}$

(d) $\lim\limits_{n \to \infty} \dfrac{n^4 - 2n^3 + n^2 + n - 1}{-2n^4 + n^3 - n^2 - n + 5}$

(e) $\lim\limits_{n \to \infty} \dfrac{n^5 - 3}{n^4 + 100}$

(f) $\lim\limits_{n \to \infty} \dfrac{n^{10} - n^5 - 1}{n^{11} - n^6 + 3}$

3.2.2. Evaluate each of the following by using algebraic rationalization techniques:

(a) $\lim_{n\to\infty} (\sqrt{n+1} - \sqrt{n}) = \lim_{n\to\infty} \frac{\sqrt{n+1} - \sqrt{n}}{1}$

(*Hint:* Multiply numerator and denominator by $(\sqrt{n+1} + \sqrt{n})$.)

(b) $\lim_{n\to\infty} (\sqrt{n+c} - \sqrt{n})$

(c) $\lim_{n\to\infty} n(\sqrt{n^2+1} - n)$

(d) $\lim_{n\to\infty} (\sqrt{n+\sqrt{n}} - \sqrt{n-\sqrt{n}})$

3.2.3. Evaluate $\lim_{n\to\infty} (1 + x + x^2 + x^3 + \cdots + x^n)$ for $|x| < 1$.

3.2.4. Evaluate the following limits:

(a) $\lim_{n\to\infty} [(1/n^2) + (2/n^2) + (3/n^2) + \cdots + (n/n^2)]$

(b) $\lim_{n\to\infty} [(1^2/n^3) + (2^2/n^3) + (3^2/n^3) + \cdots + (n^2/n^3)]$

(c) $\lim_{n\to\infty} [(1^3/n^4) + (2^3/n^4) + (3^3/n^4) + \cdots + (n^3/n^4)]$

3.2.5. Write the first five terms starting with $n = 1$ of the infinite sequences whose general term is given by:

(a) $A_n = 1 - (1/2^n)$ (b) $B_n = (-1)^n$

(c) $D_n = n[1 + (-1)^n] + (1/n)$ (d) $[1 - (-1)^n]/2 + (1/n)$

(e) $(-1)^n/n$

3.2.6. Which of the sequences of Prob. 3.2.5 have limits?

3.2.7. Find the corresponding rational number for each of the following decimals:

(a) .12 12 12 12 ...   (b) .01 01 01 01 ...

(c) .123 123 123 ...   (d) .001 001 001 ...

3.2.8. Consider the sum:

$$S_N = \left(1 - \frac{1}{2}\right) + \left(\frac{1}{2} - \frac{1}{3}\right) + \left(\frac{1}{3} - \frac{1}{4}\right) + \cdots + \left(\frac{1}{N} - \frac{1}{N+1}\right)$$

(a) Use (3.1.4) to evaluate S_N.

(b) Find $\lim_{n\to\infty} S_N$.

3.2.9. Find

$$\lim_{n\to\infty} \sum_{k=1}^{n} \frac{1}{2^k}$$

[*Hint:* Use (3.2.1).]

3.2.10. A ball is dropped from a height of 10 ft. Each time the ball bounces, it rises 3/5 the distance it had previously fallen. Assuming the ball perfectly elastic, what is the total distance traveled by the ball?

Some problems relating *to sequences arising in psychology* follow.

3.2.11. In Ex. 1.1.10, the reliability of a lengthened test in terms of the original reliability r was given by $f_n(r) = nr/[1 + (n - 1)r]$ for $0 \le r \le 1$. Show that $\lim_{n \to \infty} f_n(r) = 1$ for each fixed r. What does this say about reliability?

3.2.12. Thurston's learning function (see Ex. 1.1.9) is given by

$$G(x) = [a(x + b)]/(x + c)$$

Since x denotes the number of practise acts, x is actually a positive integer, so the learning function is actually a sequence $\{G(n)\} = \{A_n\}$ where

$$A_n = [a(n + b)]/(n + c)$$

Show that $\lim_{n \to \infty} (1/a) \cdot A_n = 1$.

3.2.13. Let $\{a_k\}$ be a sequence with the property that $\lim_{n \to \infty} a_n = 2$. Show that

$$\lim_{n \to \infty} \sum_{k=1}^{n} (a_{k+1} - a_k)$$

exists, and find its value.

3.2.14. A formal definition of $\lim_{n \to \infty} a_n = L$ is that corresponding to each open interval J containing L there is a positive integer N (which depends on J) such that if $n > N$, then a_n will be in J.

(a) Show that if $\lim_{n \to \infty} a_n = L$, then every open interval containing L must contain all except perhaps a finite number of the sequence $\{a_n\}$.

(b) Show that if $\lim_{n \to \infty} a_n = L$, then L is unique; i.e., if $\lim_{n \to \infty} a_n = L^*$ as well as L, then $L = L^*$.

3.2.15. Let $f(x)$ be continuous on $a \le x \le b$. We know that $f(x)$ attains its maximum at some value u with $a \le u \le b$. We then write $\max_{a \le x \le b} f(x) = f(u)$. Let $\{f_n(x)\}$ be a sequence of functions, each defined and continuous on $a \le x \le b$. We say $f_n(x)$ converges uniformly to $f(x)$ if

$$\lim_{n \to \infty} \left(\max_{a \le x \le b} |f_n(x) - f(x)| \right) = 0$$

Let $g_n(x) = x^n(1 - x)^n$, $0 \le x \le 1$.

(a) Without any calculations, explain why each $g_n(x)$ must attain an absolute maximum in $0 < x < 1$. Observe that $g_n(x) \ge 0$, $0 \le x \le 1$.

(b) Show that $g_n(x)$ converges uniformly to $g(x) = 0$, $0 \le x \le 1$. (*Hint:* Use the methods of §2.4.)

3.3. Anti-derivatives.

In Chapter 1, we considered the following problem: Given a differentiable function $G(x)$, find $f(x)$ such that $DG(x) = f(x)$; i.e., find $f(x)$, the derivative of $G(x)$. We now consider a closely related problem: Given $f(x)$, find $G(x)$ such that $DG(x) = f(x)$; i.e., find a function $G(x)$ which has a *given* derivative. We call a function G which solves the equation $DG(x) = f(x)$ [for the given $f(x)$], **an anti-derivative** of $f(x)$, and use the symbol $\int f(x)dx$ to represent an anti-derivative of $f(x)$. Summarizing, we have

Definition 3.3.1. A function $G(x)$ is said to be *an anti-derivative of $f(x)$*,

$$G(x) = \int f(x)\, dx$$

if the derivative of $G(x)$ is $f(x)$; i.e.,

(3.3.1) $\displaystyle\int f(x)\, dx = G(x)$ means $(d/dx)G(x) = f(x)$

The symbol $\int (\ ) dx$ is read "an anti-derivative with respect to x." dx indicates only that anti-differentiation is to take place with respect to x, just as the symbol d/dx means that differentiation is to take place with respect to x. Some authors prefer to replace the symbol $\int f(x)dx$ by the symbol $D^{-1}f(x)$.

Example 3.3.1.

$$\int x\, dx = x^2/2$$

i.e., $x^2/2$ is an anti-derivative of $f(x) = x$. This is because $D\frac{1}{2}x^2 = x$. Observe that $D(\frac{1}{2}x^2 + 1) = x$, and $D(\frac{1}{2}x^2 - 7) = x$, so $\frac{1}{2}x^2 + 1$ and $\frac{1}{2}x^2 - 7$ are *also* anti-derivatives of $f(x) = x$. In fact, if c is any constant, $D(\frac{1}{2}x^2 + c) = x$, so $\frac{1}{2}x^2 + c$ is an anti-derivative of $f(x) = x$.

Example 3.3.2.

$$\int (x^2 + x - 3)\, dx = \tfrac{1}{3}x^3 + \tfrac{1}{2}x^2 - 3x + C$$

because $D(\frac{1}{3}x^3 + \frac{1}{2}x^2 - 3x + C) = x^2 + x - 3$, where C is *any* constant.

From Ex. 3.3.1 and Ex. 3.3.2, it is apparent that if

$$G(x) = \int f(x)\, dx$$

[and hence $DG(x) = f(x)$], then, for any constant c

$$G(x) + c = \int f(x)\, dx$$

because $D[G(x) + c] = DG(x) = f(x)$. In fact,

Theorem 3.3.1. Let $G(x)$ be *any* anti-derivative of $f(x)$; then the most general anti-derivative is given by $G(x) + c$ where c is an arbitrary constant. Equivalently, if $G(x)$ and $F(x)$ are any two anti-derivatives of $f(x)$ (i.e., if $G'(x) = F'(x)$), then there is a constant k such that

(3.3.2) $$F(x) = G(x) + k$$

Remark. This theorem asserts that, if $G(x)$ is any particular anti-derivative of $f(x)$, then as c takes on arbitrary real values we get every possible anti-derivative of $f(x)$ from the expression $G(x) + c$. Also observe that the most general anti-derivative is not one function but a *set* of functions $G(x) + c$, depending on c.

The proof of Thm. 3.3.1 is a consequence of the mean value theorem, and appears in the Appendix.

Example 3.3.3.

$$\int x\sqrt{x^2 + 1}\, dx = \tfrac{1}{3}(x^2 + 1)^{3/2} + c$$

because $D\{\tfrac{1}{3}(x^2 + 1)^{3/2} + c\} = x\sqrt{x^2 + 1}$.

Example 3.3.4.

$$\int x^n\, dx = \frac{x^{n+1}}{n+1} + c, \qquad n \neq -1$$

since

$$D\left[\frac{x^{n+1}}{n+1} + c\right] = \frac{1}{n+1} Dx^{n+1} = \frac{n+1}{n+1} x^{(n+1)-1} = x^n$$

The anti-derivative has the following geometrical interpretation. The set of functions $\int f(x)dx$ may be thought of as all functions whose graphs have tangent lines with slope $f(x)$ at the point x, since, if $y = G(x)$ is a function whose graph has a tangent line with slope $m = f(a)$ at $x = a$, where a is in the domain of $f(x)$ and $G(x)$, then $G'(a) = f(a)$ for each such a. Thus, $G(x) = \int f(x)\, dx$.

Example 3.3.5. Find all functions whose graphs have tangent lines with slope $2x$ at each value x. By our above remarks, if $G(x)$ is such a function, then $G(x) = \int 2x\, dx = x^2 + c$, and so we see that all functions $G(x) = x^2 + c$ have the required slope $2x$.

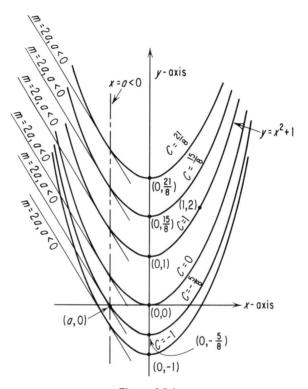

Figure 3.3.1

Example 3.3.6. In the set of all functions with slope $2x$, find the one which passes through the point $(1, 2)$. From Ex. 3.3.5, the set of functions is of the form $G(x) = x^2 + c$. Since $(1, 2)$ is on the graph of $G(x)$, we have

$$2 = G(1) = 1^2 + c$$

so $c = 1$, and the function we want is $G(x) = x^2 + 1$. By specifying $G(1) = 2$ we have fixed the value of c; in fact, specifying a point through which the graph of the anti-derivative must pass fixes the constant. Some of the functions $x^2 + c$ are graphed in Fig. 3.3.1. Observe that the tangent lines drawn to any point $x = a$ are parallel; i.e., $D(x^2 + c)|_{x=a} = 2a$.

Example 3.3.7. Find the function $F(x)$ whose graph has a tangent line with slope $x^3 - x^2 + 1$ at any x, if $F(0) = -3$ also [i.e., the graph is to pass through

(0, -3)]. The "line tangent to the graph of $F(x)$ has slope $x^3 - x^2 + 1$" means that $F'(x) = x^3 - x^2 + 1$, so $F(x) = \int (x^3 - x^2 + 1)\, dx$. We can directly verify that $F(x) = (\frac{1}{4})x^4 - (\frac{1}{3})x^3 + x + C$ is the required class of functions. Since $F(0) = -3$, we have $-3 = F(0) = C$, so $C = -3$. Hence the desired function is $F(x) = (\frac{1}{4})x^4 - (\frac{1}{3})x^3 + x - 3$.

The reader is probably aware that all the anti-derivatives we have evaluated so far were found by knowing derivatives first, and that the calculations often seem to be good guesses verified by differentiation. In fact the techniques for anti-differentiation are not as easy or as systematic or as comprehensive as the techniques for differentiation. Nevertheless, we can prove

Theorem 3.3.2. Given $\int f(x)\, dx$ and $\int g(x)\, dx$, and an arbitrary constant A,

(3.3.3)

(i) $\quad \displaystyle\int \{f(x) + g(x)\}\, dx = \int f(x)\, dx + \int g(x)\, dx$

(ii) $\quad \displaystyle\int Af(x)\, dx = A \int f(x)\, dx$

Proof. (i) Set

$$F(x) = \int f(x)\, dx \quad \text{and} \quad G(x) = \int g(x)\, dx$$

[we will suppose the arbitrary constants are already in the expressions $F(x)$ and $G(x)$]. Then $DF(x) = f(x)$ and $DG(x) = g(x)$. Hence,

$$D[F(x) + G(x)] = f(x) + g(x)$$

From (3.3.1) we see that $D[F(x) + G(x)] = f(x) + g(x)$ implies

$$F(x) + G(x) = \int (f(x) + g(x))\, dx$$

and substituting the values of $F(x)$ and $G(x)$ we finally obtain

$$\int f(x)\, dx + \int g(x)\, dx = \int [f(x) + g(x)]\, dx$$

(ii) Let $H(x) = \int Af(x)\, dx$. Hence, $DH(x) = Af(x)$, so for $A \neq 0$,

$$(1/A)DH(x) = f(x)$$

But $(1/A)DH(x) = D(H(x)/A)$, so we have $D(H(x)/A) = f(x)$. From (3.3.1), we get $H(x)/A = \int f(x)\, dx$, so $H(x) = A \int f(x)\, dx$. Comparing the two equal values of $H(x)$ gives the desired result. The case $A = 0$ is obvious.

In words, Thm. 3.3.2(i) states that the anti-derivative of a sum is the sum of anti-derivatives, and Thm. 3.3.2(ii) says that the anti-derivative of a constant times a function is that constant times the anti-derivative of the function.

Theorem 3.3.2 coupled with Ex. 3.3.4 gives a way to find the anti-derivative of polynomials.

Example 3.3.8. $\int 1\,dx = x + c$ since $D(x + c) = 1$. We let $\int dx = \int 1\,dx$.

Example 3.3.9.

$$\int (3x^7 - 4x^5 + 2x^2 - 7)\,dx = 3\int x^7\,dx - 4\int x^5\,dx + 2\int x^2\,dx - 7\int dx$$

$$= 3(x^8/8) - 4\cdot(x^6/6) + 2(x^3/3) - 7x + c$$

$$= \tfrac{3}{8}x^8 - \tfrac{2}{3}x^6 + \tfrac{2}{3}x^3 - 7x + c$$

Observe that each of the anti-derivatives gave rise to an arbitrary constant, but that all the arbitrary constants have been combined in the single arbitrary constant c.

In §1.3 we established the relationship between distance at time t, $s(t)$, instantaneous velocity at time t, $v(t)$, and instantaneous acceleration at time t, $a(t)$, given by

(1.3.5) $$v(t) = D_t s(t) \quad a(t) = D_t v(t)$$

From (3.3.1) we get the corresponding anti-derivatives

(3.3.4) $$s(t) = \int v(t)\,dt$$

(3.3.5) $$v(t) = \int a(t)\,dt$$

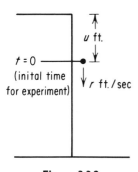

Figure 3.3.2

Example 3.3.10. An early experiment on the effect of gravity on objects falling under free fall indicated that (close to the surface of the earth) all objects, from lead bricks to small pebbles, (ignoring air resistance, etc.) experience the same acceleration. It was measured to be about 32 ft/sec², often abbreviated by the symbol g.

Now suppose an object is dropped off a building so that at time $t = 0$, the object moves r ft/sec and is u units from the top of the building; i.e., $v(0) = r$ and $s(0) = u$ (see Fig. 3.3.2). We shall determine the laws of motion of the object. From (3.3.5), since $a(t) = g$, a *constant*, we have

$$v(t) = \int a(t)\,dt = \int g\,dt$$

From (3.3.3), we have $\int g\,dt = g\int dt$.

From Ex. 3.3.8, $\int dt = \int 1\, dt = t + c$ since $D_t(t + c) = 1$. (Observe that t may systematically replace x used throughout our previous work.) Hence,

$$v(t) = \int g\, dt = g \int dt = gt + k$$

where $k = gc$. Since $v(0) = r$, we have

$$r = v(0) = g \cdot 0 + k = k$$

so $k = r$, the velocity at time $t = 0$. Hence

$$v(t) = gt + r$$

Next from (3.3.4), we have

$$s(t) = \int v(t)\, dt = \int (gt + r)\, dt$$

Using (3.3.3), since g and r are known constants,

$$s(t) = \int (gt + r)\, dt = g \int t\, dt + r \int dt$$
$$= g(t^2/2) + rt + A$$

Since $s(0) = u$, we have $u = s(0) = g \cdot (0^2/2) + r \cdot 0 + A$, so $u = A$. Hence,

$$s(t) = (\tfrac{1}{2})gt^2 + rt + u$$

where $u = s(0)$ and $r = v(0)$.

PROBLEMS

3.3.1. Evaluate each of the following anti-derivatives: (The reader should keep these answers for later use.)

(a) $\displaystyle\int 2x\, dx$ (b) $\displaystyle\int 7\, dx$

(c) $\displaystyle\int (t^3 - 1)\, dt$ (d) $\displaystyle\int (u^{10} - 5u^7 + 4u)\, du$

(e) $\displaystyle\int (x + 1)^2\, dx$ (f) $\displaystyle\int \left(u^{3/2} - \sqrt{u} + \frac{1}{u^{10}}\right) du$

3.3.2. A particle moves in such a way that its acceleration is given by $a(t) = t$. It is also known that $v(1) = 2$ and $s(2) = 4$. Find $v(t)$ and $s(t)$.

3.3.3.
(a) Find the set of functions whose graphs have tangent lines with slope at any x given by $x^{-1/2}$
(b) Find the function whose graph has tangent lines with slope given by $x^{-1/2}$ and which passes through $(1, 0)$.
(c) Find the function whose graph has tangent lines with slope given by $x^{-1/2}$ and passes through $(1, 1)$.
(d) Find the function whose graph has tangent lines with slope $x^{-1/2}$ and passes through $(1, -3)$.
(e) Sketch the graph of the functions of (b), (c), and (d).

3.3.4. Find $f(x)$ if $f'(x) = x^5 - x^{\sqrt{2}} + x^{-3/2} - 5/x^{25}$.

3.3.5. Find each of the six following functions, if the graph of each one is to have a tangent line with slope of $2x - 5$, and the first passes through $(0, 0)$, the second $(1, 1)$, the third through $(0, 1)$, the fourth through $(0, 2)$, the fifth through $(1, 0)$, and the sixth through $(2, 0)$. Sketch their graphs.

3.3.6. Suppose the marginal cost of an item is given by $(x^2 - 1)/x^2$ [see (1.3.3)], and the marginal cost is known to be 1 when 1 unit has been produced. Find the total cost of production.

3.3.7. Find $f(x)$ if $f''(x) = \sqrt{x} + (1/\sqrt{x})$, given that $f'(1) = 2$ and $f(0) = 0$.

3.3.8. Starting from rest, with what constant acceleration must a car proceed to go 360 ft in 6 sec?

3.3.9.
(a) If an object is projected vertically upward, it is clear that for the first moments of flight the velocity is strictly decreasing. What does this imply about the sign of g (the acceleration due to gravity)?
(b) Suppose an object is projected vertically upward from rest with an initial velocity of 16 ft/sec. What is the maximum height attained? When does it reach the ground again?

3.4. The area problem. The definite integral.

Suppose we are given a non-negative function $y = f(x)$ continuous on the closed interval $a \le x \le b$, which means that $f(x)$ is continuous at every point of $a \le x \le b$, with the appropriate definition of continuity at the end points [see §1.7]. We wish to determine the area bounded by the graph of $y = f(x)$, the vertical lines $x = a$ and $x = b$ and the horizontal line $y = 0$ (i.e., the x-axis) (see Fig. 3.4.1). We will sometimes refer to this simply as the area "under $f(x)$ from a to b." The continuity requirement, though not necessary, is sufficient to guarantee that such an area is always meaningful, but we shall not prove this.

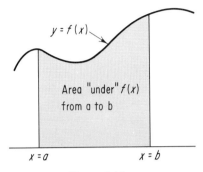

The problem is that in general the curve described by the graph of $f(x)$ is not suited to the methods of plane geometry. Our initial efforts will be to approximate the area under $f(x)$ from a to b by the area of rectangles, using the formula area $= B \cdot H$ where B is the base and H is the height.

Figure 3.4.1

Consider the function $y = f(x)$ graphed in Fig. 3.4.2. We are interested in a first approximation to the area under $f(x)$ from a to b. We proceed as follows. Bisect the interval from a to b. Each subinterval so constructed has length $(b - a)/2$, and the coordinate of the midpoint is $a + (b - a)/2 = (a + b)/2$.

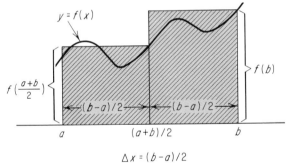

Figure 3.4.2

At the right endpoint of each subinterval, construct a line segment which is perpendicular to the x-axis and which extends from the x-axis to the graph of $y = f(x)$. Consider the two rectangles with equal base $(b - a)/2$ and heights $f([a + b]/2)$ and $f(b)$. The total area of the two rectangles is

$$\frac{(b - a)}{2} f\left(\frac{a + b}{2}\right) + \frac{(b - a)}{2} f(b)$$

An equivalent way to write this area is as

$$f\left(a + \frac{b - a}{2}\right) \cdot \frac{b - a}{2} + f\left(a + 2\frac{b - a}{2}\right) \cdot \frac{b - a}{2}$$

If we abbreviate $(b - a)/2$ by the symbol Δx (read "delta-x"), the sum becomes

$$\sum_{k=1}^{2} f(a + k\,\Delta x) \cdot \Delta x$$

A casual inspection of Fig. 3.4.2 shows that the area of the rectangles so constructed is in general a crude approximation to what one feels is the area under $f(x)$ from a to b.

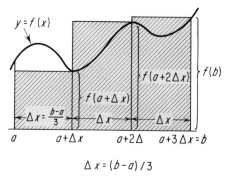

$$\Delta x = (b-a)/3$$

Figure 3.4.3

To improve the estimate, we next trisect the interval from a to b. Call the length of each subinterval so constructed Δx (we still use the symbol Δx to denote the length of a typical subinterval, though its numerical value has changed); then $\Delta x = (b - a)/3$. The x-coordinate of the first trisection point is $a + \Delta x$, the second trisection point is $a + 2\,\Delta x$, and the third and final trisection point is $a + 3\,\Delta x = b$ (see Fig. 3.4.3). At each of these trisection points construct verticals to the graph; the verticals will have values $f(a + \Delta x)$,

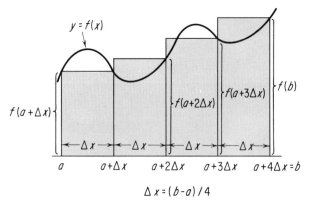

$$\Delta x = (b-a)/4$$

Figure 3.4.4

$f(a + 2\,\Delta x)$, and $f(a + 3\,\Delta x)$, respectively. The sum of the areas of the rectangles is

$$f(a + \Delta x)\,\Delta x + f(a + 2\,\Delta x)\,\Delta x + f(a + 3\,\Delta x)\,\Delta x = \sum_{k=1}^{3} f(a + k\,\Delta x)\cdot\Delta x$$

To continue to refine our estimate, we next subdivide the interval $a \le x \le b$ into four parts, each of length $\Delta x = (b - a)/4$. Then, as in Fig. 3.4.4, consecutive points are labeled $a + \Delta x$, $a + 2\,\Delta x$, $a + 3\,\Delta x$, and $a + 4\,\Delta x$ (we continue our policy of using right endpoints of intervals), and the corresponding heights are $f(a + \Delta x), f(a + 2\,\Delta x), f(a + 3\,\Delta x)$, and $f(a + 4\,\Delta x) = f(b)$. The sum of the areas of the rectangles is now

$$\sum_{k=1}^{4} f(a + k\,\Delta x)\cdot\Delta x$$

As we increase the number of subdivisions, we improve the approximation. Suppose we divide the interval from a to b into N equal parts, each of length $\Delta x = (b - a)/N$. See Fig. 3.4.5. The consecutive x values obtained, still using the right end of each interval, are

$$a + \Delta x, \quad a + 2\,\Delta x, \quad \ldots,$$

$$a + N\,\Delta x = a + N\cdot(b - a)/N = b$$

and the sum of the areas of the rectangles is given by

$$\sum_{k=1}^{N} f(a + k\,\Delta x)\cdot\Delta x$$

Then we *define* the area under $f(x)$ from $x = a$ to $x = b$ to be the limit of this sum as $N \to \infty$. We shall summarize our procedure.

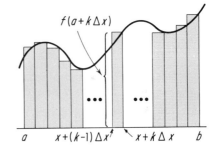

$\Delta x = (b-a)/N$

Figure 3.4.5

Definition 3.4.1. Let $y = f(x)$ be a non-negative continuous function on $a \le x \le b$. Subdivide $a \le x \le b$ into N equal parts, each of length

$$\Delta x = (b - a)/N$$

The *area under $f(x)$ from a to b*, A_a^b is defined to be

(3.4.1)
$$A_a^b = \lim_{N \to \infty} \sum_{k=1}^{N} f(a + k\,\Delta x)\,\Delta x$$

Remark. Since $f(x)$ is continuous on $a \le x \le b$, it can be proved that the limit in (3.4.1) always exists.

Example 3.4.1. We shall use (3.4.1) to find the area of a right triangle of base B and height H. First put the triangle in the xy-plane with its base along the x-axis and its height parallel to the y-axis as in Fig. 3.4.6; the hypotenuse is then the line segment between $(0, 0)$ and (B, H). The *line* passing through $(0, 0)$ and (B, H) has slope $m = H/B$, and hence has equation $y = Hx/B$ [see (1.4.3)]. The problem now can be rephrased as the problem of finding the area under $f(x) = Hx/B$ from $x = 0$ to $x = B$ (see Fig. 3.4.6).

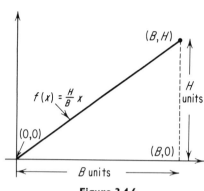

Figure 3.4.6

In terms of notation from Def. 3.4.1, $a = 0$ and $b = B$, so

$$\Delta x = (B - 0)/N = B/N$$

Also,

$$f(a + k\,\Delta x) = f(k\,\Delta x) = \frac{H}{B}\,k\,\Delta x = \frac{Hk}{N}$$

so (3.4.1) becomes

$$\sum_{k=1}^{N} \frac{Hk}{N} \cdot \frac{B}{N} = \sum_{k=1}^{N} \frac{HB}{N^2} \cdot k$$

Since HB/N^2 does not involve k, it can be considered constant with respect to k, so by (3.1.3) it follows that

$$\sum_{k=1}^{N} \frac{HB}{N^2}\,k = \frac{HB}{N^2}\sum_{k=1}^{N} k$$

From (3.1.5) we have that

$$\frac{HB}{N^2}\sum_{k=1}^{N} k = \frac{HB}{N^2} \cdot \frac{N(N+1)}{2} = \frac{HB}{2}\cdot\frac{N}{N}\cdot\frac{N+1}{N} = \frac{HB}{2}\left(1 + \frac{1}{N}\right)$$

From (3.4.1), the area is given by

$$\lim_{N \to \infty} \frac{HB}{2}\left(1 + \frac{1}{N}\right) = \frac{HB}{2}$$

which is precisely what we would expect from plane geometry.

If $f(x)$ is continuous, it turns out that the limit on the right side of (3.4.1) exists even if $f(x)$ is negative for some values of x. Of course what we have asserted is a theorem, but we shall not prove it. We use it to define

Definition 3.4.2. The **DEFINITE INTEGRAL** *from* $x = a$ *to* $x = b$, symbolically

$$\int_a^b f(x)\,dx \quad \text{or} \quad \int_a^b f$$

is defined for continuous $f(x)$ as

(3.4.2)
$$\int_a^b f = \lim_{N \to \infty} \sum_{k=1}^N f(a + k\,\Delta x)\,\Delta x$$

where $\Delta x = (b - a)/N$.

Remarks.

(1) The limit in (3.4.2) exists if $f(x)$ is continuous in $a \le x \le b$.

(2) The symbol used in (3.4.2) very closely resembles the symbol $\int f(x)\,dx$ used for anti-derivatives [see (3.3.1)]. However, *the concepts they represent are completely distinct.* The definite integral is the limit of a sum, whereas the anti-derivative is related to a derivative. The student should make a determined effort to separate the concepts represented by these symbols. An amazing fact is that these two conceptually distinct ideas are related by a theorem which we shall see later.

(3) If $f(x) \ge 0$ on $a \le x \le b$, then $\int_a^b f = A_a^b$.

(4) $\int_a^b f$ is a *real number*; if $f \ge 0$, then $\int_a^b f$ is the *real number* identified as the *area* under f from a to b.

(5) Definition 3.4.2 is not the most general definition of the definite integral, but it is completely adequate for continuous functions. Because different forms of the definite integral are used, we shall outline a more general definition in the next section.

Example 3.4.2.

$$\int_0^B \frac{H}{B} x\,dx = \frac{1}{2} HB$$

as we determined in Ex. 3.4.1.

Example 3.4.3. Evaluate $\int_0^1 (x + 1)\, dx$. Appealing to (3.4.2) above with $a = 0$, $b = 1$, we see that

$$f(x) = x + 1, \quad \Delta x = 1/N, \quad f(a + k\,\Delta x) = f(k/N) = (k/N) + 1$$

and

$$\int_0^1 (x + 1)\, dx = \lim_{N \to \infty} \sum_{k=1}^{N} \left[\frac{k}{N} + 1 \right] \frac{1}{N}$$

$$= \lim_{N \to \infty} \sum_{k=1}^{N} \left(\frac{k}{N^2} + \frac{1}{N} \right) = \lim_{N \to \infty} \left\{ \sum_{k=1}^{N} \frac{k}{N^2} + \sum_{k=1}^{N} \frac{1}{N} \right\}$$

$$= \lim_{N \to \infty} \left(\frac{1}{N^2} \sum_{k=1}^{N} k + \frac{1}{N} \sum_{k=1}^{N} 1 \right)$$

$$= \lim_{N \to \infty} \left(\frac{N(N + 1)}{2N^2} + 1 \right) = \lim_{N \to \infty} \left\{ \left[\frac{1}{2} \cdot \frac{N}{N} \cdot \frac{N + 1}{N} \right] + 1 \right\}$$

$$= \tfrac{1}{2} + 1 = \tfrac{3}{2}$$

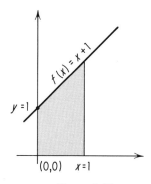

Figure 3.4.7

(Keep in mind that $1/N$ and $1/N^2$ do not depend on k, and so (3.1.3) applies.)

The value of this definite integral can of course be interpreted geometrically as the area under $f(x) = x + 1$ from $x = 0$ to $x = 1$ (see Fig. 3.4.7).

Example 3.4.4. We next evaluate $\int_0^2 (-x)\, dx$.

In this example, $a = 0$, $b = 2$, and $f(x) = -x$. Observe $f(x) \leq 0$ in $0 \leq x \leq 2$, so we are not dealing with an area problem. Again using (3.4.2), with $\Delta x = 2/N$,

$$f(a + k\,\Delta x) = f(2k/N) = -2k/N$$

$$\int_0^2 (-x)\, dx = \lim_{N \to \infty} \sum_{k=1}^{N} -\frac{2k}{N} \cdot \frac{2}{N} = \lim_{N \to \infty} \frac{-4}{N^2} \sum_{k=1}^{N} k$$

$$= \lim_{N \to \infty} -2 \cdot \frac{N}{N} \cdot \frac{N + 1}{N} = -2$$

If we plot graph of the function $f(x) = -x$ for $0 \leq x \leq 2$, as in Fig. 3.4.8, we see that the region bounded by the graphs of $x = 0$, $x = 2$, and $f(x) = -x$ is a right triangle with area $\frac{1}{2}BH$. Taking $H = y = -2$ units, then "area" is $(\frac{1}{2}) \cdot 2 \cdot (-2) = -2$ "square units." This of course is *not* the usual way we

think of area; our usual idea of area *requires* that $A \geq 0$. So, $\int_0^2 (-x)\,dx$
does not give us the usual area. It should be clear that the area of the region
is 2 square units.

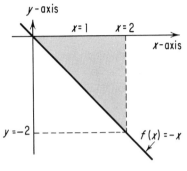

Figure 3.4.8

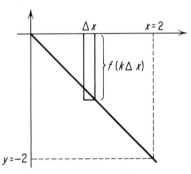

Figure 3.4.9

In Ex. 3.4.4, suppose we wanted to get the area in the usual sense (i.e., a
positive area) of the region bounded by the graphs of $f(x) = -x$, $x = 0$, and
$x = 2$. Since the base is positive (2 units), we would take $\frac{1}{2}B|H|$; i.e.,

$$\tfrac{1}{2} \cdot (2) \cdot |-2| = 2 \text{ square units}$$

If we look at the kth subinterval obtained by dividing the interval $0 \leq x \leq 2$
into N equal parts, and construct the rectangle whose area appears as the kth
summand in (3.4.1), the rectangle will have base $\Delta x = 2/N$ and height
$f(k\,\Delta x) = -2k/N$ (see Fig. 3.4.9). To make everything *positive*, we take
as the *area* of this rectangle

$$A = \text{base} \times |\text{height}| = |f(k\,\Delta x)| \cdot \Delta x = \left| \frac{-2K}{N} \right| \cdot \frac{2}{N} = \frac{4k}{N^2}$$

Our limit then looks like

$$\lim_{N \to \infty} \sum_{k=1}^{N} \left| \frac{-2k}{N} \right| \cdot \frac{2}{N} = \lim_{N \to \infty} \frac{4}{N^2} \sum_{k=1}^{N} k = +2$$

This leads us to define

Definition 3.4.3. If $f(x)$ is any continuous function on $a \leq x \leq b$, then the
area bounded by the graphs of $y = f(x)$, the x-axis and the lines $x = a$ and
$x = b$ is given by

(3.4.3)

$$A_a^b = \int_a^b |f(x)|\,dx$$

Remark. If $f(x) \geq 0$, then $|f(x)| = f(x)$, and the area is given by

$$\int_a^b f(x)\, dx$$

both in terms of (3.4.3) and remark (3) following Def. 3.4.2.

Example 3.4.5. Evaluate $\int_{-2}^{2} (-x)\, dx$; then find the *area* bounded by the graphs of the x-axis, the graph of $f(x) = -x$ and the lines $x = 2$ and $x = -2$.

To evaluate $\int_{-2}^{2} (-x)\, dx$, we use (3.4.2) with $a = -2$, $b = 2$,

$$\Delta x = [2 - (-2)]/N = 4/N, \quad f(x) = -x$$

$$f(a + k\, \Delta x) = f(-2 + [4k/N]) = -2 + (4k/N)$$

Hence,

$$\int_{-2}^{2} (-x)\, dx = \lim_{N \to \infty} \sum_{k=1}^{N} \left(-2 + \frac{4k}{N}\right) \cdot \frac{4}{N}$$

$$= \lim_{N \to \infty} \sum_{k=1}^{N} (-8/N + 16k/N)$$

$$= \lim_{N \to \infty} \left[(-8\backslash N) \sum_{k=1}^{N} 1 + (16/N^2) \sum_{k=1}^{N} k\right]$$

$$= \lim_{N \to \infty} (-8 + [16N(N + 1)/2]) = 8 - 8 = 0$$

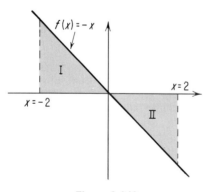

Figure 3.4.10

Let us try to interpret this result geometrically. From Fig. 3.4.10, we see that the region bounded by the graphs of $f(x) = -x$, the x-axis and the lines $x = -2$ and $x = 2$ consists of two right triangles, labeled I and II. Triangles I and II are equal in area (area is positive of course), but their numerical contributions are opposite in sign (see Ex. 3.4.4), and hence there is a net effect of 0 when we add.

Next we find the area bounded by the graphs of $f(x) = -x$, the x-axis, and the lines $x = -2$, $x = +2$. This, of course, is just the area of triangles I and II. Again from Ex. 3.4.4 we expect each area to be 2, so the total area to be 4. We proceed analytically by using (3.4.3).

The desired area is given by $\int_{-2}^{2} |-x| \, dx$. In the interval $-2 \le x \le 0$, $f(x) = -x \ge 0$ (see Fig. 3.4.10), so $|f(x)| = |-x| = -x$. But in the interval $0 \le x \le 2$, $f(x) = -x \le 0$, so $|f(x)| = |-x| = x$. We have graphed $|f(x)| = |-x|$ in Fig. 3.4.11. Now

$$\int_{-2}^{2} |-x| \, dx =$$

$$\int_{-2}^{0} (-x) \, dx + \int_{0}^{2} x \, dx$$

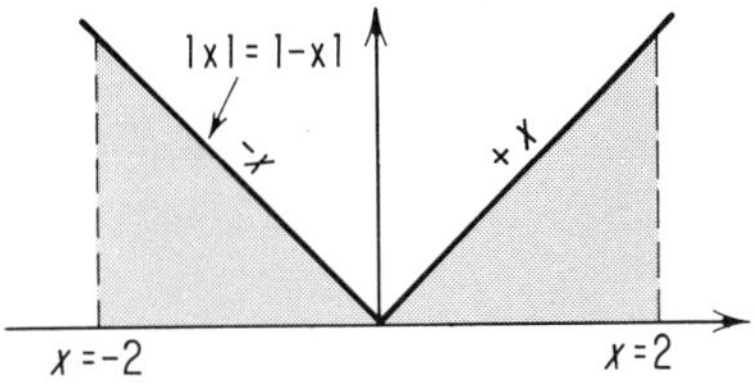

We leave it as an exercise at the end of this section to verify that

Figure 3.4.11

$$\int_{-2}^{0} (-x) \, dx = \int_{0}^{2} x \, dx = 2$$

We conclude this section with an important theorem on the definite integral.

Theorem 3.4.1. Let $f(x)$ and $g(x)$ be continuous on the closed interval $a \le x \le b$. Let A be any real number. Let c be any real number between a and b; i.e., $a < c < b$. Then $Af(x)$ and $f(x) + g(x)$ are continuous on $a \le x \le b$ (see Thm. 1.7.1) and

(i) $$\int_{a}^{b} [f(x) + g(x)] \, dx = \int_{a}^{b} f(x) \, dx + \int_{a}^{b} g(x) \, dx$$

i.e., the definite integral of a sum is the sum of definite integrals;

(ii) $$\int_{a}^{b} Af(x) \, dx = A \int_{a}^{b} f(x) \, dx$$

i.e., a *constant* can be removed from the integral sign:

(iii) $$\int_{a}^{b} f(x) \, dx = \int_{a}^{c} f(x) \, dx + \int_{c}^{b} f(x) \, dx$$

Proof. To prove (i), set $F(x) = f(x) + g(x)$, so $\int_{a}^{b} F = \int_{a}^{b} (f + g)$ (recall that $\int_{a}^{b} F = \int_{a}^{b} F(x) \, dx$). Observe that

$$F(a + k \, \Delta x) = f(a + k \, \Delta x) + g(a + k \, \Delta x)$$

so, by (3.4.2)

$$\int_a^b (f + g) = \int_a^b F = \lim_{N \to \infty} \sum_{k=1}^{N} F(a + k\, \Delta x)\, \Delta x$$

$$= \lim_{N \to \infty} \sum_{k=1}^{N} \{f(a + k\, \Delta x) + g(a + k\, \Delta x)\}\, \Delta x$$

$$= \lim_{N \to \infty} \sum_{k=1}^{N} \{f(a + k\, \Delta x)\, \Delta x + g(a + k\, \Delta x)\, \Delta x\}$$

$$= \lim_{N \to \infty} \left[\sum_{k=1}^{N} f(a + k\, \Delta x)\, \Delta x + \sum_{k=1}^{N} g(a + k\, \Delta x)\, \Delta x \right]$$

[by (3.1.2)]

$$= \lim_{N \to \infty} \sum_{k=1}^{N} f(a + k\, \Delta x)\, \Delta x + \lim_{N \to \infty} \sum_{k=1}^{N} g(a + k\, \Delta x)\, \Delta x$$

(see Thm. 3.2.1)

$$= \int_a^b f + \int_a^b g$$

(ii) Write $G(x) = Af(x)$, so, $\displaystyle\int_a^b G = \int_a^b A \cdot f$, and observe

$$G(a + k\Delta x) = A \cdot f(a + k\, \Delta x)$$

Hence, by (3.4.2)

$$\int_a^b A \cdot f = \int_a^b G = \lim_{N \to \infty} \sum_{k=1}^{N} G(a + k\, \Delta x)\, \Delta x$$

$$= \lim_{N \to \infty} \sum_{k=1}^{N} Af(a + k\, \Delta x)\, \Delta x$$

$$= \lim_{N \to \infty} A \sum_{k=1}^{N} f(a + k\, \Delta x)\, \Delta x \qquad \text{[by (3.1.3)]}$$

$$= A \int_a^b f$$

(iii) We shall not give a formal proof of (iii), but merely observe that geometrically it states that for $f(x) > 0$, the total area is the sum of its parts. See Fig. 3.4.12.

For the sake of completeness, we add the following useful definition:

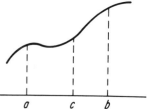

Figure 3.4.12

Definition 3.4.4. (i) If $a \neq b$, then $\displaystyle\int_a^b f = -\int_b^a f$. (ii) $\displaystyle\int_a^a f = 0$.

The reader should observe that we could have defined $\int_a^b f = -\int_b^a f$ for any a and b; then by setting $a = b$, we would have $\int_a^a f = -\int_a^a f$. But the only number A with the property that $A = -A$ is 0; hence, we would conclude that $\int_a^a f = 0$, which is consistent with our definitions.

Example 3.4.6.

(i) $$\int_{-2}^2 -10x \, dx = -10 \int_{-2}^2 x \, dx = 0$$

(See Ex. 3.4.5.)

(ii) From Ex. 3.4.4, $\int_0^2 (-x) \, dx = -2$. But

$$\int_0^2 (-x) \, dx = -\int_0^2 x \, dx$$

so

$$-\int_0^2 x \, dx = -2 \quad \text{implies} \quad \int_0^2 x \, dx = 2$$

(iii) In Ex. 3.4.2,

$$\int_0^B \frac{Hx}{B} \, dx = \tfrac{1}{2}HB$$

Multiply both sides by B/H to get:

$$\frac{B}{H} \int_0^B \frac{H}{B} x \, dx = \tfrac{1}{2}HB \cdot \frac{B}{H} = \tfrac{1}{2}B^2$$

But by Thm. 3.4.1(ii),

$$\frac{B}{H} \int_0^B \frac{H}{B} x \, dx = \int_0^B \frac{B}{H} \cdot \frac{H}{B} x \, dx = \int_0^B x \, dx$$

Hence, $\int_0^B x \, dx = (\tfrac{1}{2})B^2$ for *any* B. In particular, $\int_0^2 x \, dx = (\tfrac{1}{2}) \cdot 4 = 2$, as was observed in part (ii) of this example.

PROBLEMS

3.4.1. Use (3.4.2) to show that

$$\int_{-2}^0 (-x) \, dx = \int_0^2 x \, dx = 2$$

3.4.2. Use (3.4.2) to evaluate

$$\int_0^T x^2 \, dx, \quad \int_a^b 1 \, dx \quad (T, a, \text{ and } b \text{ constants}) \quad \text{and} \quad \int_0^2 (2x^2 + x - 1) \, dx$$

3.4.3. Evaluate

$$\int_{-1}^1 x^3 \, dx \quad \text{and} \quad \int_0^1 x^3 \, dx$$

(see Ex. 3.1.3). Then find the area bounded by the graphs of $f(x) = x^3$, the x-axis, and the lines $x = -1$ and $x = 1$.

3.4.4. Find the area bounded by the graphs of $f(x) = x$, the x-axis and the lines $x = 2$ and $x = -2$. Compare this with $\int_{-2}^2 x \, dx$. Then compare all these results with Ex. 3.4.5.

3.4.5. Given that

$$\int_0^1 x^5 \, dx = \tfrac{1}{6} \quad \text{and} \quad \int_0^1 x^6 \, dx = \tfrac{1}{7}$$

find

(i) $$\int_0^1 \{24x^5 - 49x^6\} \, dx$$

(ii) $$\int_1^0 \{30x^5 + 7x^6\} \, dx$$

3.4.6. Find the area of the region bounded by the x-axis, the y-axis, and the line $x + y = 1$.

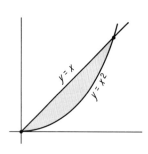

3.4.7. Find the area of the region bounded by the curve given by $y = 4 - x^2$ and the x-axis. Then find the area of the region bounded by the curve given by $y = x^2 - 4$ and the x-axis. Explain the similarity.

3.4.8. Find the area bounded by the curves given by $y = x$ and $y = x^2$. See Fig. 3.4.13.

3.4.9. Find the area bounded by the graphs of $f(x) = x^2 - 1$, the x-axis, and the lines $x = -1$ and $x = 2$. Then find $\int_{-1}^2 (x^2 - 1) \, dx$.

Figure 3.4.13

3.4.10. Find the area enclosed by the graphs of $y = 2x^3$ and $y = 8x$.

3.5. The definite integral. A more general form.

We have already remarked that the integral in (3.4.2) of §3.4 is completely adequate for continuous functions, but it is not the most general definition of the definite integral. We present a more general definition in this section, but first, we need the following definition.

Definition 3.5.1. A function $f(x)$ is *bounded on a set* (of numbers) S if there is a positive constant A such that $|f(x)| < A$ for every x in S.

We can rephrase this definition in two ways: $f(x)$ is bounded on S if (1) there is a constant $A > 0$ such that the graph of $f(x)$ lies entirely between two lines, $y = A$ and $y = -A$ for every x in S, or (2) there is a constant $A > 0$ such that $-A < f(x) < A$ for every x in the set S. In Fig. 3.5.1, the set S is the interval $a \le x \le b$.

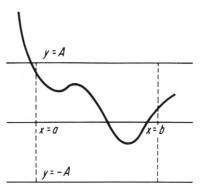

Figure 3.5.1

Example 3.5.1. In Ex. 2.4.1, page 81, the function $f(x)$ is *not* bounded on the set $0 \quad x \quad 1$, since the range of $f(x)$ is the set $y \quad 0$ and $y \quad 1$ (i.e., no matter what "horizontal" line $y \quad A$ is drawn in Fig. 2.4.2, there are points of the graph "above" the line). On the other hand, the function $g(x)$ defined in Ex. 2.4.2 is bounded on the set $0 \le x \le 1$, and, in fact, $-2 < g(x) < 2$ (we are required to exhibit at least *one* $A > 0$ such that $-A < g(x) < A$, and $A = 2$ is such a possible choice). Neither of the functions in Ex. 2.4.3 or Ex. 2.4.4 are bounded on their domains, whereas the reader should convince himself that the functions in Ex. 2.4.5 and Ex. 2.4.6 are bounded on their respective domains. A consequence of Thm. 1.7.4 is that a function that is defined and continuous on a closed interval I is bounded on that interval I, but a function which is not continuous can be bounded (e.g., see Ex. 2.4.2).

We turn now to the construction of the integral. Let $y = f(x)$ be any function defined and bounded on a closed interval $a \le x \le b$. Subdivide the interval $a \le x \le b$ into n not necessarily equal subdivisions. Let the corresponding points on the x-axis be $a = x_0 < x_1 < \cdots < x_n = b$. Let Δx_i denote the length of the ith subinterval; i.e.,

$$\Delta x_1 = x_1 - x_0 = x_1 - a, \quad \Delta x_2 = x_2 - x_1$$

and in general, $\Delta x_k = x_k - x_{k-1}$ for $k = 1, 2, ..., n$. In Fig. 3.5.2, $n = 6$. Call δ the largest of the numbers $\Delta x_1, \Delta x_2, ..., \Delta x_n$.

Next pick an *arbitrary* point x_1' in the first subinterval, and an *arbitrary* point x_2' in the second subinterval, and so on, so that in the kth subinterval we pick the *arbitrary* point x_k'. In Fig. 3.5.2 we indicate one such possible choice for the x_1', x_2', ..., x_n'. Of course the values x_k', where $k = 1, 2, ..., n$, need not be endpoints. We next evaluate f at each x_i', where $i = 1, ..., n$, and obtain products of the form $f(x_1') \Delta x_1$, $f(x_2') \Delta x_2$, ... If $f > 0$, then each $f(x_i') \Delta x_i$ is simply the area of a rectangle.

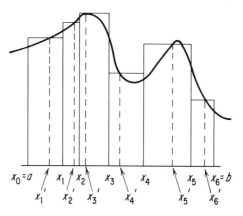

Figure 3.5.2

In Fig. 3.5.2, we picture an f for which $f > 0$. In general, some of these rectangles will appear *below* the x-axis, as in Fig. 3.5.3. Next form the sums

$$\sum_{k=1}^{N} f(x_k') \Delta x_k$$

In Fig. 3.5.2, we see that this is some approximation to an area, but in Fig. 3.5.3 we are not dealing with an area problem. In any event we investigate

$$(3.5.1) \qquad \lim_{\substack{N \to \infty \\ \delta \to 0}} \sum_{k=1}^{N} f(x_k') \Delta x_k$$

We define

Definition 3.5.2. If (3.5.1) exists and has a unique value I for every possible choice of subdivisions of $a \le x \le b$ (and every resulting choice of Δx_k) and for every possible choice of x_k' (arbitrarily chosen in the kth subinterval), then we say that $\int_a^b f(x)\, dx$ exists, and equals I.

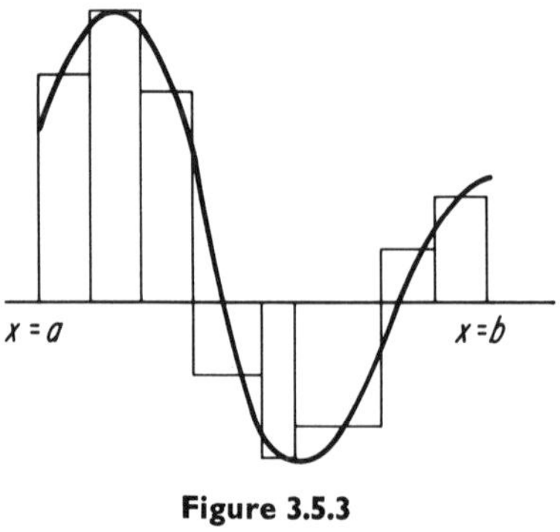

Figure 3.5.3

Observe that Def. 3.5.2 does *not* require that $f(x)$ be continuous on $a \le x \le b$. The most general conditions under which the definite integral exists are far beyond the scope of this book. The interested reader might consult Taylor, *Advanced Calculus*,[*] Chapter 16, especially §16.11 and §16.12. We assert the following theorem without proof.

Theorem 3.5.1. If $f(x)$ is continuous on $a \le x \le b$, then $\displaystyle\int_a^b f(x)\,dx$ exists (in the sense of Def. 3.5.2).

Since, with $f(x)$ continuous on $a \le x \le b$, (3.5.1) exists for *any* subdivision, it certainly exists *a fortiori* if we choose the subdivisions of equal size with

$$\Delta x_k = \Delta x = \frac{b-a}{N}$$

(i.e., all the Δx_k's equal), and if we pick $x_k' = a + k\,\Delta x$. Hence we have Def. 3.4.2 for *continuous* functions.

In fact, it is not necessary that $f(x)$ be continuous in the entire closed interval $a \le x \le b$. An interesting result (which we shall not prove) is

Theorem 3.5.2. If $f(x)$ is defined and bounded and has at most a finite number of discontinuities on the interval $a \le x \le b$, then $\displaystyle\int_a^b f$ exists in the sense of Def. 3.5.2.

More will be said of this later.

PROBLEMS

3.5.1. In evaluating the definite integral of a continuous function, we could use the left endpoint of each interval and obtain, using subintervals of equal length,

$$\int_a^b f = \lim_{N \to \infty} \sum_{k=1}^N f(a + (k-1)\,\Delta x)\,\Delta x$$

Use this form to find $\displaystyle\int_0^T x^2\,dx$ and compare this with Prob. 3.4.2.

3.5.2. Let $f(x)$ be continuous on $a \le x \le b$. If we subdivide $a \le x \le b$ into N equal parts, $a = x_0 < x_1 < x_2 < \cdots < x_N = b$, we could use the midpoint of each subinterval to evaluate $\displaystyle\int_a^b f$, as in Fig. 3.5.4.

(a) Verify that the midpoint of the kth subinterval is given by $(\frac{1}{2})(x_k + x_{k-1})$.

---

[*] See the bibliography.

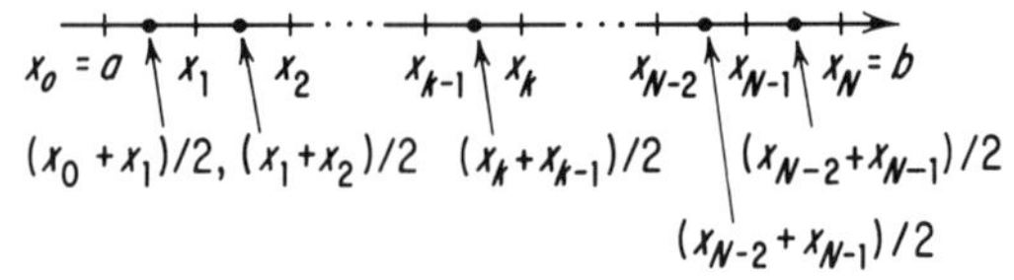

$$x_0 = a \quad x_1 \quad x_2 \qquad x_{k-1} \quad x_k \qquad x_{N-2} \quad x_{N-1} \quad x_N = b$$

$$(x_0 + x_1)/2, \ (x_1 + x_2)/2 \quad (x_k + x_{k-1})/2 \quad (x_{N-2} + x_{N-1})/2$$

$$(x_{N-2} + x_{N-1})/2$$

Figure 3.5.4

(b) Verify that

$$x_k = a + k \, \Delta x \quad \text{and} \quad x_{k-1} = a + (k-1) \, \Delta x$$

where $k = 1, 2, 3, \ldots, N$, with $\Delta x = (b - a)/N$.

(c) Verify that (3.5.1) with $x_k' = (\tfrac{1}{2})(x_k + x_{k-1})$ becomes

$$\int_a^b f = \lim_{N \to \infty} \sum_{k=1}^{N} f\left(a + \frac{2k-1}{2} \, \Delta x\right) \Delta x$$

where, as always $\Delta x = (b - a)/N$.

(d) Use the form of $\displaystyle\int_a^b f$ given in (c) to find

$$\int_0^1 x^2 \, dx$$

3.5.3. Let $f(x)$ be continuous on $a \leq x \leq b$. Divide the interval $a \leq x \leq b$ into N equal parts by $a = x_0 < x_1 < x_2 < \cdots < x_N = b$. Trisect the kth sub-interval, and choose x_k' as the first trisection point, measuring from the left endpoint of the subinterval. Write the appropriate form of (3.5.1), and use it to evaluate $\displaystyle\int_0^1 x \, dx$.

3.5.4. Verify that the functions in Ex. 2.4.5 and Ex. 2.4.6 are bounded on their domains, whereas the functions in Ex. 2.4.3 and Ex. 2.4.4 are not.

3.6. The fundamental theorem of calculus.

The reader has no doubt already observed that evaluating

$$\int_0^1 \left\{ x^{17} - 3x^5 + \frac{1}{(x-5)^2} + \sqrt{x} \right\} dx$$

using (3.4.2) is arduous; if you don't believe it, write down the limit of the sum in (3.4.2). But the function $x^{17} - 3x^5 + (x-5)^{-2} + \sqrt{x}$ is continuous on $0 \leq x \leq 1$, so the integral exists. What we need is a theorem to simplify our calculations.

Let $f(x)$ be continuous on $a \leq x \leq b$. Define

(3.6.1)
$$F(x) = \int_a^x f$$

where x is a number in the interval $[a, b]$. What we are doing is to let the upper limit of integration vary over $a \leq x \leq b$. If $f(x) > 0$, then $F(c)$ is just the area under $f(x)$ from $x = a$ to $x = c$; $F(d)$ is the area under $f(x)$ from $x = a$ to $x = d$; and $F(b)$ is the area under $f(x)$ from $x = a$ to $x = b$ (see Fig. 3.6.1). Also, if $f \geq 0$, then $F(c + h) - F(c)$, $h > 0$, is the area under $f(x)$ between $x = c$ and $x = c + h$, and hence, by (3.4.3), can be written as

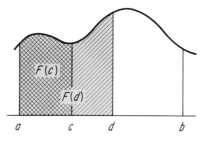

Figure 3.6.1

(3.6.2)
$$F(c + h) - F(c) = \int_c^{c+h} f$$

We assume $c \neq a$, $c \neq b$, and $h \neq 0$, with h so small that $a \leq c + h \leq b$. If $c = a$ (or $c = b$, respectively), we shall choose $h > 0$ (or $h < 0$, respectively) but so small that $a \leq c + h \leq b$.

But even if $f(x)$ is *not* always positive on $a \leq x \leq b$, $F(x) = \int_a^x f$ is still meaningful, but of course the arguments used above would have to be modified. Using Thm. 3.4.1(iii), we have for $h \neq 0$:

$$\int_c^{c+h} f = \int_a^{c+h} f - \int_a^c f = F(c + h) - F(c)$$

which is exactly (3.6.2).

We next investigate $\int_c^{c+h} f$. First we consider $h > 0$. We divide the interval $c \leq x \leq c + h$ into N equal parts by $c = x_0 < x_1 < x_2 < \cdots < x_N = c + h$, each of length

$$\Delta x = \frac{(c + h) - c}{N} = \frac{h}{N}$$

Let I_1 be the first closed interval (i.e., I_1 is the set of all x such that $x_0 \leq x \leq x_1$); let I_2 be the second closed subinterval (i.e., I_2 is the set of all x such that $x_1 \leq x \leq x_2$; x_1 is in both I_1 and I_2, but there is no harm in this); in general, let I_k be the kth closed interval (i.e., I_k is the set of all x such that

$$x_{k-1} \leq x \leq x_k)$$

Since $c \le x \le c + h$ (with $h > 0$) is closed, and $f(x)$ is continuous on $a \le x \le b$ and hence on the smaller interval $c \le x \le c + h$, we can apply Thm.

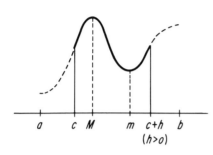

1.7.4 to assert the existence of numbers M and m in the interval $c \le x \le c + h$ such that $f(M)$ is the maximum value of $f(x)$ on $c \le x \le c + h$ and $f(m)$ is the minimum value of $f(x)$ on $c \le x \le c + h$ (see Fig. 3.6.2). As h becomes smaller, the interval $c \le x \le c + h$ becomes smaller. Moreover, the right endpoint $c + h$ tends to the left endpoint c as $h \to 0$. But $c \le M \le c + h$, and $c \le m \le c + h$, and hence $M \to c$

Figure 3.6.2

as $h \to 0$, and $m \to c$ as $h \to 0$, if $h > 0$.

A similar argument can be applied to the case $h < 0$. Combining the cases $h > 0$ and $h < 0$, and since f is continuous, we have

Lemma 1. $\lim\limits_{h \to 0} f(M) = f(c)$ and $\lim\limits_{h \to 0} f(m) = f(c)$.

Remark. If $c = a$ or $c = b$, the limits in the above lemma are taken in the sense of Def. 1.5.2.

We shall also need the following lemma which we shall not prove.

Lemma 2. If three functions f, g, and h are defined in some open interval I containing a point c, if $f(x) \le g(x) \le h(x)$ for all x in I, and if $\lim\limits_{x \to c} f(x) = \lim\limits_{x \to c} h(x) = A$, then $\lim\limits_{x \to c} g(x)$ exists and has value A.

The proof requires the ε–δ definition of limit found in §1.6.

Again we shall begin by assuming $h > 0$ (though everything we say will also be true for $h < 0$). In I_k, the contribution to (3.4.2) toward finding $\int_{c}^{c+h} f$ will be $f(c + k \, \Delta x) \, \Delta x$, where $\Delta x = (c + h - c)/N = h/N > 0$. By the way M and m are defined, we have

$$f(m) \le f(c + k \, \Delta x) \le f(M)$$

and hence

$$f(m) \, \Delta x \le f(c + k \, \Delta x) \, \Delta x \le f(M) \, \Delta x$$

$$\sum_{k=1}^{N} f(m) \, \Delta x \le \sum_{k=1}^{N} f(c + k \, \Delta x) \, \Delta x \le \sum_{k=1}^{N} f(M) \, \Delta x$$

Since $f(m)$, $f(M)$ and $\Delta x = h/N$ are constant with respect to k, we use (3.1.3) to obtain

$$\frac{h}{N} f(m) \sum_{k=1}^{N} 1 \leq \sum_{k=1}^{N} f(c + k\,\Delta x)\,\Delta x \leq \frac{h}{N} f(M) \sum_{k=1}^{N} 1$$

Since

$$\sum_{k=1}^{N} 1 = N$$

then

$$f(m) \cdot h \leq \sum_{k=1}^{N} f(c + k\,\Delta x)\,\Delta x \leq f(M)h$$

so

$$f(m) \leq \frac{1}{h} \sum_{k=1}^{N} f(c + k\,\Delta x)\,\Delta x \leq f(M)$$

As $N \to \infty$, we have

$$f(m) \leq \frac{1}{h} \int_{c}^{c+h} f \leq f(M)$$

or

(3.6.2) $$f(m) \leq \frac{F(c + h) - F(c)}{h} \leq f(M)$$

The inequality (3.6.2) is the same if $h < 0$. The details are completely analogous and are left to the reader. Hence, as $h \to 0$ in (3.6.2) using the lemmas above (and Def. 1.5.5 if $c = a$ or $c = b$) we obtain $F'(c)$ exists and $f(c) \leq F'(c) \leq f(c)$, and hence $F'(c) = f(c)$, where c was arbitrarily chosen, $a \leq c \leq b$. Replacing c by x, we have

Theorem 3.6.1. Let $f(x)$ be continuous in $a \leq x \leq b$, and define $F(x) = \int_{a}^{x} f$. Then, $F'(x) = f(x)$.

Theorem 3.6.1 tells us that the function $F(x)$ defined by $\int_{a}^{x} f$ is *an anti-derivative of* $f(x)$. Unfortunately, we do not know *which* anti-derivative. We next remedy this situation.

Let $G(x)$ be *any known* anti-derivative of $f(x)$. How does $G(x)$ relate to $F(x)$? By (3.3.2) there must exist a constant K such that $F(x) = G(x) + K$. By Def. 3.4.4, $F(a) = \int_{a}^{a} f = 0$. Hence, $0 = F(a) = G(a) + K$, or, $K = -G(a)$. Therefore,

$$G(x) - G(a) = F(x) = \int_{a}^{x} f$$

and so

$$G(b) - G(a) = \int_a^b f$$

If we define

(3.6.3)
$$G(x) \Big]_a^b = G(b) - G(a)$$

we can summarize our results in the following remarkable theorem.

Theorem 3.6.2 (The Fundamental Theorem of Calculus). Let $f(x)$ be continuous on $a \le x \le b$. Then

(3.6.4)
$$\int_a^b f = \int_a^b f(x)\,dx = G(x)\Big]_a^b$$

where $G(x)$ defined on $a \le x \le b$ is any anti-derivative of $f(x)$; i.e., where $G(x)$ is any function such that $G'(x) = f(x)$ on $a \le x \le b$.

If we think of $\int f(x)\,dx$ as *any anti-derivative* or the most general, we can write (3.6.4) as

(3.6.5)
$$\int_a^b f(x)\,dx = \int f(x)\,dx \Big]_a^b$$

We now show the power of this theorem.

Example 3.6.1. We evaluate

$$\int_0^B \frac{Hx}{B}\,dx$$

From Thm. 3.4.1, we write this first as

$$\frac{H}{B}\int_0^B x\,dx$$

Now

$$\int_0^B x\,dx = \int x\,dx \Big]_0^B = \frac{x^2}{2}\Big]_0^B$$

$$= \frac{B^2}{2} - \frac{0^2}{2} = \frac{B^2}{2}$$

and hence

$$\frac{H}{B}\int_0^B x\,dx = \frac{H}{B}\frac{B^2}{2} = \tfrac{1}{2}HB$$

Compare this with Ex. 3.4.1.

Example 3.6.2. Evaluate $\int_0^1 (x + 1)\, dx$. By the fundamental theorem,

$$\int_0^1 (x + 1)\, dx = \int (x + 1)\, dx \Bigg]_0^1$$

Clearly,

$$\int (x + 1)\, dx = \int x\, dx + \int dx = \tfrac{1}{2}x^2 + x$$

and hence

$$\int_0^1 (x + 1)\, dx = (\tfrac{1}{2}x^2 + x) \Bigg]_0^1 = (\tfrac{1}{2} + 1) - \left(\frac{0^2}{2} + 0\right) = \tfrac{3}{2}$$

Compare this with Ex. 3.4.3.

Suppose in Ex. 3.6.2 we had used a different anti-derivative for $x + 1$; e.g., suppose we had written $\int (x + 1)\, dx = \tfrac{1}{2}x^2 + x + c$ where c is some constant that we can choose to suit ourselves. We would then obtain

$$\int_0^1 (x + 1)\, dx = \tfrac{1}{2}x^2 + x + c \Bigg]_0^1 = (\tfrac{1}{2} + 1 + c) - \left(\frac{0^2}{2} + 0 + c\right) = \tfrac{3}{2}$$

i.e., in evaluating the anti-derivative from $x = 0$ to $x = 1$, the constant c is first added and then subtracted and so never appears in the final result. We shall therefore henceforth always take $c = 0$ when using the fundamental theorem.

Example 3.6.3. Find $\int_0^2 (-x)\, dx$. Here

$$\int_0^2 (-x)\, dx = \int (-x)\, dx \Bigg]_0^2 = -\tfrac{1}{2}x^2 \Bigg]_0^2 = (-4/2) - (-0/2) = -2$$

Compare this with Ex. 3.4.4.

Example 3.6.4.

$$\int_{-2}^2 (-x)\, dx = \int (-x)\, dx \Bigg]_{-2}^2 = -\tfrac{1}{2}x^2 \Bigg]_{-2}^2 = (-4/2) - (-4/2) = 0$$

Compare this with Ex. 3.4.5.

Example 3.6.5.

$$\int_{-2}^2 |-x|\, dx = \int_{-2}^0 (-x)\, dx + \int_0^2 x\, dx$$

(see Ex. 3.4.5). Now,

$$\int_{-2}^{0} (-x)\, dx = \int (-x)\, dx\Big]_{-2}^{0} = -\tfrac{1}{2}x^2\Big]_{-2}^{0} = (-0/2) - (4/2) = 2$$

and

$$\int_{0}^{2} x\, dx = \int x\, dx\Big]_{0}^{2} = \tfrac{1}{2}x^2\Big]_{0}^{2} = (4/2) - (0/2) = 2$$

so

$$\int_{-2}^{2} |-x|\, dx = 2 + 2 = 4$$

Again compare this with Ex. 3.4.5.

Example 3.6.6. Find

$$\int_{0}^{1} \{x^{17} - 3x^5 + (x-5)^{-2} + x^{1/2}\}\, dx$$

the integral at the beginning of this section. Here, we evaluate

$$\int \{x^{17} - 3x^5 + (x-5)^{-2} + x^{1/2}\}\, dx\Big]_{0}^{1}$$

$$= \tfrac{1}{18}x^{18} - \tfrac{1}{2}x^6 - 1/(x-5) + \tfrac{2}{3}x^{3/2}\Big]_{0}^{1}$$

$$= (\tfrac{1}{18} - \tfrac{1}{2} + \tfrac{1}{4} + \tfrac{2}{3}) - (0 - 0 + \tfrac{1}{5} + 0)$$

The reader should not waste his time carrying out the arithmetic.

If $f(x)$ has certain symmetry properties, the problem of evaluating certain integrals is simplified. Suppose, for example, that the graph of $f(x)$ on the

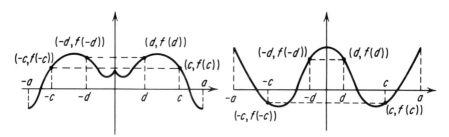

Figure 3.6.3

interval $-a \le x \le a$, with $a > 0$, can be obtained by reflecting in the y-axis the graph of $f(x)$ on the interval $0 \le x \le a$ (see Fig. 3.6.3). Such functions have the property that for each x in $-a \le x \le a, f(x) = f(-x)$. It is possible to prove (as Fig. 3.6.3 leads us to believe) that

$$\int_{-c}^{0} f = \int_{0}^{c} f = \tfrac{1}{2} \int_{-c}^{c} f$$

Another type of symmetry occurs if the graph of $f(x)$ in $-a \le x \le a$ can be obtained by reflecting the graph of $f(x)$ on $0 \le x \le a$ first in the y-axis and then in the x-axis (see Fig. 3.6.4). Such functions are characterized by

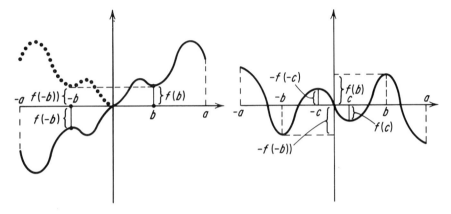

Figure 3.6.4

the relationship $f(x) = -f(-x)$. It is possible to prove (as Fig. 3.6.4 leads us to believe) that

$$\int_{-a}^{0} f = -\int_{0}^{a} f \quad \text{and} \quad \int_{-a}^{a} f = 0$$

We formalize these statements in the following theorem (the reader is cautioned to realize that our geometrical observations are *not* proofs).

Theorem 3.6.3. Let $f(x)$ be continuous in $-a \le x \le a$ $(a > 0)$.
(i). If $f(x) = f(-x)$ for every x in $-a \le x \le a$ (such functions are called *even* on the interval), then

$$\int_{-a}^{a} f = 2 \int_{0}^{a} f = 2 \int_{-a}^{0} f$$

(ii). If $f(x) = -f(-x)$ for every x in $-a \le x \le a$ (such functions are called *odd* on the interval), then

$$\int_{-a}^{a} f = 0$$

Example 3.6.7. Consider $f(x) = |-x|$, $-2 \leq x \leq 2$. Here $f(x) = |-x|$, $f(-x) = |-(-x)| = |x|$. But $|-x| = |x|$, so $f(x) = f(-x)$ and the function is even. Hence,

$$\int_2^2 |-x|\, dx = 2 \int_0^2 |-x|\, dx$$

In the interval $[0, 2]$, $|-x| = x$, so

$$\int_2^2 |-x|\, dx = 2 \left\{ \int_0^2 x\, dx \right\} = x^2 \Big]_0^2 = 4$$

Compare this with Ex. 3.6.5.

Example 3.6.8. Evaluate $\int_{-2}^2 (-x)\, dx$. Here, $f(x) = -x$, $-2 \leq x \leq 2$. Since $f(x) = -x$, $f(-x) = -(-x) = x$. Hence, $f(x) = -x = -f(-x)$, so $f(x)$ is odd. Hence,

$$\int_{-2}^2 (-x)\, dx = 0$$

Compare this with Ex. 3.4.5.

Example 3.6.9. Let f be a continuous function of x. Suppose we know the function $P(x)$ is related to the function $f(x)$ by the formula

(3.6.6) $$P(x) = \int_{a-bx}^c f$$

where a, b, and c are certain fixed constants. Observe that this integral is a function of x alone. Such an integral arises in application in a mental test theory proposed by Lord in which he attempts to derive an estimate of an examinee's true ability (see F. M. Lord, *An application of confidence intervals of maximum likelihood to the estimation of an examinee's ability*, Psychometrica, 1953: **18**, 57–76).

We wish to determine $D_x P(x)$. We shall do so by use of the fundamental theorem.

First, write $y = g(x)$ where $g(x) = a - bx$. Writing

$$Q(y) = \int_y^c f = -\int_c^y f$$

we see that our original integral formula (3.6.6) can now be written as $P(x) = Q[g(x)]$. By the chain rule (Thm. 1.10.1), we see that $D_x P(x) = D_y Q[g(x)] \cdot D_x g(x)$. Since f is continuous for all x, and so in particular in the interval $c \leq x \leq y$, we see by Thm. 3.6.1 that $D_y Q(y) = -f(y)$. Also, $D_x g(x) = -b$. Hence, $D_x P(x) = -f[g(x)] \cdot (-b) = bf(a - bx)$, which is the desired derivative.

•

PROBLEMS

3.6.1. Use Thm. 3.6.2 to solve Probs. 3.4.2 and 3.4.3.

3.6.2. Use Thm. 3.6.2 to solve Probs. 3.4.4 through 3.4.6.

3.6.3. Use Thm. 3.6.2 to solve Probs. 3.4.7 through 3.4.9.

3.6.4. Evaluate:

(a) $\displaystyle\int_{-3}^{5} 2x\, dx$ 　　　　　　(b) $\displaystyle\int_{-10}^{10} 7\, dx$

(c) $\displaystyle\int_{0}^{2} (t^3 - 1)\, dt$ 　　　　　(d) $\displaystyle\int_{0}^{1} (u^{10} - 5u^7 + 4u)\, du$

(*Hint:* See Prob. 3.3.1.)

3.6.5. Use Thm. 3.6.3 to evaluate:

(a) $\displaystyle\int_{-2}^{2} (x^6 + x^2)\, dx$ 　　　　(b) $\displaystyle\int_{-1}^{1} (x^{10} - 5x^2)\, dx$

(c) $\displaystyle\int_{-25}^{25} (x^{15} - 4x^{11})\, dx$ 　　(d) $\displaystyle\int_{-1}^{1} (x^{15} + x^2)\, dx$

3.6.6. Evaluate:

(a) $\displaystyle\int_{0}^{1} (x^2 - 2x + 5)\, dx$ 　　　(b) $\displaystyle\int_{1}^{3} (x - 1)^2\, dx$

(c) $\displaystyle\int_{1}^{2} \frac{(x + 1)}{\sqrt{x}}\, dx$ 　　　　　(d) $\displaystyle\int_{1}^{2} \frac{(x^3 + 1)}{x^2}\, dx$

(e) $\displaystyle\int_{0}^{1} x(x^2 - 3)\, dx$ 　　　　(f) $\displaystyle\int_{0}^{1} \sqrt{x}(1 - \sqrt{x})\, dx$

(g) $\displaystyle\int_{-1}^{1} \sqrt[3]{x}\, dx$ 　　　　　　(h) $\displaystyle\int_{a}^{b} (Ax^2 + Bx + C)\, dx$

(i) $\displaystyle\int_{-2}^{0} \sqrt{-x}\, dx$ 　　　　　(j) $\displaystyle\int_{1}^{2} \left(\frac{1}{\sqrt{x}} + \frac{1}{x^2} + \frac{1}{x^4}\right) dx$

3.6.7. Find the area of the region bounded by the graphs of:

(a) $f(x) = x^2 + 1$, $x = -1$, $x = 1$, and the *x*-axis

(b) $f(x) = \sqrt{x}$, $x = 0$, $x = 1$, and the *x*-axis

(c) $f(x) = x^3$, $x = -1$, $x = 1$, and the x-axis

(d) $f(x) = \sqrt[3]{x}$, $x = -2$, $x = +2$, and the x-axis

(e) $f(x) = -x^2$, $x = -1$, $x = 1$, and the x-axis

(f) $f(x) = \sqrt{1 - x}$, $x = 0$, $y = 0$

(g) $f(x) = x^2 - 1$, $x = -1$, $x = 2$, and the x-axis

(*Hint:* To find $|f(x)|$, investigate the inequalities $f(x) > 0$ and $f(x) < 0$.)

(h) $f(x) = x(x + 2)(x - 1)$, $x = -2$, $x = 2$, and the x-axis.

(*Hint:* See the hint in (g) above.)

3.6.8. Evaluate

$$\lim_{N \to \infty} \frac{1}{N} \sum_{k=1}^{N} \sqrt{k/N}$$

3.6.9. Evaluate

$$\lim_{N \to \infty} \frac{1}{N} \sum_{k=1}^{N} \left(\frac{k}{N}\right)^{\sqrt{2}}$$

3.6.10. Let $f(x)$ be continuous on $a \le x \le b$, and define

$$F(x) = \int_a^x f \qquad a \le x \le b$$

Explain when $F(x)$ is a continuous function on $a \le x \le b$. State some stronger properties possessed by $F(x)$.

3.6.11. Let

$$G(x) = \int_a^{x^2 - 5x + 1} f$$

where $f(x)$ is continuous for all x. Find $dG(x)/dx$.

3.6.12. Let

$$G(x) = \int_{x^2}^{0} \sqrt{t^2 + t} \, dt$$

Find $G'(x)$.

3.6.13. Find $P'(x)$ in Ex. 3.6.9 if $f(x) = \sqrt[3]{x^2 - 1}$.

3.6.14. Let $f(x)$ be a function defined on the entire real line.

(a) Show that $F(x) = \frac{1}{2}\{f(x) + f(-x)\}$ is even on the interval $-a \le x \le a$ for *any* $a > 0$.

(b) Show that $G(x) = \frac{1}{2}\{f(x) - f(-x)\}$ is odd on the interval $-a \le x \le a$ for *any* $a > 0$.

(c) Verify that $f(x) = F(x) + G(x)$, and hence every function defined on the entire real line is the sum of an even and odd function.

3.7. Area between curves. Distance and velocity.

Let $f(x)$ and $g(x)$ be two functions each continuous on $a \le x \le b$, and suppose first that $f(x) > g(x) > 0$, as in Fig. 3.7.1. Then the area between the curves is just the area under $f(x)$ minus the area under $g(x)$; i.e.,

$$\text{area between curves} = \int_a^b f - \int_a^b g$$

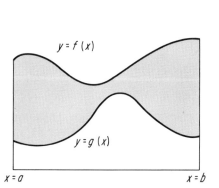

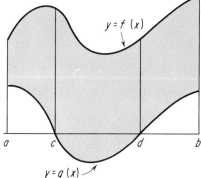

Figure 3.7.1   **Figure 3.7.2**

But by Thm. 3.4.1,

$$\int_a^b f - \int_a^b g = \int_a^b (f - g)$$

so the area between the curves is just

(3.7.1) $$\int_a^b (f - g)$$

Next, what happens if $g(x)$ is sometimes negative on $a \le x \le b$? Specifically, for illustration, suppose $g(x) < 0$ in $c \le x \le d$ as in Fig. 3.7.2. For $a \le x \le c$ and $d \le x \le b$, we are in the same situation as we first considered, so the area between the curves in these regions is given by

$$\int_a^c (f - g) \quad \text{and} \quad \int_d^b (f - g)$$

respectively.

In the interval $c \le x \le d$ we wish to add the contributions of $g(x)$ to the area bounded by the graphs of $y = f(x)$, the x-axis, and the lines $x = c$ and

$x = d$. By Def. 3.4.3, the area bounded by the graphs of $y = g(x)$, the x-axis, and the lines $x = c$ and $x = d$ is given by $\int_c^d |g(x)|\, dx$. But since $g(x) < 0$, $|g(x)| = -g(x)$. Hence the area between the graphs of $f(x)$ and $g(x)$ from $x = c$ to $x = d$ is the sum of the areas

$$\int_c^d f(x)\, dx + \int_c^d |g(x)|\, dx = \int_c^d f + \int_c^d (-g) = \int_c^d f - \int_c^d g$$

$$= \int_c^d (f - g)$$

The *total* area is given by the sum

$$\int_a^c (f - g) + \int_c^d (f - g) + \int_d^b (f - g) = \int_a^b (f - g)$$

as before.

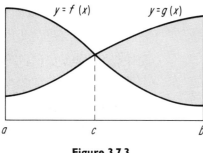

$y = f(x)$ $y = g(x)$

a c b

Figure 3.7.3

Another possibility is that $0 > f > g$. But in this case $f - g$ is still positive, and the reader should convince himself the *same* integral (3.7.1) applies.

Finally, what if $f > g$ sometimes but $g > f$ at other times in $a \le x \le b$, as in Fig. 3.7.3? The area is given by

$$\int_a^c (f - g) + \int_c^b (g - f) = \int_a^b |f - g|$$

It turns out that in all cases, the *area between the graphs of $f(x)$ and $g(x)$ from $x = a$ to $x = b$ is given by*

(3.7.2)
$$\int_a^b |f - g|$$

In the following examples, we will use methods of §1.1 to solve inequalities.

Example 3.7.1. Find the area bounded by the graphs of $f(x) = x$ and $g(x) = x^2$ (see Fig. 3.7.4). To find where the graphs intersect, set $f(x) = g(x)$. This gives $x = x^2$, or $x^2 - x = x(x - 1) = 0$. Hence, the graphs intersect at $x = 0$ and at $x = 1$. If we graph $f(x)$ and $g(x)$, it is apparent that in the interval $0 < x < 1$, $f(x) = x > x^2 = g(x)$. We can also show this analytically by investigating the sign of $f(x) - g(x) = x - x^2 = x(1 - x)$. Hence, $f(x) -$

$g(x) > 0$ when $0 < x < 1$ (see Fig. 3.7.5). Consequently, $f(x) > g(x)$ when $0 < x < 1$. Using (3.7.2), $f - g > 0$ implies $|f - g| = f - g$, so the desired area

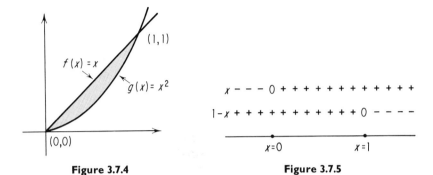

Figure 3.7.4   **Figure 3.7.5**

is given by

$$\int_0^1 (x - x^2)\, dx = \tfrac{1}{2}x^2 - \tfrac{1}{3}x^3 \Big]_0^1 = \tfrac{1}{2} - \tfrac{1}{3} = \tfrac{1}{6}$$

Example 3.7.2. Find the area bounded by the parabola given by $y = f(x) = x^2 - 2$ and the straight line $y = g(x) = -x$. To find where the graphs intersect, set $f(x) = g(x)$. This becomes $x^2 - 2 = -x$, or $x^2 + x - 2 = 0$. This factors into $(x - 1)(x + 2) = 0$. Hence the graphs intersect at $x = 1$ and $x = -2$ (see Fig. 3.7.6). To find $|f - g|$, we must know when $f - g > 0$ and when $f - g < 0$. We see that $f(x) - g(x) = x^2 + x - 2 = (x - 1)(x + 2) > 0$ when $x > 1$ and when $x < -2$; and $f - g < 0$ when $-2 < x < 1$ (see Fig. 3.7.7). Hence, in the region of interest, $-2 < x < 1$,

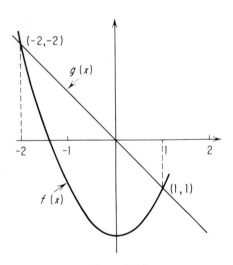

Figure 3.7.6

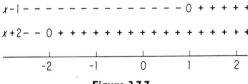

Figure 3.7.7

$g - f > 0$, so $|f - g| = g - f$, and the required area is

$$\int_{-2}^{1} (-x - x^2 + 2)\, dx = -\frac{x^2}{2} - \frac{x^3}{3} + 2x \Bigg]_{-2}^{1} = \frac{9}{2}$$

We conclude this section with a discussion of rectilinear motion. Let $s(t)$, $v(t)$, and $a(t)$ denote distance, velocity, and acceleration, respectively. First we investigate $\int_{a}^{b} v(t)\, dt$. Using the fundamental theorem 3.6.2,

$$\int_{a}^{b} v(t)\, dt = G(b) - G(a)$$

where $G(t)$ is any anti-derivative of $v(t)$ defined on $a \leq t \leq b$. Since $s(t)$ is an anti-derivative of $v(t)$, we have

(3.7.3)
$$s(b) - s(a) = \int_{a}^{b} v(t)\, dt$$

where $s(a)$ is distance at time $t = a$ and $s(b)$ is distance at time $t = b$. The quantity $s(b) - s(a)$ may be thought of as the **net distance traveled.**

Example 3.7.3. Suppose a particle travels in such a way that its velocity is $v(t) = (t - 1)^3$. What is the net distance traveled over the time interval $0 \leq t \leq 2$; i.e., what is the value of $s(2) - s(0)$? From (3.7.2),

$$s(2) - s(0) = \int_{0}^{2} v(t)\, dt = \int_{0}^{2} (t - 1)^3\, dt$$

$$= \frac{(t - 1)^4}{4} \Bigg]_{0}^{2} = \frac{1}{4} - \frac{1}{4} = 0$$

Physically, from $t = 0$ to $t = 1$, we have that $v < 0$; at $t = 1$, $v = 0$, so the particle has stopped, and from $t = 1$ to $t = 2$, $v > 0$ so the particle is going in a direction exactly opposite to its direction in $0 \leq t \leq 1$. Hence the *net* effect is 0 motion (see Fig. 3.7.8).

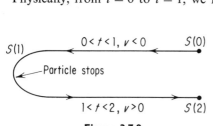

Figure 3.7.8

To find the *total* distance traveled, we simply replace negative values of velocity by their corresponding positive values, thus treating the motion as if it were only in *one* direction. Hence **total distance traveled** from time $t = a$ to time $t = b$ is

(3.7.4)
$$\int_{a}^{b} |v(t)|\, dt$$

Example 3.7.4. The total distance traveled by the particle in Ex. 3.7.3 is given by

$$\int_0^2 |(t-1)^3|\, dt$$

Since $(t-1)^3 < 0$ in $0 \le t < 1$, we have that $|(t-1)^3| = -(t-1)^3$ in this interval. Since $(t-1)^3 > 0$ on $1 < t \le 2$, we have that $|(t-1)^3| = (t-1)^3$ in this interval. Consequently,

$$\int_0^2 |(t-1)^3|\, dt = \int_0^1 -(t-1)^3\, dt + \int_1^2 (t-1)^3\, dt = \tfrac{1}{2}$$

It is interesting to observe that the *total* distance traveled from time $t = a$ to $t = b$ is the area bounded by the graph of the velocity, the t-axis, and the lines $t = a$ and $t = b$.

PROBLEMS

3.7.1. Find the area bounded by each of the following curves:
(a) $f(x) = 2 - x^2$ and $g(x) = -x$
(b) $f(x) = x^2$ and $g(x) = x^3$
(c) $f(x) = x$ and $g(x) = \sqrt{x}$
(d) $f(x) = x^2$ and $g(x) = \sqrt[3]{x}$
(e) $f(x) = x$ and $g(x) = x^3$
(f) $f(x) = x^2 - 4$ and $g(x) = 2$
(g) $f(x) = x^4 - 3x^2$ and $g(x) = 6x^2$
(h) $f(x) = x^3 - x^2$ and $g(x) = 6x$
(i) $\sqrt{x} + \sqrt{y} = 1$ and the coordinate axes.

3.7.2. The area bounded by the x-axis, the curve $y = f(x)$, and the lines $x = a$ and $x = b$ is given by $\sqrt[3]{b^3 - a^3}$ for *every* $b > a$, with a fixed. Find $f(x)$.

3.7.3. A particle moves so that its velocity is given by $v(t) = (t-2)^5$. Find the net and total distance traveled over the time interval $0 \le t \le 4$.

3.7.4. A particle moves so that its velocity is given by $v(t) = t^2 - 4$. Find the net and total distance traveled over the time period $-1 \le t \le 2$.

3.8. The exponential function.

We will devote this and the next section to defining some new functions of special interest. First we wish to define the function $f(x) = 2^x$ for all real numbers x. Though it is clear that $f(3) = 2^3 = 8$, how should we define

$f(\pi) = 2^\pi$? Recall from §1.1 that the number systems leading to the reals are the integers, the rationals, and the irrationals, the reals being numbers which are rational or irrational. **By defining 2^x for each of these number systems, we shall ultimately define 2^x for all reals.** Let us proceed by cases.

Case 1. x is a positive integer, say $x = n$. Then $f(n) = 2^n = \underbrace{2 \cdot 2 \cdot 2 \cdots 2}_{n \text{ times}}$. So, $f(1) = 2, f(3) = 8, f(37) = 2^{37}$, etc.

Case 2. x is a non-positive integer. For $x = -n$, $n > 0$, $f(-n) = 2^{-n} = 1/2^n$; also $f(0) = 2^0 = 1$ (see §1.8). Hence, $f(-1) = 2^{-1} = \frac{1}{2}$, $f(-2) = 2^{-2} = \frac{1}{4}$, $f(-37) = 2^{-37} = \frac{1}{2}^{37}$, etc.

Case 3. x is rational, say $x = p/q$, where p and q are integers, with $q > 0$. Recall from algebra that $a^{p/q} = \sqrt[q]{a^p}$ when the symbol is meaningful. Hence, $f(p/q) = 2^{p/q} = \sqrt[q]{2^p}$. For instance,

$$f(1/2) = 2^{1/2} = \sqrt{2} \qquad f(-1/2) = 2^{-1/2} = 1/2^{1/2} = 1/\sqrt{2}$$

$$f(5/7) = \sqrt[7]{2^5} \qquad f(-4/3) = 1/\sqrt[3]{16}$$

Remark. Since every integer is rational, all three cases can be subsumed under the heading "x rational."

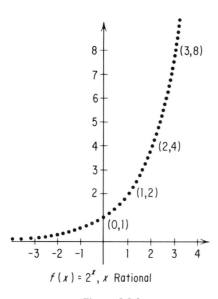

$f(x) = 2^x$, x Rational

Figure 3.8.1

Suppose we graph $f(x) = 2^x$ for Cases 1 through 3 by plotting a large number of rational values of 2^x. We see from Fig. 3.8.1 that the graph of $f(x) = 2^x$ for x rational is monotone increasing and is above the x-axis.

Case 4. x is irrational. We define $f(\delta) = 2^\delta$ at δ irrational so as to make the function continuous. Roughly, to find 2^δ for δ irrational we can consider a sequence $r_1 < r_2 < \cdots < r_n < \cdots$ of rational numbers such that $r_n \to \delta$ as $n \to \infty$. Since $f(x)$ is a strictly increasing function of x for x rational, we have that $2^{r_1} < 2^{r_2} < \cdots < 2^{r_n} < \cdots$. We define $2^\delta = \lim_{n \to \infty} 2^{r_n}$. That this limit really exists, is independent of the particular choice of sequence, and that this makes 2^x continuous is beyond the scope of this book. The interested reader might consult Courant, *Differential and Interval Calculus*, Vol. 1, appendix to Ch. 1, §3; or Taylor, *Advanced Calculus*, Theorem III of Chapter 2 and Theorem II of Chapter 15.*

The graph of $f(x) = 2^x$ is now defined for all real x, and is strictly increasing and continuous everywhere (see Fig. 3.8.2).

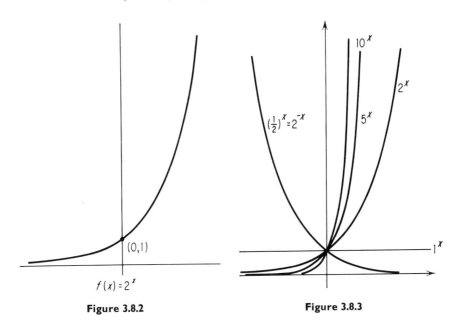

Figure 3.8.2   **Figure 3.8.3**

For any positive number a, we can investigate the function g given by $g(x) = a^x$ in the same way as $f(x) = 2^x$. The curve for $y = 3^x$ will become steeper more rapidly than the curve for $y = 2^x$ as x increases through positive values; for instance, $3^2 = 9 > 4 = 2^2$, $3^3 = 27 > 8 = 2^3$, and in general, $3^x > 2^x$ if $x > 0$. If $x < 0$, we have, for instance, $3^{-1} = (\frac{1}{3}) < (\frac{1}{2}) = 2^{-1}$, $3^{-2} = (\frac{1}{9}) < (\frac{1}{4}) = 2^{-2}$; in general, $3^x < 2^x$ if $x < 0$. In all cases, $3^0 = 2^0 = a^0 = 1$, when $a > 0$. Some typical graphs are drawn in Fig. 3.8.3.

We turn now to an investigation of the derivative of $f(x) = a^x$. We must resort to the definition of derivative as a limit. We have:

$$Da^x = \lim_{h \to 0} \frac{a^{x+h} - a^x}{h} = \lim_{h \to 0} a^x \left[\frac{a^h - 1}{h} \right] = a^x \lim_{h \to 0} \left[\frac{a^h - 1}{h} \right]$$

We define the number e as the result of solving the equation

$$\lim_{h \to 0} \frac{a^h - 1}{h} = 1$$

_____

* See the bibliography.

for the unknown a; i.e.,

$$(3.8.1) \qquad \lim_{h \to 0} \frac{e^h - 1}{h} = 1$$

The reader should realize that we are deliberately evading the issue of whether such a solution exists at all; we claim that it does.

With this value of $a = e$, we have

$$(3.8.2) \qquad De^x = e^x \quad \text{or} \quad \frac{d}{dx} e^x = e^x$$

We shall find another expression for e when we discuss the logarithm in §3.9. We shall anticipate this and state that e is *approximately* 2.7183. The reader should observe that e is a real number, in some ways similar to π. That fact that $y = e^x$ is **S.I.** implies that

$$(3.8.3) \qquad e^a = e^b \quad \text{if and only if } a = b.$$

The function $f(x) = e^x$ obeys the usual laws for exponents. Specifically, if a and b are any real numbers, then

$$(3.8.4) \qquad \begin{aligned} e^a e^b &= e^{a+b} \\ e^{-a} &= 1/e^a \\ (e^a)^b &= e^{ab} \end{aligned}$$

That (3.8.4) holds for a and b rational is well known from algebra. That the rules are still valid for a and b any real numbers depends on the definition of e^x for arbitrary real x; we shall not give a proof here.

We next consider $e^{f(x)}$ where $f(x)$ is some function of x. Because the notation $e^{f(x)}$ is rather clumsy, we shall often replace it by the symbol $\exp f(x)$, called **exponential** of $f(x)$. We define $\exp(x) = e^x$, and hence $\exp f(x) = e^{f(x)}$.

We wish to evaluate $D_x \exp f(x)$ where $f(x)$ is any differentiable function. Define $g(u) = e^u$; by (3.8.2), $D_u e^u = e^u$. Next let $u = f(x)$. We use the chain rule (see Thm. 1.10.1) to conclude that

$$D_x g[f(x)] = D_u g(u) \cdot D_x f(x) = e^u D_x f(x) = [\exp f(x)] \cdot D_x f(x)$$

Summarizing:

$$(3.8.5) \qquad D_x \exp f(x) = [\exp f(x)] \cdot D_x f(x)$$

Example 3.8.1. $D_x \exp(x^3 + x) = [\exp(x^3 + x)][3x^2 + 1]$.
From (3.8.2), we see that

$$(3.8.6) \qquad \int e^x \, dx = e^x + C$$

Example 3.8.2.

$$\int_0^1 e^x \, dx = \left[\int e^x \, dx \right]_0^1 = e^x \Big|_0^1 = e - 1$$

PROBLEMS

3.8.1. Find $f'(x)$ if:

(a) $f(x) = xe^x$

(b) $f(x) = e^{-3x}$

(c) $f(x) = \exp \sqrt{x - 1}$

(d) $f(x) = [\exp (x + 1)] \cdot [\exp (x - 1)]$

(e) $f(x) = \exp [x\sqrt{x + 1}]$

(f) $f(x) = x^2 e^x$

(g) $f(x) = \exp (-1/x^2)$

(h) $f(x) = \exp \sqrt{x/(x - 1)}$

(i) $f(x) = \exp [x^2 + 1]^{10}$

3.8.2. Use the appropriate result of Prob. (1) to find:

(a) $\displaystyle \int_2^5 \frac{\exp \sqrt{x - 1}}{\sqrt{x - 1}} \, dx$

(b) $\displaystyle \int_0^1 xe^x \, dx$

[*Hint:* Use Prob. 3.8.1(a).]

(c) $\displaystyle \int_0^1 e^{-3x} \, dx$

(d) $\displaystyle \int_1^2 \frac{1}{x^3} \exp \frac{-1}{x^2} \, dx$

(e) $\displaystyle \int_0^1 x^2 e^x \, dx$

[*Hint:* Use Prob. 3.8.1(f) and Prob. 3.8.2(b).]

3.8.3. Find Dy if $xe^y + ye^x = 2x$.

3.8.4. Find $f'(x)$ and sketch the curve if

(a) $f(x) = \frac{1}{2}[e^x - e^{-x}]$

(b) $f(x) = \frac{1}{2}[e^x + e^{-x}]$

(c) $f(x) = \dfrac{e^x - e^{-x}}{e^x + e^{-x}}$

3.8.5. Find the absolute extrema for the function

$$f(x) = (1/s\sqrt{2\pi}) \exp(-(x - u)^2/2s^2)$$

where $s > 0$ and u are fixed constants (this function is important in statistics).

3.8.6. If the demand law for a certain commodity is $p = 9e^{-x/3}$, find the maximum total revenue.

3.8.7. Let $f(x) = e^{-ax}$ and $g(x) = e^{-bx}$. Show that each of these functions satisfies the differential equation

$$y''(x) + (a + b)y'(x) + aby(x) = 0$$

where a and b are constants.

3.9. The inverse of a function. The natural logarithm.

Definition 3.9.1. Given the function $y = f(x)$, the *inverse function* of $f(x)$ is a function $g(x)$ which satisfies the equations

(3.9.1)

$$\boxed{f[g(x)] = x} \qquad \text{for all } x \text{ in the domain of } g$$

$$\boxed{g[f(x)] = x} \qquad \text{for all } x \text{ in the domain of } f$$

There are functions which have no inverse functions; we will see one such instance in Ex. 3.9.2.

Example 3.9.1. We find the inverse function of $f(x) = 6x - 1$. First we solve the equation $f[g(x)] = x$ for $g(x)$. For our particular $f(x)$, we have $f[g(x)] = 6[g(x)] - 1$. Hence the equation $f[g(x)] = x$ becomes $6[g(x)] - 1 = x$. Solving for $g(x)$, we obtain $6[g(x)] = x + 1$, or finally $g(x) = (\frac{1}{6})(x + 1)$. According to (3.9.1), if $g(x)$ is to be the inverse, it must *also* satisfy the equation $g[f(x)] = x$. To see that it does, observe first that since $g(x) = (\frac{1}{6})(x + 1)$, it follows that $g[f(x)] = (\frac{1}{6})(f(x) + 1)$. But, of course, $f(x)$ is the same $f(x)$ we began with; i.e., $f(x) = 6x - 1$. So finally we have

$$g[f(x)] = \tfrac{1}{6}(f(x) + 1) = \tfrac{1}{6}(\{6x - 1\} + 1) = x$$

Summarizing, we began with $f(x) = 6x - 1$, then solved the equation $f[g(x)] = x$ to find that $g(x) = (\frac{1}{6})(x + 1)$. Hence, if $f(x) = 6x - 1$ has an inverse function, it must be $g(x) = (\frac{1}{6})(x + 1)$. To qualify as the inverse function, $g(x)$ must satisfy the second equation in (3.9.1). Expanding $g[f(x)]$, we found that $g[f(x)] = x$ was valid, so $g(x) = (\frac{1}{6})(x + 1)$ is the inverse function of $f(x) = 6x - 1$.

Geometrically, the problem of finding an inverse function to $f(x)$ is the problem of viewing the graph of $y = f(x)$ with the x-axis and the y-axis *inter-changed*, and if the graph so obtained is the graph of a function, to label the function the inverse function for $f(x)$. We shall illustrate this using the function $f(x) = 6x - 1$ of Ex. 3.9.1.

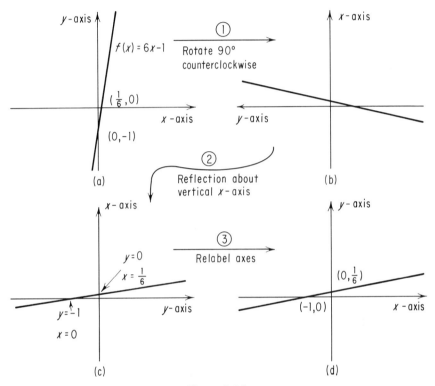

Figure 3.9.1

In Fig. 3.9.1(a) we sketch the graph of the function $f(x) = 6x - 1$, a straight line with slope 6 and y-intercept -1. We next set about interchanging the axes. First rotate the xy-plane 90 deg counterclockwise, of course, rotating the straight line with the plane. The result is pictured in Fig. 3.9.1(b). The problem now is that the y-axis points from right to left; this implies that with the y-axis as our new horizontal axis, the numbers increase as we go from right to left. But this has destroyed the orientation of the horizontal axis on which numbers should increase as we go from *left* to *right*, as the arrow indicates in Fig. 3.9.1(a). However, the vertical axis still points correctly after the rotation.

To re-establish the proper orientation, we reflect the graph about the new vertical x-axis; i.e., with the vertical x-axis as an axis of rotation, pivot the graph. The vertical axis does not change, but the horizontal y-axis changes direction, as desired. This is pictured in Fig. 3.9.1(c).

Finally, we simply replace every occurence of the symbol x by the symbol y, and we replace every occurence of the symbol y by the symbol x [see Fig. 3.9.1(d)] so that we have interchanged the axes.

Observe that the graph in Fig. 3.9.1(d) is essentially the same as the graph in Fig. 3.9.1(a), but viewed with the axes interchanged. The graph in Fig. 3.9.1(d) represents a function, and so is the graph of the inverse function to $f(x) = 6x - 1$. It is a straight line with slope $\frac{1}{6}$ and y-intercept $\frac{1}{6}$, and so has equation $g(x) = (\frac{1}{6})x + \frac{1}{6}$. This is exactly the result of Ex. 3.9.1.

Example 3.9.2. Given $f(x) = x^2$. Find the inverse function, if one exists. First let us investigate the problem geometrically. In Fig. 3.9.2(a), we sketch $f(x) = x^2$; Fig. 3.9.2(b) represents a 90 deg rotation counterclockwise; Fig. 3.9.2(c) represents a reflection in the vertical axis; and in Fig. 3.9.2(d) we relabel the axes.

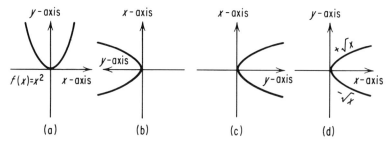

Figure 3.9.2

From Fig. 3.9.2(d), it is clear that the inverse *relation* does *not* represent a function, since to values of x, where $x > 0$, we have *two* related values of y. Hence $f(x) = x^2$ does *not* have an inverse function.

Next we will see what happens if we attempt to find an inverse function $g(x)$ by solving the equations (3.9.1). With $f(x) = x^2$, we try to solve $f[g(x)] = x$. Since $f[g(x)] = [g(x)]^2$, $f[g(x)] = x$ becomes $[g(x)]^2 = x$, whose solution is $g(x) = \pm\sqrt{x}$, which is *not* a function. Strictly speaking we should *not* write $g(x) = \pm\sqrt{x}$ at all, since we reserve the notation $g(x)$ for functions. So we have found that there is *no* function $g(x)$ such that $f[g(x)] = x$.

If we had taken $f(x) = x^2$ with $x \geq 0$, our calculations would yield $f[g(x)] = [g(x)]^2$, with $g(x) \geq 0$, so $f[g(x)] = x$ becomes $[g(x)]^2 = x$, $g(x) \geq 0$, whose solution is $g(x) = \sqrt{x}$, since only this solution is consistent with $g(x) \geq 0$ (see Fig. 3.9.3).

A similar result can be obtained for $f(x) = x^2$ with $x \leq 0$. We will let the reader verify this in a problem.

If the reader gives some careful thought to all these examples, he should realize that if the function $f(x)$ is **S.I.** (or **S.D.**), (see §2.2 for the definition of **S.I.** and **S.D.**), the graph of the inverse relation will also be **S.I.** (or **S.D.**), and hence the graph of the inverse relation will be the graph of a function.

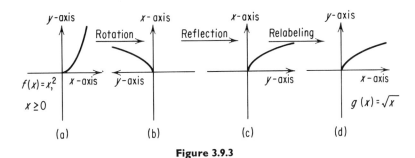

Figure 3.9.3

In §3.8 we observed that the graph of $f(x) = e^x$ is **S.I.**, and hence $f(x) = e^x$ has an inverse function, which is also **S.I.**

Definition 3.9.2. The inverse function to $f(x) = e^x$ is defined to be the function we shall call the **natural logarithm** of x, which we shall designate by ln x.

The graph of ln x is immediate, and is constructed in Fig. 3.9.4.

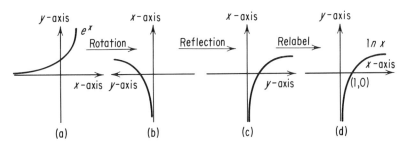

Figure 3.9.4

The natural logarithm of x is **S.I.**, has domain $x > 0$, is continuous on its domain (one can prove that in general the inverse function of a continuous function is continuous; our graphical construction of the inverse makes such a theorem reasonable). Also, since $e^0 = 1$, we have ln $1 = 0$ (see Fig. 3.9.4).

$f(x) = e^x$ and $g(x) = \ln x$ must satisfy (3.9.1); hence

$$f[g(x)] = e^{g(x)} = e^{\ln x} = x, \text{ all } x > 0$$

and

$$g[f(x)] = \ln f(x) = \ln e^x = x, \text{ all } x$$

We therefore have the identities:

(3.9.2) $\begin{cases} e^{\ln x} = x \quad (\text{or } \exp(\ln x) = x) \quad \text{all } x > 0 \\ \ln e^x = x \qquad \text{all } x \end{cases}$

It is also apparent from (3.9.2) that $0 = \ln e^0 = \ln 1$, and $1 = \ln e^1 = \ln e$. Since $\ln x$ is **S.I.**, it follows that $\ln a = \ln b$ if and only if $a = b$ (i.e., different values for $\ln x$ must come from different values of x).

We prove next a theorem on the fundamental algebraic properties of the natural logarithm.

Theorem 3.9.1. Let $a > 0$, $b > 0$ be any real (positive) numbers. Then,
(a) $\ln ab = \ln a + \ln b$ (b) $\ln 1/a = -\ln a$
(c) $\ln (a/b) = \ln a - \ln b$ (d) $\ln \{a^c\} = c \ln a$ c arbitrary

Proof. The proof relies heavily on (3.8.3), (3.8.4), and (3.9.2).
(a) Set $u = \ln a$ and $v = \ln b$. Then $e^u = a$ and $e^v = b$ [by (3.9.2)]. Then $a \cdot b = e^u \cdot e^v = e^{u+v}$. Hence, $\ln a \cdot b = \ln e^{u+v} = u + v$, again by (3.9.2). But $u + v = \ln a + \ln b$, so $\ln a \cdot b = \ln a + \ln b$.
(b) Let $w = \ln (1/a)$. Then $e^w = e^{\ln (1/a)} = 1/a$ by (3.9.2). Hence $a = 1/e^w = e^{-w}$, and so $\ln a = \ln e^{-w} = -w = -\ln (1/a)$, so (b) is proved.
(c) $\ln (a/b) = \ln (a \cdot b^{-1})$, and by (a), $\ln (ab^{-1}) = \ln a + \ln b^{-1}$. By (b), $\ln b^{-1} = -\ln b$. Hence $\ln (a/b) = \ln a - \ln b$.
(d) Let $u = \ln a$; then $e^u = e^{\ln a} = a$. By (3.8.4), $(e^u)^b = e^{ub}$. Consequently, $e^u = a$ implies $(e^u)^b = e^{ub} = a^b$, so $\ln e^{ub} = \ln a^b$. But $\ln e^{ub} = ub = b \ln a$, so $b \ln a = \ln a^b$, and (d) is proved.

Example 3.9.3. $\ln 16 = \ln \{2^4\} = 4 \ln 2$; $\ln 8 = \ln 4 \cdot 2 = \ln 4 + \ln 2$; with $x > 0$ and $y > 0$, $\ln x^5 y^2 = \ln x^5 + \ln y^2 = 5 \ln x + 2 \ln y$; for $z > 0$, $\ln \sqrt{z} = \ln z^{1/2} = (\frac{1}{2}) \ln z$.

Since $f(x) = e^x$ has a non-horizontal tangent line at each point of its graph (i.e., $De^x = e^x$, and e^x is never 0), we expect a non-vertical tangent line to the graph of $g(x) = \ln x$ at each point of its graph (see Fig. 3.9.4). Hence we expect $D \ln x$ to be defined everywhere in the domain of $\ln x$.

We next evaluate $D \ln x$, assuming from our geometrical considerations that it exists for all x in the domain of $\ln x$. From (3.9.2), $x = \exp(\ln x)$, $x > 0$. Differentiating yields

(a) $Dx = D \exp(\ln x)$

Clearly $Dx = 1$, and from (3.8.5), $D \exp(\ln x) = [\exp(\ln x)] \cdot D \ln x$. Since

$\exp (\ln x) = x$, (a) is equivalent to $1 = xD \ln x$, and so

(3.9.4) $$D_x \ln x = 1/x \qquad x > 0$$

Next we differentiate $\ln f(x)$ for any differentiable positive function $f(x)$. We require $f(x) > 0$ to insure the existence of $\ln f(x)$. We shall use the chain rule. To make the details more transparent, define $L(u) = \ln u$ where $u = f(x)$. Then $L[f(x)]$ is $\ln f(x)$. Applying the chain rule to $L[f(x)]$, we have

$$D_x L[f(x)] = D_u L(u) \cdot D_x f(x) = (1/u) f'(x)$$

or, since $u = f(x)$,

(3.9.5) $$D_x \ln f(x) = \frac{[D_x f(x)]}{f(x)} \qquad f(x) > 0$$

We shall apply (3.9.5) to the special positive differentiable function $f(x) = |x|$, $x \neq 0$. Recall that $D|x| = 1$ if $x > 0$ and $D|x| = -1$ if $x < 0$ (see §1.2). We consider two cases:

Case 1.

$$x > 0 \qquad D \ln |x| = \frac{1}{|x|} \cdot 1 = \frac{1}{x}$$

Case. 2.

$$x < 0 \qquad D \ln |x| = \frac{1}{|x|}(-1) = \frac{-1}{x}(-1) = \frac{1}{x}$$

In both cases, we have

(3.9.6) $$D \ln |x| = \frac{1}{x} \qquad x \neq 0$$

Repeating the steps leading to (3.9.5) with $f(x)$ replaced by $|f(x)|$ yields

(3.9.7) $$D_x \ln |f(x)| = \frac{D_x f(x)}{f(x)} \qquad f(x) \neq 0$$

Equations (3.9.6) and (3.9.7) lead to the anti-derivatives

$$\int \frac{1}{x} \, dx = \ln |x| + c, \qquad \int \frac{f'(x)}{f(x)} \, dx = \ln |f(x)| + c$$

Example 3.9.4.

$$D \ln |x^2 + 2x + 7| = \frac{D(x^2 + 2x + 7)}{x^2 + 2x + 7}$$

$$= \frac{2x + 2}{x^2 + 2x + 7}$$

Example 3.9.5.

$$D \ln \sqrt[3]{(x + 1)/(x - 1)} = D \ln \left[\frac{x + 1}{x - 1}\right]^{1/3}$$

$$= D\tfrac{1}{3} \ln \left[\frac{x + 1}{x - 1}\right]$$

$$= \tfrac{1}{3}D[\ln (x + 1) - \ln (x - 1)]$$

$$= \tfrac{1}{3}\left[\left(\frac{1}{x + 1}\right) - \left(\frac{1}{x - 1}\right)\right]$$

$$= -\tfrac{2}{3}\left[\frac{1}{(x + 1)(x - 1)}\right]$$

Of course the differentiation in Ex. 3.9.5 might have been done other ways [e.g., using (3.9.5)], but the example illustrates how the properties of the natural logarithm can simplify the calculations.

The exponential and logarithmic functions give a technique for differentiating certain functions of a complex nature. We shall call this technique *logarithmic differentiation*. The next example illustrates the technique.

Example 3.9.6. Consider $G(x) = x^x$, $x > 0$. We wish to find $G'(x)$. Since the exponent is also a variable and *not a constant*, (1.11.4) does *not* apply. Use (3.9.2) to write

$$G(x) = x^x = \exp (\ln x^x) = \exp (x \ln x)$$

and consequently

$$G'(x) = D \exp (x \ln x) = [\exp (x \ln x)]D(x \ln x)$$
$$= x^x(1 + \ln x)$$

Hence,

$$G'(x) = D(x^x) = x^x(1 + \ln x) \qquad x > 0$$

Theorem 1.11.4. For any fixed real number r and any differentiable function $f(x)$,

(a) $$Dx^r = rx^{r-1},$$
(b) $$D[f(x)]^r = r[f(x)]^{r-1}Df(x).$$

Proof. Write $x^r = \exp \ln x^r = \exp (r \ln x)$, so $Dx^r = D \exp (r \ln x) = \exp (r \ln x)Dr \ln x = [\exp (r \ln x)][r/x] = rx^{r-1}$. To prove (b), set $G(u) = u^r$, where $u = f(x)$, so $G(u) = G[f(x)] = [f(x)]^r$. Use the chain rule and the result in (a).

Finally we shall express e as a limit from which rational approximations to its value can be made. We differentiate $\ln x$:

(a) $\dfrac{1}{x} = D \ln x = \lim\limits_{h \to 0} \dfrac{\ln (x + h) - \ln x}{h} = \lim\limits_{h \to 0} \dfrac{1}{h} \ln \left(\dfrac{x + h}{x} \right)$

$= \lim\limits_{h \to 0} \ln [1 + (h/x)]/h$

If we set $x = 1$ in (a), we obtain

$$1 = \lim\limits_{h \to 0} \dfrac{1}{h} \ln (1 + h) = \lim\limits_{h \to 0} \ln (1 + h)^{1/h}$$

Since e^x is a continuous function of x, it follows that

$$e = \lim\limits_{h \to 0} \exp [\ln (1 + h)^{1/h}] = \lim\limits_{h \to 0} (1 + h)^{1/h}$$

i.e.,

$$e = \lim\limits_{h \to 0} (1 + h)^{1/h}$$

We might next choose $h = 1/n$, where $n = 1, 2, 3, \ldots$. Then $h \to 0$ is equivalent to $n \to \infty$. Since $\lim\limits_{h \to \infty} (1 + h)^{1/h}$ exists, so does $\lim\limits_{n \to \infty} [1 + (1/n)]^n$, and the limits are the same; i.e.,

$$\boxed{e = \lim\limits_{n \to \infty} [1 + (1/n)]^n}$$

By taking large values of n, we get e is approximately 2.7183, as was mentioned in §3.8.

PROBLEMS

3.9.1. Consider $f(x) = x^2$, with $x < 0$. Find the inverse function. Construct its graph beginning with the graph of x^2, $x < 0$, and rotating, reflecting, and relabeling.

3.9.2. Use (3.9.2) to find the inverse function (if it exists) of each of the following; then use graphical methods to investigate the inverse, and graph both functions.
  (a) $f(x) = 3x$
  (b) $f(x) = 4x - 5$
  (c) $f(x) = ax + b$, $(a, b$ constant, $a \neq 0)$
  (d) $f(x) = x^3$
  (e) $f(x) = x^4$
  (f) $f(x) = 1/x$, $x \neq 0$ (This function is neither S.D. nor S.I., but an inverse function exists)
  (g) $f(x) = x^4$, $x > 0$.

3.9.3. Consider the function $f(x) = (ax + 1)/(bx - 1)$. Find values of a and b such that $f(x)$ is its *own* inverse; i.e., such that $f(f(x)) = x$.

3.9.4. For the reliability function $f_n(r)$ given in Ex. 1.1.10, show that if $R = f_n(r)$, then $r = f_{1/n}(R)$. What does this say about inverses?

3.9.5. Find dy/dx if

(a) $y = \ln \sqrt{x}$

(b) $y = \ln |x^3 - 3x^2 + 2x + 5|$

(c) $y = \ln (xe^x)$

(d) $y = \ln x(x + 1)^5$

(e) $y = \ln \sqrt{x(x^2 + 1)^3}$

(f) $y = \ln \sqrt{x(x + 1)(x + 2)}$

(g) $y = \ln (\ln x)$

(h) $y = \ln (e^x) + e^x \ln x$

3.9.6. Use logarithmic differentiation to find dy/dx if:

(a) $y = x^{x^2 + x - 2}$, $x > 0$

(b) $y = x^{\ln x}$, $x > 0$

(c) $y = (\ln x)^{\ln x}$, $x > 0$

(d) $y = (x^2 + x + 1)^{2x - 7}$, $x > 0$

(e) $y = (\sqrt{x})^{\sqrt{x}}$, $x > 0$

3.9.7. Find when $f(x) = (\ln x)/x$, $x > 0$, is **S.I.** and when it is **S.D.** Discuss the extrema of $f(x)$.

3.9.8. Psychologists believe that a person's childhood ability to memorize, measured by $G(t)$ where t is measured in years, is given by

$$G(t) = \begin{cases} t \ln t + 1, & 0 < t \le 4 \\ 1, & t = 0 \end{cases}$$

Find the extrema of $G(t)$.

3.9.9. Let f be the inverse function of g. What relation exists between the range and domain of f and the range and domain of g?

3.9.10. Let $y = f(u)$ be a differentiable function on its domain, and let $u = g(x)$ be such that each u in the range of $g(x)$ is in the domain of $f(u)$. (Why is this necessary?) Let g be a differentiable function of x, and let $f[g(x)] = x$. Prove that

$$\frac{dg(x)}{dx} = \frac{1}{\dfrac{df(u)}{du}\bigg]_{u = g(x)}}$$

3.9.11. Another proof that $\ln ax = \ln a + \ln x$, where $a > 0$ is some constant and $x > 0$, supposes one already knows the differentiation rules for $\ln f(x)$. It proceeds as follows. First, $D_x \ln ax = D_x \ln x$ (Why?). Hence there is a constant k such that $\ln ax = \ln x + k$ (Why?). Set $x = 1$ and finish the proof.

3.10. Techniques for integration.

In §1.9 we found that it was possible to evaluate many derivatives explicitly without using the definition of the derivative as a limit. The fundamental theorem discussed in §3.6 is not a complete analogue; indeed, the theorem is useful only when we can explicitly exhibit an anti-derivative for the continuous function whose definite integral we wish to evaluate. For instance, though it is routine to evaluate $D[(x + 1)\sqrt[3]{x^2 + 2x + 5}]$, we see that to evaluate $\int_0^1 (x + 1)\sqrt[3]{x^2 + 2x + 5}\, dx$ requires finding an anti-derivative of $(x + 1)\cdot\sqrt[3]{x^2 + 2x + 5}$, and the fundamental theorem does not tell us how to do this. We shall exhibit in this section two new techniques for integrating complicated functions; this will be a *partial* answer to the problem of evaluating integrals.

Theorem 3.10.1 (The method of substitution or change of variables). Let $f(w)$ be a continuous function and let $g(x)$ be a function such that $g'(x)$ exists. Then, under the substitution $w = g(x)$,

$$(3.10.1) \qquad \int f(w)\, dw = \int f[g(x)]g'(x)\, dx$$

Proof. Set $F(w) = \int_a^w f$; by Thm. 3.6.1, $F(w)$ is an anti-derivative of $f(w)$. Next set $w = g(x)$, and observe that $F(w) = F[g(x)]$ is a function of x; call it $G(x)$. So

$$G(x) = F[g(x)]$$

By the chain rule,

$$(3.10.2) \qquad \frac{dG(x)}{dx} = \frac{dF(w)}{dw}\cdot\frac{dg(x)}{dx}$$

But $dF/dw = f(w)$, so (3.10.2) becomes (where $'$ means differentiation with respect to x)

$$(3.10.3) \qquad G'(x) = f(w)g'(x) = f[g(x)]g'(x)$$

Taking anti-derivatives, this becomes

$$(3.10.4) \qquad \int f(w)\, dw = \int G'(x)\, dx = \int f[g(x)]g'(x)\, dx$$

since an anti-derivative of $G'(x)$ is $G(x) = F(w) = \int f(w)\, dw$.

Example 3.10.1. Find $\int 2x\sqrt{x^2 + 1} \, dx = \int 2x(x^2 + 1)^{1/2} \, dx$. The more complicated part of the function we wish to anti-differentiate is $\sqrt{x^2 + 1}$. We shall simplify this by setting

$$g(x) = x^2 + 1, \qquad f(w) = \sqrt{w}$$

so

$$f[g(x)] = \sqrt{g(x)} = \sqrt{x^2 + 1}$$

Clearly, $g'(x) = 2x$, and it exists for all x. From the integral on the right side of (3.10.1), we see that

$$\int f[g(x)]g'(x) \, dx = \int \sqrt{x^2 + 1} \cdot 2x \, dx$$

which is what we wish to evaluate. From (3.10.1),

$$\int f[g(x)]g'(x) \, dx = \int f(w) \, dw = \int w^{1/2} \, dw$$

$$= \tfrac{2}{3} w^{2/3} + c$$

and, since $w = g(x) = x^2 + 1$, we finally obtain

$$\int 2x\sqrt{x^2 + 1} \, dx = \tfrac{2}{3}(x^2 + 1)^{3/2} + c$$

Example 3.10.2. We shall evaluate $\int (x + 1)\sqrt[3]{x^2 + 2x + 5} \, dx$. We shall evaluate the *definite integral* later. Set $g(x) = x^2 + 2x + 5$; then $g'(x) = 2(x + 1)$, which certainly exists for all x. Next, set $f(w) = w^{1/3}$. With these choices, $f[g(x)] = [g(x)]^{1/3} = (x^2 + 2x + 5)^{1/3}$, part of the function we are trying to anti-differentiate. Comparing our specific problem with (3.10.1) it becomes evident that our technique will work if $(x + 1)$ of our problem can somehow be accounted for by $g'(x)$ of (3.10.1). But with our choice of $f(w) = w^{1/3}$ and $g(x) = x^2 + 2x + 5$, the right side of (3.10.1) yields

$$\int f[g(x)]g'(x) \, dx = \int 2(x + 1)(x^2 + 2x + 5)^{1/3} \, dx$$

and so (3.10.1) implies

$$\int w^{1/3} \, dw = 2 \int (x + 1)(x^2 + 2x + 5)^{1/3} \, dx$$

or

$$\int (x + 1)(x^2 + 2x + 5)^{1/3} \, dx = \tfrac{1}{2} \int w^{1/3} \, dw$$

$$= \tfrac{1}{2} \cdot \tfrac{3}{4} \cdot w^{4/3} + c$$

$$= \tfrac{3}{8} w^{4/3} + c$$

Since $w = g(x) = x^2 + 2x + 5$, we finally have

$$\int (x + 1)\sqrt[3]{x^2 + 2x + 5}\ dx = \tfrac{3}{8}(x^2 + 2x + 5)^{4/3} + c$$

Example 3.10.3. Evaluate

$$\int 10\,\frac{x}{\sqrt{x^2 + 1}}\,dx$$

We shall simplify the denominator by setting $g(x) = x^2 + 1$ and $f(w) = w^{-1/2}$, $w > 0$, so that

$$f[g(x)] = [g(x)]^{-1/2} = 1/\sqrt{x^2 + 1}$$

and $g'(x) = 2x$. Hence,

$$\int \frac{10x}{\sqrt{x^2 + 1}}\,dx = \int \frac{5\cdot 2x}{\sqrt{x^2 + 1}}\,dx = 5\int \frac{g'(x)}{\sqrt{g(x)}}\,dx$$

$$= 5\int g'(x)f[g(x)]\,dx, \qquad g(x) > 0$$

By (3.10.1),

$$\int \frac{10x}{\sqrt{x^2 + 1}}\,dx = 5\int g'(x)f[g(x)]\,dx$$

$$= 5\int f(w)\,dw = 5\int w^{-1/2}\,dw$$

$$= 10w^{1/2} + c = 10\sqrt{x^2 + 1} + c$$

What information does Thm. 3.10.1 give concerning the evaluation of definite integrals? We continue to assume $g'(x)$ exists. If we analyze the proof of Thm. 3.10.1, we find that (3.10.4) must be defended. It is always true that $\int G'(x)\,dx = G(x)$ (this is a statement about anti-derivatives, and says simply $G'(x) = G'(x)$, which is always true!), but when is

$$\int_a^b G'(x)\,dx = \left[\int G'(x)\,dx\right]_a^b\ ?$$

If we look at the fundamental theorem, we see we must have $G'(x)$ *continuous* on $a \le x \le b$; from (3.10.3), we can ensure the continuity of $G'(x)$ by assuming the continuity of $f[g(x)]$ and $g'(x)$. Hence,

Theorem 3.10.2. If $g(x)$, $g'(x)$, and $f[g(x)]$ are all continuous on $a \le x \le b$, then Thm. 3.10.1 applies to definite integrals. To evaluate $\displaystyle\int_a^b f[g(x)]g'(x)\,dx$, we can evaluate $\int f(w)\, dw$, change this back to an expression in x, and evaluate this from $x = a$ to $x = b$.

Theorem 3.10.2 gives a technique for evaluating definite integrals which is rather clumsy at times, since it requires first evaluating $\int f(w)\, dw$ and then changing this back to an expression in x and then finally evaluating this from $x = a$ to $x = b$. If we analyze (3.10.4), we see that as the integral on the right goes from $x = a$ to $x = b$, and since $w = g(x)$, the integral on the left goes from $w = g(a)$ to $w = g(b)$, so we obtain:

Theorem 3.10.3. Under the hypotheses of Thm. 3.10.2,

$$(3.10.5) \qquad \int_{g(a)}^{g(b)} f(w)\, dw = \int_a^b f[g(x)]g'(x)\, dx$$

Example 3.10.4. Find $\displaystyle\int_0^1 2x\sqrt{x^2 + 1}\, dx$. We use the same substitutions as in Ex. 3.10.1. Here $g(x) = x^2 + 1$, $g'(x) = 2x$ and $f[g(x)] = \sqrt{x^2 + 1}$; all three functions are continuous on $0 \le x \le 1$. Hence, from Ex. 3.10.1,

$$\int_0^1 2x\sqrt{x^2 + 1}\, dx = \tfrac{2}{3}(x^2 + 1)^{3/2}\Big|_0^1 = \tfrac{2}{3}(2^{3/2} - 1)$$

To apply Thm. 3.10.3, we can use the details of Ex. 3.10.1 to observe that in that example, with $w = g(x) = x^2 + 1$,

$$\int_0^1 2x\sqrt{x^2 + 1}\, dx = \int_{g(0)}^{g(1)} w^{1/2}\, dw = \int_1^2 w^{1/2}\, dw$$

$$= \tfrac{2}{3}w^{3/2}\Big|_1^2$$

$$= \tfrac{2}{3}(2^{3/2} - 1)$$

Example 3.10.5 We next evaluate $\displaystyle\int_0^1 (x + 1)\sqrt[3]{x^2 + 2x + 5}\, dx$. If we repeat the calculations in Ex. 3.10.2, with $g(x) = x^2 + 2x + 5$, we find that

$$\int_0^1 (x + 1)\sqrt[3]{x^2 + 2x + 5}\, dx = \tfrac{1}{2}\int_{g(0)}^{g(1)} w^{1/3}\, dw$$

$$= \tfrac{1}{2}\int_5^8 w^{1/3}\, dw$$

$$= \tfrac{3}{8}w^{4/3}\Big|_5^8 = \frac{48 - 3\sqrt[3]{5^4}}{8}$$

The final technique we shall exhibit is given by

Theorem 3.10.4 (Integration by parts). Let $f(x)$, $g(x)$, $f'(x)$, and $g'(x)$ be continuous. Then,

$$(3.10.6) \qquad \int f(x)g'(x)\,dx = f(x)g(x) - \int g(x)f'(x)\,dx$$

or, for definite integrals,

$$(3.10.7) \qquad \int_a^b f(x)g'(x)\,dx = f(x)g(x)\Big]_a^b - \int_a^b g(x)f'(x)\,dx$$

Proof. The astute reader will observe that the hypotheses on the continuity of $f(x)$, $g(x)$, $f'(x)$, and $g'(x)$ are needed for the definite integrals in (3.10.7); for (3.10.6) we could actually assume less. We shall prove (3.10.6), making parenthetical remarks on the definite integral case to indicate how (3.10.7) follows. For convenience we shall use the notation $(f(x)g(x))'$ to mean $D[f(x)g(x)]$.

From the product rule for derivatives we have

$$(f(x)g(x))' = f'(x)g(x) + f(x)g'(x)$$

Hence, $(f(x)g(x))'$ is continuous, and so $\int_a^b (f(x)g(x))'\,dx$ exists and by the

fundamental theorem equals $f(x)g(x)\Big]_a^b$. Next observe that

$$\int (f(x)g(x))'\,dx = \int \{f'(x)g(x) + f(x)g'(x)\}\,dx$$

$$= \int f'(x)g(x)\,dx + \int f(x)g'(x)\,dx$$

Since $\int (f(x)g(x))'\,dx = f(x)g(x) + c$ [keep in mind that this is a statement about anti-derivatives, and is true simply because the derivative of $f(x)g(x) + c$ is $(f(x)g(x))'$], (3.10.6) is proved. The constant c has been omitted in (3.10.3) since it will arise when any of the anti-derivatives of (3.10.3) are actually computed. [By the fundamental theorem,

$$\int_a^b f'(x)g(x)\,dx = \int f'(x)g(x)\,dx\Big]_a^b$$

$$\int_a^b f(x)g'(x)\,dx = \int f(x)g'(x)\,dx\Big]_a^b$$

so (3.10.7) follows.]

Remark. The $g(x)$ that occurs on the right side of (3.10.6) and (3.10.7) is *any* anti-derivative of the $g'(x)$ that appears on the left side of (3.10.6) and (3.10.7), so the constant which arises when we anti-differentiate $g'(x)$ to get the $g(x)$ on the right side of (3.10.5) and (3.10.7) may be chosen to be any convenient value. It is usually chosen to be 0, though occasionally a different choice is efficacious.

Example 3.10.6. We shall use (3.10.6) to find $\int xe^x \, dx$. Set $f(x) = x$ and $g'(x) = e^x$. Then

$$\int xe^x \, dx = \int f(x)g'(x) \, dx$$

Clearly $f'(x) = 1$ and $g(x) = e^x$ [$g(x)$ is any anti-derivative, so we choose $c = 0$ in the general anti-derivative $e^x + c$]. Hence, by (3.10.6),

$$\int xe^x \, dx = xe^x - \int 1 \cdot e^x \, dx = xe^x - e^x + c$$

Example 3.10.7. From Ex. 3.10.6,

$$\int_0^1 xe^x \, dx = \int xe^x \, dx \Big]_0^1 = (xe^x - e^x) \Big]_0^1 = 1$$

Another way to write this is (still from Ex. 3.10.6)

$$\int_0^1 xe^x \, dx = xe^x \Big|_0^1 - \int_0^1 1 \cdot e^x \, dx$$

$$= e - \left(e^x \Big]_0^1 \right) = 1$$

Example 3.10.8. Find $\int \ln x \, dx$. We have a choice to make: Either set $f(x) = \ln x$ and $g'(x) = 1$ or set $f(x) = 1$ and $g'(x) = \ln x$. If we choose $g'(x) = \ln x$ and $f(x) = 1$, then to use (3.10.6) we must find $g(x)$; but to find $g(x)$ we must anti-differentiate $\ln x$; and to do this involves already knowing $\int \ln x \, dx$, which is, unfortunately, exactly our problem in this example.

Hence, set $f(x) = \ln x$ and $g'(x) = 1$. Then $f'(x) = 1/x$, and $g(x) = x$, so (3.10.6) becomes

$$\int \ln x \, dx = x \ln x - \int x \cdot \frac{1}{x} \, dx$$

$$= x \ln x - \int dx = x \ln x - x + c$$

PROBLEMS

3.10.1. Use (3.10.1) or (3.10.5) to evaluate each of the following:

(a) $\displaystyle\int \frac{x^2}{\sqrt{x^3 + 2}}\, dx$

(b) $\displaystyle\int \frac{x^2}{x^3 + 2}\, dx$

(c) $\displaystyle\int \frac{x - 3}{\sqrt[3]{x^2 - 6x + 15}}$

(d) $\displaystyle\int_0^1 \frac{x^5}{x^6 + 1}\, dx$

(e) $\displaystyle\int_0^1 \frac{x^5}{(x^6 + 1)^2}\, dx$

(f) $\displaystyle\int xe^{x^2}\, dx$

(g) $\displaystyle\int_1^e \frac{\ln x}{x}\, dx$

(h) $\displaystyle\int \frac{1}{x \ln x}\, dx$

(i) $\displaystyle\int_1^e \frac{\ln \sqrt{x}}{x}\, dx$

(j) $\displaystyle\int \frac{x + 1}{\sqrt{8 - 2x - x^2}}\, dx$

(k) $\displaystyle\int \frac{x \ln (1 + x^2)}{1 + x^2}\, dx$

(l) $\displaystyle\int \frac{(\ln x)^4}{x}\, dx$

(m) $\displaystyle\int \frac{\ln \ln x}{x \ln x}\, dx$

(n) $\displaystyle\int \frac{(x + 3) \ln (x^2 + 6x + 8)}{x^2 + 6x + 8}\, dx$

(o) $\displaystyle\int \frac{e^{2x}}{1 + e^{2x}}\, dx$

(p) $\displaystyle\int \frac{e^x - e^{-x}}{e^x + e^{-x}}\, dx$

3.10.2. Use (3.10.6) or (3.10.7) to evaluate each of the following:

(a) $\displaystyle\int x^2 e^x\, dx$

(*Hint:* Use (3.10.7) twice, with the result of Ex. 3.10.6.)

(b) $\displaystyle\int_0^1 xe^{-x}\, dx$

(c) $\displaystyle\int_1^e x(\ln x)\, dx$

(*Hint:* Set $f(x) = \ln x$ and $g'(x) = x$.)

(d) $\displaystyle\int \sqrt{x}(\ln x)\, dx$

(e) $\displaystyle\int_0^4 x^2\sqrt{4 - x}\, dx$

(*Hint:* Use (3.10.7) twice, beginning with $f(x) = x^2$ and $g'(x) = \sqrt{4-x}$.)

$$\text{(f)} \quad \int_{-1}^{0} x^2\sqrt{x^2+1} \; dx$$

(*Hint:* Set $f(x) = x$ and $g'(x) = x\sqrt{x^2+1}$, and use (3.10.1) at the appropriate time.)

3.10.3. If marginal revenue is known to be $x/\sqrt{9-x}$, find the revenue function $R(x)$ if it is also known that $R(0) = 1$.

3.10.4. Let $P(x)$ be any polynomial. Prove the formula

$$\int e^x P(x) \; dx = e^x\{P(x) - P'(x) + P''(x) - P'''(x) + \cdots\}$$

3.10.5. Suppose that we wish to evaluate $\int (1/x) \, dx$ by using (3.10.6) as follows; Set $f(x) = (1/x)$ and $g'(x) = 1$; then $f'(x) = -1/x^2$ and $g(x) = x$, so by (3.10.6) we obtain

$$\int \frac{1}{x} \, dx = 1 + \int \frac{1}{x} \, dx$$

which seems to assert that $0 = 1$. Does this contradict (3.10.6)? Explain.

3.10.6. Show that

$$\int x^n(\ln x) \, dx = \frac{x^{n+1}}{n+1}\left(\ln x - \frac{1}{n+1}\right)$$

(*Hint:* Set $f(x) = x^n$ and $g'(x) = \ln x$, and use the result of Ex. 3.10.8. Terms involving $\int x^n(\ln x) \, dx$ will appear on both sides of the expression analogous to (3.10.6); combine them and solve for $\int x^n(\ln x) \, dx$.)

3.10.7. Let $f(x)$ be defined, continuous, and even on $-a \le x \le a$, where $a > 0$. Use the method of substitution to prove

$$\int_{-a}^{a} f(x) \, dx = 2 \int_{0}^{a} f(x) \, dx$$

This is part of the proof of Thm. 3.6.3. (*Hint:* Write

$$\int_{-a}^{0} f(x) \, dx + \int_{0}^{a} f(x) \, dx = \int_{-a}^{a} f(x) \, dx$$

In the first integral on the left, set $x = g(t) = -t$.)

3.10.8. Let $f''(x)$ be continuous on $a \le x \le b$.
(a) Why are $f(x)$ and $f'(x)$ continuous on $a \le x \le b$?
(b) Use integration by parts to show that

$$\int_{a}^{b} xf''(x) \, dx = bf'(b) - f(b) + f(a) - af'(a)$$

Chapter 4

SOME APPLICATIONS

OF

INTEGRATION

4.1. Volumes of revolution.

If we take a region in the xy-plane that is enclosed by curves and revolve this region about a straight line not passing through the region, the volume so generated is called a **volume of revolution.** Specifically, we shall take the region enclosed by the graph of some function $f(x)$, continuous and non-negative on $a \leq x \leq b$, the x-axis, and the lines $x = a$ and $x = b$, and we shall describe two types of volumes of revolution and methods for obtaining the volumes so generated: the "disk method" if the region is revolved about the x-axis, and the "method of cylindrical shells" if the region is of the form $0 \leq a \leq x \leq b$, and is revolved about the y-axis.

In Fig. 4.1.1, the region sketched in (a) is revolved about the x-axis to get the volume described in (b); then the region in (a) is revolved about the y-axis to get the region sketched in (c).

First we consider the problem of revolving about the x-axis; we shall describe the *disk method.* We approach the problem in the same spirit as the problem in §3.4 of finding the area bounded by curves. Divide the interval from $x = a$ to $x = b$ into N equal parts, each of length $\Delta x = (b - a)/N$. On the first subinterval construct a rectangle of base Δx and height $f(a + \Delta x)$; on the second subinterval construct a rectangle of base Δx and height $f(a + 2 \Delta x)$; and so on. The kth rectangle will have base Δx and height $f(a + k \Delta x)$ (see Fig. 4.1.2). Now revolve about the x-axis the regions enclosed by these rectangles. We obtain a set of consecutive solid right circular cylinders, or disks, whose total volume approximates the volume we want [see Fig. 4.1.3(a)].

If we isolate the kth disk, as in Fig. 4.1.3(b), we see that it has a radius $f(a + k \Delta x)$ and a height Δx, and hence a volume $\pi \cdot (\text{radius})^2 \cdot \text{height} = \pi[f(a + k \Delta x)]^2 \Delta x$. The total volume of all the disks is

$$\pi \sum_{k=1}^{N} [f(a + k \Delta x)]^2 \Delta x$$

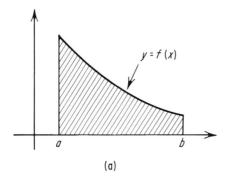

(a)

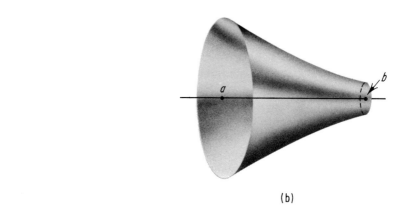

(b)

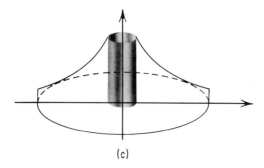

(c)

Figure 4.1.1

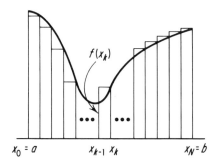

$$\Delta X = X_k - X_{k-1} = (b-a)/N$$

Figure 4.1.2

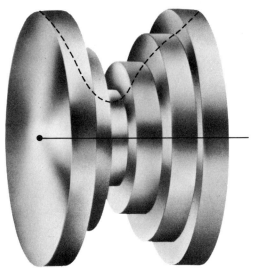

(a)

$f(a + k \Delta x)$

Δx

(b)

Figure 4.1.3

Since $f(x)$ is continuous on $a \le x \le b$, so is $(f(x))^2$. Taking limits, we see by (3.4.2) that

$$\pi \lim_{N \to \infty} \sum_{k=1}^{N} [f(a + k \, \Delta x)]^2 \, \Delta x = \pi \int_a^b [f(x)]^2 \, dx$$

so we take the volume of revolution obtained by revolving about the x-axis the region bounded by the graph of the continuous non-negative function $f(x)$, the x-axis, and the lines $x = a$ and $x = b$, to be this limit:

(4.1.1)
$$V = \pi \int_a^b [f(x)]^2 \, dx$$

Example 4.1.1. Let R and H be fixed positive constants. Use the disk method to find the volume generated by revolving about the x-axis the region bounded by the graph of $f(x) = Rx/H$, the x-axis, and the lines $x = 0$ and $x = H$ (see Fig. 4.1.4). Clearly, $[f(x)]^2 = R^2x^2/H^2$ is continuous on $0 \le x \le H$ (in fact, it is continuous everywhere). The desired volume is

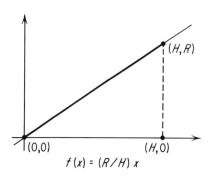

$f(x) = (R/H) x$

Figure 4.1.4

$$V = \pi \int_0^H \frac{R^2x^2}{H^2} \, dx = \frac{\pi R^2}{H^2} \int_0^H x^2 \, dx$$

Applying the fundamental theorem, this becomes

$$V = \frac{\pi R^2}{H^2} \frac{x^3}{3} \Big]_0^H = \frac{\pi R^2}{H^2} \cdot \frac{H^3}{3} = \tfrac{1}{3}\pi R^2 H$$

If we examine the geometrical object obtained by revolving this triangle, we see that it is a right circular cone of radius R and height H.

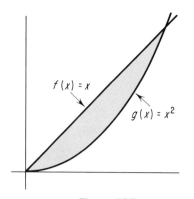

$f(x) = x$

$g(x) = x^2$

Figure 4.1.5

Example 4.1.2. Find the volume generated by revolving about the x-axis the area bounded by the graphs of $f(x) = x$ and $g(x) = x^2$ (see Fig. 4.1.5). The reader can easily verify that $f(x) = g(x)$ at $x = 0$ and $x = 1$, and hence the graphs intersect at $(0, 0)$ and $(1, 1)$. If we call V_2 the volume obtained by revolving about the x-axis the area under $f(x) = x$ from $x = 0$ to $x = 1$, and V_1 the volume obtained by revolving about the x-axis the area under $g(x) = x^2$, from $x = 0$ to $x = 1$, the desired volume V is given by $V = V_2 - V_1$. Using the disk method we obtain

$$V = V_2 - V_1 = \pi \int_0^1 x^2 \, dx - \pi \int_0^1 x^4 \, dx$$

$$= \left. \frac{\pi x^3}{3} \right]_0^1 - \left. \frac{\pi x^5}{5} \right]_0^1 = \frac{2\pi}{15}$$

We observe in passing that we might have written

$$V = V_2 - V_1 = \pi \int_0^1 [f(x)]^2 \, dx - \pi \int_0^1 [g(x)]^2 \, dx$$

$$= \pi \int_0^1 \{[f(x)]^2 - [g(x)]^2\} \, dx$$

Again consider a function $f(x)$ that is continuous and non-negative on $a \le x \le b$. We wish to take the area bounded by the graph of $f(x)$, the x-axis, and the lines $x = a$ and $x = b$, and revolve this area about the y-axis, thus generating a volume; the method this time is called the *method of cylindrical shells*. To insure that our region does not cross the y-axis, we assume that $a \ge 0$.

Again divide the interval from $x = a$ to $x = b$ into N equal parts, each of length $\Delta x = (b - a)/N$. Construct the same rectangles as were constructed for the disk method, but this time revolve them about the y-axis. This time we obtain a set of concentric cylindrical shells (a typical shell is drawn in Fig. 4.1.6), whose total volume approximates the volume of revolution we want. Our plan is to take a limit of the volumes of these shells.

We next find the volume of a typical shell. In general, if we have two concentric cylinders of the same height h, the inside cylinder having radius r and the outside cylinder having radius R, the volume of the shell is just the difference in volumes of the cylinders; i.e., $\pi R^2 h - \pi r^2 h$ (see Fig. 4.1.7). If we compare this to Fig. 4.1.6, we see that $h = f(a + k\,\Delta x)$, $R = a + k\,\Delta x$, $r = a + (k - 1)\,\Delta x$, so the volume of the shell is

$$\pi h(R^2 - r^2) = \pi f(a + k\,\Delta x)[(a + k\,\Delta x)^2 - (a + (k-1)\,\Delta x)^2]$$

When we perform the algebra, we find

$$(a + k\,\Delta x)^2 - (a + (k-1)\,\Delta x)^2 = 2(a + k\,\Delta x)\,\Delta x - (\Delta x)^2$$

Hence, the volume of a typical shell is

$$2\pi(a + k\,\Delta x)f(a + k\,\Delta x)\,\Delta x - \pi f(a + k\,\Delta x)(\Delta x)^2$$

and the sum of such volumes (giving the volume of the approximation to the

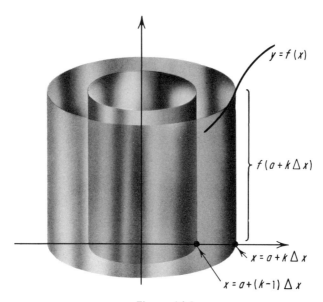

Figure 4.1.6

volume of revolution) is

(4.1.2) $2\pi \sum_{k=1}^{N} (a + k\,\Delta x)f(a + k\,\Delta x)\,\Delta x - \pi \sum_{k=1}^{N} f(a + k\,\Delta x)(\Delta x)^2$

Let $G(x) = 2\pi x f(x)$. Then $G(x)$ is continuous on $a \le x \le b$. (Why?) From (3.4.2), we see that

$$\int_a^b G(x)\,dx = \lim_{N \to \infty} \sum_{k=1}^{N} G(a + k\,\Delta x)\,\Delta x$$

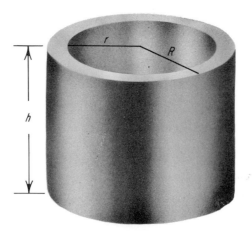

Figure 4.1.7

But $G(a + k\,\Delta x) = 2\pi(a + k\,\Delta x)f(a + k\,\Delta x)$, and $G(x) = 2\pi x f(x)$, so

$$2 \int_a^b xf(x)\,dx = \lim_{N \to \infty} 2\pi \sum_{k=1}^{N} (a + k\,\Delta x)f(a + k\,\Delta x)\,\Delta x$$

Hence, the first sum in (4.1.2) has as its limit

$$2\pi \int_a^b xf(x)\,dx$$

We next investigate the limit of the second sum in (4.1.2). Remember that $\Delta x = (b - a)/N$. We have

$$\pi \sum_{k=1}^{N} f(a + k\,\Delta x)(\Delta x)^2 = \frac{\pi(b - a)}{N} \sum_{k=1}^{N} f(a + k\,\Delta x)\,\Delta x$$

Again using (3.4.2), we have

$$\lim_{N \to \infty} \frac{\pi(b - a)}{N} \sum_{k=1}^{N} f(a + k\,\Delta x)\,\Delta x = 0 \cdot \int_a^b f(x)\,dx = 0$$

Thus, the limit of the expression in (4.1.2), and hence the volume of revolution obtained by revolving about the y-axis the region bounded by the graphs of $y = f(x)$, the x-axis, and the lines $x = a$ and $x = b$ is given by

(4.1.3)
$$\boxed{V = 2\pi \int_a^b xf(x)\,dx}$$

Example 4.1.3. Use the method of cylindrical shells to find the volume of the solid obtained by revolving about the y-axis the region bounded by the graph of $f(x) = x^2$, the x-axis and the lines $x = 0$ and $x = 1$. The desired volume is given by

$$2\pi \int_0^1 x \cdot x^2\,dx = 2\pi \left. \frac{x^4}{4} \right]_0^1 = \frac{\pi}{2}$$

Example 4.1.4. Find the volume obtained by revolving about the y-axis the region bounded by the graphs of $f(x) = x$ and $g(x) = x^2$. As in Ex. 4.1.2, the graphs intersect at $(0, 0)$ and $(1, 1)$, and on $0 \le x \le 1, f(x) \ge g(x)$. If V_2 is the volume obtained by revolving about the y-axis the area under $y = f(x)$ from $x = 0$ to $x = 1$, and V_1 is the volume obtained by revolving about the y-axis the area under $y = g(x)$ from $x = 0$ to $x = 1$, the desired volume is $V_2 - V_1$ which is

$$2\pi \int_0^1 x \cdot x\,dx - 2\pi \int_0^1 x \cdot x^2\,dx = 2\pi(\tfrac{1}{3} - \tfrac{1}{4}) = \pi/6$$

In passing we might observe that $V_2 - V_1$ can also be written as

$$2\pi \int_0^1 xf(x)\,dx - 2\pi \int_0^1 xg(x)\,dx = 2\pi \int_0^1 x\{f(x) - g(x)\}\,dx$$

In conclusion we should remark that in both the disk method and the method of cylindrical shells, we have tacitly assumed that our "approximations to the true volume" found by constructing disks or cylindrical shells actually do approach the true volume as the number of subdivisions becomes arbitrarily large; i.e., we have tacitly assumed that the integrals in (4.1.1) and (4.1.3) give the correct volumes. Since we have no definition of the "true" volume, we have nothing with which to check our constructions. We simply assert that the volumes obtained are the correct volumes. The precise definition of volume involves the concept of "double-integral" and is beyond the scope of this book.

PROBLEMS

4.1.1. Find the volume of revolution obtained by revolving about the y-axis the region bounded by the graph of $f(x) = -(H/R)(x - R)$ and the coordinate axes. Interpret your result geometrically. (H and R are positive constants.)

4.1.2. A semi-circle of radius R has equation $y = \sqrt{R^2 - x^2}$. Obtain the volume of a sphere by revolving this semi-circle about the x-axis.

4.1.3. Use the disk method to find the volumes obtained by revolving about the x-axis the region bounded by the graphs of :
(a) $f(x) = \sqrt{x}$, the x-axis, $x = 0$ and $x = 1$
(b) $f(x) = x + \sqrt{x}$, the x-axis, $x = 0$ and $x = 1$
(c) $f(x) = \sqrt{x}(x^2 + 1)^{1/4}$, the x-axis, $x = 0$ and $x = 1$
(d) $f(x) = |x^3|$, the x-axis, $x = -1$ and $x = 1$
(e) $f(x) = xe^{\sqrt{x}}$, the x-axis, $x = 0$ and $x = 1$
(f) $f(x) = x(x^3 + 5)^\pi$, the x-axis, $x = 0$ and $x = 1$

4.1.4. Use the method of cylindrical shells to find the volume obtained by revolving about the y-axis the region bounded by the graphs of:
(a) $f(x) = \sqrt{x}$, the x-axis, $x = 0$ and $x = 1$
(b) $f(x) = x + \sqrt{x}$, the axis, $x = 0$ and $x = 1$
(c) $f(x) = \sqrt{16 - x^2}$, the x-axis, $x = 0$ and $x = 4$
(d) $f(x) = x(x^3 + 5)^\pi$, the x-axis, $x = 0$ and $x = 1$
(e) $f(x) = 1/\sqrt{x^2 + 3}$, the x-axis, $x = 1$ and $x = \sqrt{6}$
(f) $f(x) = xe^x$, the x-axis, $x = \ln 2$ and $x = \ln 3$

4.1.5. Find the volume obtained by revolving the area bounded by each of the following curves about the prescribed axis:

(a) $f(x) = x^2$, $g(x) = x^3$, each axis
(b) $f(x) = x^2$, $g(x) = 3$, the x-axis
(c) $f(x) = 4 - x^2$, $g(x) = 0$, the x-axis
(d) $f(x) = 4 - x^2$, $g(x) = -1$, $x \geq 0$, the y-axis
(e) $f(x) = x^{1/3}$, $g(x) = x^2$, each axis
(f) $f(x) = \frac{1}{8}(12x - x^3)$, $y = 2$, $x = 0$ and $x = 2$, each axis.

4.1.6. Find the volume obtained by revolving the region bounded by $f(x) = 1 - x^2$ and the x-axis about the line $y = -1$.

4.2. Survival functions and renewal theory.

We shall consider a population of some sort for which we know that there is some function $f(x)$ to be determined, which gives the number of objects in the population at time x. We are therefore thinking of populations that change with time, such as a population of bacteria in a culture, or the population of vacuum tubes in a television set. Though we do not know $f(x)$ for general x, we do know the population at time $x = 0$, that is, the initial population, which we designate as $f(0)$. Our objective is to determine $f(x)$.

Suppose we look at our population at time $x > 0$. First we ask how many of the original population survived at time x. It is often possible to express this value as a proportion of the initial population; e.g., perhaps the number that survive at some instant is $\frac{1}{2} \cdot f(0)$ or $\frac{3}{4} \cdot f(0)$. We can often determine, perhaps empirically, a **survival function** $s(x)$ with the property that at time x, $f(0) \cdot s(x)$ is the population which has survived. Typically, $s(0) = 1$ (i.e., at time 0, our population is just $f(0)$), and $0 \leq s(x) \leq 1$. Very often, $s(x)$ is **S.D.** (see §2.1), and $\lim_{x \to \infty} s(x) = 0$ (see Def. 1.5.4).

We now consider a situation in which new objects are added to the population; we shall say that when this happens, the population is *renewed*, and call $r(x)$ for $x > 0$, the **renewal function.** We turn to an investigation of this function.

Let $A > 0$ be some time of interest, and consider the closed time interval $0 \leq x \leq A$. Divide this interval into N equal parts by means of the subdivisions $0 = x_0 < x_1 < x_2 < \cdots < x_{N-1} < x_N = A$. Hence, $\Delta x = A/N$ is the length of any one of the subintervals. Then $x_k = (kA)/N$. In the notation (3.4.2), $x_k = a + k \Delta x$, where in our specific problem, $a = 0$ and $\Delta x = A/N$ (see Fig. 4.2.1). We shall suppose that at time x_k, $r(x_k) \Delta x$ new objects are *added* to the population. Let $s(x)$ be the survival function for the original population, and suppose that the new population after objects are added is subject to the same survival function $s(x)$.

At time x_1, $r(x_1)\,\Delta x$ objects are added to the population; thinking of this as a new initial population, we find that at $A - x_1$ time units later (i.e., when we are at time A),

$$s(A - x_1) \cdot r(x_1) \cdot \Delta x$$

of the population that was added at time x_1 has survived. At time $x = x_2$, we

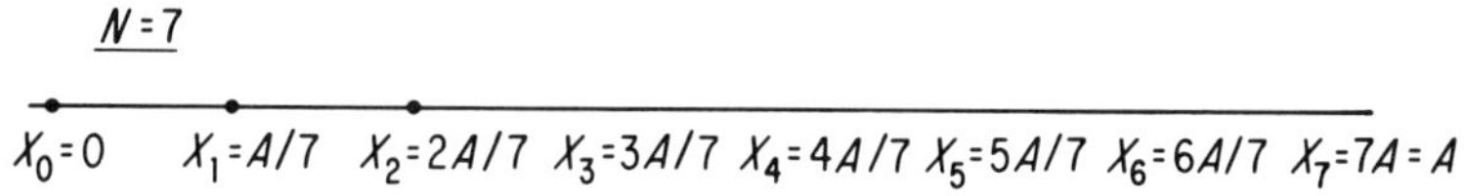

$$N = 7$$

$$X_0 = 0 \quad X_1 = A/7 \quad X_2 = 2A/7 \quad X_3 = 3A/7 \quad X_4 = 4A/7 \quad X_5 = 5A/7 \quad X_6 = 6A/7 \quad X_7 = 7A = A$$

Figure 4.2.1

add $r(x_2)\,\Delta x$ objects, and of this added population, $A - x_2$ time units later (i.e., again when we are at time A), the number surviving is

$$s(A - x_2) \cdot r(x_2)\,\Delta x$$

In general, then, at time $x = x_k$, we add $r(x_k)\,\Delta x$ to the population, and the number of this added population that survive $A - x_k$ time units later is

$$s(A - x_k) \cdot r(x_k)\,\Delta x$$

Hence, the *total* population $f(A)$ at time $x = A$, due to the initial population $f(0)$ and the N additions to the population at times $x_1, \ldots, x_N$ is given by

$$(4.2.1) \qquad f(A) = f(0)s(A) + \sum_{k=1}^{N} s(A - x_k)r(x_k)\,\Delta x$$

Assuming that $s(x)$ and $r(x)$ are continuous, we see that in limit (4.2.1) becomes [using (3.4.2)]

$$(4.2.2) \qquad f(A) = f(0)s(A) + \int_0^A s(A - x)r(x)\,dx$$

This can be interpreted as meaning that *we are continuously adding to the population.* By definition of limit, this also means that for N sufficiently large, (4.2.2) is a "good" approximation to (4.2.1).

If we think of A as a variable, and replace A by t, (4.2.2) becomes

$$(4.2.3) \qquad f(t) = f(0)s(t) + \int_0^t s(t - x)r(x)\,dx$$

PROBLEMS

4.2.1. Suppose we have an initial population of 10,000 objects, and we know that the survival function is given by $s(x) = e^{-x}$ and the renewal function is $r(x) = k$ for some constant k, with x measured in hours. We assume continuous renewals. What is the size of the population at the end of 12 hours?

4.2.2. Repeat Prob. 4.2.1 with $r(x) = x^2$.

4.2.3. Repeat Prob. 4.2.1 for arbitrary time $t = A$ and $k = 1$.

4.2.4. Show that if the survival function s is given by $s(x) = \exp(-kx/m)$ and $f(0) = m$, then the population size has the constant value $f(x) = f(0) = m$ when the renewal function has the constant value k. Of course, k and m are positive constants, and we are assuming continuous renewals.

4.3. An application from economics: consumer surplus.

Let $p(x)$ be the price function for a commodity, expressed as a function of demand x (see §2.3). Suppose that whatever conditions govern the market determine the market demand to be $x = A$ with the corresponding price $p(A)$. If we are at a point x at which $p(x) > p(A)$, then the consumer has gained, since the market price is fixed at $p(A)$. That is, since the consumer is willing to pay $p(x)$ but only has to pay the smaller price $p(A)$, it is a gain for the consumer. A measure of the consumer gain is often taken to be the area between the graphs of $y = p(x)$ and $y = p(A)$ in the region in which $p(x) > p(A)$ (of course, $y = p(A)$ is a constant function whose graph is a straight line parallel to the x-axis).

Since $p(x)$ is assumed to be **S.D.** (this only assumes that as demand x increases, price $p(x)$ decreases), we have $p(x) > p(A)$ on $0 \le x < A$ (see Fig. 4.3.1). The area between the

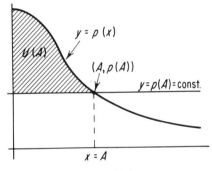

Figure 4.3.1

graphs $y = p(x)$ and $y = p(A)$ in the region in which $p(x) > p(A)$; i.e., $0 \le x \le A$, is given by

$$\int_0^A \{p(x) - p(A)\}\, dx$$

so we define the **consumer surplus** $U(A)$ related to the demand $x = A$ by

$$U(A) = \int_0^A \{p(x) - p(A)\}\, dx$$

(See Fig. 4.3.1.)

PROBLEMS

4.3.1. Suppose price as a function of demand is given by $p(x) = e^{-x}$, and the demand is fixed at $x = \ln 10$. Determine the consumer surplus.

4.3.2. Repeat Prob. 4.3.1 with price now given by $p(x) = xe^{-x}$.

4.3.3. It is known that for a certain commodity, the price is constant at $1/(2 \ln 2)$ when demand x is such that $0 \le x \le 2$, and then for demand $x > 2$, the price behaves like $1/(x \ln x)$; i.e.,

$$p(x) = \begin{cases} 1/(2 \ln 2), & 0 \le x \le 2 \\ 1/(x \ln x), & x > 2 \end{cases}$$

First verify that $p(x)$ is never increasing, and that for $x > 2$, $p(x)$ is **S.D.** Then find $U(x)$ if demand is fixed at $x = A = 5$.

4.4. A differential equation of interest.

Historically one of the most powerful mathematical tools possessed by the physicist in his efforts to describe physical phenomena has been differential equations; i.e., equations in which derivatives occur. Vast numbers of technical articles and texts at all levels have been devoted exclusively to a systematic investigation of such equations. We shall confine ourselves now to the investigation of a single such equation; namely, with $f(x)$ and $g(y)$ continuous functions of x and y, respectively, we consider

(4.4.1) $$g(y) \frac{dy}{dx} = f(x)$$

A solution to such an equation is a differentiable function $u(x)$ which satisfies (4.4.1); i.e., a differentiable function $u(x)$ such that

(4.4.2) $$g[u(x)] \, Du(x) = f(x)$$

We wish to determine this function $u(x)$. Assume that (4.4.1) has $u(x)$ as its solution, so (4.4.2) holds. If we formally anti-differentiate both sides of (4.4.2), we have

(4.4.3) $$\int g[u(x)]u'(x) \, dx = \int f(x) \, dx + c$$

where c is the arbitrary constant arising through anti-differentiation. Applying (3.10.1) to the left integral in (4.4.3), we have with $y = u(x)$

$$\int g[u(x)]u'(x) \, dx = \int g(y) \, dy$$

Since $f(x)$ is continuous, Thm. 3.6.1 guarantees the existence of $\int f(x)\, dx$; namely $F(x) = \int_a^x f$ is an anti-derivative of $f(x)$. Hence, the solution to (4.4.1) must have the form

$$(4.4.4) \qquad \int g(y)\, dy = \int f(x)\, dx + c$$

Conversely, (4.4.4) is a formal solution to (4.4.1), since

$$\frac{d}{dx}\int g(y)\, dy = g(y)\frac{dy}{dx} \qquad \text{(why?)}$$

and

$$\frac{d}{dx}\int f(x)\, dx = f(x) \qquad \text{(why?)}$$

and so differentiating (4.4.4) with respect to x yields

$$g(y)\frac{dy}{dx} = f(x)$$

which is exactly (4.4.1).

Example 4.4.1. Solve the differential equation $dy/dx = x/y$. Putting this in the form (4.4.1), it becomes $y(dy/dx) = x$; so in (4.4.1), $g(y) = y$ and $f(x) = x$. By (4.4.4), the solution is

$$\int y\, dy = \int x\, dx + c$$

or, $y^2/2 = c + x^2/2$. Multiplying this by 2 and setting $k = 2c$, we have $y^2 = x^2 + k$.

Of course this yields two solutions, $y = \sqrt{x^2 + k}$ and $y = -\sqrt{x^2 + k}$. Each of these functions is defined when $x^2 + k \geq 0$ and differentiable when $x^2 + k > 0$. Hence the specific nature of the solutions depends on the value of the constant k. Some graphs for various values of k are drawn in Fig. 4.4.1.

If we differentiate implicitly with respect to x the equation $y^2 = x^2 + k$, we obtain $2y\,Dy = 2x$, or, $dy/dx = x/y$.

Example 4.4.2. Solve $Dy = x\sqrt{y}$ for y if $y = 1$ when $x = 0$. This equation takes the form $y^{-1/2}\, Dy = x$, which is (4.4.1) with $g(y) = y^{-1/2}$ and $f(x) = x$. To guarantee the continuity of $g(y)$, we must restrict its domain to $y > 0$. Then (4.4.4) becomes

$$\int y^{-1/2}\, dy = \int x\, dx + c, \qquad y > 0$$

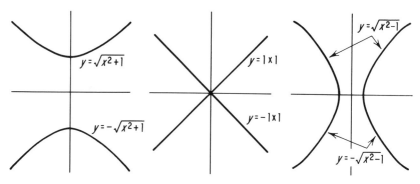

Figure 4.4.1

or

$$2\sqrt{y} = \frac{x^2}{2} + c, \qquad y > 0$$

Since $y = 1$ when $x = 0$, we have $2\sqrt{1} = 0^2/2 + c$, so $c = 2$, and our final solution is

$$2\sqrt{y} = \frac{x^2}{2} + 2, \qquad y > 0$$

Example 4.4.3. Solve

$$Dy = \frac{\sqrt{y^2 + 1}}{10y}$$

for y. This equation takes the form

$$\frac{10y}{\sqrt{y^2 + 1}} Dy = 1$$

so in (4.4.1),

$$g(y) = \frac{10y}{\sqrt{y^2 + 1}} \qquad f(x) = 1$$

Hence (4.4.4) becomes

$$\int \frac{10y}{\sqrt{y^2 + 1}} \, dy = \int 1 \, dx + c = x + c$$

By Ex. 3.10.3, the integral on the left is $10\sqrt{y^2 + 1}$ (we omit the constant which appears in Ex. 3.10.3, since it already appears on the right side of our solution). Hence the solution is implicitly given by $10\sqrt{y^2 + 1} = x + c$.

Example 4.4.4. Let A be an arbitrary real number. Solve the equation $y' = Ay$ for y. This equation takes the form $(1/y)y' = A$, so $g(y) = 1/y$ and

$f(x) = A$ in (4.4.1). To insure the existence and continuity of $g(y)$, we assume that $y \neq 0$. Then (4.4.4) becomes

(4.4.5)
$$\int \frac{1}{y} \, dy = \int A \, dx + k$$

Consequently, $\ln |y| = Ax + k$, and so

$$\exp(\ln |y|) = \exp(Ax + k) = e^{Ax} \cdot e^k$$

By (3.9.2), this simplifies to

(4.4.6)
$$|y| = e^k \cdot e^{Ax}$$

No matter what value is chosen for k, we see that $e^k > 0$. Let $c = e^k$; then $c > 0$. Also, no matter what A is, or what value of x we choose, $e^{Ax} > 0$. Hence, $ce^{Ax} > 0$. But (4.4.6) implies $y = \pm ce^{Ax}$; i.e., the solution to $y' = Ay$ is $y = ce^{Ax}$ where c is *any arbitrary* constant, not necessarily positive. To guarantee a non-zero solution, we assume $c \neq 0$.

PROBLEMS

Solve each of the following differential equations:

4.4.1. $y' = xy$

4.4.2. $Dy = -y/x$

4.4.3. $Dy = \sqrt{x/y}$,   if $y = 4$ when $x = 0$

4.4.4. $y' = y^2 \left(x + \frac{1}{x} \right)$

4.4.5. $(dy/dx) = x$,   if $y = 1$ when $x = 1$

4.4.6. $Dy = \sqrt{y e^x}$

4.4.7. $Dy = \dfrac{yx^2}{\sqrt{x^3 + 1}}$

4.4.8. $Dy = \dfrac{(\log x)\sqrt{y^2 - 1}}{xy}$

4.4.9. $yDy = xe^x + 1$

4.4.10. $Dy = \dfrac{3x^2 + 2x}{(\log y)(x^3 + x^2 + 1)^{1/5}}$

4.4.11. $Dy = y/x$,   if $y = 5$ when $x = 1$

4.4.12. $Dy = y/(x + 1)$

4.4.13. $Dy = \dfrac{1}{xy\sqrt{y + 2}}$

4.4.14. $Dy = xy(\ln x)(\ln y)$

4.5. Some applications of the differential equation of §4.

The problems we shall consider are taken mainly from the life sciences.

Example 4.5.1. **Parasites.**

We consider the situation in which a population of parasites lives on a host population. Each population exerts an influence on the other which in some cases aids and in some cases impedes the growth of that population. Hence, the time rate of change of the population of parasites at any given time depends both on the population of parasites at that time and the host population at that time; and, because of the interaction of the populations, the same statement can be made about the time rate of change of the host population.

If $x(t)$ denotes the size of the population of parasites at time t, and $y(t)$ denotes the size of the host population, with $x \geq 0$ and $y \geq 0$, then each of dx/dt and dy/dt depends on both x and y. The reader may recall that the total number of ways of pairing m distinct objects with n other distinct objects, distinct also from the first m, is $m \cdot n$; hence, x parasites can be paired with y hosts in xy distinct ways. This total pairing often contributes to dx/dt and dy/dt.

It has been determined that in many cases the differential equations which describe the populations are

(4.5.1) $$\frac{dx}{dt} = Ax + Bxy \quad \text{and} \quad \frac{dy}{dt} = Ry + Sxy$$

where A, B, R, and S are appropriate constants, $B \neq 0$, $S \neq 0$, and $x \geq 0$, $y \geq 0$.

We wish to find a relationship between x and y. Suppose the relationship is given by $y(x)$; our problem is to find $y(x)$. By the chain rule,

$$\frac{dy[x(t)]}{dt} = \frac{dy(x)}{dx} \cdot \frac{dx(t)}{dt}$$

Hence, if $dx/dt \neq 0$,

(4.5.2.) $$\frac{dy}{dx} = \frac{(dy/dt)}{(dx/dt)}$$

and consequently, substituting (4.5.1) into (4.5.2), we have

$$\frac{dy}{dx} = \frac{Ry + Sxy}{Ax + Bxy} = \frac{y(R + Sx)}{x(A + By)}$$

so

$$\left(\frac{A}{y} + B\right)\frac{dy}{dx} = \left(\frac{R}{x} + S\right)$$

Appealing to (4.4.1) with $g(y) = (A/y) + B$ and $f(x) = (R/x) + S$, (4.4.4) implies

$$\int \left(\frac{A}{y} + B\right) dy = \int \left(\frac{R}{x} + S\right) dx + c$$

$$A \ln |y| + By = R \ln |x| + Sx + c$$

This can be written as

$$\ln \frac{(y^A)}{(x^R)} = Sx - By + c$$

which implies that

$$\frac{y^A}{x^R} = \exp (Sx - By + c)$$

or finally, with $k = e^c$,

$$y^A \exp (By) = kx^R \exp (Sx)$$

which is the desired relationship.

Example 4.5.2. The diffusion equation.

We shall consider a cell which produces some substance at its center. For simplicity we assume that the rate at which this substance is produced inside the cell is q gm/cu cm/sec, and that this rate is independent of the concentration of the substance produced in the cell. The external environment in which the cell is normally found contains some normal concentration of this substance produced by the cell; call this concentration u gm/cu cm. We assume that u is smaller than the concentration in the cell. What happens is threefold. First, the substance produced diffuses from the central portion of the cell toward the cell's periphery; then the substance passes through the wall of the cell; and finally the substance interacts with the external environment. We shall investigate the equations which describe this diffusion process.

First we make some assumptions about the geometry of the cell. We suppose the cell is more or less an ellipsoid; i.e., shaped something like a football. Figure 4.5.1(a) represents a cross section with approximate length

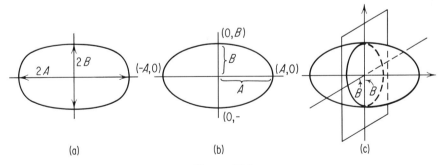

(a)   (b)   (c)

Figure 4.5.1

$2A$ and approximate width $2B$. We shall refer to PR and QS as the "ends" of the cell, and PQ and RS as its "sides." Figure 4.5.1(b) represents the geometrical idealization of the cross section of the cell, an ellipse whose equation is

(4.5.3)
$$\frac{x^2}{A^2} + \frac{y^2}{B^2} = 1$$

The idealization of the cell itself as a three-dimensional entity is the ellipsoid obtained by revolving the upper half of the ellipse of Fig. 4.5.1(b) about the x-axis, as in Fig. 4.5.1(c); the total volume of the disk can then be found by the *disk method* [see (4.1.1)].

We now compute the area of the ellipse in Fig. 4.5.1(b). By symmetry, it is clearly enough to find the area of the portion of the ellipse in the region bounded by the ellipse and the half-lines $x \geq 0$ and $y \geq 0$ (see Fig. 4.5.2), and then multiply this result by 4. Solving (4.5.3) for y, we obtain as the equation of the upper portion of the ellipse $y = (B/A)\sqrt{A^2 - x^2}$, and hence the area under the graph of the ellipse from $x = 0$ to $x = A$ is

(4.5.4)
$$\frac{1}{4}(\text{area of ellipse}) = \frac{B}{A}\int_0^A \sqrt{A^2 - x^2}\, dx$$

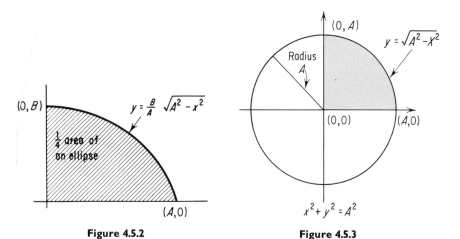

Figure 4.5.2   **Figure 4.5.3**

If we analyze the expression $y = \sqrt{A^2 - x^2}$, we see that it is exactly the equation of the top semi-circle of the circle $x^2 + y^2 = A$ (see Fig. 4.5.3), and hence $\int_0^A \sqrt{A^2 - x^2}\, dx$ is the area of 1/4 a circle of radius A; i.e.,

$$\int_0^A \sqrt{A^2 - x^2}\, dx = \tfrac{1}{4}\pi A^2$$

Substituting this into (4.5.4), we see that (4.5.4) becomes $(B/A) \cdot (1/4)\pi A^2 = (1/4)\pi AB$. Since this is 1/4 the area of the ellipse, the total area of the ellipse is πAB.

The area of the *cross section* of the cell pictured in 4.5.1(c) is exactly the area of a circle of radius B, and hence is πB^2. Each "end" of the cell has approximately the area of the circle pictured in 4.5.1(c), so:

(4.5.5) Total surface area of ends of cell $\sim 2\pi B^2$ ("$\sim$" meaning "approximately")

Each of the "sides" of the cell has surface area approximately equal to the area of the ellipse of Fig. 4.5.1(b); since there are four "sides",

(4.5.6)   total surface area of sides $\sim 4\pi AB$

If we revolve the region bounded by the graph of $y = (B/A)\sqrt{A^2 - x^2}$ and the x-axis about the x-axis, we find by the disk method that the volume of the cell is

$$V = \frac{\pi B^2}{A^2} \int_{-A}^{A} (A^2 - x^2) \, dx$$

and by symmetry (see Thm. 3.6.3),

(4.5.7) $$V = \frac{2\pi B^2}{A^2} \int_{0}^{A} (A^2 - x^2) \, dx = \frac{4}{3} \pi AB^2$$

We now have all the background information necessary, so we may turn our attention to the diffusion process. We first consider the motion in the cell of the substance produced by the cell from the region of greater concentration in the center of the cell to the region of sparser concentration at the "ends" and "sides" of the cell. Call c the average concentration of the substance in the center of the cell, and let c_1 and c_2 be the concentrations at the "ends" and "sides" of the cell, respectively. By what we have already said, $c > c_1$ and $c > c_2$.

If we move from the center of the cell to either end, the concentration drops from c to c_1 as we move over roughly A units, so the average drop in concentration in one direction is $(c - c_1)/A$. Since there are two ends, the average drop in concentration per unit length in the direction corresponding to the length of the cell is $2(c - c_1)/A$. Similarly, the average drop in concentration per unit length in the direction of the width of the cell is $2(c - c_2)/B$. This implies that the average *flow* of the substance in the direction of the length and width of the cell is

$$2M \frac{c - c_1}{A} \text{ gm/sq cm/sec}$$

(4.5.8)

$$2M \frac{c - c_2}{B} \text{ gm/sq cm/sec}$$

respectively, where M is a constant called the **diffusion constant for the substance within the cell.**

Next we look at the external environment in which the cell is suspended. As already remarked, we suppose the environment normally contains a concentration u of the substance produced in the cell. The presence of the cell causes a greater concentration of this substance in the vicinity of the cell. Let u_1 be the concentration *in the environment* corresponding to the "ends" of the cell and u_2 be the concentration *in the environment* corresponding to the "sides" of the cell. We assume that the concentrations u_1 and u_2 are significant only in that part of the environment that is *near* the cell wall; call P the distance from the cell throughout which u_1 and u_2 are significant (see Fig. 4.5.4).

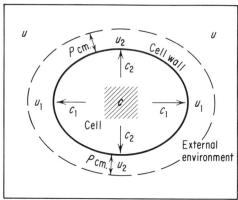

Figure 4.5.4

The flow through the cell wall is proportional to the difference in concentrations of the substance within the cell and in the environment, and so, for a constant of proportionality we shall call L (it is called the *permeability of the cell*), the flow through the "ends" and "sides" of the cell is given, respectively (see Fig. 4.5.4), by

(4.5.9) $L(c_1 - u_1)$ and $L(c_2 - u_2)$ gm/sq cm/sec

Finally we consider the situation in the environment that is within P-units of the cell. In this region, the drops in the concentration in the directions of the length and width of the cell are, respectively, $(u_1 - u)/P$ and $(u_2 - u)/P$. The equations analogous to (4.5.8) for the environment, i.e., the equations describing the flow in the environment, are

$$\frac{N(u_1 - u)}{P} \text{ gm/sq cm/sec}$$

(4.5.10)

$$\frac{N(u_2 - u)}{P} \text{ gm/sq cm/sec}$$

in the appropriate directions, where N is a constant called the **diffusion constant for the environment.**

The flow per square centimeter within the cell toward the cell wall, given by (4.5.8), must equal the flow per square centimeter through the cell wall given by (4.5.9), which in turn must equal the flow per square centimeter in the environment outside the cell wall, given by (4.5.10). Equating these expressions yields

(4.5.11) $$2M(c - c_1) = AL(c_1 - u_1)$$

(4.5.12) $$2M(c - c_2) = BL(c_2 - u_2)$$

(4.5.13) $$\frac{2M}{A}(c - c_1) = \frac{N}{P}(u_1 - u)$$

(4.5.14) $$\frac{2M}{B}(c - c_2) = \frac{N}{P}(u_2 - u)$$

The total flow through the "ends" and "sides" is the flow per square centimeter per second, multiplied by the total number of square centimeters; i.e., it is flow per square centimeter per second multiplied by surface area. The total surface area of the "ends" if the cell, given by (4.5.5), is $2\pi B^2$, and the flow per square centimeter per second, given by (4.5.9), is $L(c_1 - u_1)$, so the *total flow through the "ends" is*

(4.5.15) $$L(c_1 - u_1) \cdot 2\pi B^2 \text{ gm/sec}$$

In a similar way, appealing to (4.5.6) and (4.5.9), we see that the *total flow through the "sides" is*

(4.5.16) $$L(c_2 - u_2) \cdot 4\pi AB \text{ gm/sec}$$

Substituting from (4.5.11), (4.5.15) becomes

(4.5.17) $$\frac{4\pi MB^2(c - c_1)}{A} \text{ gm/sec}$$

and substituting from (4.5.12), (4.5.16) becomes

(4.5.18) $$8\pi MA(c - c_2) \text{ gm/sec}$$

Since the substance within the cell is produced on the average at q gm/cu cm/sec (see the first paragraph of the discussion), and the total volume of the cell, given by (4.5.7), is $(\frac{4}{3})\pi AB^2$, it follows that the *total amount of substance produced in the cell per second*

(4.5.19) $$(\tfrac{4}{3})\pi AB^2 q \text{ gm/sec}$$

The dimension of volume is cubic centimeters and the dimension of density is grams per cubic centimeter; so this product gives the total amount of substance in the cell, which is $(\frac{4}{3})\pi AB^2 c$ gm, and hence the *rate of change* of the *total* amount of the substance is given by the time derivative

$$\frac{4}{3}\pi AB^2 \frac{dc}{dt} \text{ gm/sec}$$

and this must equal the total amount produced by the cell per second minus the total amounts leaving the cell per second. These amounts are given by (4.5.17), (4.5.18), and (4.5.19). Consequently,

$$\frac{4}{3}\pi AB^2 \frac{dc}{dt} = \frac{4}{3}\pi AB^2 q - \left[\frac{4\pi MB^2(c - c_1)}{A} + 8\pi MA(c - c_2)\right]$$

Multiplying this expression by $3/4\pi AB^2$ and factoring out $3M$, this expression becomes

$$(4.5.20) \qquad \frac{dc}{dt} = q - 3M\left(\frac{c - c_1}{A^2} + 2\frac{c - c_2}{B^2}\right)$$

and this is the differential equation which describes the diffusion process.

Equation (4.5.20) can be modified at the expense of introducing some rather lengthy computations. Without explicitly carrying out the details, we indicate what can be done. From (4.5.11) and (4.5.13) it is possible to eliminate u_1 and to express c_1 in terms of M, N, P, L, c, A, and u. From (4.5.12) and (4.5.14) we can eliminate u_2 and express c_2 in terms of M, N, P, L, c, B, and u. These expressions for c_1 and c_2 give us new expressions for $c - c_1$ and $c - c_2$ which can be substituting into (4.5.20) yielding a form equivalent to (4.5.20), namely,

$$(4.5.21) \qquad dc/dt = q - (c - u)/w$$

where w is the rather cumbersome constant

$$(4.5.22) \qquad w = \frac{AB(2MN + 2PML + ALN)(2MN + 2PML + BLN)}{2(2MN + 2PML + ALN)A + (2MN + 2PML + BLN)B}$$

We shall finally solve (4.5.21). We put it into the form (4.4.1) by writing it as

$$(4.5.23) \qquad \frac{w}{(qw + u) - c}\frac{dc}{dt} = 1$$

where the expressions w, $(qw + u)$ are independent of time t, and hence constant. By (4.4.4), the solution is of the form

$$(4.5.24) \qquad w\int \frac{1}{(qw + u) - c}\,dc = \int 1\,dt - k$$

Setting $z = (qw + u) - c$, and hence $dz/dc = -1$, the integral on the left of

(4.5.24) becomes $-w \int (1/z) \, dz$ [see (3.10.1)], so (4.5.24) becomes

(4.5.25)
$$\int \frac{1}{z} \, dz = \frac{-1}{w} \int dt + k$$

This is exactly the form (4.4.5) in Ex. 4.4.4. Hence, from Ex. 4.4.4, the solution to (4.5.25) is

(4.5.26)
$$z = a \exp(-t/w)$$

where a is an arbitrary constant. By replacing z by $(qw + u) - c$ in (4.5.26) we finally obtain as the solution to (4.5.21)

(4.5.27)
$$c = u + qw - a \exp(-t/w)$$

where a is determined by the initial value of c.

Example 4.5.3. **Exponential growth and decay.**

In a vast selection of problems drawn from the physical sciences and the life sciences, experimental evidence based on observations of a given population, such as the amount of radium in a given sample or the size of the population of bacteria in a culture indicates that the rate of change of the size of the population at any given instant of time is directly proportional to the size of the population at that instant. Mathematically, if we set $y(t)$ equal to the size of the population at time t, then we have $dy(t)/dt$ is directly proportional to $y(t)$, or, for a constant of proportionality A,

(4.5.28)
$$\frac{dy(t)}{dt} = Ay(t)$$

In (4.5.28), if $A > 0$, then the population is growing, whereas if $A < 0$, the population is decreasing in size with time (this latter is the case in radioactive decay, a situation in which radioactive substances emit particles).

Equation (4.5.28), is exactly the differential equation appearing in Ex. 4.4.4, and hence has solution

(4.5.29)
$$y = ce^{At}$$

where c is a constant related to the initial population. Because of the nature of (4.5.29), we say we have **exponential growth** if $A > 0$ and **exponential decay** if $A < 0$.

We illustrate with the following representative though fanciful example. Suppose that a population grows so that its rate of growth is directly proportional to its size. Suppose that its initial size is 1000 objects, and in 10 days, it has 2000 objects. Find the number of objects at an arbitrary time t. Clearly, (4.5.28) describes the growth of the population (t measured in days), and so $y = c \cdot \exp(At)$ is the size of the population at time t. We must determine c and A.

Since the initial size of the population is 1000, we have $y(0) = 1000$. But $y(0) = ce^{A \cdot 0} = c$. Hence $c = 1000$, so (4.5.29) becomes $y = 1000 \exp{(At)}$. In 10 days we have 2000 objects; hence $2000 = y(10) = 1000\, e^{10A}$; or, $2 = e^{10A}$. Hence $10A = \ln 2$, so $A = (\ln 2)/10$. The population at time t is therefore

$$y(t) = 1000 \exp \frac{t(\ln 2)}{10}$$

Example 4.5.4. We return to Thm. 2.3.1 on elasticity of demand, which we only partially proved in §2.3. We are now in a position to prove (in the notation of §2.3) that if $\eta = 1$ for all p in $a \le p \le b$, then $p \cdot x(p)$ is constant. We recall that $\eta = 1$, $a \le p \le b$, means

(4.5.30)
$$\left[-\frac{p}{x(p)} \right] \left[\frac{dx(p)}{dp} \right] = 1$$

holds for all p in $a \le p \le b$ [recall (2.3.4)]. To put this in the form (4.4.1), we write (4.5.30) as

(4.5.31)
$$\frac{1}{x(p)} \frac{dx(p)}{dp} = -\frac{1}{p}$$

with solution from (4.4.4)

$$\int \frac{1}{x} dx = - \int \frac{1}{p} dp$$

whose evaluation yields $\ln x = - \ln p + c$, where c is an arbitrary constant. This becomes $\ln x + \ln p = c$, which implies $\ln(x \cdot p) = c$, which in turn implies $\exp{(\ln xp)} = \exp c$; i.e., $xp = \exp c$. If we write A for $\exp c$, we finally obtain $x \cdot p(x) = A$, which is the desired conclusion.

Example 4.5.5. We now complete the proof of Thm. 2.3.2; i.e., in the notation of §2.3, if $\eta > 1$, then $p \cdot x(p)$ (the total consumer expenditure) is **S.D.** We shall need (but shall not prove) the proposition: *If $f(x)$ and $g(x)$ are continuous on the interval $a \le x \le b$, and $f(x) < g(x)$ on $a \le x \le b$, then*

$$\int_a^b f < \int_a^b g$$

If $f \ge 0$ and $g \ge 0$, the integrals can be interpreted as areas, and we assert that $f(x) < g(x)$ on $a \le x \le b$ implies that the area under $f(x)$ does not exceed the area under $g(x)$, though the theorem is true regardless of the sign of $f(x)$ and $g(x)$. To say $\eta > 1$ is to say $-[p/x(p)]x'(p) > 1$. Dividing by p yields $-[1/x(p)]x'(p) > [1/p]$. Suppose that $b > a > 0$. By the above proposition, we have

(4.5.32)
$$- \int_a^b \frac{1}{x(p)} x'(p)\, dp > \int_a^b \frac{1}{p}\, dp$$

By (3.10.2), with $w = x(p)$ and $f(w) = 1/w$, $w > 0$,

$$\int_a^b \frac{1}{x(p)} x'(p)\, dp = \int_{x(a)}^{x(b)} \frac{1}{w}\, dw$$

$$= \ln w \Big]_{x(a)}^{x(b)} = \ln x(b) - \ln x(a)$$

Hence, (4.5.32) becomes

$$\ln x(a) - \ln x(b) > \ln b - \ln a$$

or

$$\ln x(a) + \ln a > \ln x(b) + \ln b$$

By Thm. 3.9.1 (a), this implies

$$\ln [a \cdot x(a)] > \ln [b \cdot x(b)]$$

and hence, since $\ln s$ is a **S.I.** function of s,

$$ax(a) > bx(b)$$

Summarizing, if $a < b$, then $ax(a) > bx(b)$; i.e., $p \cdot x(p)$ is a **S.D.** function of p.

PROBLEMS

4.5.1. It is known that for large samples of radium, the rate at which the radium decreases is proportional to the amount of radium. If it takes 1 gm of radium 1700 years to decrease to half its original size, find the amount of the original 1 gm of radium present after 2000 years.

4.5.2. A population is known to grow exponentially. During the first 10 minutes of observation, the population grows from 1000 objects to 5000 objects. When will the population contain 6000 objects? (Leave your answer in terms of the natural logarithm.) What will be the population at the end of 20 minutes?

4.5.3. The following is a theory of nerve excitation evinced by H. A. Blair (see *Journal of General Physiology*, **15**, 1932, 7–9). If a current V is applied to a nerve, ionization occurs, which in turn leads to excitation. If ε (epsilon) denotes the concentration of the ion causing excitation in excess of the normal concentration, then ε is a measure of the excitation. It is assumed that the time rate of change of ε increases proportionally with the voltage and decreases proportionally with ε; i.e., $d\varepsilon/dt = aV - b\varepsilon$ where $a > 0$ and $b > 0$ are proportionality constants. Determine ε as a function of time t, $\varepsilon(t)$, assuming constant current V.

4.5.4. (a) The following technique is used to date once-living objects. It is known that a living organism is composed of stable carbon C_1 and radioactive carbon C_2 in such a way that the ratio of the amount of C_2 to the amount of C_1 in the tissue is approximately constant, no matter what part of the tissue you investigate. When the organism dies, C_2 experiences exponential decay in such a way that in about 5550 years, only half as much C_2 is present. Find the number of grams, $y(t)$, of C_2, t years after the organism has died. (Use the fact that $\ln 2 \sim 0.693$.)

(b) A piece of ancient charcoal is found to have only 12 per cent of its original C_2 content. How many years ago did the tree from which the charcoal came die?

4.5.5. The following is a model proposed by L. F. Richardson to describe the spread of war fever (see Richardson, "War-Moods: I", *Psychometrica*, 1948, 13). Let $y(t)$ represent the proportion of the population advocating war at time t. Then for some constant c, $y(t)$ satisfies the differential equation $(dy/dt) = cy(1 - y)$ where $y(0) = 1/(e + 1)$. Find $y(t)$. (*Hint:* Observe that $1/[y(1 - y)] = [1/y] + [1/(1 - y)]$.)

4.5.6. Let $x(p)$ be a demand function with domain $a \le p \le b$, and for that function, suppose that the associated elasticity of demand, η, is constant, say $\eta = k$. Determine $x(p)$.

4.6. Further remarks on the integral. Improper integrals.

In the construction of the definite integral $\int_a^b f$, we were always careful to assume that $f(x)$ is continuous at each point on the closed interval $a \le x \le b$. Although continuity is certainly a strong enough condition to guarantee the existence of the definite integral, it is actually more than one needs. For instance, suppose that $f(x)$ is continuous at each point of the interval $a \le x \le b$ except at the point $x = c$ (where, necessarily, $a \le c \le b$), and $f(x)$ *is bounded on $a \le x \le b$* (i.e., there is a constant A such that $|f(x)| < A$ for every x in $[a, b]$); then no matter how $f(x)$ is defined at $x = c$, and, in fact, even if $f(x)$ is not defined at $x = c$, it is possible to prove that $\int_a^b f$ exists, and

(4.6.1)
$$\int_a^b f = \int_a^c f + \int_c^b f$$

where the integrals have the usual meaning as found in §3.5. In fact, if $f(x)$ is continuous except at a finite number of points $x = c_1, x = c_2, \ldots, x = c_N$, all points satisfying $a \le c_i \le b$, $i = 1, 2, \ldots, N$, with $c_1 < c_2 < \ldots < c_N$, and $f(x)$ is bounded on $a \le x \le b$, then $\int_a^b f$ exists (see Thm. 3.5.2), and

$$(4.6.2) \qquad \int_a^b f = \int_a^{c_1} f + \int_{c_1}^{c_2} f + \int_{c_2}^{c_3} f + \cdots + \int_{c_{N-1}}^{c_N} f + \int_{c_N}^b f$$

Example 4.6.1. Consider each of the following functions:

$$f(x) = \begin{cases} x, & 0 \le x < 1 \\ \tfrac{1}{2}, & x = 1 \\ 2, & 1 < x \le 2 \end{cases}$$

$$g(x) = \begin{cases} x, & 0 \le x \le 1 \\ 2, & 1 < x \le 2 \end{cases}$$

$$h(x) = \begin{cases} x, & 0 \le x < 1 \\ 2, & 1 < x \le 2 \end{cases}$$

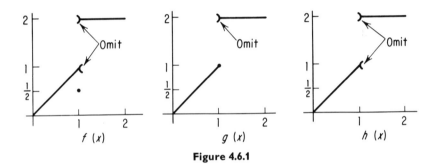

Figure 4.6.1

Each function is continuous at each point of $0 \le x \le 2$, except $x = 1$, and the functions are identical except at their common point of discontinuity. (See Fig. 4.6.1.) Clearly, no functional value exceeds 2 or is smaller than -2; i.e.,

$$|f(x)| < 2, \quad |g(x)| < 2, \quad \text{and} \quad |h(x)| < 2 \quad \text{for all } x \text{ in } [0,2]$$

Hence, we are assured that each integral exists, and

$$\int_0^2 f = \int_0^2 g = \int_0^2 h$$

Since the integrals are completely independent of the value of $f(x)$, $g(x)$, or $h(x)$ at $x = 1$, we can just as well take the functions $F(x) = x$, $0 \le x \le 1$, and $G(x) = 2$, $1 \le x \le 2$, each of which is continuous on its respective domain; then

$$\int_0^2 f = \int_0^1 F + \int_1^2 G = \int_0^1 x \, dx + \int_1^2 2 \, dx$$

The continuity of F on $[0, 1]$ guarantees that the fundamental theorem applies, and

$$\int_0^1 x\, dx = \frac{x^2}{2}\Big]_0^1 = \frac{1}{2}$$

Similarly we can apply the fundamental theorem, or use the definition of the integral directly to verify that $\int_1^2 2\, dx = 2$. Hence,

$$\int_0^2 f = \int_0^2 g = \int_0^2 h = \frac{5}{2}$$

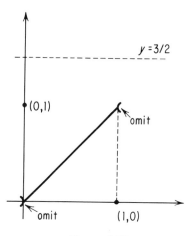

Figure 4.6.2

Example 4.6.2. Let $f(x) = x$ $(0 < x < 1)$, $f(0) = 1$, and $f(1) = 0$. Then $f(x)$ is continuous at each x of $[0, 1]$ except at $x = 0$ and $x = 1$. Clearly, $-\frac{3}{2} < f(x) < \frac{3}{2}$ for every x in $[0, 1]$ (see Fig. 4.6.2). Hence, $|f(x)| < \frac{3}{2}$, and so

$$\int_0^1 f = \int_0^1 x\, dx = \frac{x^2}{2}\Big|_0^1 = \frac{1}{2}$$

i.e., since the integral does not depend on the value of $f(x)$ at the endpoints 0 and 1, we have replaced $f(x)$ by the *continuous* function $F(x) = x$, with $0 \le x \le 1$ and used the fundamental theorem.

Example 4.6.3. Let $g(x) = x$, with $0 < x < 1$. Then $g(x)$ is continuous everywhere on $0 < x < 1$ except at $x = 0$ and $x = 1$, where it is not defined. Hence, the entire argument of Ex. 4.6.2 for $f(x)$ carries over to $g(x)$, and

$$\int_0^1 g = \int_0^1 f = \frac{1}{2}$$

A more serious problem involves functions $f(x)$ that are discontinuous at a finite number of points on some closed interval $a \le x \le b$, for which $|f(x)|$ assumes arbitrarily large values as x tends to the point of discontinuity. We call such a function **unbounded** at the point of discontinuity. We shall list a few functions of this type in the next example.

Example 4.6.4. Consider $F(x) = x^{-1/2} = 1/\sqrt{x}$, $0 < x \le 1$; $G(x) = 1/x$, $0 < x \le 1$; $H(x) = (x-1)^{-2/3}$, $0 \le x < 1$. Observe that $F(x)$ and $G(x)$ are continuous at each point of $0 < x \le 1$, but $1/\sqrt{x}$ and $1/x$ become arbitrarily large as x tends to 0, with $x > 0$. Observe that since F and G have their discontinuities at the end points of their domains, we use the concept "tends to 0" in the sense of Def. 1.5.2. Similarly, $H(x)$ is continuous on $0 \leq x < 1$, but as $x \to 1$ $(x < 1)$, $H(x)$ becomes arbitrarily large.

What, if any, meaning can be given the symbols

$$\int_0^1 F, \quad \int_0^1 G, \quad \text{and} \quad \int_0^1 H?$$

It turns out that these symbols are *not* meaningful in the sense of Thm. 3.5.1.

Let us, for illustration, consider $\int_0^1 F$.

Example 4.6.5. As in Ex. 4.6.4, let $F(x) = x^{-1/2}$, $0 < x \leq 1$ (see Fig. 4.6.3). For any number c on $0 < c < 1$, observe that F is continuous everywhere in the closed interval $c \leq x \leq 1$. Hence, with respect to the interval, $c \leq x \leq 1$, $\int_c^1 F$ exists in the sense of (3.4.2) or Def. 3.5.2, and, in fact, the fundamental theorem 3.6.2 applies to this function in this interval. Consequently,

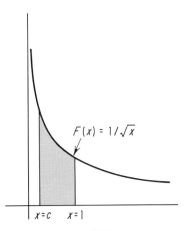

$F(x) = 1/\sqrt{x}$

$x = c$ $x = 1$

Figure 4.6.3

$$\int_c^1 x^{-1/2} \, dx = 2x^{1/2} \Big|_c^1 = 2 - 2\sqrt{c}$$

Since $\lim_{c \to 0} (2 - 2\sqrt{c}) = 2$ (in the sense of Def. 1.5.2), we say that the integral $\int_0^1 F$ exists *in the limiting sense*; we call the integral an improper integral; and we write

$$\int_0^1 \frac{1}{\sqrt{x}} \, dx = 2$$

Definition 4.6.1. Let $f(x)$ be defined and continuous everywhere in $a < x \leq b$, and let $f(x)$ have a discontinuity at $x = a$ at which $f(x)$ is unbounded. Then we say that $\int_a^b f$ exists as an *improper integral* and is equal to A if

$$\lim_{\substack{c \to a \\ c > a}} \int_c^b f = A$$

(i.e., if the limit exists in the sense of Def. 1.5.2), and we write simply

(4.6.3)
$$\int_a^b f = \lim_{\substack{c \to a \\ c > a}} \int_c^b f$$

to indicate the equality with respect to this endpoint limit. If the limit does not exist, we call $\int_a^b f$ *divergent*.

Example 4.6.5 now can be rephrased to read: for $c > 0$,

$$\int_0^1 \frac{1}{\sqrt{x}}\, dx = \lim_{\substack{c \to 0 \\ c > 0}} \int_c^1 x^{-1/2}\, dx = \lim_{\substack{c \to 0 \\ c > 0}} \left(2x^{1/2}\Big]_c^1\right) = \lim_{c \to 0}\, (2 - 2\sqrt{c}) = 2$$

Example 4.6.6. We next investigate the improper integral (with $1 > c > 0$)

$$\int_0^1 \frac{1}{x}\, dx = \lim_{c \to 0} \int_c^1 \frac{1}{x}\, dx = \lim_{c \to 0} \left(\ln x\Big]_c^1\right) = \lim_{c \to 0}\, (-\ln c)$$

This limit does not exist. Hence, $\int_0^1 (1/x)\, dx$ is divergent.

Definition 4.6.2. Let $f(x)$ be defined and continuous everywhere in $a \le x < b$, and let $f(x)$ have a discontinuity at $x = b$, at which $f(x)$ is unbounded. Then $\int_a^b f$ exists as an *improper integral* and is equal to B if

$$\lim_{\substack{c \to b \\ c < b}} \int_a^c f = B$$

(i.e., if the limit exists in the sense of Def. 1.5.2), and we write

(4.6.4)
$$\int_a^b f = \lim_{\substack{c \to b \\ c < b}} \int_a^c f$$

If the limit does not exist, we say the improper integral *diverges*.

Example 4.6.7. We investigate the improper integral

$$\int_0^1 (x - 1)^{-2/3}\, dx$$

To emphasize some of our previous remarks, the function $G(x) = (x - 1)^{-2/3}$ is continuous on each interval $0 \le x \le c$ for c fixed and $c < 1$. Hence we can apply the fundamental theorem to obtain

$$\int_0^c (x - 1)^{-2/3}\, dx = 3(x - 1)^{1/3}\Big]_0^c = 3(c - 1)^{1/3} + 3$$

and so, by Def. 4.6.2 above, we see that,

$$\int_0^1 (x-1)^{-2/3}\,dx = \lim_{\substack{c\to 1 \\ c<1}} \int_0^c (x-1)^{-2/3}\,dx = \lim_{c\to 1}[3(c-1)^{1/3}+3] = 3$$

Another possibility is that the function is unbounded at a point c in the interior of the interval; i.e., at a point c such that $a < c < b$.

Definition 4.6.3. Let $f(x)$ be defined and continuous at each point of the closed interval $a \le x \le b$ except at $x = c$, with $a < c < b$, where $f(x)$ is unbounded (see Fig. 4.6.4). Then we say that $\int_a^b f$ exists as an improper integral if

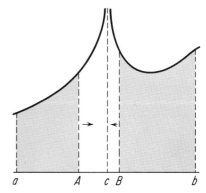

(i) $\qquad \lim_{\substack{A\to c \\ A<c}} \int_a^A f \qquad$ exists

(ii) $\qquad \lim_{\substack{B\to c \\ B>c}} \int_B^b f \qquad$ exists

and then we define

Figure 4.6.4

$$(4.6.5) \qquad \int_a^b f = \lim_{A\to c}\int_a^A f + \lim_{B\to c}\int_B^b f, \qquad A < c \text{ and } B > c$$

Example 4.6.8. Let $f(x) = x^{-2/3}$ on $-1 \le x \le 1$ with $x \ne 0$ (see Fig. 4.6.5). Clearly $f(x)$ is continuous at each x in $[-1, 1]$ except at $x = 0$, where it is unbounded. We wish to investigate

$$\int_{-1}^1 f = \int_{-1}^1 x^{-2/3}\,dx$$

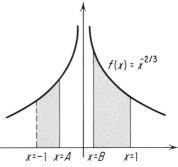

$f(x) = x^{-2/3}$

The improper integral, if it exists at all, must be evaluated in terms of (4.6.5). Since $f(x)$ is defined and continuous at all points $-1 \le x \le A$, $B \le x \le 1$, $A < 0 < B$, the definite integrals exist over these intervals in the sense of §3.4 and the fundamental theorem applies over these intervals.

$x=-1 \quad x=A \qquad x=B \qquad x=1$

Figure 4.6.5

Hence,

$$\int_{-1}^A x^{-2/3}\,dx = 3x^{1/3}\Big]_{-1}^A = 3A^{1/3}+3, \qquad A < 0$$

and

$$\int_B^1 x^{-2/3}\, dx = 3x^{1/3}\Big]_B^1 = 3 - 3B^{1/3}, \qquad B > 0$$

so, by (4.6.5),

$$\int_{-1}^1 x^{-2/3}\, dx = \lim_{\substack{A \to 0 \\ A < 0}} (3A^{1/3} + 3) + \lim_{\substack{B \to 0 \\ B > 0}} (3 - 3B^{1/3}) = 6$$

It is possible, of course, to have an improper integral of a so-called "mixed" type; i.e., one with discontinuities at more than one point, with the function unbounded at each of the discontinuities. For such problems, the integral must exist in the sense of each definition that applies. We shall illustrate with

Example 4.6.9. We wish to evaluate $\displaystyle\int_0^1 f$, where

$$f(x) = \begin{cases} x^{-1/2}, & 0 < x < \tfrac{1}{2} \\ (1 - x)^{-1/2}, & \tfrac{1}{2} \le x < 1 \end{cases}$$

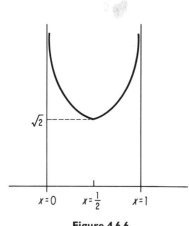

$x=0 \qquad x=\tfrac{1}{2} \qquad x=1$

Figure 4.6.6

Observe that this function *is* continuous at $x = \tfrac{1}{2}$. It has an unbounded discontinuity at $x = 0$ and $x = 1$, the endpoints of the interval (see Fig. 4.6.6). At $x = 0$, (4.6.3) applies, whereas at $x = 1$, (4.6.4) applies. Hence, the integral must exist as an improper integral at $x = 0$ in the sense of Def. 4.6.1, *and it must exist* at $x = 1$ as an improper integral in the sense of Def. 4.6.2; if *either* (4.6.3) *or* (4.6.4) fails to exist, then $\displaystyle\int_0^1 f$ is divergent.

Specifically, we take any convenient point of continuity of $f(x)$ that is between the two "bad" points, 0 and 1. By the way our particular function is defined, $x = \tfrac{1}{2}$ is a reasonable point to choose. Then,

$$\int_0^1 f = \int_0^{1/2} x^{-1/2}\, dx + \int_{1/2}^1 (1 - x)^{-1/2}\, dx$$

If we glance at Ex. 4.6.5, we see that for $c > 0$,

$$\int_0^{1/2} x^{-1/2} dx = \lim_{\substack{c \to 0 \\ c > 0}} \int_c^{1/2} x^{-1/2} \, dx$$

$$= \lim_{c \to 0} \left(2x^{1/2} \Big]_c^{1/2} \right)$$

$$= \lim_{c \to 0} \left(\frac{2}{\sqrt{2}} - 2\sqrt{c} \right) = \frac{2}{\sqrt{2}}$$

By (4.6.4), with $c < 1$,

$$\int_{1/2}^1 (1 - x)^{-1/2} \, dx = \lim_{c \to 1} \int_{1/2}^c (1 - x)^{-1/2} \, dx$$

Applying the rule of substitution to the integral on the right (see Thm. 3.10.2), we set $g(x) = 1 - x$, $F(w) = w^{-1/2}$, where $g(\frac{1}{2}) = \frac{1}{2}$, $g(c) = 1 - c$, and observe that

$$\int_{1/2}^c (1 - x)^{-1/2} \, dx = -\int_{1/2}^{1-c} w^{-1/2} \, dw$$

$$= -2w^{1/2} \Big]_{1/2}^{1-c} = -2(1 - c)^{1/2} + \frac{2}{\sqrt{2}}$$

Hence, with $c < 1$,

$$\int_{1/2}^1 (1 - x)^{-1/2} \, dx = \lim_{\substack{c \to 1 \\ c < 1}} \left[-2(1 - c)^{1/2} + \frac{2}{\sqrt{2}} \right] = \frac{2}{\sqrt{2}}$$

Consequently,

$$\int_0^1 f = \frac{2}{\sqrt{2}} + \frac{2}{\sqrt{2}} = \frac{4}{\sqrt{2}}$$

Example 4.6.10. Consider

$$g(x) = \begin{cases} x^{-1}, & 0 < x \le 1 \\ (2 - x)^{-1/2}, & 1 \le x < 2 \end{cases}$$

We wish to investigate $\int_0^2 g$. The reader should verify that $g(x)$ is continuous everywhere except at $x = 0$ and $x = 2$. We write

$$\int_0^2 g = \int_0^1 g + \int_1^2 g$$

$$= \int_0^1 x^{-1} \, dx + \int_1^2 (2 - x)^{-1/2} \, dx$$

provided each of the integrals

$$\int_0^1 x^{-1}\, dx, \quad \int_1^2 (2-x)^{-1/2}\, dx$$

exists, the first in the sense of Def. 4.6.1 and the second in the sense of Def. 4.6.2. But by Ex. 4.6.6,

$$\int_0^1 x^{-1}\, dx = \int_0^1 \frac{1}{x}\, dx$$

does not exist, and so $\displaystyle\int_0^2 g$ *does not exist.*

PROBLEMS

4.6.1. Let $f(x)$ be defined by

$$f(x) = \begin{cases} x, & 0 \le x < 1 \\ 10, & x = 1 \\ -x + 2, & 1 < x < 2 \end{cases}$$

(a) Sketch the graph of $f(x)$.

(b) Evaluate $\displaystyle\int_0^2 f$, if it exists. Is this an improper integral?

4.6.2. Define $g(x)$ by

$$g(x) = \begin{cases} 1, & x = 0 \\ x, & 0 < x < 1 \\ 0, & x = 1 \\ -x + 2, & 1 < x < 2 \\ 1, & x = 2 \end{cases}$$

Graph the function. Evaluate $\displaystyle\int_0^2 g$. Compare this with Prob. 4.6.1.

4.6.3. Define

$$h(x) = \begin{cases} x^{-1/2}, & 0 < x < 1 \\ 5, & x = 1 \end{cases}$$

In view of Ex. 4.6.5, evaluate $\displaystyle\int_0^1 h$.

4.6.4. Define

$$f(x) = \begin{cases} 0, & 0 \le x < 1 \\ 1, & 1 \le x < 2 \\ 2, & 2 \le x < 3 \end{cases}$$

Find $\displaystyle\int_0^3 f$.

For Prob. 4.6.5 through 4.6.14, evaluate the integrals, if they exist.

4.6.5. $\displaystyle\int_0^1 \frac{1}{x^{1/5}}\, dx$

4.6.6. $\displaystyle\int_0^1 \frac{1}{x^{0.99}}\, dx$

4.6.7. $\displaystyle\int_{-1}^1 \frac{1}{x^{1/5}}\, dx$

4.6.8. $\displaystyle\int_0^1 \ln x\, dx$

4.6.9. $\displaystyle\int_0^1 x \ln x\, dx$

(*Hint:* Assume that $\lim_{x \to 0} x \ln x = 0$.)

4.6.10. $\displaystyle\int_0^1 \exp\left(-\tfrac{1}{2} \ln x\right) dx$

4.6.11. $\displaystyle\int_{-1}^1 \frac{1}{\sqrt{|x|}}\, dx$

4.6.12. $\displaystyle\int_0^1 \frac{x}{\sqrt{1-x^2}}\, dx$

4.6.13. $\displaystyle\int_1^2 \frac{x}{\sqrt{x^2-1}}\, dx$

4.6.14. $\displaystyle\int_0^1 \frac{x}{1-x^2}\, dx$

4.6.15. For what values of p does $\displaystyle\int_0^1 (1/x^p)\, dx$ exist? Evaluate the integral for the appropriate p.

4.6.16. Discuss the following calculation:

$$\int_{-1}^1 \frac{1}{x^2}\, dx = \int_{-1}^1 x^{-2}\, dx = \frac{-1}{x}\Big]_{-1}^1 = -[1-(-1)] = -2$$

4.7. Some other types of improper integrals.

In §4.6 the integrals were improper because of difficulties in the function. We next consider integrals which are improper because of the limits of integration; i.e., because of the region over which integration takes place. Specifically, we shall define integrals of the form

$$\int_a^\infty f(x)\, dx, \quad \int_{-\infty}^b f(x)\, dx, \quad \int_{-\infty}^\infty f(x)\, dx$$

Definition 4.7.1. Let $f(x)$ have an integral, either in the sense of Def. 3.4.2 or of §4.6, on every finite interval $a \le x \le b$. Then

(4.7.1)
$$\int_a^\infty f(x)\, dx = \lim_{T \to \infty} \int_a^T f(x)\, dx$$

if the integral on the right exists. If the integral on the right does not exist, then $\int_a^\infty f(x)\,dx$ does not exist, and is said to be **divergent**;

(4.7.2)
$$\int_{-\infty}^b f(x)\,dx = \lim_{S \to -\infty} \int_S^b f(x)\,dx$$

if the integral on the right exists. If the integral on the right does not exist, then $\int_{-\infty}^b f(x)\,dx$ does not exist, and is said to be divergent.

Remark. To discuss integrals of the form (4.7.1) or (4.7.2), the domain of the function must be at least $x \geq a$ or $x \leq b$, respectively. It would suffice in either case for the domain of the function to be the entire real line. Also, if $f(x)$ is continuous, say on the real line, then it will certainly have an integral on every finite interval $a \leq x \leq b$.

Example 4.7.1. We shall investigate $\int_1^\infty (1/x^2)\,dx$. By (4.7.1),

$$\int_1^\infty \frac{1}{x^2}\,dx = \lim_{T \to \infty} \int_1^T x^{-2}\,dx$$

The function $f(x) = x^{-2}$ is continuous on $1 \leq x \leq T$ for every $T > 1$. Hence, on the interval $1 \leq x \leq T$, the fundamental theorem applies, and

$$\int_1^T x^{-2}\,dx = -\frac{1}{x}\Big]_1^T = -\frac{1}{T} + 1$$

Consequently,

$$\int_1^\infty \frac{1}{x^2}\,dx = \lim_{T \to \infty} \left(-\frac{1}{T} + 1\right) = 1$$

Example 4.7.2. We next consider $\int_1^\infty (1/x)\,dx$. By (4.7.1),

$$\int_1^\infty \frac{1}{x}\,dx = \lim_{T \to \infty} \int_1^T \frac{1}{x}\,dx$$

The function $f(x) = 1/x$ is continuous on $1 \leq x \leq T$ for every $T > 1$. Hence, on the interval $1 \leq x \leq T$, the fundamental theorem applies, and

$$\int_1^T \frac{1}{x}\,dx = \ln x\Big]_1^T = \ln T - \ln 1 = \ln T$$

but

$$\int_1^\infty \frac{1}{x}\, dx = \lim_{T \to \infty} \ln T$$

does not exist.

Example 4.7.3. Define the function $G(x)$ by

$$G(x) = \begin{cases} x^{-1/2}, & 0 < x \le 1 \\ x^{-2}, & 1 < x \end{cases}$$

We investigate $\displaystyle\int_0^\infty G(x)\, dx$. The integral is of a mixed type. Because of the upper limit, the integral is of the form (4.7.1); because $G(x)$ has an unbounded discontinuity at $x = 0$, the integral is also of the form (4.6.3). We write

$$\int_0^\infty G(x)\, dx = \int_0^1 G(x)\, dx + \int_1^\infty G(x)\, dx$$

$$= \int_0^1 x^{-1/2}\, dx + \int_1^\infty \frac{1}{x^2}\, dx$$

provided each integral on the right exists. By Ex. 4.6.5 and Ex. 4.7.1,

$$\int_0^\infty G(x)\, dx = 3$$

Example 4.7.4. Evaluate $\displaystyle\int_{-\infty}^0 e^x\, dx$. By (4.7.2), we must consider

$$\lim_{s \to -\infty} \int_s^0 e^x\, dx$$

The function given by e^x is continuous on $s \le x \le 0$ for every $s < 0$. Hence, the fundamental theorem applies, and

$$\int_s^0 e^x\, dx = e^x \Big|_s^0 = 1 - e^s$$

Consequently,

$$\int_{-\infty}^0 e^x\, dx = \lim_{s \to -\infty} (1 - e^s) = 1$$

Definition 4.7.2. Suppose $\displaystyle\int_a^\infty f(x)\, dx$ and $\displaystyle\int_{-\infty}^a f(x)\, dx$ each exists in the sense of (4.7.1) and (4.7.2), respectively. Then

(4.7.3) $$\int_{-\infty}^\infty f(x)\, dx = \int_{-\infty}^a f(x)\, dx + \int_a^\infty f(x)\, dx$$

If either of the integrals on the right is divergent, then so is the integral on the left.

Remark. The value of a in (4.7.3) is arbitrary, and chosen for convenience. It is often chosen to be 0.

Example 4.7.5. We shall investigate $\int_{-\infty}^{\infty} \exp{(-|x|)}\, dx$. First observe that

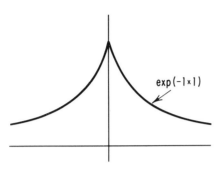

$$\exp{(-|x|)} = \begin{cases} e^{-x}, & x \geq 0 \\ e^{x}, & x < 0 \end{cases}$$

and the function is continuous everywhere (see Fig. 4.7.1). Since the form of the function changes at $x = 0$, it is natural to choose $a = 0$ in (4.7.3). Hence,

Figure 4.7.1

$$\int_{-\infty}^{\infty} \exp{(-|x|)}\, dx = \lim_{s \to -\infty} \int_{s}^{0} e^{x}\, dx + \lim_{T \to \infty} \int_{0}^{T} e^{-x}\, dx$$

By Ex. 4.7.4, $\int_{-\infty}^{0} e^{x}\, dx = 1$. Also,

$$\lim_{T \to \infty} \int_{0}^{T} e^{-x}\, dx = \lim_{T \to \infty} \left(-e^{-x} \Big|_{0}^{T} \right) = \lim_{T \to \infty} \left(-e^{-T} + 1 \right) = 1$$

So

$$\int_{-\infty}^{\infty} \exp{(-|x|)}\, dx = \int_{-\infty}^{\infty} e^{-|x|}\, dx = 2$$

PROBLEMS

In Prob. 4.7.1 through 4.7.10 evaluate each of the integrals whenever they exist. Assume that you already know $\lim_{x \to \infty} x^{n}e^{-x} = 0$ for all positive integers n.

4.7.1. $\int_{1}^{\infty} \frac{1}{x^{3}}\, dx$

4.7.2. $\int_{1}^{\infty} \frac{1}{x^{1.01}}\, dx$

4.7.3. $\int_{0}^{\infty} xe^{-x}\, dx$

4.7.4. $\int_{0}^{\infty} x^{2}e^{-x}\, dx$

4.7.5. $\int_{-\infty}^{0} xe^{x}\, dx$

4.7.6. $\int_{2}^{\infty} \frac{x}{(x^{2}-1)^{10}}\, dx$

4.7.7. $\displaystyle\int_0^\infty \frac{1}{\sqrt{x}}\,dx$

4.7.8. $\displaystyle\int_{-1}^\infty \frac{2x+1}{(x^2+x+10)^\pi}\,dx$

4.7.9. $\displaystyle\int_{-\infty}^\infty x\exp(-|x|)\,dx$

4.7.10. $\displaystyle\int_{-\infty}^\infty x\exp(-x^2)\,dx$

4.7.11. $\displaystyle\int_1^\infty \frac{1}{x^{0.99}}\,dx$

4.7.12. Let $f(x)$ be defined by

$$f(x) = \begin{cases} 1/x^2, & x \geq 1 \\ 1, & -1 \leq x < 1 \\ e^{x+1}, & x < -1 \end{cases}$$

Sketch the graph. Then, if it exists, evaluate

$$\int_{-\infty}^{+\infty} f(x)\,dx$$

4.7.13. For what numbers p does $\displaystyle\int_1^\infty (1/x^p)\,dx$ exist? Evaluate the integral for those p.

4.7.14. We have already seen that $\displaystyle\int_1^\infty (1/x)\,dx$ is divergent. Show that $\displaystyle\int_a^\infty (1/x)\,dx$ is divergent no matter what real number $a > 0$ is chosen. What happens if $a = 0$? if $a < 0$?

4.7.15. Show that

$$\int_2^\infty \frac{1}{x\ln x}\,dx$$

is divergent, but

$$\int_2^\infty \frac{1}{x(\ln x)^2}\,dx$$

exists, and find its value. Then find the values of p such that

$$\int_2^\infty \frac{1}{x(\ln x)^p}\,dx$$

exists, and the value of the integral for these p.

4.7.16. A painter with a good mathematical background is given the task of painting the region bounded by the graph of $f(x) = (1/x)$ and the x-axis, with the additional requirement that $x \geq 1$. In view of Ex. 4.7.2, the painter realizes the task is futile, so he decides to revolve the graph about the x-axis, taking as his volume (in the spirit of §4.1) $\pi \int_1^\infty [f(x)]^2 \ dx$. Use Ex. 4.7.1 to show that this volume is finite. Hence, all our painter has to do is pour the paint into the container formed by revolving $f(x) = (1/x)$, $x \geq 1$, about the x-axis, and then take a cross section, and in so doing, he has painted the required region (or has he?).

4.8. An introduction to probability.

We shall illustrate the probability concept by some simple examples, and then sort out the various ingredients of interest. [We shall refer to the various experiments by "exp." and continue to use "Ex." as an abbreviation for example.]

Experiment 1. The die experiment.

We consider the experiment of rolling an "honest" die; i.e., a die that is not "loaded." We can consider this as an experiment with six possible outcomes. The possible outcomes can be abbreviated by:

$$0_1 = \text{the event that a single dot appears on the die}$$
$$0_2 = \text{the event that two dots appear on the die}$$
$$\vdots$$
$$0_6 = \text{the event that six dots appear on the die}$$

Since the die is assumed to be honest, any one of the six faces is equally likely to appear in a single roll of the die.

Suppose that an experiment can have any of N distinct equally likely outcomes, and that an event of interest, say the event A, can happen in any one of M ways. We define the *probability* of A as the number M/N, and write $P[A] = M/N$. Since the event 0_1 can happen in exactly one way (namely, 0_1 occurs if and only if a single dot appears on the roll of the die, and there is only one way for the die to show a single dot), and there is a total of six distinct equally likely outcomes to the throw of our die, we see that $P[0_1] = 1/6$. Roughly, this means that if we roll the die enough times, we can expect a single dot to show on the die about one sixth of the time. Similarly, $P[0_2] = \frac{1}{6}$, $P[0_3] = \frac{1}{6}$, ..., $P[0_6] = \frac{1}{6}$. Hence to each outcome, 0_1, ..., 0_6, we have attached a probability; namely, the number $\frac{1}{6}$.

Set E be the event "an odd number appears on the roll of a die." Observe that E is just another possible outcome of our die rolling experiment. E can occur if one, three, or five dots appear after rolling the die. Hence, $P[E] = \frac{3}{6} = \frac{1}{2}$. We should observe that E is just the event that 0_1 occurs *or* 0_3 occurs *or* 0_5

occurs. Each of the events $0_1, 0_3$, and 0_5 is thought of as "elementary," since no one of them can be decomposed into more simple events, whereas E is an event which is a combination of the events $0_1, 0_3$, and 0_5. The complete set of elementary events for our experiment is the set $\{0_1, 0_2, 0_3, 0_4, 0_5, 0_6\}$. We remark that *events and only events have probability.*

Definition 4.8.1. An *event* is a possible outcome of an experiment; it has a real number between 0 and 1 (inclusive) assigned to it called its *probability.*

Loosely speaking, the elementary events are those that cannot be decomposed into combinations of more simple events, like $0_1, \ldots, 0_6$ in Exp. 1. A possible analogy might be to compare an elementary event to a point on the line, whereas an event might be compared to a set of points on the line. A more precise definition of elementary event will be given later. The set of elementary events will be called the *sample space* and we shall assume that the probability of the sample space (which is an event) is 1.

Definition 4.8.2. Two events are said to be *mutually exclusive* or *disjoint* if they cannot occur simultaneously.

Remark. Elementary events are always mutually exclusive.

Example 4.8.1. $0_1, 0_2, \ldots, 0_6$ are all the elementary events in Exp. 1, each with assigned probability $\frac{1}{6}$. We can write the previous probability statement as $P[0_k] = 1/6$, $k = 1, 2, \ldots, 6$. It should be clear that in any roll of the die, 0_1 or 0_2 or ... or 0_6 must occur, so $P[0_1 \text{ or } 0_2 \text{ or } \cdots \text{ or } 0_6] = 1$. But $0_1, 0_2, \ldots, 0_6$ are not the only events of the experiment. E, as defined in Exp. 1, is also an event, with assigned probability $\frac{1}{2}$. The sample space of the experiment is the set $\{0_1, 0_2, 0_3, \ldots, 0_6\}$.

Calculus, as we have developed it, is concerned with functions $f(x)$ whose domain is some set of *real numbers.* A sample space is not necessarily such a set. To apply the concepts and techniques of calculus we will identify our abstract sample space with some set of real numbers. In the case of our die rolling experiment, a reasonable identification would be to associate the real number 1 with the elementary event 0_1, the real number 2 with the elementary event 0_2, and in general, the real number i with the event 0_i as i takes on values from $i = 1$ to $i = 6$.

Hence we have defined a function W whose domain is the sample space of all elementary events and whose range is the set of real numbers $\{1, 2, 3, 4, 5, 6\}$, such that $W(0_1) = 1$, $W(0_2) = 2$, and in general $W(0_i) = i$ for each $i = 1, \ldots, 6$.

We can now identify all our previous probability statements made for our original sample space with corresponding statements for the real numbers

$i = 1, 2, \ldots, 6$ by observing that the event $W = 1$ is merely the counterpart of the event 0_1, so $P[W = 1] = P[0_1] = \frac{1}{6}$, and in general $P[W = i] = P[0_i] = \frac{1}{6}$, $i = 1, 2, \ldots, 6$. Observe also that $W(E)$ is undefined, since E is *not* an elementary event, and hence E is *not* in the domain of W.

Definition 4.8.3. A function whose domain is the entire sample space and whose range is some set of real numbers, or some set of points in the plane, is called a ***random variable***.

Remark. In Exp. 1 the range of the random variable W was a set of real numbers; namely, the set $\{1, 2, \ldots, 6\}$. Later we shall give an example of a random variable whose range is a set of points in the xy-plane. Our ultimate concern in these notes will be for random variables whose range is some set of real numbers, usually an interval or half line, or possibly the entire real line.

Experiment 2. A certain sorority has 18 pledges: 3 hazel-eyed redheads, 6 blue-eyed redheads, and 9 blue-eyed blondes. Fraternity pledges, to be perfectly fair, put the names of the girls in a box. We will consider the first drawing from the box. To simplify notation, let R = redhead, Y = blonde, B = blue eyes, and H = hazel eyes.

Since there are 18 names in the box and it is equally possible to pick any name, the probability of picking any particular girl is $1/18$. We now have a choice of sample spaces. For instance, since each girl is distinct, our elementary event might be that we pick some particular girl on the first drawing. This sample space has 18 elements, and is determined essentially by the names of the girls. Another possible sample space can be based on eye and hair color of the girls instead of names. Any girl can be represented by a pair of symbols, such as (H, R) for hazel-eyed redhead, (B, R) for blue-eyed redhead, and (B, Y) for blue-eyed blonde, and these three pairs exhaust all possibilities. This gives us the three element sample space $\{(\overline{H, R}), (\overline{B, R}), \text{and } (\overline{B, Y})\}$, where $(\overline{H, R})$ is the *event* that we pick (H, R) on the drawing; $(\overline{B, R})$ the event that we pick (B, R) on the drawing; and $(\overline{B, Y})$ the event that we pick (B, Y) on the drawing.

Since there are three ways for $(\overline{H, R})$ to occur, $P(\overline{H, R}) = \frac{3}{18} = \frac{1}{6}$. Similarly, $P(\overline{B, R}) = \frac{6}{18} = \frac{1}{3}$ and $P(\overline{B, Y}) = \frac{9}{18} = \frac{1}{2}$.

We next investigate relationships between events. We shall illustrate the following definitions in subsequent examples.

Definition 4.8.4. (i) We write $A \subset B$; i.e., A is a ***subevent*** of B or event A is contained in event B, to mean that whenever event A has happened, so has event B.

(ii) The ***null event*** is one that cannot occur in an experiment; i.e., it is impossible for this event to be realized. It is designated by $\varnothing$, and we take $P[\varnothing] = 0$. For convenience, we assume the null-event is a subevent of every event; i.e., $\varnothing \subset A$ for any event A.

Definition 4.8.5. The event A is an *elementary event* if the only subevents of A are A itself and the null-event $\varnothing$.

Example 4.8.2. In Exp. 1, $\varnothing$ might be the event that seven dots appear on the roll of a die; and $0_3 \subset E$, since whenever a three appears in a die, an odd number of dots have appeared. Observe, however, that it is false that $E \subset 0_3$, since E has occurred if 0_5 occurs, but if 0_5 has occurred, 0_3 certainly has not.

Definition 4.8.6. Let A and B be any events, not necessarily elementary.

(i) the event "A has *not* occurred" is called the event *complementary* to A, and will be designated by $\bar{A}$. Hence, $\bar{A}$ is the set of all elementary events which exclude A.

(ii) The *union* of A and B, written $A \cup B$, is the event that either A has occurred or B has occurred, *or both A and B have occurred.

(iii) The *intersection* of A and B, written $A \cap B$, is the set of all events common to A *and* B.

(iv) If A_1, A_2, ..., A_N are events

$$\bigcup_{i=1}^{N} A_i \qquad \text{means} \qquad A_1 \cup A_2 \cup \cdots \cup A_N$$

Remark. That A and B are mutually exclusive (or disjoint) can be written $A \cap B = \varnothing$.

Example 4.8.3. Recalling the event E as defined in Exp. 1, $E = 0_1 \cup 0_3 \cup 0_5$. Let F be the event: an even number of dots appear on the throw of the die. Then, $F = 0_2 \cup 0_4 \cup 0_6$ and $E \cap F = \varnothing$. $E \cap 0_1 = 0_1$, since 0_1 is common to both E and 0_1. The event $\bar{0}_1$ is the set of all elementary events which exclude 0_1, so $\bar{0}_1 = \{0_2, 0_3, 0_4, 0_5, 0_6\}$. The realization of any of the events $0_2, 0_3, 0_4, 0_5,$ or 0_6 is equivalent to the failure of 0_1 to occur.

Example 4.8.4. The elementary events in Exp. 2, (H, R), (B, R), and (B, Y), can be compared with points in the plane (x, y) whose first coordinate is "color of eyes" and second coordinate is "color of hair." If we identify $x = 1$ with blue eyes, $x = 2$ with hazel eyes, $y = 1$ with red hair, and $y = 2$ with blonde hair, we can define the random variable F by:

$$F\overline{(B, R)} = (1, 1), \quad F\overline{(B, Y)} = (1, 2), \quad \text{and} \quad F\overline{(H, R)} = (2, 1)$$

(see Fig. 4.8.1). The expression $F = (1, 2)$ now represents the event that the

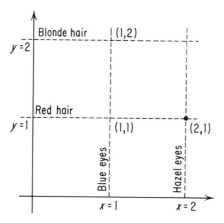

Figure 4.8.1

girl chosen is a blue-eyed blonde. The associated probabilities, as shown in our original discussion in Experiment 2, are:

$$P[F = (1, 1)] = \tfrac{1}{3}, \quad P[F = (1, 2)] = \tfrac{1}{2}, \quad \text{and} \quad P[F = (2, 1)] = \tfrac{1}{6}$$

By the way Exp. 3 was designed, no girl is both a blue-eyed redhead and a blue-eyed blonde. This can be expressed by $(\overline{B, R}) \cap (\overline{B, Y}) = \varnothing$, or, $\{F = (1, 1)\} \cap \{F = (1, 2)\} = \varnothing$.

We state the following theorem without proof:

Theorem 4.8.1. Let A and B be two events (not necessarily elementary). Then (i) $P[A \cup B] = P[A] + P[B] - P[A \cap B]$; (ii) If A and B are mutually disjoint; i.e., $A \cap B = \varnothing$, then $P[A \cup B] = P[A] + [B]$.

Example 4.8.5. In Exp. 2, we seek the probability that our arbitrarily chosen girl has blue eyes. This can happen only in two disjoint ways, namely, if she has blue eyes and red hair or if she has blue eyes and blonde hair. We can write the event "the girl has blue eyes" as $(\overline{B, \cdot})$ where the " $\cdot$ " signifies that the second coordinate hair color is not specified. Hence, since $(\overline{B, R}) \cap (\overline{B, Y}) = \varnothing$ we see by Thm. 4.8.1 that

$$P[\overline{B, \cdot}] = P[(\overline{B, R}) \cup (\overline{B, Y})] = P[\overline{B, R}] + P[\overline{B, Y}] = \tfrac{5}{6}$$

In terms of the random variable F, this event can be written as $\{F = (1, \cdot)\} = \{F = (1, 1)\} \cup \{F = (1, 2)\}$ and since the points $(1, 1)$ and $(1, 2)$ are distinct, $\{F = (1, 1)\} \cap \{F = (1, 2)\} = \varnothing$ so by Thm. 4.8.1, $P[F = (1, \cdot)] = P[F = (1, 1)] + P[F = (1, 2)] = \tfrac{5}{6}$. It is interesting to observe that the event "the girl has blue eyes" is transformed by the random variable to the event that we are looking at a point in the plane with first coordinate 1; i.e., that we are looking at all points in the range of F that are on the line $x = 1$ (see Fig. 4.8.1).

Example 4.8.6. Find $P(E \cup 0_1)$ in Exp. 1. First, observe that $E \cup 0_1 = E$, since if E occurs, 0_1 must occur; i.e., E or 0_1 occurs when E occurs. Hence, $P[E \cup 0_1] = P[E] = \frac{1}{2}$. By Thm. 4.8.1, $P[E \cup 0_1] = P[E] + P[0_1] - P[E \cap 0_1]$, and since $E \cap 0_1 = 0_1$, this says that $P[E \cup 0_1] = P[E] + P[0_1] - P[0_1] = P[E]$, as expected. Observe that when we take $P(E) + P(0_1)$, we have added the contribution of 0_1 to the probability of $E \cup 0_1$ *twice*, and that subtracting $P(E \cap 0_1)$ simply subtracts the extra contribution.

Example 4.8.7. In Exp. 1 we saw that $E = 0_1 \cup 0_3 \cup 0_5$. Since $(0_1 \cup 0_3) \cap 0_5 = \varnothing$, it follows that

$$P[(0_1 \cup 0_3) \cup 0_5] = P[0_1 \cup 0_3] + P(0_5)$$

Since $0_1 \cap 0_3 = \varnothing$, it follows that $P[0_1 \cup 0_3] = P[0_1] + P[0_3]$. Hence,

$$P[0_1 \cup 0_3 \cup 0_5] = P(0_1) + P(0_3) + P(0_5)$$

Example 4.8.6. is a special case of a more general theorem which we now state. The example also suggests a method of proof based on Thm. 4.8.1.

Theorem 4.8.2. Let $A_1, A_2, \ldots, A_N$ be N mutually disjoint events. Then

$$P\left[\bigcup_{i=1}^{N} A_i\right] = \sum_{i=1}^{N} P[A_i]$$

Example 4.8.6. In Exp. 1,

$$P\left[\bigcup_{i=1}^{6} 0_i\right] = \sum_{i=1}^{6} P[0_i] = 1$$

Our sample space consisted of six elementary events. In Exp. 2 the sample space consisted of three elementary events. We next consider an experiment in which our sample space is infinite.

Experiment 3. Suppose we have constructed a machine which, whenever a button is pushed, gives us a positive integer. The elementary events can be written

$\quad N_1 =$ the event that the machine registers a 1

$\quad N_2 =$ the event that the machine registers a 2 ...

$N_{1156} =$ the event the machines registers the positive integer 1156 ...

$\quad N_K =$ the event the machine registers the positive integer K

We shall suppose further that as the integer becomes larger, the probability that the machine selects that integer becomes smaller. Specifically, suppose

$P[N_1] = 1/2$, $P[N_2] = 1/2^2 = 1/4$, $P[N_3] = 1/2^3 = 1/8$, ..., $P[N_K] = 1/2^K$. Observe that it is *not* equally likely that we pick one integer rather than another. We will soon see that the probability just defined is nevertheless a legitimate probability function (see Def. 4.9.2). An obvious random variable is the function g where $g(N_K) = K$. So, for $K \geq 1$, $P[g = K] = 2^{-K}$. Finally observe that

$$\bigcup_{k=1}^{\infty} N_K$$

is merely the event that when we push the button, the machines registers a "1" or a "2" or a "3," etc.; i.e., it is simply the event that the machine registers *some* integer. Since the machine is designed to register some integer whenever the button is pushed, we expect that

$$P\left[\bigcup_{K=1}^{\infty} N_K\right] = 1$$

If we recall the discussion of geometric series (see §3.1 and §3.2), we see that

$$\lim_{N \to \infty} \sum_{K=1}^{N} 1/2^K = 1$$

(see Prob. 3.2.9). Consequently

$$\lim_{N \to \infty} \sum_{K=1}^{N} P[N_K] = 1$$

Combining these remarks, we have

$$P\left[\bigcup_{K=1}^{\infty} N_K\right] = \lim_{N \to \infty} \sum_{K=1}^{N} P(N_K) = 1$$

In terms of the random variable g, this can be written

$$P\left[\bigcup_{K=1}^{\infty} \{g = K\}\right] = \lim_{N \to \infty} \sum_{K=1}^{N} P[g = K]$$

The range of our random variable is the set of all positive integers, and to each positive integer k, we have assigned a *probability* $f(k)$, where

$$f(k) = P[g = k]$$

i.e., $f(k)$ is the probability of the event $g = k$, which is equivalent to the probability of the event N_k that our machine chooses a k. If we plot the range of the random variable on the x-axis; i.e., if we look at values of x that are positive integers, and plot the corresponding probabilities on the y-axis, we obtain a function $f(k)$, $k = 1, 2, 3, ...$, with corresponding graph $(k, f(k))$ pictured in Fig. 4.8.2. The function $f(k)$ is the probability function associated with our experiment.

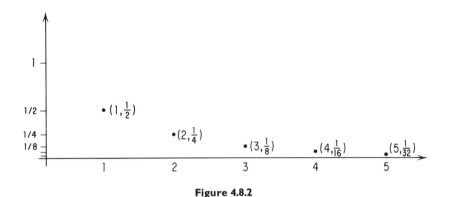

Figure 4.8.2

PROBLEMS

4.8.1. In Exp. 2, write the event "the girl has red hair" in terms of the random variable F, and find the probability of this event.

4.8.2. In Exp. 3, find the probability that the machine chooses an integer ≤ 20. (*Hint:* Use Thm. 4.8.2.) What is the probability the number chosen is > 20?

4.8.3. In Exp. 1, is W^2 a random variable? Explain your answer.

4.8.4. Suppose an event A has probability $\frac{1}{4}$, an event B has probability $\frac{1}{3}$, and the probability of A and B occurring together is $\frac{1}{10}$. Find $P(A \cup B)$.

4.8.5. Suppose we have a device which picks an arbitrary real number on the interval $0 \leq x \leq 2$. Consider the events that the number picked, x, is such that $E_1: 0 \leq x < 1$; $E_2: 0 < x \leq 2$; $E_3: 1 < x < 2$; $E_4: 1 \leq x < \frac{3}{2}$; $E_5: 0 \leq x \leq 2$; $E_6: x = 1$; $E_7: x = 3$. Describe: $E_1 \cap E_2$; $E_3 \cap E_5$; $E_1 \cup E_3$; $E_4 \cup E_6$; $\bar{E}_5$; $E_1 \cup E_2$; $(E_3 \cap E_4) \cup E_6$; $E_1 \cap E_3$; $E_6 \cap E_7$; $\bar{E}_4 \cup E_1$; $(\overline{E_1 \cup E_4})$; $E_3 \cap E_4$. What is the event E_7?

4.8.6. A penny, a nickel, and a dime are dropped simultaneously on a table. For each coin, it is equally likely that a head or tail will appear.
   (a) It is known that if one event can occur in m ways and a different disjoint event can occur in n ways, the two together can occur in $m \cdot n$ ways. Use this to determine all the ways the coins can land.
   (b) Let p_0 and p_1 be the events that a head or tail appears, respectively, on the penny, with n_0, n_1, d_0, d_1 be analogous events for the nickel and dime. Verify that the triples (p_i, n_j, d_k), $i = 0, 1$; $j = 0, 1$; $k = 0, 1$, form a sample space.

(c) Assuming all outcomes equiprobable, find $P(p_i, n_j, d_k)$, i, j, k equal to 0 or 1, where P represents probability; i.e., find the probability of an elementary event.

(d) Verify that the event p_0, "the penny lands heads," can be written in terms of the experiment "drop three coins simultaneously" as $(p_0, {}^x, {}^x)$ where ^{x} signifies that the event does not specify the coordinates representing the outcome of dropping the nickel and dime. Verify that

$$(p_0, {}^x, {}^x) = (p_0, n_0, d_0,) \cup (p_0, n_0, d_1) \cup (p_0, n_1, d_0) \cup (p_0, n_1, d_1)$$

(e) Find the probability that the penny lands heads, $P(p_0, {}^x, {}^x)$.

(f) Write the event "exactly one coin lands tails" as the appropriate union, and find its probability.

(g) Define the random variable F by $F(p_i, n_j, d_k) = i + j + k$. Observe F counts the number of tails which appears on a throw of the coins. Describe the event $F = 1$, and find $P[F = 1]$, the probability that $F = 1$.

4.8.7. It is known that the number of ways to take k distinct objects out of a larger population of n distinct objects is $\binom{n}{k}$, where $\binom{n}{k}$ is the binomial coefficient found in Def. 1.8.1. This selection process does not discriminate between different orderings, but only between distinct objects. For example, if we were picking two objects, the objects (A, B) and (B, A) would be counted only once, since both represent picking the distinct elements "A" and "B."

(a) Count the total number of ways of taking three letters out of the English alphabet (disregarding order).

(b) Count the total number of ways in which one of the three letters chosen is a "W." (Disregard the order.)

(c) Find the probability that one of the three letters is a "W." (Disregard the order.)

4.9. More probability. Some general properties.

Let us stop for a moment and summarize what we have determined so far. We have constructed a sample space of elementary events for a given experiment. We have observed that for a given experiment, it is often possible to construct different sample spaces, depending on what outcomes of the experiment interest us. When we pick the elementary events, we simultaneously assign probabilities. To get away from the abstract sample space, we created a function which identifies the elementary events with certain sets of points on the line (i.e., real numbers) or sometimes points in the plane. We then assigned the corresponding probabilities to these points and found we could completely describe the experiment in terms of these points on the line or in the plane.

We also found that the elementary events were not the only events, but that "unions" and "complements," for instance, were also events. We ask now: What are *all* conceivable events in our experiments?

Definition 4.9.1. Let S be the sample space of elementary events, $A_1, A_2, \ldots$ (not necessarily finite). The set of all conceivable events, which we shall call the *event space*, obeys the following axioms:
   (i) Each A_i is in the event space
   (ii) $\emptyset$ is in the event space
   (iii) S is in the event space (this is simply the event that some one of elementary events has occurred)
   (iv) If $E_1, E_2, \ldots$ are in the event space, so is $E_1 \cap E_2 \cap \cdots$ in the event space
   (v) If $E_1, E_2, \ldots$ are in the event space, so is $E_1 \cup E_2 \cup \cdots$
   (vi) If E is in the event space, so is $\bar{E}$ (the complement of E; i.e., the set of elementary events not in E)

Next we determine what properties a function must have to qualify as a probability function. If we had N equally likely elementary events, $A_1, \ldots, A_N$, we said $P[A_1] = P[A_2] = \cdots = P[A_N] = 1/N$. But in Exp. 3, the events were *not* equally likely. What we wish to know is what the probability function in experiments 1, 2, and 3 have in common; in fact, we wish to know what all possible probability functions defined on any event space have in common. To avoid confusion we shall use S to designate the sample space, and the German letter $\mathfrak{S}$ for the event space.

Definition 4.9.2. Let S be a sample space, and $\mathfrak{S}$ be the corresponding event space. Then the function P is a *probability function on* $\mathfrak{S}$ if:
   (i) the domain of P is all of $\mathfrak{S}$ (i.e., every event has probability)
   (ii) for each event B in $\mathfrak{S}$, $P[B]$ is a real number with $0 \le P[B] \le 1$
   (iii) $P[S] = 1$ and $P[\emptyset] = 0$
   (iv) if $B_1, B_2, \ldots, B_N$ are N disjoint events in $\mathfrak{S}$, then

$$P\left[\bigcup_{i=1}^{N} B_i\right] = \sum_{i=1}^{N} P[B_i]$$

   (v) if $\mathfrak{S}$ is infinite and $\{B_i\}$ is a sequence of disjoint events, then

$$P\left[\bigcup_{i=1}^{\infty} B_i\right] = \lim_{N \to \infty} \sum_{i=1}^{N} P[B_i]$$

The reader should convince himself that the probability functions defined in Exp. 1, 2, and 3 satisfy the properties in Def. 4.9.2. We shall prove the following theorem.

Theorem 4.9.1. Let B be any event and $\bar{B}$ be its complementary event. Then $P[\bar{B}] = 1 - P[B]$.

Proof. Since $\bar{B}$ is the event B has not happened, $\bar{B} \cap B = \varnothing$. Since either B or $\bar{B}$ must occur, $B \cup \bar{B} = S$ where S is the sample space. By Thm. 4.8.1, $P[B \cup \bar{B}] = P[B] + P[\bar{B}]$. But $P[B \cup \bar{B}] = P[S] = 1$ by Def. 4.9.2. Hence, $P[B] + P[\bar{B}] = 1$, which implies the theorem.

Example 4.9.1. In Exp. 1, what is the probability that a one does *not* appear on the roll of the die, $P[\bar{0}_1]$? It has already been observed that $\bar{0}_1$ is a rather complicated event. Its probability, however, is easy to find by using Thm. 4.9.1. In fact,

$$P[\bar{0}_1] = 1 - P(0_1) = \tfrac{5}{6}$$

We shall use the next example to illustrate all the ideas so far presented in a cohesive unified fashion.

Experiment 4. The roll of two dice. Suppose we have two distinguishable dice, say one blue and one yellow. Our experiment will be a single roll of the dice. There are at least two outcomes which are of interest:
  (1) the elementary event that the blue die shows n dots and yellow die shows k dots, $1 \leq n \leq 6$, $1 \leq k \leq 6$;
  (2) the elementary event that the *sum* of the number of dots shown on the dice is m, with $2 \leq m \leq 12$.

If we pick (1) as our elementary events, then we can express (2) in terms of (1), whereas if we pick (2) as our elementary events, we can express (1) in terms of (2). We shall show that both (1) and (2) give rise to sample spaces.

Let (B_n, Y_k) be the event that n dots appear on the blue die and k dots appear on the yellow die. Since on a single roll of the dice, it is impossible for the events (B_1, Y_1) and (B_5, Y_1) to occur simultaneously, these events are disjoint. Since each die can land in 6 distinct equally probable ways, the two dice can land in $6 \cdot 6 = 36$ equally probable distinct combinations. The events (B_n, Y_k) form a sample space with 36 elements, and

$$P[B_n, Y_k] = 1/36, \text{ where } n = 1, 2, \ldots, 6; \text{ and } k = 1, 2, \ldots, 6$$

Next consider the event $T_j =$ the sum of the number of dots on the dice is j with $2 \leq j \leq 12$. Since on one roll of the dice, the sum of the number of dots on the dice cannot be 5 and 7 simultaneously, $T_5 \cap T_7 = \varnothing$. In fact $T_i \cap T_j = \varnothing$ for $i \neq j$, so all these events are disjoint. Furthermore,

$$P\left[\bigcup_{j=2}^{12} T_j\right] = 1$$

since on a roll of the dice *some* sum must appear. The space $S = \{T_2, T_3, T_4, \ldots, T_{12}\}$ is an eleven element sample space for Exp. 4.

We shall investigate $P[T_j]$ in terms of $P[B_n, Y_k]$. There is exactly one way for the event T_2 to occur, namely the event (B_1, Y_1) must occur. Hence, $P[T_2] = P[B_1, Y_1] = 1/36$. But T_3 can happen if (B_1, Y_2) or (B_2, Y_1) occurs; hence $P[T_3] = P[(B_1, Y_2) \cup (B_2, Y_1)] = P[B_1, Y_2] + P[B_2, Y_1] = 2/36 = 1/18$ (we have used Thm. 4.8.1). Similarly,

$$P[T_4] = P[(B_1, Y_3) \cup (B_2, Y_2) \cup (B_3, Y_1)]$$
$$= P[B_1, Y_3] + P[B_2, Y_2] + P[B_3, Y_1]$$
$$= 3/36 = 1/12$$

using Thm. 4.8.2. We shall simply record the rest of the probabilities (the reader will be asked to verify them in the problem set):

$$P[T_5] = 1/9, \quad P[T_6] = 5/36, \quad P[T_7] = 1/6$$
$$P[T_8] = 5/36, \quad P[T_9] = 1/9, \quad P[T_{10}] = 1/12$$
$$P[T_{11}] = 1/18, \quad P[T_{12}] = 1/36$$

We shall now restrict our attention to the experiment "the sum of the dice is m" with sample space $\{T_2, T_3, ..., T_{12}\}$. Define the random variable $z(T_j) = j$. Then the event $z = j$ corresponds to the event that the sum of the number of dots on the dice is j. By our previous discussion, $P(z = 1) = 0, P(z = 2) = 1/36$, $P(z = 3) = 1/18, P(z = 4) = 1/12$, etc. (see Fig. 4.9.1). The range of the random variable is plotted on the x-axis, the corresponding probabilities on the y-axis.

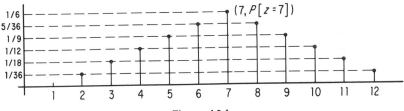

Figure 4.9.1

Each ordered pair of the graph is of the form (x, y) where $y = P[z = x]$. Observe that the values $x = 2$, $x = 3$, ..., $x = 12$ correspond with our original sample space $T_2, T_3, ..., T_{12}$. The graph of $y = P[z = x]$ represents a *function*, since to each x, there corresponds at most one $y = P[z = x]$. Hence, we are entitled to write $f(x) = P[z = x]$. To illustrate, $f(2) = P[z = 2] = 1/36$, $f(6) = P[z = 6] = 5/36, f(12) = P[z = 12] = 1/36$.

Let a and b be any two real numbers, $a < b$. We shall define the event $a \le x \le b$ to be the event that z takes on those integer values of x for which $a \le x \le b$. With similar definitions, we see that each of the sets $a < x \le b$, $a \le x < b$, $a < x < b$, $x < a$, $x \le a$, $x > b$, $x \ge b$ is an event! With this notation our discussion of events becomes a discussion of intervals and half-lines. In the same spirit, when we write the event "$x = c$" we shall mean the event the random variable z takes on the value $x = c$. For example,

$$P[\tfrac{5}{2} < x \le 5] = P[(x = 3) \cup (x = 4) \cup (x = 5)]$$
$$= P[x = 3] + P[x = 4] + P[x = 5] = f(3) + f(4) + f(5)$$
$$= \tfrac{1}{18} + \tfrac{1}{12} + \tfrac{1}{9} = \tfrac{1}{4}$$

$$P[x > 5] = P[(x = 6) \cup (x = 7) \cup \cdots \cup (x = 12)] = \sum_{k=6}^{12} f(k) = \tfrac{8}{9}$$

Observe also that

$$P\left[\bigcup_{i=2}^{12} \{z = i\}\right] = \sum_{k=2}^{12} f(k) = 1$$

This also can be written

$$P[2 \le x \le 12] = \sum_{k=2}^{12} f(k) = 1$$

Summarizing, we have the theorem:

Theorem 4.9.2. Let the range of a random variable G be a finite set. Let $f(x) = P[G = x]$; i.e., $f(x)$ is the probability that the random variable assumes the value x. Then

(4.9.1)
$$P[a < x < b] = \sum_{a < x < b} f(x)$$

where $\sum\limits_{a < x < b}$ is the sum of all integer values of x between a and b. Also,

(4.9.2) $$P[-\infty < x < \infty] = \left\{ \sum_{-\infty < x < \infty} f(x) \right\} \equiv \sum_{0 < x < \infty} f(x) + \sum_{0 \ge x > -\infty} f(x)$$

$$= \lim_{N \to \infty} \sum_{k=1}^{N} f(k) + \lim_{M \to -\infty} \sum_{k=0}^{M} f(k) = 1$$

PROBLEMS

4.9.1. Verify that the probability function described in Exp. 3 satisfies the conditions of Def. 4.9.2.

4.9.2. In Exp. 4, use Thm. 4.9.1 to evaluate $P[z \ge 10]$.

4.9.3. Suppose three distinguishable dice, one red, one yellow, and one blue, are rolled. Let (R_i, Y_j, B_k) be the event that the red die shows i dots, the yellow j dots, and the blue k dots, with $1 \le i \le 6$, $1 \le j \le 6$, $1 \le k \le 6$.
(a) How many ways can the dice land?
(b) Find the probability of the event (R_i, Y_j, B_k); i.e., find $P[R_i, Y_j, B_k]$.
(c) Define the random variable $S(R_i, Y_j, B_k) = i + j + k$. Observe that

$S = N$ if the sum of the dots on the dice is N. Evaluate $P[S = N]$ where $N = 2, 3, 4$, and 5.

(d) Show that the events $S = N$, with $3 \leq N \leq 18$, are disjoint, and are elementary events for a sample space.

(e) Find $P[\{S = 1\} \cup \{S = 2\}]$.

(f) Find $\bigcup\limits_{i=3}^{18} \{S = i\}$.

(g) Find $P[S \leq 17]$. (*Hint:* Use Thm. 4.9.1.).

4.9.4. In Exp. 4, find each of the indicated probabilities:

(a) $P[z < 1]$ (b) $P[8.5 \leq z \leq 9.5]$

(c) $P[z \leq 12]$ (d) $P[z \geq 1]$

(e) $P[\{z = \frac{1}{2}\} \cup \{z = 3\}]$ (f) $P[z \leq 3.41]$

(g) $P[z \geq 3.9]$

4.9.5. Let S be a sample space, and let A and B be two events in the corresponding event space. Show that the following are valid identities:

(a) $A \cap \emptyset = \emptyset$ (b) $A \cup \emptyset = A$

(c) $\bar{S} = \emptyset$ (d) $\bar{\emptyset} = S$

(e) $\overline{A \cup B} = \bar{A} \cap \bar{B}$ (f) $\overline{A \cap B} = \bar{A} \cup \bar{B}$

(g) $\bar{\bar{A}} = A$

4.9.6. In Prob. 4.9.3 find

(a) $P[S = 6]$ (b) $P[(S = 6) \cup (S = 7)]$

4.9.7. In Exp. 3, in which we had a machine that gave us integers, find:

(a) $P[0 \leq g \leq 4]$ (b) $P[g > 4]$

(c) $G(1)$ and $G(2)$, if $G(x) = P[g \geq x]$

4.9.8. Verify Fig. 4.9.1. Is the graph the correct one for the probability function of Exp. 4?

4.10. Continuous random variables. The normal distribution.

The random variables considered so far have been of a special type. In Exp. 1, 2, and 4, the range of each random variable is a finite set. Specifically, in Exp. 1 the range of W was the set of six integers, 1, 2, 3, 4, 5, 6; in Exp. 2, the range of F is the set of three points (1, 1), (1, 2) and (2, 1); and in Exp. 4, the range of z is the set of integers between 2 and 12, inclusive. In Exp. 3, the range of g is the set of all positive integers. Such a set, though infinite, can nevertheless be "counted"; i.e., to each element in the range of g, we can match precisely one integer, and vice versa. In general, we say a set is **countable** if it is possible to match each element of the set with precisely one element of the set of positive integers, and vice versa. It can be proved that the set of all real numbers on any interval (open or closed) is *not* countable (see, for example, Taylor, *Advanced Calculus*, Chapter 14).*

Definition 4.10.1. A random variable is called *discrete* if its range is finite or countable, and if every finite interval contains, at most, a finite number of points from the range.

Let G be some discrete random variable, and let P be a probability function. Let $f(x)$ be the function defined by

(4.10.1)
$$f(x) = P[G = x]$$

Definition 4.10.2. Let $f(x)$ be defined by (4.10.1). Then we say that $f(x)$ is the *probability distribution* associated with the random variable G.

Example 4.10.1. In Exp. 1, the function $f(x) = P[W = x]$ is

$$f(x) = \begin{cases} \frac{1}{6}, & x = 1, 2, 3, 4, 5, 6 \\ 0, & \text{otherwise} \end{cases}$$

and $f(x)$ is the probability distribution associated with the random variable W. To see that $f(x) = 0$ when x is not one of the numbers 1, 2, 3, 4, 5, or 6, it is enough to observe that for such an x, the event $W = x$ is a null event (e.g., the event " $W = 7$ " is null), so $\{W = x\} = \emptyset$, and so $f(x) = P[W = x] = P(\emptyset) = 0$.

We shall next consider an experiment that is quantitatively different from experiments previously considered.

Experiment 5. A manufacturer of light bulbs is interested in knowing the probable life of a light bulb. A reasonable procedure to test the life of a typical bulb is to line up a large number of bulbs, light them all at once, and then record the number of hours each bulb burns. Our sample space is composed of elementary events of the form "the bulb burns out at the end of t hours"; call this event B_t. We take as our random variable v defined by $v(B_t) = t$. The range of the random variable is the set of all $t \geq 0$. This is an uncountable set, and hence v is not a discrete random variable.

Suppose for the sake of argument that 10,000 bulbs are lit at time $t = 0$. Suppose further that our count of light bulbs is the one given in Table 1.

At the end of 80 hours, 100 per cent of the bulbs have burned out, so the probability that a bulb has burned out at the end of 80 hours is 1. Therefore, we write $P(v \leq 80) = 1$. Then the probability that a bulb has burned out,

---

* See the bibliography.

during the first 30 hours of the experiment is $P(v \le 30) = 0.15$ since 15 per cent of the bulbs have burned out in that line. To look more closely at the various probabilities, let us graph Table 1 in Fig. 4.10.1. We use the x-axis

TABLE 1

Number of bulbs burned out in given time interval	Time interval in which specified bulbs burned out	% of Total
500	between 10 and 20 hours	5
1000	between 20 and 30 hours	10
2000	between 30 and 40 hours	20
3000	between 40 and 50 hours	30
2000	between 50 and 60 hours	20
1000	between 60 and 70 hours	10
500	between 70 and 80 hours	5
Total: 10,000	between 10 and 80 hours	100

for the range of v; i.e., we plot hours on the x-axis. Over each time interval we place a rectangle whose area represents the fraction corresponding to the per cent of the total number of bulbs which have burned out over that

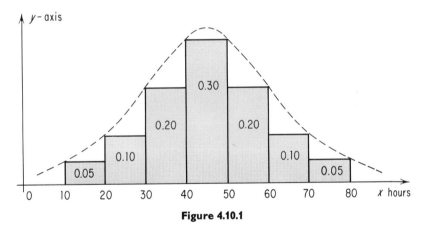

Figure 4.10.1

time interval. In terms of Fig. 4.10.1, we make the *additional assumption* that *within the time interval* $10n < x < 10(n + 1)$, *the percentage of bulbs burned out is proportional to the area*; e.g., in $20 \le x \le 22$, we assume that 2 per cent of the bulbs burned out, and in $22 \le x \le 30$, we assume that 8 per cent burned out.

With this formulation of the problem, we have

$$P(v \le 80) = \text{sum of areas of all rectangles where } 0 \le x \le 80$$
$$= 0.05 + 0.10 + 0.20 + 0.30 + 0.20 + 0.10 + 0\,05 = 1$$

$P(v \le 30) =$ sum of areas of all rectangles where $0 \le x \le 30$
$$= 0.05 + 0.10 = 0.15$$

Let $G(x)$ be the function associated with the graph in Fig. 4.10.1; i.e.,

$$\int_{10}^{20} G = 0.05, \quad \int_{20}^{30} G = 0.10, \qquad \text{etc.}$$

The graph of $G(x)$ appears in Fig. 4.10.2. Also, $G(x) = 0$ for $x \le 10$ and for

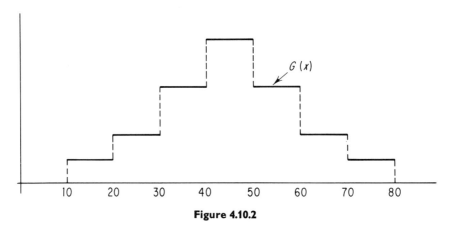

Figure 4.10.2

$x \ge 80$, since no bulbs burned out before 10 hours and all the bulbs are burned out past 80 hours. We can then write

$$\int_{-\infty}^{10} G = \int_{80}^{\infty} G = 0$$

the integrals taken as improper. In terms of $G(x)$, again with improper integrals, some typical probabilities are:

$$P[v \le 80] = \int_{-\infty}^{\infty} G = 1$$

$$P[v \le 30] = \int_{-\infty}^{30} G = 0.15$$

$$P[v \le 35] = \int_{-\infty}^{35} G$$

$$P[16 \le v \le 47] = \int_{16}^{47} G$$

Unlike Exp. 1 through Exp. 4, the probability in this example is given by an area. In fact,

(4.10.2)
$$P(v \leq x) = \int_{-\infty}^{x} G$$

(4.10.3)
$$P(a \leq v \leq b) = \left(\int_{-\infty}^{b} G \right) - \left(\int_{-\infty}^{a} G \right) = \int_{a}^{b} G$$

Compare these equations with (4.9.1) and (4.9.2), and compare Fig. 4.10.1 with Fig. 4.9.2. To find $P(z \leq 3)$ in Exp. 4, we found

$$P(z \leq 3) = \sum_{x \leq 3} f(x) = f(1) + f(2) + f(3) = \tfrac{1}{36} + \tfrac{1}{18} = \tfrac{1}{12}$$

i.e., we *added* the values of $f(x)$ at the integer values of $x \leq 3$. But to find $P(v \leq 30)$ here, we found

$$P(v \leq 30) = \int_{-\infty}^{30} G = 0.15$$

i.e., we found the *area* under the graph of $G(x)$ for all real $x \leq 30$. In Exp. 4, $f(x)$ was directly related to the probability. In fact,

$$f(x) = P[z = x]$$

In this experiment, the *area under $G(x)$ is related to the probability.* In fact,

(4.10.4)
$$\int_{-\infty}^{x} G = P[v \leq x]$$

so if we define

(4.10.5)
$$F(x) = \int_{-\infty}^{x} G$$

the function $F(x)$ closely resembles $f(x) = P[z = x]$.

The function v is called a **continuous random variable** and $G(x)$ is called the **probability density function** (abbreviated by p.d.f.), or simply **density function**, associated with v. The function $F(x)$ of (4.10.5) is called the **distribution function** associated with v; from (4.10.4), with Thm. 3.6.1,

(4.10.6)
$$F'(x) = G(x)$$

at all points of continuity of $G(x)$. We can then write (4.10.3) as

$$P[a \leq v \leq b] = F(b) - F(a)$$

In fact, looking at the improper integrals, it should be clear that

$$P[a \leq w < b] = P[a < w \leq b] = P[a < w < b] = F(b) - F(a)$$

Of course, the functions v, G, and F in our light-bulb experiment are special examples of a continuous random variable, a density function, and distribution function, respectively. More generally,

Definition 4.10.3. A random variable u whose range is contained in the real line $-\infty < x < \infty$ will be called **continuous** if its related **distribution function** $f(x)$ is defined and continuous for all x, and if the **density function** $f'(x) = g(x)$ exists and is continuous for all x except possibly at a number of points, with every finite interval containing at most a finite number of such points. We shall agree to set $g(x) = 0$ for all x not in the range of u. We then have

(i)
$$f(x) = P(u \le x) = \int_{-\infty}^{x} g$$

(ii)
$$P(a < x < b) = f(b) - f(a) = \int_{a}^{b} g$$

(iii)
$$\int_{-\infty}^{\infty} g = 1$$

A continuous random variable of particular interest is the one whose density function is

(4.10.7)
$$N(x) = \frac{1}{[\sigma\sqrt{2\pi}]} \exp\left[\frac{-(x - \mu)^2}{2\sigma^2}\right]$$

where σ and μ are certain constants, and $\sigma > 0$. The function $N(x)$ is called the **normal density function** *with parameters μ and σ*. The particular choice of μ and σ depends on the problem of interest. The graph of $N(x)$ is illustrated in Fig. 4.10.3. The random variable Y whose density function is $N(x)$ is said to be **normally distributed**, and for any values $x = a$ and $x = b$,

$$P[a \le Y \le b] = \int_{a}^{b} N$$

and is represented in Fig. 4.10.3 by the shaded area.

We shall state some important properties of the normal distribution (some of which will appear as exercises in the problem set at the end of this section): For any μ and any $\sigma > 0$,

(1) $N(x)$ is symmetric with respect to the vertical line $x = \mu$

(2) $N(x) > 0$ for all x, and

$$\int_{-\infty}^{\infty} N = 1$$

(this is part of the requirement that N is a density function).

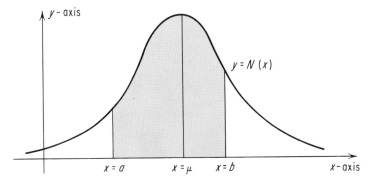

Figure 4.10.3

(3) $N(x)$ has an absolute and local maximum at $x = \mu$, and hence, the maximum value of $N(x)$ is $N(\mu) = 1/\sigma\sqrt{2\pi}$

(4) If Y is a normal random variable, $P(Y \leq x) = \displaystyle\int_{-\infty}^{x} N$

(5) If Y is normally distributed (i.e., Y is a normal random variable), $P(Y < \mu) = P(Y \leq \mu) = P(Y > \mu) = P(Y \geq \mu) = 1/2$

(6) Let the symbol " $\sim$ " mean "approximately equal to"; then

$$\int_{\mu-\sigma}^{\mu+\sigma} N \sim 0.683$$

$$\int_{\mu-2\sigma}^{\mu+2\sigma} N \sim 0.955$$

$$\int_{\mu-3\sigma}^{\mu+3\sigma} N \sim 0.977$$

In terms of probability, this asserts that for a normally distributed Y,

$$P[\mu - \sigma < Y < \mu + \sigma] \sim 0.683$$
$$P[\mu - 2\sigma < Y < \mu + 2\sigma] \sim 0.955$$
$$P[\mu - 3\sigma < Y < \mu + 3\sigma] \sim 0.997$$

and hence,

$$P[(Y < \mu - 3\sigma) \cup (Y > \mu + 3\sigma)] \sim 0.003$$

This asserts that the event $\mu - 3\sigma < Y < \mu + 3\sigma$ has very large probability ~ 0.997, whereas the event $\{Y < \mu - 3\sigma\} \cup \{Y > \mu + 3\sigma\}$ has the very small probability ~ 0.003.

(7) Changing the value of μ in $N(x)$ has the effect of shifting the entire graph along the x-axis. Changing the value of σ has the effect of either compressing the graph and causing a higher peak (if σ is increased) or

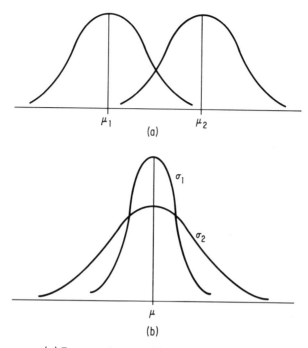

(a) Two normal curves with same σ, but $\mu_2 > \mu_1$

(b) Two normal curves with same μ, but $\sigma_1 > \sigma_2$

Figure 4.10.4

stretching the graph and lowering the peak (if σ is decreased) [see Fig. 4.10.4(a) and (b)].

(8)
$$\lim_{x \to \infty} N(x) = 0, \quad \lim_{x \to -\infty} N(x) = 0$$

If Y is normally distributed, $\mu = 0$, and $\sigma = 1$, then Y is said to be a **standard normal random variable**.

A useful theorem relating normal and standard normal random variables is

Theorem 4.10.1. Let Y be normally distributed and such that $N(x)$ has parameters μ and $\sigma > 0$. Then the new random variable

$$S = (Y - \mu)/\sigma$$

is a standard normal random variable; i.e., if

$$P[a \le Y \le b] = \frac{1}{\sigma\sqrt{2\pi}} \int_a^b \exp\left[-\frac{1}{2}\left(\frac{x - \mu}{\sigma}\right)^2\right] dx$$

then

$$P[a \le S \le b] = \frac{1}{\sqrt{2\pi}} \int_a^b \exp\left[-\frac{1}{2}x^2\right] dx$$

Proof. Since $S = (Y - \mu)/\sigma$, with $\sigma > 0$,

$$P[a \le S \le b] = P\left[a \le \frac{Y - \mu}{\sigma} \le b\right] = P[\sigma a \le Y - \mu \le \sigma b]$$

$$= P[\sigma a + \mu \le Y \le \sigma b + \mu]$$

By definition of Y,

$$P[\sigma a + \mu \le Y \le \sigma b + \mu] = \int_{\sigma a + \mu}^{\sigma b + \mu} \frac{1}{\sigma\sqrt{2\pi}} \exp\left[-\frac{1}{2}\left(\frac{x - \mu}{\sigma}\right)^2\right] dx$$

Let $g(x) = (x - \mu)/\sigma$; applying the method of substitution (see Thm. 3.10.2) with $g(\sigma a + \mu) = a$ and $g(\sigma b + \mu) = b$, $g'(x) = 1/\sigma$, the above integral becomes

$$\int_a^b \frac{1}{\sqrt{2\pi}} \exp\left[-\frac{1}{2}W^2\right] dW$$

and this is exactly the area under $N(x)$ from a to b for $\mu = 0$ and $\sigma = 1$. Since this integral is exactly $P(a < S < b)$, we see that S is a standard normal random variable.

The reader has no doubt observed a reluctance on our part to evaluate the definite integral for the normal distribution with general parameters μ and $\sigma > 0$. It turns out that it is not an elementary problem to evaluate these integrals. Extensive tables have been compiled for the *standard* normal distribution. Using Thm. 4.10.1, it is possible to translate any probability question concerning general normal distributions (i.e., with μ, $\sigma > 0$ arbitrary) to a probability question concerning the standard normal distribution, and then use the tables already compiled for that distribution.

PROBLEMS

4.10.1. Show that $N(x)$ (with parameters μ and σ) has an absolute and local maximum at $x = \mu$, and that the maximum value of $N(x)$ is $1/(\sigma\sqrt{2\pi})$.

4.10.2. Let S be a *standard* normal random variable. In the sense of Thm. 3.6.3, show that its density function is even. Use this to prove that $P[S < 0] = P[S > 0] = \frac{1}{2}$.

4.10.3. Let S be a *standard* normal random variable. Find approximate values for $P[-1 < S < 1]$; $P[-2 < S < 2]$; $P[-3 < S < 3]$; $P[0 < S < 1]$; $P[-2 < S < 0]$.

4.10.4. Let a random variable Z have as its density function

$$g(x) = \begin{cases} \dfrac{1}{\theta} e^{-x/\theta}, & \theta > 0 \text{ and constant, } x > 0 \\ 0, & x \le 0 \end{cases}$$

(a) Verify that the probability of the sample space "all real x" is 1.
(b) Find the distribution function for Z.
(c) Find the probability of each of the following events: $-10 \le Z \le 10$; $0 \le Z \le \ln \theta$; $Z \ge 100$.
(*Remark.* $g(x)$ is said to determine an ***exponential distribution***.)

4.10.5. (a) Determine the constant c such that $g(x) = c \exp(-x^2 + 4x)$, defined for all x, is a density function. [*Hint:* Consider (4.10.7).] Is this distribution normal? If so, find σ and μ.
(b) Determine the constant c such that $h(x) = c \exp(-2x^2 + 2x)$ is a density function.

4.10.6. For a constant $\theta > 0$, define

$$h(x) = \begin{cases} \theta x^{\theta - 1}, & 0 < x < 1 \\ 0, & \text{elsewhere} \end{cases}$$

Show that $h(x)$ is a density function. For any two numbers a and b with $0 < a < b < 1$, find $P[a \le T \le b]$ where h is the density function for T.

4.10.7. A real number w is to be chosen at random from the interval $a \le x \le b$. Find the density and distribution function for w, and draw their graphs. (*Hint:* $P[a \le w \le b] = 1$.)

For the next problems, make the following definitions. Let X be a continuous random variable with density function $f(x)$ and distribution function $F(x)$. We define the ***expectation of*** X, in symbols $E(X)$, as

(4.10.8)
$$E(X) = \int_{-\infty}^{\infty} x f(x) \, dx$$

and if g is some function of X, the ***expectation of*** $g(X)$ as

(4.10.9)
$$E(g(X)) = \int_{-\infty}^{\infty} g(x) f(x) \, dx$$

if these integrals exist; for technical reasons, one also often requires that the integrals of $|xf(x)|$ and $|g(x)f(x)|$, respectively, also exist on $-\infty < x < \infty$. $E(X)$ is also called the **mean of the distribution**.

The **variance** of X, symbolically, $V(X)$, is defined as

(4.10.10) $$V(X) = E\{(X - E(X))^2\}$$

4.10.8. For any constant c, show that $E(c) = c$. [*Hint:* In (4.10.9), set $g(X) = c$.]

4.10.9. Given the random variable X and two functions of the random variable, $F(X)$ and $G(X)$, show that $E[F(X) + G(X)] = E[F(X)] + E[G(X)]$, provided each expectation on the right exists. [*Hint:* In (4.10.9), set $g(X) = F(X) + G(X)$.]

4.10.10. Given a random variable X such that $E(X)$ and $E(X^2)$ each exist. Show that $V(X) = E(X^2) - [EX]^2$. [*Hint:* Use Prob. 4.10.8 and Prob. 4.10.9, remembering that $E(X)$ is a constant.]

4.10.11. If X is the standard normal random variable ($\mu = 0$ and $\sigma = 1$), show that $0 = E(X)$ and $1 = V(X)$.

4.10.12. Find the expectation and variance of the random variable whose density function is given in Prob. 4.10.6. [*Hint:* Use the result of Prob. 4.10.10 to find $V(T)$.]

4.10.13. Find the expectation and variance of the random variable of Prob. 4.10.4. (*Hint:* Use the result of Prob. 4.10.10 to find $V(Z)$.]

4.11. An application to learning theory.

We next present a brief discussion from the psychology of learning which hints at the possible applications of probability theory and calculus to learning theory. Learning often involves a series of trials, each consisting of a short interval of time during which an animal is placed in an environmental (stimulus) situation and may exhibit certain behavioral acts (responses) upon which certain environmental changes (reinforcement events) may be contingent or to which they may be correlated. The systematic change in the probability structure of classes of responses over repeated trials is often utilized to define learning. Certain theories of learning, called **stimulus sampling theories** (Estes, 1959; Bush and Estes, 1959; see bibliography), are based on the following types of assumptions which are here simplified for expositional purposes.

We assume:

(A1) An abstract set of objects called a set of **stimuli**; we shall denote this set by S. We further assume that this set has only a finite number of members.

(A2) An abstract set of objects called **responses**; we shall denote this set by R. For simplicity, we assume this set has only one member, and all other behaviors are classified as the complementary set $\bar{R}$ (where by complementary set $\bar{R}$, we mean all behavior other than those in R).

(A3) A connection relationship such that an element in S is either connected (conditioned) to R or not.

(A4) At successive times, or "trials", we extract a subset W of fixed size from the original parent set S; we call this process *sampling from S*. We assume each element in S has an equal independent opportunity to be in this subset W on each trial.

(A5) On each trial, if the response R and the reinforcement event both occur, then all elements of W, if not already connected to R, become connected (conditioned) to R with fixed probability c (of course, $0 < c \leq 1$; we shall not consider the case $c = 0$).

(A6) The probability that R occurs equals the proportion of elements in W that are connected to R.

Denote:
$N(W)$ = the number of elements (stimuli) in W
$N(W_R)$ = the number of elements in W connected to R
$N(S)$ = the number of elements in S
$N(S_R)$ = the number of elements in S that are connected to R
$N^*(S)$ = the number of elements in S in whose presence the environment allows the reinforcing event to take place; i.e., the number of elements in S which are capable of being reinforced. Observe that $N(S_R) \leq N^*(S) \leq N(S)$.

The probability that R occurs at time t, denoted by $P(t)$, is the probability that a stimulus element in our subset W is connected to R at time t, and by (A6) is given by

$$(4.11.1) \qquad P(t) = \frac{N(W_R)}{N(W)}$$

and if $N(W)$ is large it turns out that it is valid to conclude that†

$$(4.11.2) \qquad P(t) = \frac{N(S_R)}{N(S)}$$

i.e., the probability is given by the number of reinforced stimuli divided by the total number of stimuli in S.

---

† Specifically we appeal to a theorem known as the *law of large numbers*. Most of the books on probability and statistics listed in the bibliography discuss this theorem.

On any reinforced trial, i.e., a trial on which response and reinforcement occur, during an interval of time h the *change* in $N(S_R)$, denoted by $\Delta N(S_R)$, is given by

(4.11.3)
$$\Delta N(S_R) = c\frac{N(W)}{N(S)}\{N^*(S) - N(S_R)\}$$

where $N(W)/N(S)$ is the proportion of the total number of stimuli in S that are in W; $N^*(S) - N(S_R)$ is the number of stimuli that may yet become connected to R; so that $\Delta N(S_R)$ is just the proportion of the elements that may yet be connected to R that are sampled, times the probability that conditioning occurs.

Over a time interval from t to $t + h$, the change in the probability of a response or the proportion of elements in S connected to R, $\Delta P(t) = P(t + h) - P(t)$, is given by

(4.11.4)
$$\Delta P(t) = \frac{\Delta N(S_R)}{N(S)} \cdot h$$

i.e., the change in probability $\Delta P(t)$ is given by the proportion of stimuli in S becoming connected per unit interval of time (i.e., on a single trial or sampling W) times the interval of time h over which we investigate the set. Hence, in view of (4.11.3),

$$\Delta P(t) = \frac{\Delta N(S_R)}{N(S)} \cdot h = h \cdot c \cdot \frac{N(W)}{N(S)}\left\{\frac{N^*(S)}{N(S)} - \frac{N(S_R)}{N(S)}\right\}$$

and since $N(W)/N(S)$ and $N^*(S)/N(S)$ are each constant, by letting

$$\theta = N(W)/N(S), \qquad 0 < \theta \le 1$$

and

$$\lambda = N^*(S)/N(S), \qquad 0 \le \lambda \le 1$$

and by (4.11.2) we see that

(4.11.5)
$$\Delta P(t) = ch\theta(\lambda - P(t))$$

but $\Delta P(t) = P(t + h) - P(t)$, so (4.11.5) becomes

(4.11.6)
$$\frac{P(t + h) - P(t)}{h} = c\theta(\lambda - P(t))$$

and taking the limit in (4.11.6) as $h \to 0$ (assuming it exists) we get

(4.11.7)
$$P'(t) = c\theta[\lambda - P(t)]$$

which is a differential equation already discussed in §4.4.

Rewriting (4.11.7) we obtain

$$\frac{1}{P(t) - \lambda}\frac{dP}{dt} = -c\theta$$

whose solution is [see (4.4.4)]

$$\int \frac{1}{(P - \lambda)} \, dP = -\int c\theta \, dt$$

or, since $c\theta$ is constant,

$$\ln |P(t) - \lambda| = -c\theta t + k$$

and since $0 \le P(t) \le \lambda \le 1$, we have $P(t) - \lambda \le 0$, and so finally

$$|P(t) - \lambda| = \lambda - P(t)$$

Hence

$$\ln [\lambda - P(t)] = -c\theta t + k$$

and

(4.11.8) $$\lambda - P(t) = Ae^{-\theta ct} \qquad (A = e^{kt})$$

If we set $t = 0$ in (4.11.8), we see that $\lambda - P(0) = A$, so A is some constant such that $0 \le A \le 1$. Rewriting (4.11.8) as

$$P(t) = \lambda - Ae^{-c\theta t}, \qquad 0 \le A \le 1 \text{ and } 0 < c\theta \le 1$$

we see that

$$\lim_{t \to \infty} P(t) = \lambda$$

i.e., as t becomes large, the probability of a response tends to the value λ at a rate determined by $c\theta$. Since $\lambda = N^*(S)/N(S)$, this simply says in view of (4.11.2) that eventually $N(S_R) \to N^*(S)$ as $t \to \infty$; i.e., all the stimuli in whose presence reinforcement may occur eventually become conditioned. If reinforcement is made contingent upon the occurrence of the response, independent of what stimuli are available to be sampled, then $N^*(S) = N(S)$ and we have the special case of simple conditioning, for which $\lambda = 1$. So we also see that (4.11.5) states that the change in the probability of the response is some constant fraction $(c\theta)$ of that which remains to be learned, the difference between the value λ and the probability of the response already existing at time t. Thus, learning is defined in this theory by the way the change in the probability of a response over time obeys two rates: the probability of conditioning occurring c, and the proportion of elements sampled at any given time θ, and a value λ which depends on large t and indicates the maximum amount of learning possible.

It may be noted that for the simplest special case where $c = 1$ (i.e., conditioning always occurs if the response and reinforcement occur), $\lambda = 1$ and $h = 1$ (i.e., we have a unit increment of time), (4.11.6) becomes

(4.11.9) $$P(t + 1) = \theta[1 - P(t)] + P(t)$$

The form occurring in (4.11.9) is called a *finite difference*, and a mathematical theory called *the calculus of finite differences* is applicable. Since the rates c and θ are constant with respect to time, the theory of Markov chains is also applicable. These important topics are beyond the scope of this book, but some standard references are listed in the bibliography. For the general case of any c, θ, and λ, but still with $h = 1$, the solution to the difference equation

$$P(t + 1) = c\theta[\lambda - P(t)] + P(t)$$

turns out to be

$$P(t + 1) = \lambda - \{\lambda - P(1)\} \cdot \{1 - c\theta\}^t$$

which possesses the same properties as the solution (4.11.8) of the differential equation (4.11.7).

Figure (4.11.1) describes the processes referred to in this section.

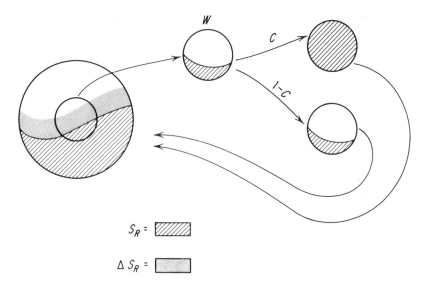

Figure 4.11.1

4.12. Expectation and an application to an optimal inventory problem.

In the problem set of §4.10, we introduced the concept of expectation of a random variable and exhibited some of the properties of expectation. Recall that, if w is a continuous random variable, if F is the probability density function (abbreviated p.d.f.) associated with w, and if g is a function, the *expected value of w*, or the *expectation* of w, is given by

$$(4.12.1) \qquad \boxed{E[w] = \int_{-\infty}^{\infty} xF(x)\, dx}$$

whenever the integral exists, and the *expected value* of (the random variable) $g(w)$ is

$$(4.12.2) \qquad \boxed{E[g(w)] = \int_{-\infty}^{\infty} g(x)F(x)\, dx}$$

whenever this integral exists (see (4.10.8) and (4.10.9)). Heuristically, the expected value of w is the value we expect w to assume on the average. For instance, if w represents the time elapsed before a lightbulb burns out, $E[w]$ can be interpreted as the average life of a lightbulb. We next present an important application of the concept of expectation to an optimal inventory problem in business.

A businessman selling perishable items (such as produce, dairy products, film, etc.) faces the problem of stocking an optimal inventory which will maximize his product. His problem is that the demand for his product fluctuates from time period to time period. To simplify the problem, we assume no penalty other than profit loss to the business if he stocks too little.

We let Q_x be the event "x units of the perishable item is sold in a time period", and associate the rather natural random variable $R(Q_x) = x$ with probability density function $F(x)$, which for the moment we can assume to be known. We shall also assume that the values of x for which $F(x)$ is non-zero is the interval $0 \le x \le T$ for the appropriate T, and hence we assume that the probability is zero that fewer than 0 items or more than T items are sold. In some instances it is feasible to let $T \to \infty$.

We suppose known the constants $c =$ *cost per unit of each unit ordered* and $s =$ *selling price of each unit*. We let $n =$ *number of units to be ordered* (inventory) and $p[R(Q_x)] = p(x)$ is the random variable *"profit from selling x units in a time period."*

The quantity xs is the total money collected on the sale of x units, and cn is the total money spent to stock the inventory. If inventory exceeds demand; i.e., if $n > x$, then profit is $sx - cn$; whereas if all units are sold; i.e., if $n \le x$, the profit is $sn - cn = (s - c)n$. Hence, $p(x)$ is the function

$$p(x) = \begin{cases} 0, & x \le 0 \\ sx - cn, & 0 < x < n \\ (s - c)n, & n \le x \le T \\ 0, & x > T \end{cases}$$

Our desire is to choose n in such a way as to maximize $E[p(x)]$. Of course, $p(x) = p[R(Q_x)]$. What we want to maximize is the profit the businessman hopes to make *on the average*; i.e., to maximize $E[p(x)]$. Keep in mind that $F(x) = 0$ for $x < 0$ and $x > T$.

To evaluate $E[p(x)]$, we think of n as fixed. From (4.12.2) we obtain

$$E[p(x)] = \int_{-\infty}^{\infty} p(x)F(x)\,dx$$

$$= \int_{0}^{n} (sx - cn)F(x)\,dx + \int_{n}^{T} (s - c)nF(x)\,dx$$

$$= s \int_{0}^{n} xF(x)\,dx - cn \int_{0}^{n} F(x)\,dx + sn \int_{n}^{T} F(x)\,dx$$

$$\quad - cn \int_{n}^{T} F(x)\,dx$$

$$= s\left[\int_{0}^{n} xF(x)\,dx + n \int_{n}^{T} F(x)\,dx \right] - cn\left[\int_{0}^{n} F(x)\,dx \right.$$

$$\left. + \int_{n}^{T} F(x)\,dx \right]$$

From Thm. 3.4.1, $\int_{0}^{n} F + \int_{n}^{T} F = \int_{0}^{T} F$, and since F is a p.d.f. and since $\int_{-\infty}^{\infty} F = \int_{0}^{T} F$, it follows that $\int_{0}^{T} F = 1$. Hence,

$$(4.12.3) \qquad E[p(x)] = s\left[\int_{0}^{n} xF(x)\,dx + n \int_{n}^{T} F(x)\,dx \right] - cn$$

The expression (4.12.3) is now a function of n which we shall maximize with respect to n. Call $E[p(x)]$ in (4.12.3) the function $G(n)$, so

$$(4.12.4) \qquad G(n) = s\left[\int_{0}^{n} xF(x)\,dx + n \int_{n}^{T} F(x)\,dx \right] - cn$$

By Thm. 3.6.1,

$$\frac{d}{dn} \int_{0}^{n} xF(x)\,dx = nF(n)$$

by Def. 3.4.4 and Thm. 3.6.1 and the product rule for derivatives,

$$\frac{d}{dn}\left[n \int_n^T F(x)\, dx \right] = \frac{d}{dn}\left[-n \int_T^n F(x)\, dx \right]$$

$$= -nF(n) - \int_T^n F(x)\, dx$$

so

$$\frac{dG(n)}{dn} = s\left[nF(n) - nF(n) - \int_T^n F(x)\, dx \right] - c$$

$$= s\int_n^T F(x)\, dx - c$$

The change of sign in the integral occurs because of the change in the order of the limits of integration. Hence,

(4.12.5) $$\frac{dG(n)}{dn} = 0 \qquad \text{when} \int_n^T F(x)\, dx = \frac{c}{s}$$

We can rewrite this by recalling $1 = \int_0^T F = \int_0^n F + \int_n^T F$, so (4.12.5) becomes $dG(n)/dn = 0$ when n satisfies

(4.12.6) $$\int_0^n F = 1 - \frac{c}{s} = \frac{s-c}{s}$$

No more explicit form of (4.12.6) can be given until a specific F is known. Observe from Def. 4.10.3 that $P[R \leq n] = \int_{-\infty}^n F = \int_0^n F$, so we have that $G(n)$ assumes a maximum for that n, call it $n = n^*$, such that $P[R \leq n^*] = (s-c)/s$; i.e., for the value $n = n^*$, such that the probability that the number of items sold is less than or equal to this optimal n^* is $(s-c)/s$. Observe also that $(s-c)/s$ is exactly the proportion of profit to selling price.

We shall not labor the point that a maximum is actually attained by $G(n) = E[p(x)]$ for this n, but shall leave it to the reader in the exercises to verify for particular choices of F.

PROBLEMS

4.12.1. Suppose the p.d.f. F for R is given by

$$F(x) = \begin{cases} 0, & x < 0 \\ 1/T, & 0 \leq x \leq T \\ 0, & x > T \end{cases}$$

the so-called *uniform* p.d.f. Find $E[p(x)]$ from (4.12.3) and use this to find the optimal inventory level. Show that you have actually attained a maximum. Check your result by using (4.12.6).

4.12.2. Repeat Prob. 4.12.1 for the p.d.f. given by

$$F(x) = \begin{cases} 0, & x < 0 \\ 2a^2x, & 0 \leq x \leq 1/a \quad (a > 0) \\ 0, & x > 1/a \end{cases}$$

4.12.3. Repeat Prob. 4.12.1. for the p.d.f. given by

$$F(x) = \begin{cases} 0, & x < 0 \\ e^{-x}, & x \geq 0 \end{cases}$$

4.13. The general linear differential equation of first order.

Let $A(x)$ and $B(x)$ be continuous functions of x. We consider the differential equation

$$(4.13.1) \qquad y'(x) + A(x)y(x) + B(x) = 0$$

the so-called **general linear differential equation of first order.** This is not immediately of the form (4.4.1), but can be put into this form by the following device. Rewrite (4.13.1) as

$$(4.13.2) \qquad y'(x) + A(x)y(x) = -B(x)$$

No matter what function $w(x)$ we choose, we can obtain from (4.13.2) by multiplying by $w(x)$:

$$(4.13.3) \qquad w(x)y'(x) + w(x)A(x)y(x) = -w(x)B(x)$$

Our object is to choose $w(x)$ judiciously. First, we wish to determine whether there exists such a function $w(x)$ such that $D[w(x)y(x)] = $ [left side of (4.13.3)]; i.e.,

$$(4.13.4) \qquad D[w(x)y(x)] = w(x)y'(x) + w(x)A(x)y(x)$$

Expanding (4.13.4), this would require

$$w(x)y'(x) + w'(x)y(x) = w(x)y'(x) + w(x)A(x)y(x)$$

or, after subtracting $w(x)y'(x)$,

$$w'(x)y(x) = w(x)A(x)y(x)$$

and finally, after dividing by $y(x)$

$$w'(x) = w(x)A(x)$$

or

$$\frac{1}{w} w' = A(x)$$

which is of the form (4.4.1), and hence, with $w \neq 0$, has solution

$$\ln |w| = \int A(x)\, dx + c$$

Since any $w(x)$ satisfying (4.13.4) will do, we choose $c = 0$. As in §4.4, we obtain

(4.13.5) $$w(x) = \exp \left[\int A(x)\, dx \right]$$

So we have determined a $w(x)$ so that (4.13.4) is satisfied. With this choice of $w(x)$, we use (4.13.4) to modify (4.13.3) to read

$$D[w(x)y(x)] = -w(x)B(x)$$

and so, by the definition of anti-derivative, we obtain

(4.13.6) $$w(x)y(x) = -\int w(x)B(x)\, dx + k$$

where k is the constant of integration. With the value $w(x)$ obtained from (4.13.5), (4.13.6) finally becomes, in terms of anti-derivatives,

(4.13.7) $$y(x) = \exp \left[-\int A(x)\, dx \right] \left\{ k - \int B(x) \exp \left[\int A(x)\, dx \right] dx \right\}$$

See Prob. 4.13.11 for the integral form of (4.13.7).

Example 4.13.1. We solve the differential equation $y' + 2y = x$. For this problem, $w(x) = \exp [\int 2\, dx] = e^{2x}$, since $A(x) \equiv 2$. Since $B(x) = x$, we obtain from (4.13.7)

$$y(x) = e^{-2x} \left\{ c - \int xe^{2x}\, dx \right\}$$

which can be evaluated by using integration by parts (recall Thm. 3.10.4).

The function $w(x) = \exp [\int A(x)\, dx]$ is called an *integrating factor* for (4.13.1).

PROBLEMS

Solve each of the following

4.13.1. $y' - xy = x$

4.13.2. $y' - y = x^2$

4.13.6. $y' + (1/x)y = e^x$, $x > 0$

4.13.7. $y' + (1/x^2)y = (1/x^2)$, $x > 0$

4.13.3. $y' - 3x^2y = x^2$ 4.13.8. $y' + 2y = x^3$

4.13.4. $y' + 2xy = x$ 4.13.9. $y' + (1/x)y = (1 + x)^2$, $x > 0$

4.13.5. $y' + y = x^2$ 4.13.10. $xy' + y = x \ln x$, $x > 0$

4.13.11. Let $A(x)$ and $B(x)$ be defined and continuous functions for $x \geq a$ for some fixed a. Show that an integral solution to (4.13.1) is

$$y(x) = \exp\left[-\int_a^x A(t)\, dt\right]\left\{y(a) - \int_a^x B(t) \exp\left[\int_a^t A(u)\, du\right] dt\right\}$$

4.14. A problem in time series.

In many applications, the problem is somehow to decide the "true" value of an unknown, basing this decision on empirical data collected; i.e., based on "measurements". We observe our unknown quantity at different times and record our measurements; we usually observe variations in our data as we make different observations, variations due to human frailty, imperfect measuring devices, etc. Each observation is assumed to be of two parts: the true value we are seeking, and some undesirable concomitant of the observation, called (because of a related engineering problem) "noise", which is reflected as a deviation from the true value in the observation. At time t, call our observation $x(t)$, the true value $y(t)$ and the "noise" $z(t)$. Then we have

$$x(t) = y(t) + z(t)$$

i.e., (observed value at time t) = (true value at time t) + (noise at time t).

The model we shall consider will assume that the true value is a constant, at least over the time interval of the experiment (possibly over long periods of time, this constant will change). So, we are assuming that during the time the experiment takes place, $y(t) \equiv A$ for the appropriate unknown constant A which we are trying to discover.

It should be observed that the requirement that $y(t) = A$; i.e., $y(t)$ is a *fixed value for all t*, is somewhat restrictive, since there are many processes in which we expect the "true value" to change with time, as for instance the position of a missile in space over a time interval. We might expect that the demand for a product at a fixed price would not change over reasonable time periods.

We shall assume that $z(t)$ is a random noise; i.e., for each t, $z(t)$ is a random variable with some unknown probability distribution. Furthermore, we assume that the expected value of $z(t)$ is 0 (i.e., $E[z(t)] = 0$ for each t); i.e., on the average, the error is small.

Our concern is to find a good estimator for $y(t) = A$; in particular we shall try to estimate $y(t) = A$ by an appropriate average. A reasonable average to use as our estimate is the arithmetic mean of our observations. Specifically, if $a_1, a_2, \ldots, a_n$ are n given numbers, the **arithmetic mean** is given by

$$(4.14.1) \qquad \frac{a_1 + a_2 + \cdots + a_n}{n} \equiv \frac{1}{n} \sum_{k=1}^{n} a_k$$

We shall show how (4.14.1) can be used in our problem in Ex. 4.14.1.

Before proceeding, we should observe that we are discussing discrete measurements or observations made sequentially over discrete values of time. So, x_1 is the first observation, made at time $t = 1$, x_2 is the second observation made 1 time unit later at time $t = 2$, and x_t is the tth observation made at time t units after the first observations. The problem is said to be one of *discrete time series*. We will end this section with the continuous analog of this problem; i.e., the problem of a continuous flow of data over say a time interval $t_1 \leq t \leq t_2$. An example of a continuous process might be the tracking of a missile in space over an interval of time.

The following example will serve to introduce the discrete time series problem.

Example 4.14.1. Suppose we have taken seven successive observations of our process of interest, and have obtained the numbers

$$x_1 = 101, \quad x_2 = 99, \quad x_3 = 102$$
$$x_4 = 101, \quad x_5 = 97, \quad x_6 = 99, \quad x_7 = 103$$

Suppose we decide in advance to average our data using sample sizes of five. We obtain the estimates

$$M_5 = \tfrac{1}{5}(x_5 + x_4 + x_3 + x_2 + x_1) = \tfrac{1}{5}(500) = 100.0$$
$$M_6 = \tfrac{1}{5}(x_6 + x_5 + x_4 + x_3 + x_2) = \tfrac{1}{5}(498) = 99.6$$
$$M_7 = \tfrac{1}{5}(x_7 + x_6 + x_5 + x_4 + x_3) = \tfrac{1}{5}(502) = 100.4$$

Observe that M_5 is the average of the first five successive observations, M_6 the second five successive observations, and M_7 the average of the five most recent observations. We can think of x_j as the observation taken at time $t = j$.

In the spirit of Ex. 4.14.1, if we call M_t the average of N observations which terminate at time t with observation $x(t) \equiv x_t$ (we shall use subscript notation, since if we are dealing with discrete time units $t = 1, t = 2, \ldots$, the corresponding observations $x(1) = x_1, x(2) = x_2, \ldots$ form a sequence, and subscript notation is more suggestive of the sequential problem), then

$$(4.14.2) \qquad M_t = \frac{x_t + x_{t-1} + \cdots + x_{t-N+2} + x_{t-N+1}}{N}$$

Observe that with $N = 5$ and $t = 5$, 6, or 7, we obtain exactly M_5, M_6, and M_7

of Ex. 4.14.1. If we replace t by $(t - 1)$ in (4.14.2), we obtain

$$M_{t-1} = \frac{x_{t-1} + x_{t-2} + \cdots + x_{t-N+1} + x_{t-N}}{N}$$

If we add x_t/N and subtract x_{t-N}/N, the above expression becomes

$$M_{t-1} + \frac{x_t}{N} - \frac{x_{t-N}}{N} = \frac{x_t + x_{t-1} + x_{t-2} + \cdots + x_{t-N+1}}{N}$$

and comparing the right side of this equation with (4.14.2) yields

(4.14.3)
$$M_{t-1} + \frac{x_t - x_{t-N}}{N} = M_t$$

Hence, we can compute the average at time t, if we know the average at time $(t - 1)$, the observation at time t and the observation taken at time $(t - N)$.

In this way we obtain a sequence of M_N, M_{N+1}, M_{N+2}, ... of averages, each one of which is an estimate of $y(t) = A$. Such averages are often called *moving averages*.

The calculations in (4.14.3) involve knowing x_{t-N}; i.e., we must keep a large inventory of previous observations. If N is large, this can require data from the distant past. Suppose we wish to compute M_t, but because of a tragic fire, all our long lists of data are gone, including x_{t-N}. However, suppose also that we still recall M_{t-1}. What should replace (4.13.3)? A reasonable estimate of M_t might be $\tilde{M}_t$ defined by

(4.14.4)
$$\tilde{M}_t = M_{t-1} + \frac{x_t - M_{t-1}}{N}$$

Example 4.14.2. With the data of Ex. 4.14.1, we suppose x_1, x_2, ..., x_6 are missing, but $M_6 = 99.6$ is still known. Then

$$\tilde{M}_7 = M_6 + \frac{x_7 - M_6}{5} = 99.6 + \frac{103 - 99.6}{5}$$

and so $\tilde{M}_7$ approximately equals 100.3, a "fairly good" estimate of 100.4.

If we do some algebra, (4.14.4), becomes

$$\tilde{M}_t = \frac{1}{N}[NM_{t-1} + x_t - M_{t-1}] = \frac{1}{N}[x_t + (N - 1)M_{t-1}]$$

$$= \frac{x_t}{N} + \left(1 - \frac{1}{N}\right)M_{t-1}$$

We extrapolate from the modified averages $\tilde{M}_t$ to construct an average $S_t(x)$ of the form

(4.14.5)
$$S_t(x) = cx_t + (1 - c)S_{t-1}(x), \qquad 0 < c < 1$$

Here, c plays the role of $(1/N)$. Looking at "averages" like $S_t(x)$ is called *exponential smoothing* of the data. Further investigation of (4.14.5) yields

$$
\begin{aligned}
S_t(x) &= cx_t + (1 - c)S_{t-1}(x) \\
&= cx_t + (1 - c)[cx_{t-1} + (1 - c)S_{t-2}(x)] \\
&= cx_t + c(1 - c)x_{t-1} + (1 - c)^2[cx_{t-2} + (1 - c)S_{t-3}] \\
&= cx_t + c(1 - c)x_{t-1} + c(1 - c)^2x_{t-2} + (1 - c)^3S_{t-3}
\end{aligned}
$$

If we continue this decomposition, we obtain

$$
S_t(x) = cx_t + c(1 - c)x_{t-1} + c(1 - c)^2x_{t-2} + \cdots \\
+ c(1 - c)^n x_{t-n} + \cdots + (1 - c)^t x_0
$$

or

(4.14.6)
$$
S_t(x) = \left[c \sum_{k=0}^{t-1} (1 - c)^k x_{t-k} \right] + (1 - c)^t x_0
$$

Since $z(t)$ is a random variable, and $x_t = x(t) = A + z(t)$, we have x_t is a random variable for each t. It is possible to prove that if X and Y have the same probability distribution, then $E(X + Y) = E(X) + E(Y)$, where E is the expectation function. If we assume each x_t has the same probability distribution, then from (4.14.6), calling $E(x_t) = E(x)$,

$$
\begin{aligned}
E[S_t(x)] &= E \left\{ \left[c \sum_{k=0}^{t-1} (1 - c)^k x_{t-k} \right] + (1 - c)^t x_0 \right\} \\
&= c \sum_{k=0}^{t-1} (1 - c)^k E[x_{t-k}] + (1 - c)^t E(x_0) \\
&= cE[x] \cdot \sum_{k=0}^{t-1} (1 - c)^k + E(x)(1 - c)^t
\end{aligned}
$$

Since $0 < c < 1$, we have $0 < 1 - c < 1$, so, with $r = 1 - c$ in (3.2.1), we have

$$
\lim_{t \to \infty} \sum_{k=0}^{t-1} (1 - c)^k = \frac{1}{1 - (1 - c)} = \frac{1}{c}
$$

and so, also using Thm. 3.2.2,

(4.14.7)
$$
\lim_{t \to \infty} E[S_t(x)] = E(x)
$$

and so the limiting expectation of the "smoothing function" $S_t(x)$ is just the expectation of any of the observations. In our specific model, $E[z(t)] = 0$, and consequently $E[x(t)] = E[A + z(t)] = E[A] + E[z(t)] = A$ (see Prob. 4.14.4).

We turn now to the continuous analog of (4.14.6). The analog of (4.14.5) is

(4.14.8)
$$
s(t) = cx(t) + (1 - c)s(t - 1)
$$

or

$$\text{(4.14.9)} \qquad \frac{s(t) - s(t-1)}{1} = c[x(t) - s(t-1)]$$

corresponding to changes in s from time $t - 1$ to t. If our process is in some sense continuous, s no longer changes over discrete values of time; we can ask about changes in s as time varies from $t - h$ to t for real numbers h. If time changes from $t - h$ to t, and the constant c is replaced by some constant β, a reasonable analog of (4.14.9) is

$$\text{(4.14.10)} \qquad \frac{s(t) - s(t-h)}{h} = \beta[x(t) - s(t-h)]$$

Assuming that $s(t)$ has a derivative, and hence is continuous, for all $t \geq 0$, we obtain from (4.14.10), by taking the limit as $h \to 0$,

$$\text{(4.14.11)} \qquad \frac{ds(t)}{dt} = \beta[x(t) - s(t)]$$

or, with $'$ denoting differentiation with respect to t,

$$s'(t) + \beta s(t) = \beta x(t)$$

which is a linear differential equation of first order of type (4.13.2). We obtain from (4.13.7) the solution in anti-derivative form

$$s(t) = \exp\left[-\int \beta \, dt \left\{ k + \int \beta x(t) \exp\left[\int \beta \, dt\right] dt\right\}\right.$$

or, in the form of an integral,

$$s(t) = e^{-\beta t}\left\{ k + \beta \int_0^t x(u)e^{\beta u} \, du\right\}$$

$$\text{(4.14.12)} \qquad\qquad = \beta \int_0^t x(u)e^{-\beta(t-u)} \, du + ke^{-\beta t}$$

PROBLEMS

4.14.1. Suppose in an experiment, the following measurements were observed

$$x_1 = 0.32, \quad x_2 = 0.37, \quad x_3 = 0.28$$
$$x_4 = 0.31, \quad x_5 = 0.29, \quad x_6 = 0.22$$
$$x_7 = 0.39, \quad x_8 = 0.33, \quad x_9 = 0.20, \quad x_{10} = 0.33$$

Based on sample sizes of $N = 5$, compute M_5, M_6, M_7, M_8, M_9, and M_{10}, using (4.14.3). Then find $\tilde{M}_6$, $\tilde{M}_7$, $\tilde{M}_8$, $\tilde{M}_9$, and $\tilde{M}_{10}$.

4.14.2. Using the data of Prob. 4.14.1, with $c = 0.2$, find $s_{10}(x)$ (assume $x_0 = 0$).

4.14.3. Find the function $s(t)$ which satisfies the differential equation

$$\frac{ds(t)}{dt} = \frac{1}{2}[t - s(t)]$$

4.14.4 Let A be a constant and u a random variable such that $E[u]$ exists. Show that $E[A + u] = A + E[u]$. (Hint. Let f be the p.d.f. associated with u. Then

$$E(A + u) = \int_{-\infty}^{\infty} (A + x)f(x)\, dx.$$

Expand this and use the fact that $\int_{-\infty}^{\infty} f(x)\, dx = 1$.)

APPENDIX

A. A proof of the chain rule.

In Chapter 1, we defined the derivative $f'(x)$ by

$$f'(x) = \lim_{h \to 0} \frac{f(x+h) - f(x)}{h}$$

whenever the limit exists. Let us compare the expressions $f'(x)$ and $(1/h)\{f(x+h) - f(x)\}$. We see that with $\lim_{h \to 0}$ omitted, there is a value $\alpha = \alpha(h)$ such that for any $h \neq 0$,

$$(A.1) \qquad \frac{f(x+h) - f(x)}{h} = f'(x) + \alpha$$

where $\alpha \to 0$ as $h \to 0$. (A.1) is merely a restatement of the definition of derivative. If we rewrite (A.1), we obtain for $h \neq 0$,

$$(A.2) \qquad f(x+h) - f(x) = f'(x)h + \alpha h$$

where

$$(A.3) \qquad \lim_{h \to 0} \alpha = 0$$

(A.2) and (A.3) are useful expressions for characterizing the derivative and yield a rather elegant proof of the chain rule:

Theorem. Let $g(y)$ be a differentiable function of y, and let $y = f(x)$ be a differentiable function of x, and suppose the range of f is contained in the domain g (this is to insure that $g[f(x)]$ is meaningful). Then, $(d/dx)g[f(x)]$ exists, and

$$\frac{d}{dx} g[f(x)] = \left[\frac{d}{dy} g(y) \right] \cdot \left[\frac{d}{dx} f(x) \right]$$

Proof. First we introduce the abbreviation $\Delta y = f(x+h) - f(x)$. Since

$f'(x)$ exists by assumption, it follows that $f(x)$ is continuous, and hence $\Delta y \to 0$ as $h \to 0$. It is possible of course that Δy will be 0 for $h \neq 0$. Applying (A.2) and (A.3) to $g(y)$, we obtain

(A.4) $g(y + \Delta y) - g(y) = g'(y)\,\Delta y + \alpha\,\Delta y = (g'(y) + \alpha)\,\Delta y$

where $\alpha \to 0$ as $\Delta y \to 0$. (A.4) remains valid even if $\Delta y = 0$, since if $\Delta y = 0$, both the left and right sides of (A.4) are equal to 0. (Why?). Applying (A.2) and (A.3) to f, we obtain

(A.5) $\Delta y = f(x + h) - f(x) = f'(x)h + \beta h$

where $\beta \to 0$ as $h \to 0$.

We substitute Δy from (A.5) into (A.4) to obtain

$$g(y + \Delta y) - g(y) = \left(\frac{dg}{dy} + \alpha\right)\left(\frac{df}{dx}\,h + \beta h\right)$$

$$= \frac{dg}{dy}\cdot\frac{df}{dx}\cdot h + \left(\frac{dg}{dy}\,\beta + \frac{df}{dx}\cdot\alpha + \alpha\beta\right)h$$

from which it follows that for $h \neq 0$,

(A.6) $\dfrac{g(y + \Delta y) - g(y)}{h} = \dfrac{dg}{dy}\dfrac{df}{dx} + \left\{\beta\dfrac{dg}{dy} + \alpha\dfrac{df}{dx} + \alpha\beta\right\}$

A direct evaluation shows that $y + \Delta y = f(x) + \{f(x + h) - f(x)\} = f(x + h)$, so (A.6) becomes

(A.7) $\dfrac{g[f(x + h)] - g[f(x)]}{h} = \dfrac{dg(y)}{dy}\cdot\dfrac{df(x)}{dx} + \left\{\beta\dfrac{dg}{dy} + \alpha\dfrac{df}{dx} + \alpha\beta\right\}$

As $h \to 0$, we see that $\beta \to 0$ and $\Delta y \to 0$, and so $\alpha \to 0$. Hence

$$\lim_{h\to 0}\left\{\frac{dg}{dy}\cdot\beta + \frac{df}{dx}\cdot\alpha + \alpha\beta\right\} = 0$$

and as $h \to 0$, the left side of (A.7) is exactly

$$\frac{dg[f(x)]}{dx}$$

Hence, letting $h \to 0$ in (A.7), we obtain the desired result of the theorem.

We conclude this section with a proof of a modified version of Thm. 1.10.2, the theorem that asserts that if $f(y)$ and $g(x)$ are each continuous, then $f[g(x)]$ is continuous. The proof depends on §1.6.

Theorem. If $f(y)$ is continuous on the open interval $A < y < B$ and if $y = g(x)$ is continuous on the open interval $a < x < b$, and if the range of

$g(x)$ is the open interval $A < y < B$ (i.e., the range of $g(x)$ is the same as the open interval on which $f(y)$ is defined), then $f[g(x)]$ is continuous on the open interval $a < x < b$.

Proof. Pick c such that $a < c < b$. It is necessary to prove that for any $\varepsilon > 0$, there is a $\delta > 0$ such that $|f[g(x)] - f[g(c)]| < \varepsilon$ whenever $|x - c| < \delta$. Let $g(c) = d$. Since d is in the interval $A < y < B$, and $f(y)$ is continuous on this interval, we know that for any $\varepsilon' > 0$, there is a $\delta' > 0$ such that $|f(y) - f(d)| < \varepsilon'$ if $|y - d| < \delta'$, and since $g(x)$ is continuous at $x = c$, we know that for every $\varepsilon'' > 0$ there is a $\delta'' > 0$ such that $|g(x) - g(c)| < \varepsilon''$ if $|x - c| < \delta''$. We know by our choice of the range of $g(x)$ that to each y satisfying $|y - d| < \delta'$ there is an x in $a < x < b$ such that $y = g(x)$, and hence $|y - d| < \delta'$ can be written $|g(x) - g(c)| < \varepsilon'$ and $|f(y) - f(d)| < \varepsilon'$ can be written $|f[g(x)] - f[g(c)]| < \varepsilon'$. We choose $\varepsilon' = \varepsilon$ ($\varepsilon > 0$ is given), $\delta' = \varepsilon''$; the required δ is then δ'', and the theorem is proved.

B. The mean value theorem.

In our discussion of increasing and decreasing functions in §2.2, reference was first made to a very powerful theorem called the mean value theorem. In Prob. 2.2.4 a statement of the theorem first appeared. In Thm. 3.3.1 reference was again made to this theorem. The theorem is most easily proved as a consequence of Rolle's theorem, which we shall state and prove first. For each theorem, we shall first state the geometrical version, then the equivalent analytical version which we shall prove.

Theorem (Rolle). (i) *Geometrical form.* Let $f(x)$ be continuous on the closed interval $a \le x \le b$, and suppose that at each c, $a < c < b$, a non-vertical tangent line can be drawn to the graph of $f(x)$ at $(c, f(c))$. Suppose also that $f(a) = 0 = f(b)$. Then we can conclude that there exists at least one value w (possibly more), $a < w < b$, such that the tangent line drawn at $(w, f(w))$ is parallel to the x-axis.

(ii) *Analytical form.* Let $f(x)$ be continuous on the closed interval $a \le x \le b$, with $f(a) = 0 = f(b)$, and suppose that at each c, $a < c < b$, $f'(c)$ exists. Then we

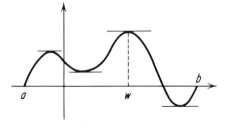

Figure B.1

can conclude that there exists at least one value w, $a < w < b$, such that $f'(w) = 0$ (see Fig. B.1).

Proof. Case 1. $f(x) = 0$ on $a \le x \le b$ (i.e., $f(x) = 0$ for *every* x in the interval $a \le x \le b$). Then no matter what w we pick in $a < x < b$, $f'(w) = 0$.

Case 2. For some values of x, $f(x)$ is not zero. Suppose we assume that for some values of x, $f(x) > 0$. From Thm. 1.7.4, we know that since $f(x)$ is continuous, $f(x)$ must attain its maximum value somewhere in $a \le x \le b$. Since $f(a) = 0 = f(b)$ and for some x, $f(x) > 0$, it must attain this maximum not at an endpoint $x = a$ or $x = b$ but at some w within the interval (i.e., at a w for which $a < w < b$). But in §2.4 we proved that if $f'(x)$ exists at a point z in (a,b) at which $f(x)$ assumes a maximum, then $f'(z) = 0$. Since $f'(x)$ is *assumed* to exist for all x in $a < x < b$, and w is such that $a < w < b$, and at $x = w$ our function assumes a maximum, we have proved that $f'(w) = 0$. A similar proof can be constructed if we assume that for some values x, $f(x) < 0$.

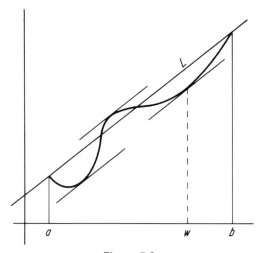

Figure B.2

The Mean Value Theorem. (i) *Geometrical form.* Let $f(x)$ be continuous on the closed interval $a \le x \le b$, and suppose that at each c, $a < c < b$, a non-vertical tangent line can be drawn to the graph of $f(x)$ at $(c, f(c))$. Draw the straight line L through the two points $(a, f(a))$ and $(b, f(b))$. Then we conclude that there exists at least one value w, $a < w < b$, such that the tangent line drawn to the graph of $f(x)$ at $(w, f(w))$ is parallel to L (see Fig. B.2).

(ii) *Analytical form.* Let $f(x)$ be continuous on the closed interval $a \le x \le b$, and suppose that at each c, $a < c < b$, $f'(c)$ exists. Then we conclude that there exists at least one value w, $a < w < b$, at which

(B.1) $$\frac{f(b) - f(a)}{b - a} = f'(w)$$

or equivalently

(B.2) $f(b) - f(a) = (b - a)f'(w)$

Remark. The reader should observe that in this theorem, as well as in Rolle's theorem, we do not exhibit the explicit w which satisfies the conclusion of the theorem, but merely assert the existence of such a value of x. Such theorems are called "existence theorems."

Proof of the mean value theorem. We first construct a special function $G(x)$ as follows. The equation of the straight line L through $(a, f(a))$ and $(b, f(b))$ is

$$y = g(x) = \frac{f(b) - f(a)}{b - a}(x - a) + f(b)$$

[see (1.4.2)]. The function $G(x)$ is defined as the function $f(x)$ minus the

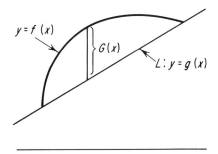

Figure B.3

corresponding y value on L; i.e., $G(x) = f(x) - g(x)$ (see Fig. B.3) and hence, after substituting,

(B.3) $G(x) = f(x) - f(b) - \frac{f(b) - f(a)}{b - a}(x - a)$

If we call

$$k = \frac{f(b) - f(a)}{b - a}$$

then clearly k is a constant. Our function $G(x)$ is then the sum of three functions, specifically, the functions $f(x)$, the constant function $y = -f(b)$, and the straight line $y = k(x - a)$. Each of these three functions is continuous on $a \le x \le b$ (the last two are actually continuous everywhere), and each function is differentiable in $a < x < b$ (the last two are actually differentiable everywhere). Hence, $G(x)$ is continuous on $a \le x \le b$ and differentiable on $a < x < b$. Furthermore, $G(a) = 0 = G(b)$ [the reader should verify this from

(B.3)]. Hence $G(x)$ satisfies all the hypotheses of Rolle's theorem and consequently there exists at least one value w, $a < w < b$, at which $G'(w) = 0$. From (B.3),

$$G'(x) = f'(x) - \frac{f(b) - f(a)}{b - a}$$

and so

$$0 = G'(w) = f'(w) - \frac{f(b) - f(a)}{b - a}$$

from which we obtain the desired result

$$f'(w) = \frac{f(b) - f(a)}{b - a}$$

for the appropriate w, $a < w < b$.

The following are some important consequences of the mean value theorem.

Corollary B.1. Let $f(x)$ be continuous on $a \le x \le b$, and suppose $f'(x) = 0$ for each x in $a < x < b$ ($f'(x)$, therefore, necessarily exists on $a < x < b$). Then $f(x)$ is constant on $a \le x \le b$; i.e., there is a constant k such that $f(x) = k$ holds throughout the interval $a \le x \le b$.

Proof. Pick the numbers r and s arbitrarily from the interval $a \le x \le b$. We must show $f(r) = f(s)$; i.e., that *all values of the function are equal*. Since all the hypotheses of the mean value theorem are satisfied by the function of our corollary, we are assured by (B.2) that $f(r) - f(s) = (r - s)f'(w)$ where w is the appropriate value between r and s. But then w is on the interval $a < x < b$, and hence $f'(w) = 0$. Consequently, $f(r) - f(s) = 0$, so $f(r) = f(s)$; since r and s are arbitrary on the interval $[a, b]$, $f(x)$ is a constant on this interval, and $f(x) \equiv f(r) = f(s)$.

Corollary B.2. Let $f(x)$ and $g(x)$ be continuous on $a \le x \le b$, and suppose $f'(x) = g'(x)$ for each x in $a < x < b$. Then there is some constant k such that $f(x) = g(x) + k$ for x in $a \le x \le b$.

Proof. Since $f'(x) = g'(x)$ on $a < x < b$, it follows that $f'(x) - g'(x) = 0$ on $a < x < b$. But

$$f'(x) - g'(x) = \frac{d}{dx}\{f(x) - g(x)\}$$

so

$$\frac{d}{dx}\{f(x) - g(x)\} = 0 \qquad \text{on } a < x < b$$

By corollary B.1 applied to $f(x) - g(x)$, we see that there is a constant k

such that $f(x) - g(x) = k$ holds throughout the interval $a \leq x \leq b$. This is the desired conclusion.

Corollary B.2 was stated (unproved) as Thm. 3.3.1.

Corollary B.3. Let $f(x)$ be continuous on $a \leq x \leq b$, and suppose that $f'(x) > 0$ on $a < x < b$. Then $f(x)$ is **S.I.** on $a \leq x \leq b$ (see §2.2).

Proof. We are required to show that for any numbers c and d satisfying $a \leq c < d \leq b$, we have $f(c) < f(d)$ (see Fig. B.4). Since $f(x)$ satisfies all the

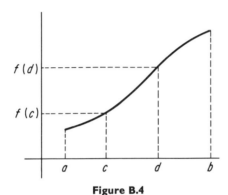

Figure B.4

hypotheses of the mean value theorem, we know that for any c and d satisfying $a \leq c < d \leq b$, $f(d) - f(c) = (d - c)f'(w)$ where w is the appropriate value, $c < w < d$. Since $c < d$, it follows that $d - c > 0$. Since $f'(x) > 0$ on $a < x < b$, it follows that $f'(w) > 0$. Consequently, $(d - c)f'(w) > 0$, and so $f(d) - f(c) > 0$, or finally, $f(d) > f(c)$. Summarizing, if $a \leq c < d \leq b$, then $f(c) < f(d)$, which is the desired result.

Corollary B.4. Let $f(x)$ be continuous on $a \leq x \leq b$, and suppose $f'(x) < 0$ on $a < x < b$. Then $f(x)$ is **S.D.** on $a \leq x \leq b$.

Proof. The proof is left to the reader.

PROBLEMS

B.1. Consider a function $f(x)$ with the following properties: $f(x)$ is continuous and differentiable for all x, $f(0) = 0$, $|f'(x)| \leq A$ for some positive constant A. Prove that $|f(x)| \leq A|x|$, for all x.

B.2. Let $f(x)$ be defined, have a continuous derivative, and $f''(x)$ exist for all x. Furthermore assume there are three distinct values $a < b < c$ such that $f'(a) = f'(b) = f'(c) = 0$ Explain why there must be at least two solutions to the equation $f''(x) = 0$.

B.3. Let $f(x)$ be continuous and differentiable on $0 \le x \le 1$, and suppose also that $f(0) = 0$ and $\lim_{x \to 0} f'(x) = 1$.   Show that $\lim_{x \to 0} [f(x)/x] = 1$.

FORMULAS FROM ALGEBRA AND GEOMETRY

1. The quadratic equation $ax^2 + bx + c = 0$ $(a \neq 0)$ has solutions

$$x = \frac{-b \pm \sqrt{b^2 - 4ac}}{2a}$$

   (a) If $b^2 - 4ac = 0$, there is only one solution (it is said to have multiplicity 2)
   (b) If $b^2 - 4ac > 0$, there are two distinct solutions
   (c) If $b^2 - 4ac < 0$, there are no (real) solutions

2. Right circular cylinder: $h = $ altitude, $r = $ radius of base.
   (a) Volume $= \pi r^2 h$
   (b) Lateral surface area $= 2\pi r h$
      (This does not include the areas of the "top" or "bottom".)

3. Right cone: $h = $ altitude, $r = $ radius of base.
   (a) Volume $= (\pi/3)r^2 h$
   (b) Lateral surface area $= \pi r \sqrt{r^2 + h^2}$
      (This does not include the circular area at the end.)

4. Sphere: $r = $ radius.
   (a) Volume $= (\frac{4}{3})\pi r^3$
   (b) Surface area $= 4\pi r^2$

5. (a) (Area of a circle of radius r) $= \pi r^2$
   (b) (Circumference of circle of radius r) $= 2\pi r$

6. (Area of a triangle with base b and altitude h) $= (\frac{1}{2})bh$

BIBLIOGRAPHY

Agnew, M. W., *Differential Equations* (2nd ed.). New York: McGraw-Hill Book Co., Inc., 1960.

Baumol, W. J., *Economic Theory and Operations Analysis.* Englewood Cliffs, N.J.: Prentice-Hall, Inc., 1961.

Brown, R. G., *Smoothing, Forecasting and Prediction of Discrete Time Series.* Englewood Cliffs, N.J.: Prentice-Hall, Inc., 1963.

Brunk, H. D., *An Introduction to Mathematical Statistics.* New York: Ginn and Co., 1960.

Bush, R. R., R. Abelson, and R. Hyman, *Mathematics for Psychologists: Examples and Problems.* New York: Social Science Research Council, 1956.

Bush, R. R. and W. K. Estes, editors, *Studies in Mathematical Learning Theory.* Stanford, Calif.: Stanford University Press, 1959.

Courant, R., *Differential and Integral Calculus*, Vol. I and II (especially Vol. I). New York: Interscience Publishers, Inc., 1937.

Cramer, H., *Mathematical Methods of Statistics.* Princeton, N.J.: Princeton University Press, 1951.

Daus, P. H. and W. Whyburn, *Introduction to Mathematical Analysis.* Reading, Mass.: Addison-Wesley Publishing Co., Inc., 1958.

Feller, W., *An Introduction to Probability Theory and its Applications*, Vol. I (2nd ed.). New York: John Wiley and Sons, Inc., 1957.

Hoel, P. G., *Elementary Statistics.* New York: John Wiley and Sons, Inc., 1960.

Howell, J. E. and D. Teichroew, *Mathematical Analysis for Business Decisions.* Homewood, Ill.: Richard D. Irwin, Inc., 1963.

Koch, S., *Psychology, a Study of Science*, Vol. 2. New York: McGraw-Hill Book Co., 1959 (especially the article *Statistical Learning Theory* by W. K. Estes).

Mack, S. F., *Elementary Statistics.* New York: Holt, Rinehart and Winston, 1960.

McBrien, V. O., *Introductory Analysis.* New York: Appleton-Century-Crofts, Inc., 1961.

Rachevsky, N., *Mathematical Biophysics.* Chicago, Ill.: University of Chicago Press, 1938.

Stern, M. E., *Mathematics for Management.* Englewood Cliffs, N.J.: Prentice-Hall, Inc., 1963.

Taylor, A. E., *Advanced Calculus.* New York: Ginn and Co., 1955.

Thomas, G. B., *Calculus and Analytic Geometry*. Reading, Mass.: Addison-Wesley, Inc., 1961.

Some references to *Markov chains*:

Kemeny, J. G., L. J. Snell, and G. L. Thompson, *Introduction to Finite Mathematics*. Englewood Cliffs, N.J.: Prentice-Hall, Inc., 1957.

Rosenblatt, M., *Random Processes*. New York: Oxford University Press, 1962. (This is an advanced work.)

Some references to *finite differences*:

Miller, K. S., *An Introduction to the Calculus of Finite Differences and Difference Equations*. New York: Holt, Rinehart and Winston, 1960.

Richardson, C. H., *An Introduction to the Calculus of Finite Differences*. New York: D. Van Nostrand Co., Inc., 1954.

ANSWERS TO SELECTED PROBLEMS

CHAPTER 1

§1.1. Page 10.

1.1.1. $f(0) = 1$, $f(-1) = -2$, $f(-2) = -13$.   **1.1.3.** No.   **1.1.6.** Use the fact that if a, b, and c are the lengths of the sides of a triangle and $c^2 = a^2 + b^2$, then the triangle is a right triangle with hypotenuse corresponding to c and legs corresponding to a and b.   **1.1.9.** 1 if $h > 0$, -1 if $h < 0$.   **1.1.11.** center $(1, 2)$, radius $\sqrt{6}$.   **1.1.13.** (a) $x \le 5/2$; (b) $x \ge 5/2$.   **1.1.15.** (a) $x > 1$ or $x < 0$; (c) $-2 \le x \le 2$; (e) $x < 1$ or $2 < x < 3$.   **1.1.21.** $a = b + (a - b)$; hence by (1.1.4), $|a| = |b + (a - b)| \le |b| + |a - b|$; and hence $|a| - |b| \le |a - b|$.   The problem is completed by a similar argument, noting that $|b| = |a + (b - a)| \le |a| + |a - b|$.

§1.2. Page 18.

1.2.1. Use similar triangles.   **1.2.2.** Because of Prob. 1.2.1, you can assume all the lines pass through $(0, 0)$. (Why?) Let the other point you use to compute $m(L)$ be (a, b), and observe that in the first quadrant, $a > 0$, $b > 0$; in the second quadrant, $a < 0$ and $b > 0$; on the x-axis, $b = 0$ and on the y-axis, $a = 0$.   **1.2.3.** Use the result of Prob. 1.1.9 to show that $f(x)$ is not differentiable at $x = 0$.   **1.2.5.** The slopes at $x = -1, 1, 2$, and -2 are -1, -1, $-\frac{1}{4}$, and $-\frac{1}{4}$, respectively.   **1.2.7.** $f'(0) = 0$, $f'(1) = 2$.   **1.2.8.** Hint: Use (1.2.4).   **1.2.9.** $f(x)$ is not differentiable at $x = 1$.

§1.3. Page 22.

1.3.1. $v = 1/2\sqrt{t}$, $a = -1/4\sqrt{t^3}$, $\bar{v} = \frac{1}{2}$, $\bar{a} = -\frac{1}{168}$ **1.3.3.** 20 units of area per unit of length.   **1.3.5.** $\pi t^2/2$.   **1.3.7.** $v = 2at + b$, acceleration $= 2a$ (the a here, of course, is the a of the problem, and does not represent acceleration).

§1.4. Page 25.

1.4.1. (a) $y = -3x + 7$; (c) $y = \frac{2}{3}(x - 2)$; (e) $y = [(b - d)/a]x + d$.   **1.4.3.** (a) $y = 4x - 3$; (c) $y = -x + 2$; (e) $y = (2a + b)x + (c - 2a)$.

§1.5. Page 32.

1.5.1. 4.   **1.5.3.** 1/2.   **1.5.5.** 0.   **1.5.7.** 10.   **1.5.9.** 0, 1, and 2, respectively. **1.5.11.** $\lim\limits_{x \to m} f(x)$ does not exist.   **1.5.13.** 0.   **1.5.15.** Multiply the numerator and denominator of $\dfrac{\sqrt{x^2 + 1} - x}{1}$ by $\sqrt{x^2 + 1} + x$; i.e., rationalize. The limit is 0. **1.5.17.** $f'(0) = 0, f'(1) = 2$.

§1.6. Page 36.

1.6.1. Set $\delta = \varepsilon$.   **1.6.3.** First assume $|x - 1| < 1$; i.e., assume that $0 < x < 2$. Hence, $3 < x + 3 < 5$, so $|x + 3| < 5$. Write $|x^2 - 9| = |x + 3| \, |x - 3| < 5|x - 3|$. and observe $5|x - 3| < \varepsilon$ if $\delta = \varepsilon/5$. Pick δ the smaller of the numbers 1 and $\varepsilon/5$. **1.6.5.** $x^3 - 8 = (x - 2)(x^2 + 2x + 4)$. First suppose $|x - 2| < 1$, find a bound for $x^2 + 2x + 4$ (e.g., $|x^2 + 2x + 4| \le |x|^2 + 2|x| + 4 \le 19$ by (1.1.4) if $|x - 2| < 1$). Proceed as in Prob. 1.6.3.   **1.6.7.** We must show that for any $\varepsilon > 0$, there exists a $\delta > 0$ such that $|[f(x) + g(x)] - [A + B]| < \varepsilon$ if $0 < |x - c| < \delta$. For the given $\varepsilon > 0$, there are numbers δ_1 and δ_2 such that $|f(x) - A| < \varepsilon/2$ if $0 < |x - c| < \delta_1$ and $|g(x) - B| < \varepsilon/2$ if $0 < |x - c| < \delta_2$ (this simply asserts that the individual limits exist). Write $|[f(x) - g(x)] - [A + B]| = |[f(x) - A] + [g(x) - B]| \le |f(x) - A| + |g(x) - B| < \varepsilon/2 + \varepsilon/2 = \varepsilon$ if $0 < |x - c| < $ (smaller of the numbers δ_1 and δ_2).   **1.6.9.** For any $\varepsilon > 0$ there is a $\delta > 0$ such that $|f(x) - L| < \varepsilon$ if $0 < x - a < \delta$ (or $a < x < a + \delta$).

§1.7. Page 41.

1.7.1. Yes.   **1.7.3.** (a) $f(x)$ is continuous at $x = -1$ and $x = 1$, but not at $x = 0$; (c) $F(x)$ is continuous at all points indicated; (e) $W(x)$ is continuous at $x = -3$. **1.7.5.** $c = 0, d = 1$. No extrema in $(0, 1)$.   **1.7.7.** No.   **1.7.9.** $f(a) > g(a)$, so a is in the domain of W. Finish, using Thm. 1.5.1.

§1.8. Page 44.

1.8.1. $(a + b)^4 = a^4 + 4a^3b + 6a^2b^2 + 4ab^3 + b^4$.   **1.8.3.** $(2a - 3b)^5 = 32a^5 - 240a^4b + 270a^3b^2 - 1080a^2b^3 + 810ab^4 - 2430b^5$.

§1.9. Page 48.

1.9.1. $y = 4x - 6$.   **1.9.3.** marginal cost $= 297$.   **1.9.5.** $x = 2$ and $x = -1$.
1.9.7. $8x(x^2 - 1)^3$ and $8(x^2 - 1)^2(7x^2 - 1)$.   **1.9.9.** $x = -2$ and $x = 1$.
1.9.11. $7x^6 - 18x^5 + 5x^4 + 2x$.   **1.9.13.** Apply (1.2.4) to $1/f(x)$, find a common denominator and take the limit.   **1.9.15.** Let $f(x) = c$, all x in $[a, b]$.

$$f'(x) = \lim_{h \to 0, \, h > 0} \frac{f(a + h) - f(a)}{h} = \lim_{h \to 0, \, h > 0} \frac{[c - c]}{h} = 0$$

§1.10. Page 53.

1.10.1. (a) $f[g(x)] = 4x^2 + 10x + 3$, $(d/dx)f[g(x)] = 8x + 10$; (c) $f[g(x)] = x^3 + 3x^2 + x - 4$.   **1.10.3.** $g(x) = (x + 7)/3$.   **1.10.5.** (a) First verify that if two functions are equal, so are their derivatives. Then differentiate both sides of the equation $f[g(x)] = x$ (i.e., the functions $f[g(x)]$ and $h(x) = x$ are equal and, hence, so are their derivatives).   **1.10.7.** Consider the hint for Prob. 1.10.6.

§1.11. Page 57.

1.11.1. (a) $-[1/(x - 1)^2]$; (c) $-2[(x + 3)/(x + 2)^3]$; (e) $10x^3(5x - 4) \cdot (x^5 - x^4 + 1)^9$; (j)

$$\frac{1}{4}\left[\frac{(1 + 2\sqrt{x})}{\sqrt{x^2 + x\sqrt{x}}}\right]$$

1.11.3. Slope for $x = 0$ is 1, for $x = 1$ is 0. Tangent lines: $y = x$ and $y = 1/2$, respectively.   **1.11.5.** $1/3x^{2/3}$ and $1/3(x - 5)^{2/3}$, respectively.   **1.11.7.** $f'(x) = 2/(1 - x)^2$, $f''(x) = 4/(1 - x)^3$, $f'''(x) = 9/(1 - x)^4$.   **1.11.9.** $20(1 + 2x)^9$.
1.11.13. total revenue $= 8 - 2p$, marginal revenue $= -2$.

§1.12. Page 64.

1.12.1. (a) The functions are $f(x) = \sqrt{x/(1 + x)}$ and $g(x) = -\sqrt{x/(1 + x)}$ with derivatives $1/[2\sqrt{x}(1 + x)^{3/2}]$ and $-1/[2\sqrt{x}(1 + x)^{3/2}]$ respectively. (b) $F'(x) = (1 - y^2)/[2y(1 + x)]$, $F' = \pm\sqrt{2}/8$ at $x = 1$, and $f'(1) = \sqrt{2}/8$, $g'(1) = -\sqrt{2}/8$.
1.12.3. (a) $y' = -2xy/(4y^2 + 2x^2)$ for $y \neq 0$; (c) $y' = -1/[y(x - 1)^2]$; (e) $y' = -(y^2 + 2xy)/(x^2 + 2xy)$.   **1.12.5.** $-8/3$ ft/sec.   **1.12.7.** $4/3$ ft/sec.   **1.12.9.** 50 m.p.h.   **1.12.11.** -40 ft/sec.   **1.12.13.** 4 ft/sec.

CHAPTER 2

§2.1. Page 68.

2.1.1. $f(1) = -1$, $f(2) = 64$.   **2.1.3.** $f''(2) = 132$, $f'''(2) = 210$.   **2.1.5.**
$P(6) = 12$.

§2.2. Page 73.

2.2.1. (a) **S.I.** for $x > 0$, **S.D.** for $x < 0$, horizontal tangent at $(0, -1)$; (c) **S.I.**
for $x > 2$, **S.D.** for $x < 2$, horizontal tangent at $(2, -1)$; (e) **S.I.** for all x, with
horizontal tangent at $(0, 0)$; (g) **S.I.** for $x < -1$, and $x > 1/3$, **S.D.** for $-1 < x < 1/3$,
with horizontal tangent at $x = -1$ and $x = 1/3$; (i) **S.I.** for $x < -1$ and for $x > 1$,
S.D. for $-1 < x < 1$, with horizontal tangents at $x = 1$ and $x = -1$; (k) **S.I.** for
$x > -1$, **S.D.** for $x < -1$, with horizontal tangents at $x = 0$ and $x = -1$; (m) **S.I.**
for all x, with horizontal tangents at $x = 0$ and $x = 1$.   **2.2.3.** We must show
that if $a < b$, then $a^{1/3} < b^{1/3}$. $a < b$ is equivalent to $a - b < 0$. Set $a^{1/3} = A$
and $b^{1/3} = B$. Then $a = A^3$ and $b = B^3$, and $a - b < 0$ implies $A^3 - B^3 < 0$.
Write $A^3 - B^3 = (A - B)(A^2 + AB + B^2) < 0$.   But $A^2 + AB + B^2 =$
$[A + (B/2)]^2 + (\frac{3}{4})B^2 \geq 0$, and so $A^3 - B^3 < 0$ implies $A - B < 0$ implies
$a^{1/3} < b^{1/3}$.   **2.2.4.** See Corollary B.3 in the appendix.   **2.2.5.** Pick any points
$x = u$ and $x = v$ such that $a \leq u \leq v \leq b$. By the mean value theorem $f(v) -$
$f(u) = f'(w)(v - u)$ for some w satisfying $u < w < v$. Show this implies $f(u) = f(v)$.
Since u and v are arbitrarily chosen in $a \leq x \leq b$, this implies $f(x)$ is constant on
this interval.   **2.2.9.** *Hint:* Consider the closed interval $[A, B]$ where $B > A > 0$,
and apply Thm. 2.2.1(i) to $g(x)$ on this interval. Since B and $A > 0$ are arbitrary,
this shows that $g(x)$ is **S.I.** for all $x > 0$.

§2.3. Page 80.

2.3.3. $\eta = -(1 + x^2)/2x^2$.   **2.3.5.** $Q = -0.21$.   **2.3.7.** To prove (a), duplicate the proof of (b), making appropriate adjustments.   **2.3.9.** Interest elasticity
of supply $= -[i/S(i)]S'(i)$.

§2.4. Page 90.

2.4.1. Absolute maximum: 0, absolute minimum: -4.   **2.4.3.** Absolute
maximum: 2, absolute minimum: -25.   **2.4.5.** Absolute maximum: $\sqrt[3]{2}$,
absolute minimum: 0.   **2.4.7.** Absolute maximum: 1, absolute minimum: $1/8$.

2.4.9. Absolute maximum: 0, absolute minimum: -4.   **2.4.11.** Absolute maximum: 11, absolute minimum: 7.   **2.4.13.** Absolute maximum: 23, absolute minimum: -21.   **2.4.15.** Absolute maximum: $\sqrt[3]{4}$, absolute minimum: $-\sqrt[3]{16}$. **2.4.17.** Absolute maximum: 119, absolute minimum: -132.   **2.4.19.** Absolute maximum: 48, absolute minimum: -28.

§2.5. Page 96.

2.5.1. $\eta = 6$ for all $p \geq 1$. Hence η assumes the same value for all $p \geq 1$.   **2.5.3.** Total revenue is maximum when $x = \frac{5}{4}$, and takes on its minimum at both $x = 0$ and $x = 5$. Marginal revenue is maximum when $x = 0$, minimum when $x = 5/2$. **2.5.5.** Minimum average cost $= -\frac{1}{4}$.   **2.5.7.** Maximum total revenue $= 2$ (observe that total revenue $\to 0$ as $x \to \infty$).   **2.5.9.** Maximum rate of change $= 180$. **2.5.11.** Maximum area $= (L^2/2)$.   **2.5.13.** Height of cylinder $= (2R/\sqrt{3})$, radius of cylinder $= (\frac{2}{3})R^2$.   **2.5.15.** Maximum area $= R^2$.   **2.5.17.** Q should be 4 miles from P, and R should be 2 miles from P.   **2.5.21.** 134 units of work per second.

§2.7. Page 104.

2.7.1. Observe that $g(-1) > 0$ and $g(0) < 0$, so by Thm. 2.7.1, $g(x) = 0$ for some x in $-1 < x < 0$; similarly for $g(0) < 0$ and $g(1) > 0$.   **2.7.3.** If $f(x)$ is continuous at $x = 1$, then it is continuous for all x in $0 \leq x \leq 1$. Since $f(0) = 1$ and $f(x) < 0$ for $0 < x \leq 1$, $f(x) = \frac{1}{2}$ must have a solution (by Thm. 2.7.1.) But this is impossible.

CHAPTER 3

§3.1. Page 110.

3.1.1. (a) 11,781; (c) $1 - (1/2^{n+1})$.   **3.1.3.** $n(n + 1)(n + 2)/3$.   **3.1.5.** 13,651. **3.1.7.** (a) $20 + (\frac{3}{4})(1 + [1/n])$.

§3.2. Page 115.

3.2.1. (a) 0; (c) -1; (e) no limit.   **3.2.2.** (a) 0; (c) Write $n(\sqrt{n^2 + 1} - n) \cdot$

$$\frac{\sqrt{n^2 + 1} + n}{\sqrt{n^2 + 1} + n} = \frac{n}{\sqrt{n^2 + 1} + n} = \frac{1}{\sqrt{1 + (1/n^2)} + 1} \to \frac{1}{2} \text{ as } n \to \infty. \quad \textbf{3.2.3. } 1/(1 - x).$$

3.2.4. (a) Hint: Write the limit as $\lim_{n \to \infty} \sum_{k=1}^{n} \frac{k}{n^2} = \lim_{n \to \infty} \frac{1}{n^2} \sum_{k=1}^{n} k$. **3.2.5.** (a) $(1/2) +$
$(3/4) + (7/8) + (15/16) + (31/32)$;   (c) $1 + (9/2) + (1/3) + (33/4) + (1/5)$;   (e)
$-1 + (1/2) - (1/3) + (1/4) - (1/5)$.   **3.2.7.** (a) $12/99$; (c) $123/999$.   **3.2.9.** 1.
3.2.11. *Hint:* Divide numerator and denominator by n. This implies that you can
make the test as reliable as you please (i.e., you can make the reliability of the test
as close to 1 as you please) by making the length of the test sufficiently long.
3.2.13. Use (3.1.4). The limit is $2 - a_1$.   **3.2.14.** (a) Let J be some open interval
containing L. By definition of limit, there is an integer N such that for $n > N$, all
the a_n's are in J; hence only $a_1, a_2, \ldots a_{N-1}$ are not in J, and there are only $N - 1$
of these. (b) Suppose $L \neq L^*$. Pick open intervals A and B containing L and L^*,
respectively, such that A and B have no points in common (e.g., A and B might be
the open intervals given by the set of all x such that $|x - L| < (L + L^*)/2$ and
$|x - L^*| < (L + L^*)/2$, respectively). Apply (a) to both A and B to show that L
must equal L^*.   **3.2.15.** (b) max $|g_n(x) - 0| = g_n(1/2) = 1/4^n \to 0$ as $n \to \infty$.

§3.3. Page 123.

3.3.1. (a) $x^2 + c$; (b) $7x + c$; (c) $(\frac{1}{4})t^4 - t + c$; (d) $(1/11)u^{11} - (\frac{5}{8})u^8 + 2u^2 + c$.
3.3.3. (a) $2\sqrt{x} + c$; (b) $2\sqrt{x} - 2$; (c) $2\sqrt{x} - 1$.   **3.3.5.** The functions are $x^2 - 5x$,
$x^2 - 5x + 5$, $x^2 - 5x + 1$, $x^2 - 5x + 2$, $x^2 - 5x + 4$, and $x^2 - 5x + 6$, respectively.   **3.3.7.** $15f(x) = 4x^{5/2} + 20x^{3/2} - 10x$.   **3.3.9.** (b) maximum height
attained $= 4$ feet. It takes one second to reach the ground.

§3.4. Page 135.

3.4.1.

$$\int_{-2}^{0} (-x)\,dx = \lim_{n \to \infty} \sum_{1}^{n} [2 - (2k/n)][2/n] = \lim_{n \to \infty} [(4/n) \sum_{1}^{n} 1 - (4/n^2) \sum_{1}^{n} k]$$

$$= \lim_{n \to \infty} [(4/n)n - (4/n^2)(1/2)n(n + 1)] = 4 - 2 = 2$$

3.4.3. 0 and $\frac{1}{4}$, respectively. The area is $1/2$.   **3.4.5.** (i) -3; (ii) 6.   **3.4.7.** Both
areas $= 22/3$ square units. The reason is that in $-2 \le x \le 2, |4 - x^2| = |x^2 - 4| = 4 - x^2$, so both functions yield the same number in (3.4.3).   **3.4.9.** The area is
$8/3$ square units, but $\int_{-1}^{2} (x^2 - 1)\,dx = 0$.

§3.5. Page 139.

3.5.3. $x'_k = a + [(k-1)(b-a)/N] + (\frac{1}{3})(b-a)/N = a + [(3k-2)/3N]$. Hence, (3.5.1) becomes

$$\lim_{N \to \infty} \sum_1^N f(a + [3k-2]/3N)[(b-a)/N]$$

and in particular,

$$\int_0^1 x \, dx = \lim_{N \to \infty} (1/3N^2) \sum_1^N (3k-2), \text{ etc.}$$

§3.6. Page 149.

3.6.1. For Prob. 3.4.2: $T^3/3$, $b-a$, and $16/3$, respectively. For Prob. 3.4.3: the integrals are 0 and 1/4, respectively.   **3.6.3.** For Prob. 3.4.8: $\int_0^1 (x - x^2) \, dx =$

$\{(\frac{1}{2})x^2 - (\frac{1}{3})x^3\} \Big]_0^1 = 1/6$.   **3.6.5.** (a) $f(x)$ is even. The integral $= 656/21$; (c) $f(x)$ is odd. The integral $= 0$.   **3.6.7.** (a) 8/3; (c) 1/2; (e) 2/3; (g) 8/3.
3.6.8. Hint: Consider (3.4.2), write the limit as an appropriate integral of $\sqrt{x}$ and use Thm. 3.6.2.   **3.6.9.** See the hint for the solution of Prob. 3.6.8. The limit equals $1/(1 + \sqrt{2})$.   **3.6.11.** Write $g(x) = x^2 - 5x + 1$ and $F(y) = \int_a^y f$ and observe $F[g(x)] = G(x)$. $G'(x) = (2x - 5)f(x^2 - 5x + 1)$.

§3.7. Page 155.

3.7.1. (a) 9/2; (c) 1/6; (e) 1/2; (g) 81/2; (i) Observe that the equation reduces to $y = 1 + x - 2\sqrt{x}$ for $0 \leq x \leq 1$; the area is 1/6.   **3.7.2.** Let $F(b) = \int_a^b f = \sqrt[3]{b^3 - a^3}$ with b thought of as variable, $b > a$. Apply the Fundamental Theorem.
3.7.3. Net distance $= 0$, total distance $= 64/3$ units.

§3.8. Page 159.

3.8.1. (a) $xe^x + e^x$; (c) $2\exp \sqrt{x-1}]/\sqrt{x-1}$; (e) $[\exp x\sqrt{x+1}][3x+2]/2\sqrt{x+1}$; (g) $(2/x^3) \exp (-1/x^2)$; (i) $20x(x^2 + 1)^9 \exp (x^2 + 1)^{10}$.   **3.8.2.**

(a) $e(e-1)$; (c) $(e^3-1)/3e^3$; (e) $D_x x^2 e^x = x^2 e^x + 2xe^x$. Hence, $\displaystyle\int_0^1 Dx^2 e^x\, dx =$

$\displaystyle\int_0^1 x^2 e^x\, dx + 2\int_0^1 xe^x\, dx$, and so $\displaystyle\int_0^1 x^2 e^x\, dx = -\left.x^2 e^x\right]_0^1 + 2\int_0^1 xe^x\, dx = 2 - e.$

3.8.3. $D_x y = (2 - e^y - ye^x)/(xe^y + e^x).$ **3.8.5.** max. $= f(u) = 1/s\sqrt{2\pi}$; no min.

§3.9. Page 167.

3.9.2. (a) $g(x) = x/3$; (c) $g(x) = (x - b)/a$; (e) no inverse function; (g) $g(x) = x^{1/4}$, $x > 0$.   **3.9.3.** $a = 1$, b arbitrary.   **3.9.5.** (a) $1/2x$; (c) $1 + (1/x)$; (e) $(1/2x) + [6x/(x^2 + 1)]$; (g) $1/(x \ln x)$.   **3.9.6.** (a) $y' = y[-(2x + 1) \ln x + (x^2 + x - 2)/x]$; (c) $y' = y(\ln \ln x + 1)/x$; (e) $y' = (y/4)(2 + \ln x)/\sqrt{x}$. **3.9.7.** S.I. for $0 < x < e$; S.D. for $x > e$; rel. max. at $x = e$.   **3.9.9.** Domain of $f =$ range of g, and domain of $g =$ range of f.   **3.9.10.** Hint: Use implicit differentiation and the chain rule on $f[g(x)] = x$.

§3.10. Page 175.

3.10.1. (a) $(\tfrac{2}{3})(x^3 + 2)^{1/2} + c$; (c) $(\tfrac{3}{4})(x^2 - 6x + 15)^{2/3} + c$; (e) $1/12$; (g) $1/2$; (i) $1/4$; (k) $(\tfrac{1}{4})[\ln (1 + x^2)]^2 + c$; (m) $(\ln \ln x)^2/2 + c$; (o) $(\tfrac{1}{2}) \ln (1 + e^{2x}) + c$. **3.10.2.** (a) $x^2 e^x - 2xe^x + 2e^x + c$; (c) $(e^2 + 1)/4$; (e) $2048/105$.   **3.10.5.** If the arbitrary constants c and d are explicitly exhibited, the equation would read

$$\int \frac{1}{x}\, dx + c = 1 + \int \frac{1}{x}\, dx + d$$

or $c = 1 + d$, *not* $0 = 1$.

CHAPTER 4

§4.1. Page 184.

4.1.1. $V = (\tfrac{1}{3})\pi R^2 H$.   **4.1.3.** (a) $\pi/2$; (c) $(\pi/3)(2\sqrt{2} - 1)$; (e) $\pi(e - 2)$. **4.1.4.** (a) $4\pi/5$; (c) $128\pi/3$; (e) 2π.   **4.1.5.** (a) $2\pi/35$ about x-axis, $\pi/10$ about y-axis; (c) $512\pi/15$; (e) $2\pi/5$ about x-axis, $10\pi/28$ about y-axis.

§4.2. Page 186.

4.2.1. $k + (10,000 - k)/e^{12}$.   **4.2.3.** $(9999/e^4) + 1$.

§4.3. Page 188.

4.3.1. $(9/10) - (\ln 10)^2$.

§4.4. Page 191.

4.4.1. $y = ce^x$.   **4.4.3.** $6\sqrt{y} - 2\sqrt{x^3} = 12$.   **4.4.5.** $y = (x^2 + 1)/2$.   **4.4.7.** $y = c \exp (2[x^3 + 1]^{3/2}/9)$.   **4.4.9.** $y^2 = 2e^x(x - 1) + x + c$.   **4.4.11.** $y = 5x$.   **4.4.13.** $6(y + 2)^{5/2} - 20(y + 2)^{3/2} - \ln x = c$.   **4.4.16.** The calculations are invalid. In fact, the integral diverges.

§4.5. Page 201.

4.5.1. $\exp (-20 \ln 2/17)$.   **4.5.3.** $[aV - c \exp (-bt)]/b$, where c is an arbitrary constant.   **4.5.5.** $y/(1 - y) = \exp (ct - 1)$.

§4.6. Page 210.

4.6.1. (b) The integral is not improper.   **4.6.3.** 2.   **4.6.5.** 5/4.   **4.6.7.** 0.   **4.6.9.** $-1/4$.   **4.6.11.** 4.   **4.6.13.** $2\sqrt{3}$.   **4.6.15.** $1/(1 - p)$ for $p < 1$.

§4.7. Page 214.

4.7.1. 1/2.   **4.7.3.** 1.   **4.7.5.** -1.   **4.7.7.** diverges.   **4.7.9.** 2.   **4.7.11.** diverges.   **4.7.13.** converges for $p > 1$ to $1/(1 - p)$.   **4.7.15.** $u = \ln x$; converges for $p > 1$ to $(\ln 2)^{1 - p}/(1 - p)$.

§4.8. Page 223.

4.8.1. $[F = (1, 1)] \cup [F = (2, 1)]$.   **4.8.3.** Yes. Observe that W^2 meets all the requirements of Def. 4.8.3.   **4.8.5.** $E_1 \cap E_2$ is the event that x is in the interval $0 < x < 1$, $E_1 \cup E_3$ is the event that x is in the interval $0 \le x < 2$, $\bar{E}_5 = E_7 = \emptyset$, $(E_1 \cap E_4) \cup E_6$ is the event that x is in the interval $1 \le x < 3/2$, $E_6 \cap E_7 = \emptyset$, $E_1 \cup E_4$ is the event that x is in the interval $3/2 \le x < 2$. Observe $E_7 = \emptyset$.   **4.8.6.** (a) The coins can fall in $2^3 = 8$ ways; (c) $P[p_i, n_j, d_k] = 1/8$ where $i, j, k = 0$ or 1; (e) 1/2; (g) 3/8.   **4.8.7.** (a) $\binom{26}{3} = 2600$; (b) $\binom{25}{2} = 300$; (c) probability $= (300/2600 = 3/26$.

§4.9. Page 228.

4.9.2. $1/6$.   **4.9.3.** (a) 216 ways; (b) $1/216$; (c) $P[S = 2] = 0$, $P[S = 3] = 1/216$, $P[S = 4] = 1/72$; (e) 0; (f) 1.   **4.9.4.** (a) 0; (c) 1; (e) $1/18$; (g) $33/36$.   **4.9.7.** (a) $15/16$; (b) $1/16$; (c) $G(1) = 1$; $G(2) = 1/2$.

§4.10. Page 237.

4.10.3. 0.683, 0.955, 0.977, 0.341, 0.477, respectively.   **4.10.4.** (b) distribution function $= 0$, $x \le 0$; $= 1 - \exp(-x/\theta)$, $x > 0$.   **4.10.5.** (a) $c = e^4/\sqrt{\pi}$, $\mu = 2$, $\sigma = 1/\sqrt{2}$.   **4.10.7.** distribution function $= 0$, $x < a$; $= (x - a)/(b - a)$, $a \le$

$x \le b$; $= 1$, $x > b$.   **4.10.8.** $E[C] = \displaystyle\int_{-\infty}^{\infty} cf(x)\,dx = c\int_{-\infty}^{\infty} f(x)\,dx = c$.   **4.10.10.**

$V[X] = E[(X - E[X])^2] = E[X^2 - 2XE(X) + (E[X]^2)]$ (Why?) $= E[X^2] -$

$2(E[X])^2 + (E[X])^2 = E[X^2] - (E[X]^2)$.   **4.10.11.** $E[X] = \displaystyle\int_{-\infty}^{\infty} xe^{-x^2/2}\,dx =$

$\displaystyle\lim_{u,\,w\to\infty} \int_{-u}^{w} x\exp(-x^2/2)\,dx$. Use substitutions. $V[X] = \displaystyle\int_{-\infty}^{\infty} x^2 \exp(-x^2/2)\,dx$.

Integrate by parts.   **4.10.13.** $E[Z] = \theta$, $V[Z] = \theta^2$.

§4.12. Page 246.

4.12.1. $n = (s - c)T/s$.   **4.12.3.** $n = \ln(p/c)$.

§4.13. Page 248.

4.13.1. $-1 + k \exp(x^2/2)$.   **4.13.3.** $(-1/3) + k \exp(x^3)$.   **4.13.5.** $x^2 - 2(x - 1) + ke^{-x}$.   **4.13.7.** $1 + k \exp(1/x)$.   **4.13.9.** $(k/x) + (x/2) + (2x^2/3) + (x^3/4)$.   **4.13.11.** *Hint:* Evaluate $y'(x)$, using facts about the exponential function and Thm. 3.6.1.

§4.14. Page 253.

4.14.1. $M_5 = 0.354$, $M_6 = M_5 + (x_6 - x_1)/5 = 0.334$, $\tilde{M}_6 \simeq 0.327$, $\tilde{M}_7 \simeq 0.345$.
4.14.3. $s(t) = k \exp(-t/2) + t - 2$.

Appendix, §B.

B.1. Observe that $|[f(x) - f(0)]/(x - 0)| = |f'(u)|$, for the appropriate u between 0 and x. Finish using the fact that $f(0) = 0$ and $|f'(u)| \leq A$.   **B.2.** Apply Rolle's theorem to $f'(x)$ twice, first to $f'(x)$ for $a \leq x \leq b$, then to $f'(x)$ for $b \leq x \leq c$. **B.3.** Apply the mean value theorem to $f(x)$.

INDEX